Journalism, Power and Investigation

Journalism, Power and Investigation presents a contemporary, trans-national analysis of investigative journalism. Beginning with a detailed introduction that examines the relationship between this form of public communication and normative conceptions of democracy, the book offers a selection of spirited contributions to current debates concerning the place, function, and political impact of investigative work. The 14 chapters, produced by practising journalists, academics, and activists, cover a range of topics, with examples drawn from the global struggle to produce reliable, in-depth accounts of public events.

The collection brings together a range of significant investigations from across the world. These include an assignment conducted in the dangerous sectarian environment of Iraq, close engagement with Spain's Memory Movement, and an account of the work of radical charity Global Witness. Other chapters examine the relationship between journalists and state/corporate power, the troubled political legacy of WikiLeaks, the legal constraints on investigative journalism in the UK, and the bold international agenda of the investigative collective *The Ferret*. This material is accompanied by other analytical pieces on events in Bermuda, Brazil, and Egypt.

Investigative journalism is a form of reportage that has long provided a benchmark for in-depth, critical interventions. Using numerous case studies, *Journalism, Power and Investigation* gives students and researchers an insight into the principles and methods that animate this global search for truth and justice.

Stuart Price is Professor of Media and Political Discourse, and Director of the Media Discourse Centre, at De Montfort University, UK. He is the author of the forthcoming title *Corbyn and the Media* and several monographs, including *Worst-Case Scenario?* (2011), *Brute Reality* (2010), and *Discourse Power Address* (2007). He is the editor, with Ruth Sanz Sabido, of *Sites of Protest* (2016) and *Contemporary Protest and the Legacy of Dissent* (2015). His well-known textbooks include *Communication Studies* (1996).

Journalism, Power and Investigation
Global and Activist Perspectives

Edited by Stuart Price

First published 2019
by Routledge
2 Park Square, Milton Park, Abingdon, Oxon OX14 4RN

and by Routledge
52 Vanderbilt Avenue, New York, NY 10017

Routledge is an imprint of the Taylor & Francis Group, an informa business

© 2019 selection and editorial matter, Stuart Price; individual chapters, the contributors

The right of Stuart Price to be identified as the author of the editorial material, and of the authors for their individual chapters, has been asserted in accordance with sections 77 and 78 of the Copyright, Designs and Patents Act 1988.

All rights reserved. No part of this book may be reprinted or reproduced or utilised in any form or by any electronic, mechanical, or other means, now known or hereafter invented, including photocopying and recording, or in any information storage or retrieval system, without permission in writing from the publishers.

Trademark notice: Product or corporate names may be trademarks or registered trademarks, and are used only for identification and explanation without intent to infringe.

British Library Cataloguing-in-Publication Data
A catalogue record for this book is available from the British Library

Library of Congress Cataloging-in-Publication Data
Names: Price, Stuart, 1958– editor.
Title: Journalism, power, and investigation : global and activist perspectives / Stuart Price.
Description: London ; New York : Routledge, 2019. | Includes bibliographical references and index.
Identifiers: LCCN 2018043492| ISBN 9781138743069 (hardback : alk. paper) | ISBN 9781138743090 (paperback : alk. paper) | ISBN 9781315181943 (ebook)
Subjects: LCSH: Investigative reporting.
Classification: LCC PN4781 .J86 2019 | DDC 070.4/3—dc23
LC record available at https://lccn.loc.gov/2018043492

ISBN: 978-1-138-74306-9 (hbk)
ISBN: 978-1-138-74309-0 (pbk)
ISBN: 978-1-315-18194-3 (ebk)

Typeset in New Baskerville
by Apex CoVantage, LLC

Printed and bound in Great Britain by
TJ International Ltd, Padstow, Cornwall

In memory of Evan and May Lake,
and William and Maud Price

Contents

List of figures ix
List of contributors x
Acknowledgements xiv

Introduction: journalism, democracy, and the critique of political culture 1
STUART PRICE

PART I
Investigative journalism, public integrity, and the state 35

1 **Investigative journalism and terrorism: the proactive legal duty to report** 37
   RICHARD DANBURY

2 **Researching the deep state: surveillance, politics, and dissent** 56
   BEN HARBISHER

3 **State, hierarchy, and executive power: journalists under duress** 73
   STUART PRICE

4 **Can you keep a secret? Legal and technological obstacles to protecting journalistic sources** 95
   RICHARD DANBURY AND JUDITH TOWNEND

PART II
Activism, investigation, and the quest for social justice 113

5 **Citizens' investigations: recovering the past in contemporary Spain** 117
   RUTH SANZ SABIDO

Contents

6 Global Witness and investigative journalism   137
ALI HINES

7 Violence and impunity in Rio de Janeiro's favelas: citizens, smartphones, and police malpractice   160
FERNANDA AMARAL

PART III
The hazards of investigation: journalists on assignment   175

8 Surviving the sectarian divide: investigative journalism in the quagmire of Iraq   179
AHMED BAHIYA

9 Co-operative international coverage? *The Ferret*'s foreign reporting   196
PETER GEOGHEGAN, BILLY BRIGGS, AND BRINDUSA IOANA NASTASA

10 After the Arab revolts: social media and the journalist in Egypt   215
ZAHERA HARB

11 Protecting the colony: Bermuda's national image and media censorship   229
DANA SELASSIE

PART IV
An industry in turmoil: fake news, leaks, and economic challenges   243

12 Fact-checking, false balance, and 'fake news': the discourse and practice of verification in political communication   245
JEN BIRKS

13 WikiLeaks and investigative journalism: the organisation's effects and unfinished legacy   265
LISA LYNCH

14 Online news video, collaboration, and social networks: the disruption of the media industry   286
DAVID HAYWARD

Index   300

Figures

5.1 A technician in the Ponferrada laboratory tracks the bullet wound that killed an unknown victim of Francoist repression — 118
5.2 The Republican flag flies above a memorial to the '17 Roses of Guillena'. The 17 women were from a small village some 14 miles from Seville, who were murdered by Falangists in 1937. The inscription below the flag reads 'Truth Justice Reparation' — 123
5.3 Images of the 'disappeared', Plaza de la Gavidia in Seville — 124
5.4 The names of some of the thousands of people executed by the Nationalists, inscribed on the memorial wall in the cemetery, Salamanca, Spain — 132
6.1 A villager rests in the shade of a felled tree inside a HAGL subsidiary company's rubber concession in Cambodia in 2013. Communities often know nothing about the deals struck for their land until the bulldozers arrive to start clearing — 148
6.2 Villagers walk through recently cleared forest inside a HAGL rubber plantation in Cambodia in 2013 — 152
8.1 Extract from notebook — 186
9.1 Five-year-old Husan was shot in west Mosul. He was being treated at the EMC in Erbil, Iraqi Kurdistan — 204
9.2 An injured Iraqi man from west Mosul being helped by Kurdish medics on the outskirts of Mosul, Iraq — 204
9.3 Al Salam Hospital, East Mosul, Iraq — 207
9.4 Boys' class in Syrian school in Istanbul, Turkey — 208
9.5 Syrian restaurant in Aksaray, Istanbul, Turkey — 209
9.6 Girl's English class in Syrian school in Istanbul, Turkey — 211

Contributors

Fernanda Amaral is currently a PhD candidate in the Media Discourse Centre at De Montfort University, Leicester, UK, studying social media use in the Brazilian favelas. Born in Rio de Janeiro, Fernanda graduated with a bachelor's degree in Journalism. Recently, she was Marketing Manager for *Passei Direto* (the Brazilian 'Facebook for students'), and spent five years working on digital behaviour research, including digital marketing, consulting, innovation, and social media. During this time, she also worked for the digital research agencies *Agência Frog* and *Agência Carambola*, and *MJV Technology & Innovation*. She is the author of 'It's not just 20 cents: how social networks helped mobilise Brazilians against injustice', in *Sites of Protest* (Price and Sanz Sabido, 2016).

Ahmed Bahiya worked as an investigative reporter In Iraq, embedded in a team of writers, providing detailed coverage of local political, social, economic, and sporting events. His stories have appeared in *Free Media Org*, the newspaper *Al-Shaarq*, the *Geraan* newspaper, the *WNA News Agency*, the *Al-Rasheed* satellite channel, and the radio stations *Al Marbad* and *Iraqhurr*. He was educated at the University of Baghdad and gained his PhD from the Media Discourse Centre at De Montfort University, UK. His thesis was a study of the ways in which Iraqi users of social media sites assume different gendered identities in their online interactions.

Jen Birks is an Assistant Professor in the Faculty of Arts, Nottingham University, UK, and co-convener of the PSA Media and Politics Group. Her most recent research has focused on media representation and discourse, but past work has also examined the relationship between the professional ideology of journalism and particular news production practices (especially campaigning) and the news reception on political elites. Her recent publications include the articles 'Tax avoidance as an anti-austerity issue' (2017) and 'Moving life stories tell us just why politics matters' (2016). She is also the author of the monograph *News and Civil Society* (2014).

Billy Briggs is a freelance journalist committed to public interest journalism. His reports have won awards from Amnesty International and the

European Union, among others. He is a co-founder and director of *The Ferret*, the award-winning investigative website.

Richard Danbury is a Research Associate in the Faculty of Law at the University of Cambridge, UK, and Programme Leader for the MA Investigative Journalism at De Montfort University, Leicester, UK. He is a member of the Media Discourse Centre and the author of a number of pieces on the law and the media. He has a background in law and broadcast journalism. He is currently the research associate on the Arts and Humanities Research Council funded study 'Appraising Potential Legal Responses to Threats to the Production of News in the Digital Environment'. Richard practised, briefly, as a criminal barrister at 9–12 Bell Yard, before spending a decade at the BBC, working mainly in TV news and current affairs, including extended periods on 'Newsnight' and 'Panorama'. He was the Deputy Editor of the BBC's 2010 Prime Ministerial Debate, and a fellow of Oxford University's Reuters Institute for the Study of Journalism, before embarking on a masters and a doctorate which studied the position of institutional journalism and journalists in English law, both from a doctrinal and theoretical point of view. Recent publications include 'Freedom of expression and protecting journalists' sources' (forthcoming), and 'Where should speech be free? Conceiving liberal theories of free speech', in M. Price and N. Stremlau's *Speech and Society in the Digital Age* (2018).

Peter Geoghegan is a co-director of *the Ferret* and Head of Investigations for openDemocracy, and a Lecturer in Journalism in the School of Media, Culture, and Society, University of the West of Scotland. As a print and broadcast journalist, he has worked on investigative TV shows for Channel 4, and is in addition the author of two books, *The People's Referendum: Why Scotland Will Never Be the Same Again* (2015) and *A Difficult Difference: Race, Religion and the New Northern Ireland* (2011).

Zahera Harb is a Senior Lecturer in International Journalism at City University, London, UK. Her recent publications include an edited collection with Dina Matar entitled narrating *Conflict in the Middle East: Discourse, Image and Communication Practices in Palestine and Lebanon* (I.B. Tauris, 2013) and a monograph called *Channels of Resistance: Liberation Propaganda, Hezbollah and the Media* (I.B. Tauris, 2011). She is the reviews editor for the *Journal of Media Practice*. Zaheera has more than 11 years' experience as a journalist in Lebanon working for Lebanese and international media organisations. She was co-producer and presenter of a popular socio-political programme (*Khamseh Ala Sabaah, 5/7*) before becoming one of the main news anchors at *Tele Liban* (the public service TV in Lebanon). At New TV, she was appointed to a news anchor-editor post and hosted the main daily political show (*Al-Hadath*). At *Future TV* (Pan Arab satellite channel), she produced and presented her own socio-political programme (Ala Madar Assaa) while assigned as satellite news editor.

She also produced several documentaries for Lebanese TV stations and completed reporting assignments for BBC Arabic service (radio), *CNN World Report*, and Dutch TV.

Ben Harbisher is a Senior Lecturer in Media Production and a member of the Media Discourse Centre at De Montfort University, Leicester, UK. He is the author of a number of journal articles on the subject of surveillance, mobile technology, social media, and public demonstrations, including 'The Million Mask March: Language, legitimacy, and dissent' (2016), which examines emerging trends in 'protest management' in the UK, and 'Radicals, revolutionaries and misanthropes, towards a brief genealogy of public order and surveillance in Nottingham, c 1200–2012' (2012). He is also an editor of the *International Journal of Media Discourse*.

David Hayward is the Director of Digital Media and Strategy at 2020 Media International, working with clients to build creative and robust digital communication strategies. He is also Senior Lecturer in Investigative Journalism at De Montfort University, Leicester, UK, and a member of the Media Discourse Centre. During a distinguished career at the BBC, David worked as a reporter, producer, and senior editor on network radio, TV, and for the BBC World Service Trust. He specialises in digital media and future trends of journalism, having led some of the BBC's most high-profile projects in multimedia, multi-skilled working. He continues to work with the BBC as a consultant producer for the BBC Fusion project, and is currently working with broadcasters and NGOs in the UK, Nigeria, Pakistan, Kosovo, Moldova, and Russia. His last role at the BBC was Head of the Strategic Journalism Programme for the BBC Academy.

Ali Hines is a Land Campaigner at the International NGO Global Witness, which uses a variety of investigative techniques to pursue the cause of environmental and social justice. She gained an MSc in environmental social science from University College London, and a BA from De Montfort University, UK. She is the author of 'The global rush for land' (in Price and Sanz Sabido, 2016), and a number of reports on land and environmental issues.

Lisa Lynch is an Associate Professor at Concordia University, Montreal, Canada, and worked from 1987 to 1992 as a magazine and newspaper journalist in the San Francisco Bay Area, and then in Pennsylvania, USA, writing on science and cultural affairs. Since beginning her academic career, Dr. Lynch has written about the prison system, Guantanamo, and nuclear policy for both academic and popular publications. She received her PhD from Rutgers University, USA, her masters from the University of California-Berkeley, USA, and her bachelors from Stanford University, USA. Her most recent book is *Native Advertising* (2018).

Brindusa Ioana Nastasa is a Romanian documentary filmmaker and multimedia journalist, co-founder of Springroll Media (.com). Her multimedia stories have been nominated for the German Reporter Award, the Scottish Refugee Media Awards and Migration Media Awards.

Stuart Price is Professor of Media and Political Discourse, and Director of the Media Discourse Centre, at De Montfort University, UK. His recent research includes a study of the libertarian tradition and Spanish history (in Fishwick and Connolly, 2018), and a critique of 'centrist' attacks on populism (in Sanz Sabido, 2017). He is the author of three monographs and three textbooks, and is also co-editor of a number of books/journal issues on protest and social movements. He is currently working on a study of the media representation of UK Labour leader Jeremy Corbyn, and the impact of the Catalan independence movement on Spanish politics. He is a founding editor of the *International Journal of Media Discourse*.

Ruth Sanz Sabido is Reader in Media and Social Inequality at Canterbury Christ Church University (UK), and the author of *Memories of the Spanish Civil War: Conflict and Community in Rural Spain* (2016). She is co-editor of *Sites of Protest* (2016), *Contemporary Protest and the Legacy of Dissent* (2015), and three journal special issues (*Critical Discourse Studies, Catalan Journal of Communication and Cultural Studies*, and *Networking Knowledge*). She also edited the collection *Representing Communities* (2017) and is the author of several book chapters and journal articles on memory and the Spanish Civil War, media discourse, conflict, and social movements. She is Chair and founder of the MeCCSA Social Movements Network (2013–present), co-editor of the book series *Protest, Media and Culture* (Rowman and Littlefield International) and a founding editor of the *International Journal of Media Discourse*. In addition, she coordinates the project *Herencias del 36* (www.herencias1936.com) and is co-ordinator of the project 'Remembering what we have not lived: approaches to postmemory analysis'.

Dana Selassie is a documentary filmmaker, and at one point was a Lecturer in Television Production and Advanced Television Production at De Montfort University, Leicester, UK. She has been involved in Bermuda's television industry for over 25 years, working locally and internationally as a television producer, film director, media strategist, educator, and researcher.

Judith Townend is a Lecturer in Media and Information Law in the School of Law, Politics and Sociology at the University of Sussex, where she specialises in research on freedom of expression and access to information. She was previously Director of the Information Law and Policy Centre at the Institute of Advanced Legal Studies, University of London. Her doctoral research, based at the Centre for Law, Justice and Journalism (CLJJ) at City University London, examined defamation and privacy law and its relationship with journalistic practice in England and Wales.

Acknowledgements

Journalism, Power and Investigation: Global and Activist Perspectives owes its origin to two events: a conversation I had in 2015 with Niall Kennedy (then a commissioning editor at Routledge) and, a year later, the initiation of the Channel 4/De Montfort University MA degree in Investigative Journalism. This course reinforced existing teaching initiatives in our Media school, but also strengthened the research culture built up, over a number of years, by the Media Discourse Centre (MDC).

The production of this book was aided by the patience and good humour of Kitty Imbert (my editor at Routledge), the enthusiasm of Niall Kennedy, and the guidance of the series editor, Margaret Farrelly. Richard Danbury, course leader for the MA, made a number of vital suggestions for contributions and provided invaluable insights into journalistic practice, while Ben Harbisher offered robust common sense and intelligent advice. Dorothy Byrne, Head of Channel 4 News and Current Affairs (and our Visiting Professor in Media Discourse and Journalism) presided over the creation of the Channel 4 degree, a task that was underpinned by the drive and commitment of my colleague Jason Lee. The MA was taken through validation by Richard Danbury, Ali Haynes of the Journalism team, and our External Examiner, Jen Birks of Nottingham University. Dominic Shellard, Vice-Chancellor of De Montfort University, ensured from the beginning that the Masters cohort to which this book is in part addressed obtained both moral and material support.

I would also like to acknowledge the dedication of all those Media Discourse Centre members who have contributed to conferences, public events, publications, and research seminars, particularly those who kept our brand of critical enquiry alive in the days when the only resource available was their own determination to continue. Prominent within this group is Ruth Sanz Sabido, now Reader in Media and Social Inequality at CCCU. Her investigative work on memory and the Spanish Civil War (see Chapter 5), and her interest in the contemporary battles being fought in Spain (over, for example, the abuse of women's rights and the iniquities of the legal system), exemplify the best qualities of activist research. Other colleagues who have, in the past, invested time in our activities include Jo Whitehouse-Hart, Margaret Montgomerie, Andrew Clay, Jilly Boyce-Kay,

Kaitlyn Mendes, Helen Wood, and Andrew Tolson. Max Hanska's three years in the Centre, and the ingenuity of his work, provided essential support for the development of new initiatives.

A number of current MDC members have produced chapters for this book: Ben Harbisher provided the guide to analysing the 'deep state' found in Chapter 2; Fernanda Amaral wrote the piece on social media use in the Brazilian favelas, which appears as Chapter 7; Ahmed Bahiya's account of the perils of investigative enquiry in Iraq can be found Chapter 8; David Hayward, a BBC journalist and colleague on the Channel 4 degree, wrote a study of the news industry for Chapter 14; and finally, Richard Danbury made two contributions, Chapter 1 on investigative journalism and the legal system, and the co-authored work in Chapter 4 which examines the difficulties inherent in protecting sources. I would like to offer my thanks to the other contributors for their hard work in producing material for this volume: Ruth Sanz Sabido (as noted above), Ali Hines (a long-standing and highly valued research associate), Zahera Harb, Jen Birks (a major influence on our work), Peter Geoghegan, Billy Briggs, Brindusa Ioana Nastasa, Dana Selassie, Lisa Lynch, and Judith Townend.

The work of other members of the Media Discourse Centre should also be noted, including Zoe Armour's highly original study, conducted among the devotees of electronic dance music; Clare Sedgwick's work on the feminist publication *Spare Rib*; Jason Lee's analysis of fascism and his work on child abuse scandals; Gurvinder Aujla-Sidhu's enquiry into race, ethnicity and the post-colonial; Jenifer Chao's critique of the geopolitical formations of contemporary culture and her work on nation branding; Yu Sui's research on rumour and the internet; Nayia Kamenou's study of the female adherents of the neo-Nazi group Golden Dawn; Nagham Naddour's work on feminism; and Marco Checci's Foucauldian analysis of resistance. Newer members and associates include Jennifer Ere, Mariam Alsulaimi, Jeremy Clay, John Coster, Paul Smith, and Jamie Lochhead, and from other Faculties, Gil Pasternak, James Tangen, John Coster, and Ben Whitham.

Finally, I think it worth noting that the 'academy' is, as we all know, a highly competitive arena, but all education workers, irrespective of the sector in which they operate, are subjected to identical pressures: in essence, these are forms of discipline dressed up as economic necessities. The existence of a 'neo-liberal' environment has not, however, extinguished the critical perspective that still endures within, and can perhaps in the future move beyond, this straitened circumstance. The difficulties we encounter may also go some way towards explaining the existence of the almost tribal loyalty that sustains those research collectives which attempt in some way to serve the 'public good'.

Stuart Price,
Leicester and Barcelona,
2018

Introduction
Journalism, democracy, and the critique of political culture

Stuart Price

Media, freedom, and democracy

Normative models of democratic politics work on the assumption that a truly informed citizenship requires the active intervention and support of a 'free' media,[1] although the meaning of freedom in this context – economic, political, or institutional – is not always described in sufficient detail. Equally, comprehensive definitions of the media (employed here as a plural noun that refers to a collection of institutions and communicative practices), are sometimes absent or underdeveloped. Yet, even when these concepts *are* properly illustrated, and their apparent worth confirmed, practical commitment to the supposedly universal principle of free, 'mediated' exchange is less than complete, and is often reduced to modest calls for diversity and 'information pluralism' within the parameters of liberal democracy, or else distorted to serve the nationalistic homilies of the authoritarian state.

This Introduction provides the broader context for the wide-ranging studies that follow, by addressing the troubled relationship between formal authority, the public (as it is variously conceived), journalists (and the media formations they inhabit), and established conceptions of democracy. Referring to a number of International case studies (including examples drawn from the UK., the United States, Spain, Brazil, Bermuda, Iraq, Iraqi Kurdistan, Syria, Egypt, and Cambodia), the book as a whole devotes particular attention to the role of journalism and its investigative variant, in part because journalistic labour is often thought more suited to the perpetuation of democratic ideals than other media activities and/or genres. The accuracy of this conventional view depends, of course, on how democracy itself (as a global phenomenon) is understood: if it is regarded as the product of 'public reasoning' (Graham and Hajru, 2011: 20), then its essential values could be stimulated by the textual/discursive intercessions produced by a variety of media categories (such as reality television) that are not usually included in those practices thought most likely to produce coherent political insights. This inclusive perspective contends that 'communicative spaces dedicated to popular forms of entertainment' make a valuable contribution to democratic life, underpinned by the assumption that all media 'play an important role in contributing to the web of informal conversations that constitutes the public sphere' (20).

Despite the persuasiveness of this notion, its circulation has not reduced the intensity of the focus on journalism which, although it can refer to a multiplicity of functions (including a craft, a 'cultural output', and a profession [Carlson, in Peters and Broersma, 2017b: 52]) is nonetheless regarded as the most 'responsible' form of communication operating within the arena of popular debate. As 'service providers for the public' (Bro, 2018: 2), journalists are held to a higher standard, reflected in Hansen's contention that they 'should not be thought of merely as those who edit, moderate and curate already ongoing dialogues', but in addition should be seen as agents of social change, allowing 'the silent voices' to be heard (2013: 678).

Investigative journalism as a mode of enquiry

Investigative journalism, though 'more discussed than practiced' (Hamilton, 2016: 14), features prominently in this argument, appearing as a mode of enquiry that seems to exemplify the rigour and intensity that many would like to see applied to the whole field of reportage. Yet, though its advocates argue that it is 'more demanding both of its subjects and its evidential standards than normal newsroom practice' (MacFadyen, in de Burgh, 2008: 138), this conviction does not guarantee that its distinctive techniques will always be employed to attain a genuinely moral goal. As de Burgh notes in his seminal account of the investigative tradition, the methods it employs 'can be put to partisan, commercial or corrupt use as much as to right wrongs or overcome evil' (2008: 3). Considered, however, as a 'genre of storytelling' that 'seeks to evoke indignation and compel action' (Ettema and Glasser, 1994: 7), its apparently more principled and determinedly adversarial critique of the unaccountable actions of powerful individuals and remote authorities, will always attract admiration, reinforcing its long-held reputation as 'journalism of the highest order' (Ettema and Glasser, 1984: 4). The disadvantage that accompanies this elevated position is that investigative enquiry can be relegated to a specialist function, supposedly relevant only when extreme forms of corruption or abuse need to be exposed to public view.

Successful research into long-term social ills cannot, however, be conjured up at short notice: serious investigations may well produce 'exclusives' and scoops, but they depend on sustained, in-depth labour. The appearance of the data that came to be known as the Panama Papers is a case in point. After the first leaks were released in 2015, by an anonymous whistleblower, the material eventually amounted to some 11.5 million documents, and was only made public after a 'secret, year-long journalistic collaboration across more than eighty countries' involving no fewer than 400 journalists (Obermayer and Obermaier, 2017: viii). The analysis of the Papers was a genuinely international phenomenon, giving weight to Berglez's argument that, if a *global* investigative journalism is to develop (at least one worthy of the name), it must go beyond a type of 'corrective' supplement that is designed to fill in the gaps that standard reportage does not pursue (2013).

The notion of a global journalistic practice has emerged because of the growth, both of an actual cultural/economic process called globalisation, and of an *awareness* of the aggregate of developments that it is supposed to encompass. In this case, the focus would be the apparent 'interconnectedness' of mediated events, and the sense that there is a need to construct trans-national institutions capable of keeping pace with, and making sense of, activities that have a serious impact on the well-being of all those who live on the planet. As Berglez asks, 'is a domestic news story in which a domestic event is connected to climate change still solely domestic news?' (2008: 845). Although significant initiatives have indeed been taken by investigative journalists and their allies, in creating a multiplicity of structures that, taken together, resemble a global public sphere (see Chapters 6, 9, and 12), it is also notable that those capital-intensive media systems that present themselves as native, patriotic forces are still powerful enough to reproduce a more limited account of public events, and in effect the survival of a national 'imaginary'.

Berglez is again useful in addressing these issues, but his position is not necessarily founded on a 'liberal' worldview: he identifies, for example, a number of complementary forms, including peace, development, and 'human rights' journalism, which he believes emerge, not from existing journalistic practices, but from 'some distant, ethical, cultural, discursive or political planet' (2013: xvi). His goal is rather to advocate 'the kind of reporting which manages to make global processes visible and tangible' (2). This, in turn, requires an attitude of mind or an 'outlook' that sees all events as essentially interconnected (2), and which is able to generate narratives that present local, regional, or national developments in their true context. The current volume represents another attempt to work towards this goal so that, for example, the Women's Strike in Spain on 8 March 2018 (see the reference in Chapter 5) is understood as part of an international phenomenon that encompasses Brazilian struggles for social justice (the subject of Chapter 7), as well as the efforts to escape the 'post-colonial' dependence on powerful states, evident in small satellite polities like Bermuda (see Chapter 11). The economic and environmental consequences of capitalist globalisation are therefore germane to this discussion, as they offer the chance to discuss the actual conditions that affect the pursuit of any serious long-term enquiry (see Chapter 3).

Meanwhile, despite its clear difference to political activism, the inherent dangers present in investigative work are clearly evident in the pronounced hostility that greets the efforts of those reporters who challenge the status quo. In 2015, the Pew Research Center, a 'non-partisan' think tank, released a report in which it revealed that 'about two-thirds of investigative journalists surveyed (64%) believe that the U.S. government has probably collected data about their phone calls, emails or online communications', while 'eight-in-ten believe that being a journalist increases the likelihood that their data will be collected' (Holcomb et al., 2015). In effect, those attempting to establish the truth about particular events were treated as the enemies of the state.

Besides the use of surveillance, the determination of the powerful to protect their assets and public reputation has led to the harassment, imprisonment, and even, in some cases, the assassination of investigative journalists. Among the murders that caused international outrage was the brutal killing of Jamal Khashoggi in October 2018. Earlier the same year, Ján Kuciak, who had scrutinised the relationship between the 'Ndrangheta (an Italian mafia clan) and Slovakian politicians, was found shot, together with his fiancée Martina Kušnírová, in Vel'ká Mača, a village some 40 miles from the capital, Bratislava (Boffey, 2018). In Slovakia, these murders caused mass protests, followed by the resignation of the country's Prime Minister, Robert Fico. According to one of Kuciak's closest colleagues, Drew Sullivan, who edits the Organized Crime and Corruption Reporting Project (OCCRP), only a handful of trustworthy individuals – besides the public agencies which had received Kuciak's requests for information – knew about the story they were pursuing, suggesting that state agencies were responsible for the leak. Although the authorities denied that they had 'tipped off the subjects of his research', Sullivan went on to note that 'murdered journalists' are victimised because they 'work at the nexus of crime and government' (2018).

The close relationship between 'legitimate' forces and criminal powers might suggest that they are functionally inseparable. The investigative journalist Daphne Caruana Galizia was another victim of this hidden partnership. Following a lead that emerged from the release of the Panama Papers, she spent a year studying allegations that the Maltese Prime Minister, Joseph Muscat, was involved in corrupt activities. In October 2017, she was killed in a car bombing. Caruana Galizia's son, Matthew, also a journalist, condemned a 'mafia state . . . where you will be blown to pieces for exercising your basic freedoms' (Dallison, 2017). This remark is especially relevant to an analysis of power structures: 'rights' may well exist in a formal sense, but the real test of any system that lays claim to political enlightenment is how it responds when civil liberties are actually taken seriously. Although Caruana Galizia had informed the police that she had received threats, this did not help prevent her assassination, after which one police sergeant had been suspended from duty for posting a message on Facebook in Maltese that 'ended with two words in English: "Feeling happy"' (2017).

Whereas some acts of violence appear to energise resistance within civil society, others seem to have a dampening effect. Over ten years before the death of Caruana Galizia made the headlines, the killing of the journalist Anna Politkovskaya was described as 'the murder that killed free media in Russia' (Walker, 2016). She had been working for the newspaper *Novaya Gazeta*, reporting from 'the killing fields of Chechnya' and exposing the outrages committed by those forced to fight Vladimir Putin's war. She had, apparently, 'received one death threat after another', and at one point was detained and beaten by Russian troops 'who threw her into a pit, threatened to rape her and performed a mock execution' (Washington Post, 2006). Politkovskaya was found shot dead in the lift that served the block of flats where she had lived.

The range of episodes just cited are sometimes explained as isolated tragedies, produced by the crude methods of repression employed in underdeveloped, undemocratic or authoritarian states. It is certainly true that some countries lack, or have departed from, the traditions associated with more sophisticated and complex democracies, but it is also clear that polities imagined as bastions of lawful conduct have proved more than willing to employ unsavoury methods in order to serve their conception of 'the national interest'. This behaviour is not only evident when state systems are placed under duress (as was the case during the British government's long war with its Republican opponents in Northern Ireland [Cadwallader, 2013; Urwin, 2016]), but also when they are engaged in the routine business of governance. Wars and insurgencies may throw repressive tendencies into sharp relief, but some of these methods are also employed whenever the political activities of the subaltern are considered subversive (see Chapter 2). From a journalistic perspective, when particular types of investigative activity are targeted, the threat to freedom of speech is always universal, rather than particular. The material presented in this book is intended to support the argument that investigative journalism, whatever its practical and procedural flaws, is the inevitable product of any society or factional activity that is steeped in the rhetoric of freedom and democracy, but which is actually ruled by secrecy and deceit.

The 'democratic deficit': investigation vs. manipulation

Not all observers would condemn 'the system' in the blunt terms used in the previous paragraph, while others may support the underlying contention that it is not only authoritarian political rule that suffers from a serious 'failure of representation', but also the liberal variant of the democratic tradition (Starr et al., 2011: Skocpol, 2013). The detachment of a popular mass from the public institutions that are meant to represent its wishes – with a consequent decline in 'public trust and confidence in politics' (Flinders, 2010: 9) – has led to calls for a more responsive and efficient system, at both the national and trans-national levels. These political/procedural entreaties are usually focussed on the wish to maximise communicative and electoral engagement, and include routine references to 'structural reform' (Grant, 2013) improved electoral mechanisms (such as proportional representation), the strengthening of public interest journalism, and the technocratic argument that the internet (see below) offers an opportunity to counter the undue influence, or moral failure, of conventional media forms.

Offered as a way of reducing a perceived chasm between the demands of the citizen and the actions of the political class,[2] these measures do not necessarily question the structures that underlie the relationship (and, in practice, the functional separation) of political subjects and public institutions. Instead, therefore, of reforming the system, the more cynical response is to focus on the *instrumental purpose* of elections and plebiscites, which is to secure and extend the rule of particular socioeconomic cabals. When this is regarded as the goal, rather than the quality of democratic debate and exchange, then professional specialists in the art of persuasion can be drafted in to 'leverage' specific outcomes: this was exactly the insight provided by investigative journalists from the *Observer*, the *Guardian* and Channel 4 from 2017 to 2018, when they revealed how a company called Cambridge Analytica had manipulated voter perception during the American presidential election (Tobitt, 2018). The scandal escalated when senior managers in the group were filmed boasting about their ability to discredit opponents through the use of honey-traps and financial inducements (Graham-Harrison et al., 2018), but the staggeringly amoral nature of the process had already been demonstrated in Cambridge Analytica's own publicity.

Describing its contribution to the Trump campaign, its website declared that, through the study of 'millions of data points', they 'consistently identified the most persuadable voters and the issues they cared about', before these individuals were 'sent targeted messages to them at key times in order to move them to action' (Cambridge Analytica, nda). The election of a man described by many as a divisive and unstable demagogue, was presented here as just another job of work, while the more poisonous negative campaigning was outsourced to entities like 'Make America Number 1', a special interest group (or 'political action committee') sufficiently removed from the official Trump campaign to allow the production of damaging attacks on Hillary Clinton, the Democratic candidate. Cambridge Analytica, for its part, was entirely upbeat about its contribution to this process, noting that it had 'delivered data modelling, television targeting and placement, digital ad targeting and delivery, list building, and polling' to support the 'Make America Number One (MAN1) project', known to all and sundry as 'Defeat Crooked Hillary (DCH)' (Cambridge Analytica, nda).

The essence of the larger controversy, of which this incident is but one example, is conflict over the appropriate uses of public communication, and the relative sanctity of political representation. This problem is not, however, confined to one nation, restricted to a particular era, or determined by technological progress: disputes over the public role of the media (McQuail, 1992; Butsch, 2007; Keane, 2013; Carpentier et al., 2013; Couldry et al., 2016), and the efficacy and trustworthiness of a party-based democratic system (see Kitschelt, 2000)[3] are universal, long-standing, and have appeared at every stage of industrial development. As the journalist Gary Younge argued, various 'social pathologies' were 'eating away at our democracies long before social media were invented' (2018: 3). Despite the variety of positions adopted on this issue, they are underpinned by the basic assumption outlined previously – that states and governments need to maintain a formal relationship with a popular 'base' in order to substantiate (or at least exhibit) their claim to legitimacy.

Notions of popular rule

The conviction that 'the ultimate decisions' in national life 'rest with the people' (Bingham, 2011: 78) may be widespread, but the practical interpretation of this belief speaks volumes about the relative commitment of various social actors to democracy as an accurate expression of collective intent: the concept is construed not only as the unhindered exercise of popular discretion, but is also deployed to support the notion that major legislative and/or deliberative organisations possess genuine civic virtue (that they are, in effect, truly 'democratic'). This form of social organisation can be admired or deplored, but once we acknowledge the acute contradiction between the claim made by 'representative' bodies – to embody democratic values – and their apparent distance from the citizen, the challenge is to give a credible account of why such an arrangement exists. One approach, described earlier, is to lament the separation of voters and politicians, while another is to present this distance as entirely appropriate, following the contention that established powers must 'stand above the fray', and should be immune to the special pleading of sectional interests.

If the structural and physical removal of elected leaders from 'the people' *is* seen as legitimate, then any basic model of socio-political performance would have to include a mechanism that can enable meaningful acts of inter-sectional communication (instructions, 'conversations', demands, and so on) to take place. This position, which emerges from a circumscribed, functionalist view of democracy, places the onus on the process of mediation. It rests, therefore, on the conviction that any productive association between formal authority, 'intermediary bodies' such as non-governmental organisations (NGOs) and trade unions (Dearman and Greenfield, 2014: 3), and the public interest they are meant in various ways to represent, cannot function without the existence of a 'media-sphere' that allows particular communities to gain insight into the system and its procedures. Barisione and Michailidou, for instance, discussing European politics and the EU, imagine the existence of a distinct process in which 'executive decision-making' addresses specific issues, which 'subsequently become politicised' because they 'acquire public visibility through the media' (2017: 2).

This rather uninspiring model of transmission, which describes the ability of formal power to set and pursue a specific agenda, is in one respect reminiscent of Manning's argument that 'official sources associated with the apparatus of government and the state' possess 'crucial advantages' in the struggle for access to news media (2001: 140). Leaving aside for a moment the vexed question of what, in the twenty-first century, actually constitutes 'news media', it is worth noting that this routine perspective leaves intact the widespread notion that the sovereignty of the people is embedded in larger formations that act as its legal or, alternatively, its *de facto* representatives. Once again, the constant re-articulation of this mundane principle is more than a simple description of an unalterable state of affairs: it is deployed on a regular basis to reinforce points of view that draw strength, both from the notion of an 'appropriate' division of powers, *and* from the existence of a functional (i.e., no more than passably adequate) connection between elites and subordinate groups.

For sincere electoral democrats, although they may chafe against its limitations, the institutional separation of popular and executive power is an acceptable state of affairs, because it requires the regular involvement of voters in prescribed contests: these occasions can at least produce a standard against which the relative health of individual polities can be measured. So, for instance, when participation is high, systemic democracy[4] is validated, and where low, corrective measures (devoted to the creation of greater engagement) can be applied. For governments and other formal bodies, the fact that there is not a complete disconnection between citizens and administrative centres provides, as I have tried to suggest, a useful moral alibi: their spokespeople can meet a variety of challenges by citing their adherence to a tenet that is meant to underpin executive decisions. For international humanitarian organisations (see Chapter 6), the existence of this principle allows them to interrogate those governments that claim to operate within ethical boundaries, but which seem to neglect the moral sensibility that is attributed to the general populace, in the name of which democracy is enacted as a public ritual.

Popular rule, media forms, and trans-national notions of democracy

Established nations, meanwhile, are keen to evoke some conception of popular rule, and a number of states call themselves democratic despite the reluctance of the 'international community' to describe them as true democracies. Article One of Cuba's constitution, for example, declares that it is 'a united, *democratic* republic' (my emphasis), dedicated to 'the enjoyment of political freedom, social justice, individual and collective welfare, and human solidarity' (1992). This utterance is not meant to disguise the absence of the standard mechanisms associated with Western democracies (in which forms of 'healthy' competition between formally distinct, but essentially similar, entities – both electoral and economic – are celebrated), but to recalibrate routine political expectation. This is the purpose of references to other qualities (especially 'human solidarity') that might, where substantiated with action, offer a powerful counter-narrative to the instrumental goals that drive established democracies.

As a value, however, 'democracy' remains a potent meme, and circulates throughout the known political universe. Even North Korea, not usually regarded as a paragon of virtue in this respect, is known officially as 'the Democratic People's Republic of Korea'. When pariahs are subjected to critique, their attitude to democracy is an essential element of the scrutiny they must bear, even where they inhabit what appears to be a multi-party system. Vladimir Putin, for instance, who dominates the Russian Federation through the use of presidential edicts, and has been criticised for manipulating electoral procedures, stands accused by his rivals of 'seizing' power (Parfitt, 2018: 33) despite his formal engagement with more superficial aspects of democratic culture.

This critique of the 'anti-democratic' democrat is fairly widespread, however, and is not confined to attacks on non-Western figureheads. Besides references to clear cases of authoritarian power, like that exercised by Putin, any tendencies that threaten to gain electoral traction can be denigrated by 'centrist' elites as in essence extreme, and are described as 'populist' despite their location in the heartlands of democracy (Price, in Sanz Sabido, 2017; Harris, 2018). These reservations provide an instructive supplement to the debate over the meaning of democracy, but also serve to reinforce the need for media forms to serve as honest brokers on behalf of an international public. This, again, is central to any mode of journalistic enquiry that tries to provide a truly global perspective on so-called democratic norms.

In China, to take an example of a country that has an ambiguous relationship to standard conceptions of democracy, the relationship between journalism, the general population, and the state is calibrated rather differently, but still draws upon the trope that the media should act as the representative of the people and are therefore allowed to undertake specific, though limited, enquiries. This resembles the notion of 'dissenting' journalism in the West, a type of investigation that does not push too far and is therefore tolerated (de Burgh, 2008: 11), but also accords with research that seems to demonstrate the existence of a widespread, trans-national awareness (if not commitment) to 'the public-service ideal', which Deuze identifies as 'a powerful component of journalism's ideology' (2005, 442).[5] In some cases, the notion of the public good can be substantiated in specific forms, while being used simultaneously as an ideological appendage of the state. Tong, in her study of the Chinese investigative tradition, identifies exactly this tendency when she describes a core principle that is supposed to guide the conduct of those journalists engaged in serious 'public interest' campaigns. The Chinese version of this principle is known as 'public opinion supervision', a concept Tong defines as 'the *supervision by the people* of the Party and the government's work . . . through the media' (2012: 25, my emphasis). The Chinese Communist Party, in Tong's opinion, allows this form of oversight for the same reason that the ancient Imperial state drew upon the opinions of Confucian intellectuals, namely to 'reinforce its rule by providing constructive criticism without fundamental revolution' (26).

Scholarly admissions that the Chinese government falls short of its own precepts might be welcomed, but when circulated by the state itself, this form of self-criticism, dressed up as 'transparency', can have another, less laudable effect – the 'normalisation' of authoritarian systems. This is achieved by conducting an apparently balanced comparative analysis of the differences between 'democracies' and one-party states, as though dissimilarities are the mere products of tradition, and moral outrages the forgivable eccentricities associated with a colourful past. Sometimes, therefore, acknowledging the existence of limited democratic tendencies within the 'People's Republic', and contrasting these with the undoubted failures of the Western system, is designed to avoid the accusation that polities like China are actually *totalitarian* in nature, rather than open to the 'democratic' reform that the West advocates (and which it should, for the sake of consistency, also undergo).[6]

Yuezhi, in an analysis of the Chinese conundrum, is even more forthright than Tong, arguing that the appearance of critical structures represents 'the tentative institutionalisation of a form of watchdog journalism that is both popular with media audiences and instrumental to the Party leadership', going on to note that the initiative is an attempt 'to reassert control over a dysfunctional bureaucracy and expose elements of bureaucratic capitalism that had become so ruthless that they have threatened the very existence of the state bureaucracy itself' (2000: 577). The public rationale offered for decisions that lead to increased centralisation, including the removal by China's Congress of the limits on Presidential terms (allowing their leader Xi Jinping[7] to occupy the post for life), is nonetheless framed as a 'democratic' process, albeit one 'with Chinese characteristics' (BBC News, 2018). In their book on the Panama Papers, Obermayer and Obermaier discuss the extent of this merciless concentration of power and money, in a land where 'more than 300 million people . . . have less than $2 a day at their disposal' while the '100 richest have accumulated fortunes' worth on average $4.5 billion each (2017: 227).

Popular rule and the 'Western' paradigm

The dissemination of 'popular rule' as a foundational principle may ring hollow when the gulf between rich and poor is considered, racism is rife, and open, widespread discrimination against women is the norm (see Chapter 3), but the point is that the concept can be detached from its 'Western' context and reapplied elsewhere, just as it can reappear as a radical socioeconomic demand (demonstrated, for example, by the global wave of protest that occurred in 2011). In other words, the various manifestations of democracy, as a 'value laden' regime, can encompass a range of paradigms, from a set of procedures that can be administered directly by 'the people', to an instrument that is supposedly employed on their behalf. Yet, within standard versions of democratic practice, the stark contrast between those positions that envision an insurgent, disordered, 'anti-state' democracy (Abensour, 2011), and those wedded to more circumscribed paradigms (like constitutionalism), is often obscured, to the definite advantage of the latter.

An interesting example of this tendency can be found in Carpentier et al.'s description of the contrast between minimalist and maximalist models of democracy, in which they attempt to reproduce an even-handed account of these two perspectives. The *minimalist* approach to democratic culture is, in their words, 'confined mainly to the processes of representation, participation to elite selection and the political to politics' [sic], while the *maximalist* tendency regards democracy 'as a more balanced combination of representation and participation' (2013: 289). This account reveals the timidity of the received wisdom that emerges from some traditions within political science. The second definition is supposed to depict the more ambitious, extensive and idealistic version of democratic engagement, but actually replicates an underwhelming discourse about 'balance' between two basic requirements thought necessary for the operation of what sounds like the more *bureaucratic* category with which Carpentier and his co-authors began their discussion. Here, a limited ideological perspective on the essential components of democratic society reappears, apparently quite innocently, in the work of writers who are attempting to provide a useful benchmark for further discussion.

Even seemingly astute commentators – those who understand that there is an overlap between 'operative' democracy and rival systems – can base their analysis on myopic assumptions about the physical/systemic location of the ideal democratic order. Chadwick's discussion of the 'messy mixtures of democracy and authoritarianism' (2017: 12) that characterise the development of various international polities, provides an interesting point of departure for understanding what is at stake, but not perhaps in the way he had intended. Citing the work of Levitsky and Way (2010), Chadwick summarises their position by noting the 'integrated coexistence of what appear to be formal democratic rules ... with religious or military elite coercion, excessive patronage, and the flouting of the rule of law by those in power' (2017: 12).

At first sight, the enumeration of these problems seems to offer a welcome practical corrective to abstract models of democracy: they are not, however, employed as a general benchmark, against which *all* pretensions to democratic virtue can be measured. They are attributed instead to *a particular set* of nations. Chadwick focuses on the 'many African, Asian, and Latin American countries' that in his opinion embarked on 'journeys toward liberal democracy' but then became 'frozen in a pseudo-democratic stasis' that people 'living in the West may find counterintuitive and normatively objectionable' (12). Chadwick's 'key theme' here is the concept of 'transition', the (failed) progression from a nascent form of democracy to a more advanced condition (12).

The quality or relative success of movement is clearly set against a Western experience that is not subjected to analysis, but simply taken as the default position. A more nuanced and less patronising approach might suggest that Western polities are also 'frozen' in a set of practices that contradict their claim to represent the pinnacle of democratic culture, like the initiation of the destructive wars visited upon Iraq (see Chapter 8). The popular notion of 'arrested democracy' must therefore be supplemented with those studies that highlight the creation of 'authoritarian neoliberalism' as a transnational principle, in which advanced, 'Western' polities are particularly adept at implementing regimes of austerity (Tansel, 2017), while appearing to follow a set of lofty principles.

The pursuit, however, of an *orthodox* democratic paradigm is, in the last analysis, supposed to require no more than the modest participation of a 'fully informed' constituency, one that is 'empowered to choose between *conflicting opinions and alternative courses of action*' (Bingham, 2011: 78, my emphasis) that are usually generated by elite social actors. If the limited empowerment mentioned here is thought to depend upon the 'crucial role' played by the media (78), this suggests that they are imagined as an essential element within a disciplinary system of didactic paternalism. Such a belief is not dissimilar to the position developed by Kovach and Rosenstiel. Echoing the 'classic' defence of the profession, these authors declare that its main function is to 'provide citizens with the information they need to be free and self-governing' (Kovach and Rosenstiel, 2014: 17).[8] Carlson's response is that this 'respectable mission' cannot explain 'the complex social relations through which [journalism] comes to have authority' (2017a: 5). He suggests instead that attention should be focused on the *normative cultures* that prevail in each era of news production, and that the analyst needs to be aware of the differences 'across geopolitical contexts, and across different media' (5).

The production of news and investigative journalism

While Carlson attempts to provide a wider context for understanding the authoritative production of news, Zelizer (enumerating the various challenges to traditional news practices) expresses the fear that 'many presume that journalism is currently at its point of exhaustion' (2017: 1). Peters and Broersma declare quite bluntly that 'most journalism is not a public good', pointing to the 'disconnect between journalism's normative assertions' and its present condition (2017b: 188). They explain this situation as the consequence of a 'rhetorical entrenchment' formed in the last century, which cultivated a 'journalistic ethos' supposedly devoted to objectivity (188), but which allowed the pursuit of a less exalted agenda. Allan stops short of this conclusion, noting that it is nonetheless 'all too often the case that public service values are reframed *on more modest terms*', in essence because of financial constraints (2013: 17, my emphasis). Commercial pressures are, in fact, cited as one of the three reasons for what Starkman calls 'the disappearance of investigative journalism' in the United States (the others are the 'dominance of access reporting' and deregulation [2014: 199]). Starkman's point is clear: in a system where 'time is money', the high costs associated with investigative work can place this type of journalism 'on the endangered species list' (McChesney and Nichols, 2010: 24). For some media owners in the contemporary period, the legal risks and the threats posed by dominant groups mean that there is no strong rationale for pursuing challenging stories.

Nonetheless, a number of organisations are robust enough to distinguish between the financial paradigm and the moral imperative that certain types of investigation obey. In the Prologue to his co-authored book on the Panama Papers, Obermayer declares that his paper, the *Süddeutsche Zeitung* 'never pays for information, not only because we don't have the money, but primarily on principle' (Obermayer and Obermaier, 2017: 4). This also, he notes, 'reduces people's temptation to fob us off with fake documents' (4). Irrespective of the financial pressures that all acknowledge (see the opening statement in Remler et al., 2014), the growth of trans-national investigative bodies demonstrates the enduring strength of a principle that, by its very nature, is impossible to confine to one country or situation. Collective endeavours like Investigative Reporters and Editors sustain their efforts with an online presence that, in this case, describes the group as 'a grassroots nonprofit organisation' dedicated to improving 'the quality of investigative reporting', and supporting 'journalists throughout the world' (Investigative Reporters and Editors, nd). Similarly, the Global Investigative Journalism Network uses its web pages to draw attention to the range of 'nonprofit and related organisations worldwide that work in support of investigative journalism' (Global Investigative Journalism Network, nd). The range of groups accepted as affiliates include 'nonprofit newsrooms, online publishers, professional associations, NGOs, training institutes, and academic centers in nearly 50 countries' (nd), which coincides with the position advocated in the current volume – that the essential element in qualifying a set of activities as 'investigative' is not their formal constitution as news organisations, but their dedication to the principle of social justice and the free exchange of information.

Meanwhile, the democratic culture imagined by Bingham (2011), and expanded by Kovach and Rosenstiel (2014), is again most probably the regulated form of political expression common within electoral systems. In this respect, the normative emphasis is on people as 'legal subjects and bearers of rights' rather than as workers embedded in a system of hierarchies (Weeks, 2011: 2). Yet, in deference to an idealised 'sovereign public', the media in general (and presumably those organisations oriented to news and current affairs in particular) seem to be assigned a particular responsibility, not only to ensure freedom of communication but, in obedience to this principle, to preserve the democratic system and the political well-being of an entire polity.

Media, citizen, and state: three problems

The idea that the media in general (both 'old' and 'new') should be responsible for the vitality of democratic culture, engenders a number of problems: three in particular are identified in the discussion that follows. The first and most obvious of these is that the media's multiple generic functionality is lost to view, created in part by the nascence of online communication, but always evident in its 'traditional' manifestation: in other words, the diversity of forms, goals, and purposes media are thought to represent could be subsumed in the assumption that all communicative activity should work towards the propagation of the 'public good'. This expectation may be worth maintaining as a 'headline' value, but the truth is that the profits to be made from the commercial exploitation of media indicate that this goal will not be fulfilled.

As a result, where *anti-egalitarian* modes of communication appear to thrive, such as public relations (Davis, 2002; Cronin, 2018), they must either be described as such and removed from the essential core of the 'media-sphere', or conflated with practices with which they have no natural affiliation: after all, the goal of the PR operative, according to C. Wright Mills (2000), was never the perfection of democracy, but the transformation of public opinion *into one of many variables* that need to be 'pacified' during the authoritarian quest for power.[9] Conversely, the notion of an undifferentiated media bloc could also cast doubt on those functions (such as journalism and its investigative mode) that do have the potential to contribute to the positive development of useful public knowledge, since they could be associated with a larger 'failure' for which they are not necessarily responsible.

A common, though rather extreme, reaction to this conundrum is to argue that the whole process of mediation, irrespective of particular examples, is essentially despotic or anti-democratic. Unless, however, we accept Debord's thesis in its entirety, in which the media, as the instruments of an all-encompassing 'spectacle', simply present 'decisions already taken... for passive admiration' (Debord, 1998: 6), then it makes sense to distinguish between the individual functions of specific media genres, although we may question the rhetorical claims made on their behalf.[10] While there is no doubt that some modes of communication (i.e., those specifically designed to humanise elite discourse, or that use fake social media accounts to promote a point of view) have an adverse impact on even unexceptional forms of public exchange, it is worth repeating the point that other types of media – in the current example, those associated with journalistic enquiry – are invested (for better or worse) with a more serious moral potential.

The second difficulty with the notion that the media are duty-bound to substantiate democratic life, is that it obviates the need to examine the executive responsibility (and generative power) of forces that are supposed to operate above and beyond the realm of media institutions, such as state,[11] quasi-state, and corporate formations. The question, however, is the degree to which these bodies can exercise their influence *without* articulating their goals through the frameworks offered by media forms, and thus to some extent taking on the agenda set (in this case) by news organisations (which, of course, rely in turn upon the discursive frames offered by formal authority).

The problem of power and representation animated by Debord (1998) returns at this point in another guise: contemporary societies have been described as 'mediatized', based on the argument that media practices have become key elements in the production and articulation of social life (Morgan, 2011; Hepp, 2013; Esser and Strömbäck, 2014; Marcinkowski, 2014). Hepp defines the concept as the process through which the 'primary meaning' of lived cultures is not only 'mediated through technical communications media', but is 'moulded' (2013: 70) by these (presumably to some degree *automated*) processes. Despite Hepp's habit of providing rather circular explanations for this development, his contention that we inhabit 'worlds that are saturated with media communication' (128) might at least suggest that the media are not completely subordinated to the whims of the state and corporate sectors (if, of course, they can really be said to operate beyond these fields of influence).

The basic notion developed by Hepp and those associated with this tendency is that, because of the supposed autonomy of media forms, all social forces must operate within a discursive and/or institutional framework that is not necessarily under their control. There are, however, some problems with this notion, difficulties that are at once practical and conceptual. Besides the argument that some governments create *dependent communicative structures* that act as mouthpieces for those in power (which to some degree avoid their imbrication within a 'mediatized' environment, since in this instance the political frame is more heavily inflected), adherence to democracy as a visible principle usually requires the formation of 'neutral' bodies that can oversee media conduct, and are thus in theory functionally independent from both governments and media institutions (hence the creation of quangos,[12] industry regulators, and governing boards). This follows the usual practice in which 'democratic' processes are entrusted to, and embedded within, hierarchical organisations, a notion interrogated above.[13]

Addressing the issue from a more nuanced theoretical perspective, Deacon and Stanyer argue that 'mediatization' has become a catch-all term used to suggest an inevitable historical process (2014), one that is supposedly responsible for the assimilation of a governing rationale into a world where the dominant ideological or attitudinal principle is somehow established by the media. This philosophical discussion is in a relatively early stage, yet is in some senses a reconstituted version of a debate that was once organised as an enquiry into the dialectical relationship between 'opposing' forces compelled, through their co-presence on the field of conflict, into collaborative though sometimes destructive actions (see Price [2010, 2011] on the existence of 'structural complicity').

The third disadvantage of the 'media-centric' perspective is that it diminishes or caricatures the (admittedly intermittent and uncertain) agency of citizenship (the diversity of which is often reduced to a normative patriarchal standard), meaning that the creation of 'autonomous' currents of thought by relatively independent social collectives can be overlooked. In the standard conception, the citizen assumes the role of an appellant, or is reduced (as previously noted) to choosing between the formal positions created by those professional organisations which seek to gain advantage from the manufacture of a 'neo-liberal' mindset. Even this model of restricted choice is a sort of idealisation, since there is an argument to be made that the essential function of the 'sovereign individual' within capitalism (Abercrombie et al., 1986) is to provide the labour that the economy is supposed to need (Weeks, 2011). Social media, sometimes assigned a lower status than traditional forms (until, in some circles at least, the latter supposedly became an unrepresentative 'mainstream' cabal dedicated to the reproduction of fake news) are then conceived as forming an appropriate platform for conducting popular (and supposedly ill-informed) incursions into political debate. In this sense, individuals are encouraged to be 'opinionated' rather than knowledgeable and effective political agents. With regard, however, to the circulation of what we might call 'news by other means', Hermida has identified 'new para-journalism forms such as microblogging' that help journalists realise that there are 'more complex ways of understanding and reporting on the subtleties of public communication' (2012, 297). He describes this as the creation of new *awareness systems* that lead to what he calls the emergence of 'ambient journalism' (297).

New media use, political agency, and the elite

The belief that the proliferation of communication networks can offset the problems that beset democracies (noted previously), continues to produce broad generalisations about the devolution (as opposed to the concentration) of political agency. Fukuyama's recent insistence (in Görlach, 2017) that 'institutions have always been controlled by elites [but] . . . through the presence of the internet they are losing their power', is a case in point. This kind of assertion retains a certain polemical energy, but it cannot (as a brief summary of a broader issue) convey the complexities of the situation. Although the internet has enabled a culture of trans-national exchange, allowing principled, tech-savvy individuals like Snowden to expose the true character of power (Greenwald, 2014), Fukuyama's position does not differentiate between the various social forces that compete for public attention, nor does it investigate the extent to which 'new media' are employed for explicitly political purposes. The belief that new media actually 'depoliticises' the public (Roberts, 2014: 93) is another current of thought that could be addressed, while the routine constitution of the public itself as a coherent conceptual entity (eliding ethnicity, class, and gendered identity, for example) should be scrutinised in depth (see Mahony et al., 2010).

Of course, the emergence of novel material from previously untapped sources might be welcomed as an improvement on the absence of meaningful dialogue, especially when a number of established media institutions seem to act as outlets for propaganda. In this respect, an increase in dialogue (of whatever kind) could be seen as a positive contribution to the enlargement of public culture. Russell, for instance, argues that, although 'mediated publics' have often to make do with meagre resources, and are inhibited by 'structural restrictions', they manage nonetheless to wield a degree of symbolic and material power (2016: 4). Beneficial increases in sociability, the enhanced power of social movements, and a greater awareness of alternative political traditions, can all be traced to the expansion of online mediation.

These advances have, however, been accompanied by poisonous, sinister, and irrational behaviours, including the appearance of 'trolling' and online bullying, increased state and corporate surveillance, the reintroduction of fascist memes into mainstream discourse, overwhelming examples of sexist abuse, and the manufacture of conspiracy theories that attempt to deny even the most incontestable facts (including, for example, the repulsive notion that the Las Vegas massacre of October 2017 was a 'false flag' operation [Levin, 2017], a bloodless performance enacted by the deep state, the purpose of which was to increase support for gun control). The notion that the moderate exercise of rationality has been eroded by a 'maelstrom of pettiness, scandal and outrage',[14] generated by 'unregulated' behaviour on a variety of sites, might suggest that it is ordinary people who bear most of the guilt. One basic challenge lies, therefore, in the ways in which the online activity of disparate groups is imagined, and the assumption that the intrusive prominence of social media exchange provides a counterweight, for better or worse, to dominant practices.

Although the web as an 'information space' does indeed provide an arena for action and debate, the 'new online cultures' identified by Beer (2008, in Trottier and Fuchs, 2015: 6) are extremely diverse and do not necessarily represent a challenge to what is, in the last analysis, a highly resilient trans-national Establishment.[15] While, therefore, the notion of a more general political 'democratisation' through internet use is not entirely risible – where for instance it is imagined as a mode of contact that can increase the political solidarity and real-world activity of oppositional collectives – many subaltern groups engage in projects that have little to do with formal political culture, while even the most determined critics cannot alter the course of regimes that depend on the discretionary use of executive powers. In addition, the world's leaders have learned to employ social media (Gainous and Wagner, 2014; Fuchs, 2018) to reinforce their position, taking advantage of yet another form of communication (Twitter is an example) that allows them to engage in the production of edicts that imitate 'ordinary' conversations with their political base.

In many cases, however, manipulative interventions are made on behalf of political figures who do not have to take responsibility for the sharp practice that benefits their cause. One investigation conducted by BBC journalists, for example, discovered the use of 'fake social media accounts and blogs' which were used to support Dilma Rousseff's presidential candidacy in Brazil, during the 2010 election campaign (Gragnani, 2018). The details provided by the BBC team are particularly instructive, and provide a useful corrective to the kind of broad claims made by Fukuyama (see earlier). In one case, a blog post called Seja Dita Verdade ('Let the Truth be Told') gained significant influence in Brazil. The author was one Armando Santiago Jr., whose profile described him as 'a Brazilian citizen outraged by the criminal actions of the opposition in the election campaign' (Gragnani, 2018), and who was also a strong supporter of Rousseff. He made a particular point of criticising the 'false e-mails against Dilma' that he claimed were being disseminated. As it turned out, 'Comrade Armando' did not exist. His blog and his social media profiles were administered by four individuals who were paid about 4,000 Brazilian reals each a month 'to write and spread the Armando posts' (2018).

Communication, new media, and class mobility: the binary character of democracy and 'insurgent' perspectives

In sum, therefore, when access to communicative techniques is conflated with the exercise of democratic rights, a major consequence is the neglect of underlying principles and an obsession with the platforms themselves.[16] Lack of 'connectivity' can then be equated with the absence of democracy, even though 'cyberspace' is known to be the product of established 'power and knowledge relations' (Isin and Ruppert, 2015: 160), and democracy itself is supposed to be more extensive than the symbolic forms it assumes. Since the usual patterns of ownership, surveillance and control, seem to be reproduced in a refreshed technological context (Trottier, 2012), a number of analysts have begun to adopt a less celebratory approach. Isin and Ruppert, following comments made by Deibert in 2009, reinforce this note of caution by noting that, where the internet 'used to be characterised as a network of networks', it is 'perhaps now more appropriate to think of it as a network of filters and chokepoints' (2015: 2). According to Greenwald, Edward Snowden (see also Chapter 2) expressed the fear that his was 'the last generation' to enjoy the freedom that the internet had once provided (2014: 46).

Some commentators still echo the general optimism of Fukuyama but are careful not to confuse access to new media with an assault on elites, or with increased social mobility. In their account of the 'new digital age', Schmidt and Cohen (respectively, the Executive Chairman of Google, and the Director of a subdivision known as Google Ideas) describe a 'boom in digital connectivity' that will 'bring gains in productivity, health, education, and quality of life, and myriad other avenues [sic] in the physical world' (2013: 12). The networks created in this realm are imagined here as the harbingers of universal improvement, despite the unlikely pairing of higher productivity and better health.

What distinguishes this conception from run-of-the-mill techno-Utopianism is the authors' insistence that the progress they conceive will not remove the impermeable division between social classes, and thus will not (as noted previously) smooth the transition of disadvantaged individuals to a more enhanced status. Although the benefits they identify will accrue to 'the most elite users' *and* 'those at the base of the economic pyramid', this development is not regarded as even-handed (13). Access to the realm of social media is not therefore regarded in this case as the chance to develop a new model of progressive communication that can address political issues, but as an opportunity to gain 'access to the same basic platforms, information and online resources' (13).

The belief that the untrammelled use of new media is already a thing of the past, returns us to the question raised at the beginning of this Introduction – the ability or otherwise of media organisations and/or platforms to demonstrate active independence from the state and capital, on behalf of a positive conception of a public that requires support because it is structurally removed from the direct exercise of power.[17] If Schmidt and Cohen (see earlier) acknowledge that an improvement in class mobility is unlikely, and that the organisation and ownership of new platforms will remain the same, this should not suggest that the media are the only source of the problem: as part of a system (commonly known as 'democracy') that is supposed to supply their basic *raison d'être*, all media are bound (in contradistinction to the position advanced within 'mediatization' theory) to assume the biases of the system they inhabit and help to recreate. Ultimately, it is the binary character of democracy itself – drawing its conceptual and practical power from the nexus of the ideal[18] and the systemic – which divides communicative practice (see Chapter 3), and which enables the schizophrenic reproduction of an imaginary that exalts the pursuit of truth and justice, while amplifying institutional power and attempting to maximise revenue.

Dean, in her analysis of the ways in which the existence of contemporary democracy is automatically assumed to fulfil the higher desires of popular sovereignty, goes further, arguing that, because it pretends to contain the solution to all political problems within itself, its very presence destroys the hope of a better, more equal society. She attacks, therefore, the notion that true democracy has already been 'realised' merely because the organisation of social life is classified as 'democratic' (2009: 2). Holston, in his study of 'insurgent citizenship' in Brazil, provides a perspective that allows us to see more clearly the 'dark side' of this equation, noting the uncomfortable coincidence of 'democratic politics' with 'widespread violence and injustice against citizens' (2008: 310). He calls into question the value of a democratic theory that, drawn from a myopic 'North Atlantic' tradition, fails to engage with the variety of global practices that constitute the lived reality of actual cultures (311).

Holston receives support from the communication theorist Tufte, who uses the Brazilian example to advance the argument that communication devoted to social change, should be 'rooted in a more inclusive, people-centred and radically participatory development paradigm' (2017: 166). Calls for an 'inclusive democracy' began to gain traction after the appearance of Takis Fotopoulos' work on the subject in 1997. He argued that both the 'grow-or-die dynamic of the market economy', and the rival 'state socialist' model, had led to the concentration of power in the hands of elites, increasing poverty and ensuring ecological disaster (1997: xi).

However we theorise the suppression of equalitarian politics by 'systemic'[19] democracy – i.e., the triumph of a culture where 'direct participation' in government is 'minimal' (Ginsborg, 2008: 23) – we should anticipate the intrusion of formal authority (whether corporate or public) into *any realm of activity* where the ownership of capital or the exercise of political influence might be at stake. As Pickard argues, the hopes raised by digital media have been dashed by the control exerted by 'oligopolies driven by a corporate libertarian logic at odds with public interest principles' (2015: 212). Although this form of corporate power plays into dominant notions of free expression and social diversity, its actual practice is less enlightened. Writing about the Cambridge Analytica/Facebook scandal, Mahdawi noted how 'Facebook presents itself to the public as a social network' but, when describing its services to the advertising industry 'is very clear about the fact that it is a surveillance system' (2018: 8). Demands, meanwhile, for a new communicative structure (one that might address these questions by developing the expressive power of the subaltern as a distinct, self-reflexive 'class', with all the attendant contradictions of gender and ethnicity) must struggle for visibility, perhaps because any coherent, principled challenge to the dominance of *capital-intensive* media formations or platforms, is in effect a call for irreversible changes in the social order as a whole.

Elasticity of liberal ideology

Where alternative perspectives do begin to gain purchase, they are often confronted with serious obstacles, not all of which appear as overt forms of obstruction. This is not to say that social actors are necessarily mistaken when they call attention to the biassed character of state media, or criticise those communicative forms that help governments to exercise discretionary power. When Anna Gabriel, one of the leaders of the anti-capitalist Catalan party the CUP (Candidatura d'Unitat Popular, or the Popular Unity Candidacy, which is committed to independence from Spain on the basis of working-class autonomy), argued that 'I am being prosecuted due to my political activities and the government press has already condemned me', this was difficult to deny (Rincón and Pérez, 2018).

Yet a truly democratic recuperation of media forms and institutions is frustrated not simply by the obdurate hostility of vested interests, but by the apparent elasticity of liberal ideology, which is flexible enough to support the development of multiple points of view, but by the same token prevents any deep-seated reform. Heretical approaches to public communication face, therefore, a complex task: they must not only consider the explicit resistance of those who advocate 'neoliberal' principles – perspectives that Haiven argues (2014: 13) are drawn from the 'narrative, metaphoric and procedural resources imported from the financial world' and then used 'to help explain and reproduce everyday life' – but must also deal with less contentious socioeconomic precepts like notions about the sanctity of private property or the belief that the profit motive is an essential driver of human activity. According to Abercrombie et al., the argument that capitalism creates 'a mentality that exalts the [pursuit] of profit as an end in itself', stems from Weber (1986: 86). These more fundamental notions, that should really be regarded as controversial, seem to underpin everyday assumptions about the nature of social reality.

The more obvious inflexibility of the political Right may, therefore, be less of a problem than the rather nebulous, discreet character of material/ideological power, enshrined (as Corner argues) in the 'broad commitment' of trans-national elites to 'capitalist development' which, at the very least, ensures that alternatives to private enterprise 'are not a strong feature of mainstream European media content' (2011: 25). The existence of elites depends, as C. Wright Mills noted, on the ability of individuals to inhabit and control major institutions, which are 'the chief means of exercising power' and of 'acquiring and retaining wealth' (2000: 9). Among those institutions, in Mills' opinion, that enable the reproduction of power, is the media, which attracts ambitious careerists. Mills goes on to identify the mass media of his day, not as a beneficent collective, but as 'an important cause of the destruction of privacy' (314), just as Snowden eventually came to believe that the commanding heights of the online economy were devoted to 'the elimination of all privacy, globally' (Greenwald, 2014: 47).

The relative absence, however, of anti-capitalist, as opposed to more diffuse forms of public discourse, does not mean that it is impossible to articulate 'progressive' tales of community and mutual solidarity, but rather that these depictions of life are embedded in wider social narratives (produced, for example, by certain types of corporate advertising) that mount a defence of consumer society, even as they gesture towards emancipatory behaviours. The overriding issue, however, is that the production of 'insurgent' perspectives can be undermined by a variety of circumstances, quite apart from the hierarchical strength of established media conglomerates or the discretionary power of the state (see Chapter 3). Identifying an 'undesirable reality' is only the first stage of a difficult process, the success of which must ultimately depend on the correspondence between the challenge being made and the quality and clarity of the alternative on offer. General parables about the iniquities of *certain types* of (usually financial) capitalism, broad critiques of 'neoliberalism' as a philosophy, campaigns against sexual abuse and rape, or attacks on the economic corruption that sustains private hierarchies, may allow social movements, feminist and anti-patriarchal activists, Left-wing academics, and radical journalists to base their claims on a form of ethical pre-eminence, but may require cross-sectoral solidarity to avoid the dangers of assimilation into a more pervasive ideological framework.

Journalism: popular, academic, and professional assessment

If we accept the arguments set out previously, it is clear that journalism, understood both as the 'independent pursuit of accurate information' and as the 'original presentation' of this material for public edification (Shapiro, 2014: 561), is placed in an unenviable position. Embedded in a system that enables its production, yet limits its ability to fulfil the higher purposes that 'the public' (and many of its practitioners) want it to achieve, it is no wonder that, when popular opinion on the subject is tested, distrust seems to be one of the dominant responses. In 2016, according to British polling agency Ipsos MORI, only 25% of UK respondents rated journalists as trustworthy (compared, for example, to the 69% who trusted hairdressers, though of course it is usually assumed that the latter, however garrulous, do not have the same ease of access to national media outlets).

In the same year, Americans' faith in the mass media to 'report the news fully, accurately and fairly' sank to 'a new low' (Swift, 2016). A year earlier, in New Zealand, journalism had managed to attain the poorest rating of all the occupations listed, finishing below the widely reviled political class (*New Zealand Herald*, 2015). Finally, an annual global index, published by the Edelman Barometer, discovered that 'public trust in traditional media has fallen to an all-time low' and that three-quarters of the 28 countries surveyed 'were categorised as "distrustful" of government, business, media and non-governmental organisations' (Nicolaou and Giles, 2016). In this case, there seems to be a general revulsion against *any* authoritative bodies that habitually make (often unsolicited) contact with the citizens of various countries.

Although this broad (though hardly irreversible) decline in confidence varies according to national and regional factors (in the United States, Trump's assault on 'mainstream' media outlets encouraged Republican voters to adopt his attitude, thus depressing the overall approval rating), the fact remains that there is a near universal disparity between the expectation that journalism, in particular, should adhere to high professional standards, and the reality of everyday practice. This general feeling of dissatisfaction is based on a cluster of factors, including the reprehensible conduct of some practitioners, the 'bias' of particular outlets and, as seen previously, general distrust of distant or unrepresentative institutions. Meanwhile, at the beginning of 2018, the loss of faith in the quality of information obtained through social media and search engines, appeared to encourage a modest recovery in the esteem accorded to traditional journalistic formats (Edelman Global Report, 2018). According to the Edelman group, only four countries placed greater trust in online platforms as opposed to traditional news sources – Malaysia, Mexico, Turkey and Brazil (for an overview of Brazilian media practices, see Chapter 7).

Conclusion: towards a global investigative journalism

Whenever journalism is imagined as a self-reflexive mode of communication (one that is supposed to acknowledge its own role as an accountable public practice), then the chasm between its ideal function and the reality of performance will continue to provoke argument, in both academic and professional circles. Conboy argued that journalism has acted as a brake on social transformation, just as often as it has acted as a medium for change (2004: 1). In his book on American newsrooms, Ryfe identifies the core of this problem as institutional, in the sense that 'news routines enact constitutive rules *for what counts as journalism*' (2012: 23, my emphasis). If this point of view is correct, then the daily interactions pursued and experienced by journalists 'ritually reproduce' the constitutive rules 'embedded in the craft' (24). In Ryfe's opinion, a key barrier to any progressive change is the fact that sources, practitioners, and the public all recognise specific practices as journalistic, while other approaches to the dissemination of information, such as blogging, fall outside the accepted category (24).

Yet the once routine separation of news production into opposing paradigms – encapsulated in the terms *serious* and *popular*, and *professional* and *amateur* – has been disrupted by the appearance of hybrid forms like *The Daily Show* (see Baym, 2005; Harrington, 2008), the growth of online platforms (described in Holton et al., 2013), and the supposed expansion of journalism and news media to include citizen practitioners (Thurman, 2008; Campbell, in Price and Sanz Sabido, 2015). In other words, the mutation of genres, the increased technological diversity of communicative channels, and a (contested) transformation in the way journalists are identified, have all contributed to major changes in our understanding of journalism as a public practice. One notable perspective is the argument that these developments reflect the growth, not only of newly synthesised forms, but of a 'hybrid media system' that has re-energised newsgathering and reporting (Chadwick, 2017). One example of this hybridity is the way in which 'bloggers are influenced by some of the norms of professional journalism' while 'some of the norms of blogging' have had an effect on professional practices (2017: 193).

In recent years, investigative journalism, quite apart from news production in general, has definitely benefitted from the opportunities provided by technological advances, both with regard to portable equipment (e.g., smartphones) and the access these provide to online resources, social media sites, and publishing opportunities. Ettema and Glasser cite Tulloch's belief in 'the emergence of *a global investigative journalism* drawing on *webs of resources*' (my emphasis), which was 'orchestrated by a shifting cast of multi-skilled journalists, some freelance, working across print, broadcast and internet media, with relationships to branded media organisations' (2007: 491). It is important, however, not to fetishise the supposed proliferation of methods and opportunities that the digital age is meant to have produced, since as Waisbord notes, just because 'all reporting is (or should be) essentially investigative', it is 'redundant to define [it] in terms of the use of certain newsgathering methods' (2002: 377).

If investigative journalism is not defined by its techniques, practical or procedural, how then should it be described? Waisbord, writing about the situation in Latin America, provides another useful insight, when he draws attention to a central assumption that underpins many evaluations of investigative activity – its apparent role in serving a generalised notion of the public interest. If this is the acid test, then 'not every public exposure is synonymous with IJ [investigative journalism]' for the simple reason that 'not all issues are similarly relevant to the public and democracy' (377). The problems that arise from this distinction are obvious: which individuals or institutions should be empowered to decide where the public interest lies, and what exactly constitutes a worthwhile moral intervention? Such a question cannot be resolved by placing our faith in the deficient institutional/electoral framework analysed in this Introduction. As Davis observes in his book on the British elite, existing infrastructures of governance are not reliable instruments of democratic renewal, since they have been hollowed out by a selfish cabal of 'leaders' who have undermined 'the very institutions they manage' (2018: 23).

The issue of the public good can, however, be addressed from another perspective. We could ask which social forces stand to benefit from recent developments, such as the hybridisation of journalistic forms (see earlier), and the rise of practices like 'citizen journalism' (Allan and Thorsen, 2009). It would be easy enough to argue for the 'democratisation' of communication, based on the routine but vacuous argument that the free exchange of ideas and information is the guarantor of a democratic culture. When UNESCO (the United Nations Educational, Scientific and Cultural Organization), for example, produced a major report, packed with international case studies, it identified the need to delve into 'matters that are concealed either deliberately, by someone in a position of power, or accidentally, behind a mass of facts and circumstances' (Kārkliņš, in Hunter, 2012). This was prefaced by the argument that critical media practices and investigative journalism are essential to democracy. Waisbord, known for a more guarded approach, sounds an important note of caution, pointing out the limitations of investigative exposés, when for instance stories on 'the working conditions for tobacco workers in Argentina, racial discrimination in the workplace in Brazil, and police corruption in Mexico' had no lasting impact on governmental or legislative policy (2002: 379).

As long as this process – social containment used to protect financial accumulation – remains a standard practice within the realm of 'democracy', capitalist social relations will be disguised through a rhetorical allegiance to prevailing models of democratic behaviour. The fact that those who identify themselves as the opponents of injustice encounter substantial risks when pursuing simple conceptions of truth, demonstrates the continued influence of an authoritarian political force that inhabits the soul of democracy. Those, therefore, who identify themselves as 'democrats' must face the challenge of classifying the central values that characterise their stance. Is their goal the defence of whatever variant of democracy prevails within the nation they inhabit (see below)? Is the target of their critique the existence of unaccountable elites, or merely the excessive use of power (Weeks, 2011: 3)? The regular appearance of complaints about 'corruption', 'criminality', and tax evasion are, of course, entirely justifiable, but they are also the product of a set of normative assumptions that reveal the apparent limits of the 'investigative' principle.

The challenge, therefore, is to push beyond the nexus of established and insurgent practices, and the restrictions of systemic democracy, in order to pursue new forms of moral endeavour. My contention here is that radical political entities (encompassing journalists, social movement advocates, feminist activists, militants from radical groups like Black Lives Matter, working-class organisations, and academic researchers) must be strive to achieve three goals: first, the exposure of the secret machinations of a socio-economic elite (an aspiration that has met with some success); second, the destruction of a governing rationale that trades on the moral resonance of democracy, but generates the amorphous and ubiquitous utterances associated with public relations; and third, the creation of an alternative system of power based on borderless economic egalitarianism, social justice, gender and racial equality, and environmentalism.

There are, meanwhile, a number of practical initiatives that attempt to supply the institutional and political deficiencies identified previously. These progressive, open-source, often non-profit endeavours attempt to overcome the regimen of borders, the blight of hierarchical control, and the narrow focus associated with instrumental models of reportage. Although this should not suggest that they are dedicated to the re-creation (and certainly not the replacement) of the liberal democratic order, it is a measure of how attempts to pursue basic moral principles almost immediately come into conflict with the goals of what I would suggest is a rapacious trans-national capitalist patriarchy, the reproduction of which is dependent upon the continued suppression of subordinate groups and thus the maintenance of the socioeconomic conditions that allow the seizure of surplus value (see Chapter 3).

It is for these reasons – the need to provide a wider context within which critical journalistic activity takes place – that this Introduction has focused on the relationship between forms of advocacy, political structures, the binary nature of democracy, and dominant conceptions of the public. In studying the affiliation between these social forces, it has tried to avoid reproducing the tropes favoured by the liberal/democratic social order, in the belief that true political inclusivity is not the goal of trans-national elites, which depend on secrecy, access to confidential networks, and global mobility (Davis, 2018: 121). If a reasonable proportion of the electorate participates in votes and referenda, then that is often deemed enough to prove the existence of democracy. This goal depends, in turn, on voters' engagement with broad thematic depictions of 'national' life. If these themes cannot be controlled – when, for instance, supposedly populist alternatives to 'progressive' globalism began to gain attention – then this is the point at which bourgeois politicians will bemoan the erosion of democratic culture (Price, in Sanz Sabido, 2017). The argument here is that dominant groups are less concerned with the fate of those who have suffered under the rule of austerity, but rather with their drift from a political 'centre' where influence can be exerted on voters.[20]

The limitations of any critical intervention are evident because, while the powerful can certainly be discomfited by the release of confidential material or the creation of alternative narratives (see Chapter 6), it retains its influence because of the structural, physical, and economic distance it maintains from the 'everyday' rituals of public life, including those enacted through social media. Yet, in a political environment that many feel is suffused with deceit, and a media ecosystem dominated by a form of 'stealth communications' that turns public relations from a visible specialism into an entirely covert activity (Jansen, 2017), it is hardly surprising that journalism as a practice should be invested with a degree of moral significance.

Alastair Read, of the Bureau of Investigative Journalism, argued that the true role of the investigative reporter is not particularly glamorous, but consists of 'hard intellectual work in pursuit of a genuine piece of public education' (2013). Although few would imagine that even the most robust forms of investigative enquiry can provide an antidote to the severity of current social problems, whenever it retains even the vestiges of a positive civic function, it will always be distinguished from media forms that are entirely subjected to the whims of the market or the edicts of the state.

Notes

1 Bingham cites a 2001 legal dispute between a solicitors' office and *Times* newspapers, in which the following principle was aired: 'the proper functioning of a modern participatory democracy requires that the media be free, active, professional and inquiring' (2011: 78).
2 A clarification should be supplied at this point – by 'class' I do not mean a socio-economic stratum, but a cabal or 'category' of functionaries that serves as the

public face of the tension between the need to embody (and visualise) the principle of political representation, and the requirements of a capitalist economy that depends, in the last analysis, on command.

3 Kitschelt offers a critique of what he calls a 'dominant' interpretive framework, which emphasises 'state failure' in Western democracies, and the cartelisation of political parties.

4 In a previous footnote dealing with this concept, I argued that systemic democracy referred to 'those political entities in which electoral mechanisms sustain and supposedly renew the legitimacy of government as a principle, but within which executive authority operates without needing to gain the approval of the electorate for either routine or extraordinary activities' (Price, in Price and Sanz Sabido, 2016: 35).

5 Deuze argues that the notion of public service is 'an ideal that journalists aspire to, and use to legitimize aggressive . . . or increasingly interpretive . . . styles of reporting' (2005: 442).

6 The bargain offered here seems to resemble the following proposition: the 'authoritarian' state will offer a critique of the Western system, but will accept that the latter is still essentially 'democratic', if it recognises in turn the supposed virtues of the Chinese system and refrains from describing its behaviour as tyrannical.

7 For Xi Jinping, see also 'Winnie the Pooh'.

8 This citation is found in Carlson, 2017a: 5. The original source can be traced to Kovach and Rosenstiel (2014).

9 See Mills (2000: 315).

10 One of the most useful elements of Debord's argument is his belief that the media are involved in the routine production of orders (1998: 6), but this is not the only outcome that is attained – limited forms of 'debate' are also generated. My position here is that the society of the spectacle is not simply a society of 'instruction' but of dramatised controversy, staged as a means of demonstrating the existence of a vital democratic culture.

11 Some theorists delineate the state quite widely, encompassing those aspects of civil society that contribute to the functioning of the social order: my interpretation is more concerned with the origin of the 'command', bearing in mind that the consciousness of those in power is inflected by their perception that any utterance or directive has to be processed by an audience that must share their values. In practice, this means that 'authority' must to some degree align itself with the outlook adopted by its subordinates, who in turn inhabit an anxious state as they strive to understand and reflect the values of those set above them, and whom they hope at some point to supplant.

12 A quango is a 'quasi-autonomous non-governmental organisation', a body appointed and funded by central government but not (officially) run by it.

13 The challenge, however, of mounting a thorough critique of institutions that follow the logic of capitalist enterprise, means that the main target of scrutiny is often the individual behaviour of media owners, managers, and employees, and the quality of the product they create. Yet, just as media outputs are composed of many different genres, not all 'media operatives' are equally culpable for the shortcomings of the institutions they serve.

14 *The Economist* (2017: 11).

15 Although executive authority does not depend solely on the control of information or opinion (since it can make discrete use of invisible command structures and informal modes of influence), public access to communication platforms will remain at the centre of any debates about the depth and quality of democratic culture.

16 See Srnicek (2016).

17 Though not always raised in this form, echoes of the debate can appear, for example, when news editors discuss the appropriate balance between the use of 'elite' sources, and material obtained through public opinion.
18 The systemic character of democracy does, of course, incorporate the 'ideal' form upon which it depends, just as the ideal form is a reference both to a perfect 'system' and to an abstract principle.
19 See Price, in Price and Sanz Sabido, 2016.
20 The panic subsided when voters opted for Right-wing politicians like Macron (who, though determinedly populist themselves, prevented the triumph of more disruptive forces).

References

Abensour, Miguel (2011) *Democracy Against the State: Marx and the Machiavellian Moment*, Malden MA and Cambridge: Polity Press.

Abercrombie, Nicholas, Hill, Stephen and Turner, Bryan S. (1986) *Sovereign Individuals of Capitalism*, London and New York: Routledge.

Allan, Stuart (2013) *Citizen Witnessing*, Cambridge, and Malden MA: Polity Press.

Allan, Stuart and Thorsen, Einar (2009) *Citizen Journalism: Global Perspectives*, New York: Peter Lang.

Barisione, Mauro and Michailidou, Asimina (2017) 'Do we need to rethink politics in the social media era?' in Barisione, Mauro and Michailidou, Asimina [editors], *Social Media and European Politics: Rethinking Power and Legitimacy in the Digital Era*, London: Palgrave Macmillan, Springer.

Baym, Geoffrey (2005) 'The daily show: Discursive integration and the reinvention of political journalism', in *Political Communication*, Vol. 22, Issue: 3, pp. 259–276.

BBC News (2018) 'China's Xi allowed to remain "president for life" as term limits removed', *BBC News*, online, www.bbc.co.uk/news/world-asia-china-43361276?intlink_from_url=www.bbc.co.uk/news/topics/c207p54mdg7t/xi-jinping&link_location=live-reporting-story [accessed 11 March 2018].

Beer, David (2008) 'Social network(ing) sites: Revisiting the story so far', in *Journal of Computer-Mediated Communication*, Vol. 13, Issue: 2, pp. 516–529.

Berglez, Peter (2008) 'What is global journalism?' in *Journalism* Studies, Vol. 9, Issue: 6, pp. 845–858, Taylor and Francis.

——— (2013) *Global Journalism: Theory and Practice*, New York: Peter Lang Publishing.

Bingham, Tom (2011) *The Rule of Law*, London and New York: Penguin.

Boffey, Daniel (2018) 'Slovakian journalist investigating claims of tax fraud linked to ruling party shot dead', *Guardian*, online, 26 February 2018, https://www.theguardian.com/world/2018/feb/26/slovakian-journalist-investigating-claims-of-tax-linked-to-ruling-party-shot-dead [accessed 12 November 2018].

Bro, Peter (2018) *Models of Journalism: Functions and Influencing Factors*, Abingdon and New York: Routledge.

Butsch, Richard [editor] (2007) *Media and Public Spheres*, Houndmills: Palgrave Macmillan.

Cadwallader, Anne (2013) *Lethal Allies: British collusion in Northern Ireland*, Cork: Mercier Press.

Cambridge Analytica (nda) 'Donald J. Trump for president', https://ca-political.com/casestudies/casestudydonaldjtrumpforpresident2016 [accessed 21 March 2018].

——— (ndb) 'Make America no. 1', https://ca-political.com/casestudies/casestudymakeamericanumber12016 [accessed 21 March 2018].

Campbell, Vincent (2015) 'Citizen journalism and active citizenship', in Price, Stuart and Sanz Sabido, Ruth [editors], *Contemporary Protest and the Legacy of Dissent*, London: Rowman and Littlefield International.

Carlson, Matt (2017a) *Journalistic Authority: Legitimating News in the Digital Era*, New York: Columbia University Press.

Carlson, Matt (2017b) 'Establishing the boundaries of journalism's public mandate', in Peters, Chris and Broersma, Marcel [editors], *Rethinking Journalism Again: Societal Role and Public Relevance in a Digital Age*, London and New York: Routledge.

Carpentier, Nico, Dahlgren, Peter and Pasquali, Francesca (2013) 'Waves of media democratization: A brief history of contemporary participatory practices in the media sphere', in *Convergence*, Vol. 19, Issue: 3, pp. 287–294.

Chadwick, Andrew (2017) *The Hybrid Media System: Politics and Power*, Oxford: Oxford University Press.

Conboy, Martin (2004) *Journalism: A Critical History*, London and New York: Sage Publications.

Corner, John (2011) *Theorising Media: Power, Form and Subjectivity*, Manchester: Manchester University Press.

Couldry, Nick, Livingstone, Sonia and Markham, Tim (2016) *Media Consumption and Public Engagement: Beyond the Presumption of Attention*, Houndmills: Palgrave Macmillan.

Cronin, Anne (2018) *Public Relations Capitalism: Promotional Culture, Publics and Commercial Democracy*, Houndmills: Palgrave Macmillan.

Cuban Constitution (1992) Cubanet, https://www.cubanet.org/htdocs/ref/dis/const_92_e.htm [accessed 12 November 2018].

Dallison, Paul (2017) 'The murder of a journalist', *Politico*, online, 19 October 2017, www.politico.eu/blogs/on-media/2017/10/murder-malta-journalist-daphne-caruana-galizia-joseph-muscat/ [accessed 17 March 2018].

Davis, Aeron (2002) *Public Relations Democracy: Politics, Public Relations and the Mass Media in Britain*, Manchester: Manchester University Press.

—— (2018) *Reckless Opportunists: Elites at the End of the Establishment*, Manchester: Manchester University Press.

Deacon, David and Stanyer, James (2014) 'Mediatization: Key concept or conceptual bandwagon?' in *Media, Culture & Society*, Vol. 36, Issue: 7, pp. 1032–1044.

Dean, Jodi (2009) *Democracy and Other Neoliberal Fantasies: Communicative Capitalism and Left Politics*, Durham and London: Duke University Press.

Dearman, Philip and Greenfield, Cathy (2014) 'Investigating communication, media and democracy', in Dearman, Philip and Greenfield, Cathy [editors], *How We Are Governed: Investigations of Communication, Media and Democracy*, Newcastle Upon Tyne: Cambridge Scholars Publishing.

Debord, Guy (1998) *Comments on the Society of the Spectacle*, London and New York: Verso.

—— (2005) *Society of the Spectacle*, Knabb, Ken [translator and editor], London: Rebel Press.

de Burgh, Hugo (2008) *Investigative Journalism*, [2nd edition], London and New York: Routledge.

Deuze, Mark (2005) 'What is journalism? Professional identity and ideology of journalists reconsidered', in *Journalism*, Vol. 6, Issue: 4, pp. 442–464.

Edelman Global Report (2018) 'Edelman Trust Barometer', https://cms.edelman.com/sites/default/files/2018-01/2018%20Edelman%20Trust%20Barometer%20Global%20Report.pdf [accessed 13 November 2018].

Economist, The (2017) Leader, 'Do social media threaten democracy?' *The Economist*, online, 3–10 November, www.economist.com/news/leaders/21730871-facebook-google-and-twitter-were-supposed-save-politics-good-information-drove-out [accessed 24 March 2018].
Esser, Frank and Strömbäck, Jesper [editors] (2014) *Mediatization of Politics: Understanding the Transformation of Western Democracies*, Houndmills: Palgrave Macmillan.
Ettema, James S. and Glasser, Theodore L. (1984) 'On the epistemology of investigative journalism', Paper presented at the Annual Meeting of the Association for Education in Journalism and Mass Communication, 5–8 August (67th, Gainesville, FL).
——— (1994) 'The irony in – and of – journalism: A case study in the moral language of liberal democracy', in *Journal of Communication*, Vol. 44, Issue: 2, pp. 5–28.
——— (2007) 'An international symposium on investigative journalism: Introduction', in *Journalism*, Vol. 8, Issue: 5, pp. 491–494, Los Angeles, London, New Delhi and Singapore: Sage Publications.
Flinders, Matthew (2010) *Democratic Drift: Majoritarian Modification and Democratic Anomie in the United Kingdom*, Oxford: Oxford University Press.
Fotopoulos, Takis (1997) *Towards an Inclusive Democracy: The Crisis of the Growth Economy and the Need for a New Liberatory Project*, London: Bloomsbury Publishing.
Fuchs, Christian (2018) *Digital Demagogue: Authoritarian Capitalism in the Age of Trump and Twitter*, London and New York: Pluto Press.
Gainous, Jason and Wagner, Kevin M. (2014) *The Social Media Revolution in American Politics*, Oxford and New York: Oxford University Press.
Ginsborg, Paul (2008) *Democracy: Crisis and Renewal*, London: Profile Books.
Görlach, Alexander (2017) 'Francis Fukuyama: Democracy needs elites', *The Huffington Post*, online, www.huffingtonpost.com/entry/francis-fukuyama-democracy-elites_us_58b5a2cfe4b0780bac2d8ea3 [accessed 20 August 2017].
Gragnani, Juliana (2018) 'Fake profiles boosted Brazilian ex-president Dilma', 21 March, *BBC News*, online, www.bbc.co.uk/news/blogs-trending-43371212 [accessed 21 March 2018].
Graham-Harrison, Emma, Cadwalladr, Carole and Osborne, Hilary (2018) 'Cambridge Analytica boasts of dirty tricks to swing elections', *The Guardian*, online, 19 March [accessed 21 March 2018].
Graham, Todd and Hajru, Auli (2011) 'Reality TV as a trigger of everyday political talk in the net-based public sphere', *European Journal of Communication*, Vol. 26, Issue: 1, pp. 18–32.
Grant, Charles (2013) 'How to reduce the EU's democratic deficit', *The Guardian*, online, 10 June, www.theguardian.com/commentisfree/2013/jun/10/how-to-reduce-eu-democratic-deficit [accessed 23 January 2018].
Greenwald, Glenn (2014) *No Place to Hide: Edward Snowden, the NSA, and the US Surveillance State*, London: Hamish Hamilton.
Haiven, Max (2014) *Cultures of Financialisation: Fictitious Capital in Popular Culture and Everyday Life*, Houndmills: Palgrave Macmillan.
Hamilton, James T. (2016) *Democracy's Detectives: The Economics of Investigative Journalism*, Cambridge, MA and London: Harvard University Press.
Hansen, Ejvind (2013) 'Aporias of digital journalism', in *Journalism*, July, Vol. 14, Issue: 5, pp. 678–694.
Harrington, Stephen (2008). 'Popular news in the 21st century: Time for a new critical approach?' *Journalism*, Vol. 9, Issue: 3, pp. 266–284.

Harris, John (2018) 'The elite's concern for the have-nots did not last long', *The Guardian*, Journal Section, 26 February, p. 1.
Hepp, Andreas (2013) *Cultures of Mediatization*, Cambridge and Malden, MA: Polity Press.
Hermida, Alfeed (2012) 'Twittering the news: The emergence of ambient journalism', in *Journalism Practice*, Vol. 4, Issue: 3, 2010, pp. 297–308.
Holcomb, Jesse, Mitchell, Amy and Page, Dana (2015) 'Investigative journalism and digital security: Perceptions of vulnerability and behaviour', in Pew Research Centre Report, in association with Columbia University's Tow Center for Digital Journalism, http://assets.pewresearch.org/wp-content/uploads/sites/13/2015/02/PJ_InvestigativeJournalists_0205152.pdf [accessed 3 August 2018].
Holston, James (2008) *Insurgent Citizenship: Disjunctions of Democracy and Modernity in Brazil*, Princeton and Woodstock: Princeton University Press.
Holton, Avery E., Coddington, Mark and Gil de Zúñiga, Homero (2013). 'Whose news? Whose values? Citizen journalism and journalistic values through the lens of content creators and consumers', in *Journalism Practice*, Vol. 7, Issue: 6, pp. 720–737.
Hunter, Mark Lee [editor] (2012) *The Global Investigative Journalism Casebook*, Paris: UNESCO.
Investigative Reporters and Editors (nd), https://www.ire.org [accessed 13 November 2018].
Ipsos MORI (2016) 'Politicians are still less trusted than estate agents, journalists and bankers', *Ipsos MORI*, online, 22 January, www.ipsos.com/ipsos-mori/en-uk/politicians-are-still-trusted-less-estate-agents-journalists-and-bankers [accessed 24 September 2017].
Isin, Engin and Ruppert, Evelyn (2015) *Being Digital Citizens*, London: Rowman and Littlefield International.
Jansen, Sue Curry (2017) *Stealth Communications*, Cambridge and Malden, MA: Polity Press.
Kārkliņš, Jānis (2012) 'Foreword: Presenting the global investigative journalism casebook', in Hunter, Mark Lee [editor], *The Global Investigative Journalism Casebook*, Paris: UNESCO.
Keane, John (2013) *Democracy and Media Decadence*, New York and Cambridge: Cambridge University Press.
Kitschelt, Herbert (2000) 'Citizens, politicians, and party cartellization: Political representation and state failure in post-industrial democracies', in *European Journal of Political Research*, Vol. 37, Issue: 2, pp. 149–179.
Kovach, Bill and Rosenstiel, Tom (2014) *The Elements of Journalism: What Newspeople Should Know and the Public Should Expect*, New York: Three Rivers Press.
Levin, Sam (2017) 'Anger as Las Vegas "hoax shooting" clips plugged by YouTube', *The Guardian*, 6 October, 18.
Mahony, Nick, Newman, Janet and Barnett, Clive [editors] (2010) *Rethinking the Public: Innovations in Research, Theory and Politics*, Bristol: Policy Press.
Marcinkowski, Frank (2014) 'Mediatisation of politics: Reflections on the state of the concept', in *Javnost-the Public*, Vol. 21, Issue: 2, pp. 5–22.
McChesney, Robert W. and Nichols, John (2010) *The Death and Life of American Journalism: The Media Revolution That Will Begin the World Again*, New York: Nation Books.
McQuail, Denis (1992) *Media Performance: Mass Communication and the Public Interest*, Los Angeles, London, New Delhi and Singapore: Sage Publications.

Mills, C. Wright (2000) *The Power Elite*, Oxford: Oxford University Press.
Morgan, David (2011) 'Mediation or mediatisation: The history of media in the study of religion', in *Culture and Religion*, Vol. 12, Issue: 2, pp. 137–152.
New Zealand Herald (2015) 'Trust survey results revealed: MPs, journalists least trusted', *New Zealand Herald*, online, 9 June, www.nzherald.co.nz/nz/news/article.cfm?c_id=1&objectid=11462191 [accessed 24 September 2017].
Nicolaou, Anna and Giles, Chris (2016) 'Public trust in media at all time low, research shows', *Financial Times*, online, www.ft.com/content/fa332f58-d9bf-11e6-944b-e7eb37a6aa8e [accessed 6 January 2018].
Mahdawi, Arwa (2018) 'The last post?' *Guardian*, G2 Section, 21 March.
Manning, Paul (2001) *News and News Sources: A Critical Introduction*, Los Angeles, London, New Delhi and Singapore: Sage Publications.
Obermayer, Bastian and Obermaier, Frederik (2017) *The Panama Papers: Breaking the Story of How the Rich and Powerful Hide Their Money*, London: Oneworld Publications.
Parfitt, Tom (2018) 'I can give Putin a way out, poll rival says', *The Guardian*, 26 February, 33.
Peters, Chris and Broersma, Marcel [editors] (2017a) *Rethinking Journalism Again: Societal Role and Public Relevance in a Digital Age*, London and New York: Routledge.
——— (2017b) 'The rhetorical illusions of news', in Peters, Chris and Broersma, Marcel [editors], *Rethinking Journalism Again: Societal Role and Public Relevance in a Digital Age*, London and New York: Routledge.
Pickard, Victor (2015) *America's Battle for Media Democracy: The Triumph of Corporate Libertarianism and the Future of Media Reform*, New York and Cambridge: Cambridge University Press.
Price, Stuart (2010) *Brute Reality: Power, Discourse and the Mediation of War*, London and New York: Pluto Press.
——— (2011) *Worst-Case Scenario? Governance, Mediation and the Security Regime*, London and New York: Zed Books.
——— (2016) 'The "Borderless State": ISIS, hierarchy and trans-spatial politics', in Price, Stuart and Sanz Sabido, Ruth [editors], *Sites of Protest*, London: Rowman and Littlefield International.
——— (2017) 'Populism, "Community", and Political Culture: The revenge of the liberal elite', in Sanz Sabido, Ruth [editor], *Representing Communities*, London: Palgrave Macmillan.
Price, Stuart and Sanz Sabido, Ruth [editors] (2016) *Sites of Protest*, London: Rowman and Littlefield International.
Read, Alastair (2013) 'How to: Get started in investigative journalism', Journalism.co.uk, www.journalism.co.uk/skills/how-to-get-started-in-investigative-journalism/s7/a555318/ [accessed 25 March 2018].
Remler, Dahlia K., Waisanen, Don J. and Gabor, Andrea (2014) 'Academic journalism: A modest proposal', in *Journalism Studies*, Vol. 15, Issue: 4, pp. 357–373.
Rincón, Reyes and Pérez, Fernando J. (2018) 'Citing "political crimes", Switzerland casts doubt on extradition of Catalan separatist leader', *El País*, online, https://elpais.com/elpais/2018/02/21/inenglish/1519204673_212715.html [accessed 24 March 2018].
Roberts, John Michael (2014) *New Media and Public Activism: Neoliberalism, the State and Radical Protest in the Public Sphere*, Bristol: University of Bristol, Policy Press.
Russell, Adrienne (2016) *Journalism as Activism: Recoding Media Power*, Cambridge and Malden, MA: Polity Press.

Ryfe, David M. (2012) *Can Journalism Survive? An Inside Look at American Newsrooms*, Cambridge and Malden, MA: Polity Press.

Schmidt, Eric and Cohen, Jared (2013) *The New Digital Age: Reshaping the Future of People, Nations and Business*, London: John Murray.

Skocpol, Theda (2013) *Diminished Democracy: From Membership to Management in American Civic Life*, New York: University of Oklahoma Press.

Shapiro, Ivor (2014) 'Why democracies need a functional definition of journalism now more than ever', in *Journalism Studies*, Vol. 15, Issue: 5, pp. 555–565.

Srnicek, Nick (2016) *Platform Capitalism*, Cambridge and Malden, MA: Polity Press.

Starkman, Dean (2014) *The Watchdog That Didn't Bark: The Financial Crisis and the Disappearance of Investigative Journalism*, New York: Columbia University Press.

Starr, Amory, Fernandez, Luiz and Scholl, Chrisitan (2011) *Shutting Down the Streets: Political Violence and Social Control in the Global Era*, New York and London: New York University Press.

Sullivan, Drew (2018) 'Jan's and Daphne's laws: How to stop the murder of journalists', *Global Investigative Journalism Network*, online, 16 March, https://gijn.org/2018/03/16/jans-daphnes-laws-stop-murder-journalists/ [accessed 18 March 2018].

Swift, Art (2016) 'Americans' trust in mass media sinks to new low', *Gallup News*, online, 14 September, http://news.gallup.com/poll/195542/americans-trust-mass-media-sinks-new-low.aspx [accessed 24 September 2017].

Tansel, Cemal Burak [editor] (2017) *States of Discipline: Authoritarian Neoliberalism and the Contested Reproduction of Capitalist Order*, London: Rowman and Littlefield International.

Thurman, Neil (2008) 'Forums for citizen journalists? Adoption of user generated content initiatives by online news media', in *New Media & Society*, Vol. 10, Issue: 1, pp. 139–157.

Tobitt, Charlotte (2018) 'The observer fought off legal threats from Facebook and Cambridge analytica before publishing data harvesting scoop', *Press Gazette*, online, 20 March, www.pressgazette.co.uk/the-observer-fought-off-legal-threats-from-facebook-and-cambridge-analytica-before-publishing-data-harvesting-scoop/ [accessed 21 March 2018].

Tong, Jingrong (2012) *Investigative Journalism in China: Journalism, Power, and Society*, New York, London, New Delhi and Sydney: Bloomsbury Publishing.

Trottier, Daniel (2012) 'Policing social media', in *Canadian Review of Sociology/Revue Canadienne de Sociologie*, Vol. 49, Issue: 4, pp. 411–425.

Trottier, Daniel and Fuchs, Christian (2015) *Social Media, Politics and the State*, New York and Abingdon: Routledge.

Tufte, Thomas (2017) *Communication and Social Change: A Citizen Perspective*, Cambridge and Malden, MA: Polity Press.

Urwin, Margaret (2016) *A State in Denial: British Collaboration with Loyalist Paramilitaries*, Cork: Mercier Press.

Waisbord, Silvio (2002) 'The challenges of investigative journalism', in *University of Miami Law Review*, pp. 377.

Walker, Shaun (2016) 'The murder that killed free media in Russia', *The Guardian*, online, 5 October, www.theguardian.com/world/2016/oct/05/ten-years-putin-press-kremlin-grip-russia-media-tightens [accessed 12 March 2018].

Washington Post (2006) 'Her own death, foretold', *Washington Post*, online, 15 October, www.washingtonpost.com/wp-dyn/content/article/2006/10/14/AR2006101400805.html [accessed 17 March 2018].

Weeks, Kathi (2011) *The Problem with Work: Feminism, Marxism, Antiwork Politics, and Postwork Imaginaries*, Durham and London: Duke University Press.

Younge, Gary (2018) 'The poison in politics runs deeper than dodgy data', *The Guardian*, Opinion Section, 23 March, 3.

Yuezhi, Zhou (2000) 'Watchdogs on party leashes? Contexts and implications of investigative journalism in post-Deng China', in *Journalism Studies*, Vol. 1, Issue: 4, pp. 577–597.

Zelizer, Barbie (2017) *What Journalism Could Be*, Cambridge and Malden, MA: Polity Press.

Part I
Investigative journalism, public integrity, and the state

This first section exemplifies the central theme of the book, concentrating on the relationships between the practitioner, the state, and other influential forces. The study begins with Richard Danbury's account in Chapter 1 of the moral and legal challenges posed when investigative journalists in the UK have to deal with controversial issues – in this case, the legal 'duty to report' any information relating to existing (and quite broad) definitions of terrorist activity. Based in part on an incident in which Danbury and a colleague were approached about an apparently palpable and immediate threat, the chapter examines the dilemmas faced by journalists who have to contend with a competing set of obligations – to their sources, to the authorities, to the public, and to themselves. Unlike those depictions of journalistic activity that confine themselves to an abstract account of the dilemmas faced in the course of an investigation, Danbury offers both a description of the practical hurdles he and his colleague had to overcome, and an analysis of the general principles that shaped their actions, warning the reader that there are 'many legal burdens imposed on journalists to reveal information to the authorities, some of which have criminal sanctions for non-compliance'. The chapter also includes interviews with journalists and legal practitioners, who discuss issues like the 'chilling effect' that some of them attribute to the pressure of anti-terror legislation.

Chapter 2, written by Ben Harbisher, draws attention to the 'massive scale' of state surveillance, which includes 'military, political, commercial, and domestic targets'. The author goes on to identify 'fusion centres', hybrid agencies that are not only dedicated to the monitoring of terrorist activity, but also of those groups and movements that might constitute a threat to capitalism and state power. This form of conflation is enshrined in the notion of 'multi-issue extremism', where 'cause-led activism and legitimate public protest' are subjected to illegal scrutiny. One of the many useful aspects of Harbisher's contribution is his discussion of the methods employed by investigators. He notes that readily available public sources and search engines, such as LexisNexis, will yield extremely valuable information for the groups he identifies as the most eager to uncover the details of surveillance – journalists, academics, and activists. He also covers the use of Freedom of Information requests and the data sets produced by whistleblowers, ending by entreating the reader to 'consider both the risks, and the inherent limitations of conducting this type of research'.

Stuart Price, in Chapter 3, examines the relationship between journalists and those forms of authority that both enable and constrain the production of news. Identifying no less than ten forms or sites of influence, Price refers to a variety of national and global contexts that affect all reporters, drawing his examples from the UK, South Africa, Canada, Libya, Malaysia, Spain, China, Uganda, and Russia. The various situations described here are used to substantiate his argument that the pressures on journalists (full-time or 'freelance') should be understood as part of a wider 'trans-national attempt to discipline workers' under the ideological aegis of managerialism. According to this perspective, 'failing' institutions may appear to be on the brink of collapse, but are still used as clearing houses for capital, at the expense of their employees. Price also takes the position that there are diametrically opposed modes of communication, one broadly propagandist, and the other that, whatever its faults, attempts to serve the public interest. This division, he argues, can be attributed to 'a structural contradiction within the information economy', and the fact that the real commitment of dominant groups is to the *appearance* of integrity and civic virtue. He argues, in conclusion, that the determined enquiries of investigative journalists 'will continue to provide a corrective to the dubious, multi-agency exercise of "discretion" on matters that should never have been hidden from public view'. Underlying this position, however, is the author's belief that journalism does not need to be unambiguously 'moral' to act as a counterweight to powerful social forces, but that it does so by virtue of the fact that it is *procedurally intrusive.*

Chapter 4 is a co-written piece by Richard Danbury and Judith Townend, which deals with the legal and technological obstacles that can prevent journalists from protecting their sources. Discussing the need to balance the interests of the authorities and other social actors, they argue that 'there is no absolute value in . . . protecting national security in itself, or the administration of justice in itself', because these goals are only worthwhile if they serve 'the protection of higher order interests'. The authors provide examples of legal complexity when they describe the practical implications of the UK's Contempt of Court Act, 1981, and the Police and Criminal Evidence Act of 1984, which provide guidance that can be interpreted in more than one way, and which can therefore serve more than one interest. Besides the opportunities provided by legislation enacted under the Regulation of Investigatory Powers Act 2000, and its updated version in 2016, the police and other state operatives have used a number of devices and avenues of enquiry, in order to discover the origin of news stories that they find objectionable. Danbury and Townend obtained useful insights into the issue of source protection, when they organised a round-table made up of journalists and legal experts, allowing them to access a wealth of practical experience and advice.

1 Investigative journalism and terrorism
The proactive legal duty to report[1]

Richard Danbury

Introduction

In the spring of 2007, BBC 'Newsnight' reporter Richard Watson received a tip-off that someone wanted to contact us about a terrorist living in the UK. At the time, I was Richard's producer, and we were both acutely aware that any lead of this nature had to be taken seriously (two years before, there had been an attack on the London transportation system in which more than 50 people were murdered). The tip-off was that a woman would be willing to speak to us about her husband who, she said, had expressed 'pro-jihadi' sympathies. She had left him and was now living elsewhere, but claimed that he had collected some disturbing material on his computers. Although that was not particularly remarkable – as there are probably thousands of people in the UK who fit this description – she also maintained that her husband was connected to active extreme militant jihadi groups. This was altogether more worrying, and prompted us to treat the matter as an urgent priority.

The first step was to meet the woman and assess her story: if credible, we had to persuade her to let us record an interview with her. We met her, and she agreed to be filmed, but only if we took a responsible attitude to her personal safety. Having discussed what that might entail, we agreed that we would take every step to help make her anonymous in our report. We chose to interview her in a car park (an indeterminate location that we thought would help protect her identity), and were careful to frame the shots so that she could not be identified from the raw footage. She spoke in a language from the Indian subcontinent, so we used a translator, and recorded half an hour or so of material. We checked she was content with what she had said, ensuring afterwards that she could follow a safe route back to her house.

In our interview she said that her husband had asked her whether she would be prepared to strap on a belt of explosives, and become Britain's first female suicide bomber. She also revealed that she thought her husband had advance knowledge of the 2005 attack on London. Although she said that she did not know his current whereabouts, she believed he had relocated to a city in the North, and was still involved with extremism.

We knew that our half-hour interview would have to be cut down to about five minutes, as that would be all the time made available for the broadcast. Most of the filming had been carried out with angled shots, carefully framed to keep her anonymous, but we still had to consider how to use the recording of her voice. When we got to the edit suite, we had to calculate how much of this to keep in the film, knowing that this kind of interview works best if snippets of the original speech are inserted before the translation is heard. In the broadcast material, we had retained some of the woman's actual voice, an action we subsequently regretted, as we discovered that some extremists who wished her ill were trying to identify her from the small excerpts of speech that we had left in the footage.

Investigative journalism and proactive duties to report to the police

This anecdote introduces an important issue facing journalists investigating terrorism, wherever they practice in the world. We had discovered information that might be relevant to a terrorist enquiry. We considered it to be in the public interest to broadcast the information, in order to contribute to debates about the state of the country, the nature of any terrorist threat, and the appropriateness of the state's response to it. However, did we also have a separate duty to inform the authorities about the results of our investigation? Did this duty exist even if the authorities had not approached us for information? If we did have some form of obligation, could it be a legal duty, backed up by the full force of the criminal law? Behind these questions was a wider normative issue applicable more generally to all journalists in any country investigating terrorism: should such duties exist in the first place?

The questions pertaining to the existence of laws were the easier to answer: in the UK at least, there are indeed definite legal duties. They arise predominantly because of section 19 and section 38B of the Terrorism Act (2000). Knowing this to be the case, after we finished the interview but before we edited it into a film for transmission, we telephoned the police. We called the National Terrorist Hotline. We told the officer who answered that we had interviewed the woman concerned, and provided a summary of what she said, while giving the authorities sufficient information to enable them to find her. We were able to do this because, before the filming started, we had already made it clear to our subject that if we conducted the interview, we would be obliged to take this course of action. Richard Watson was filmed telephoning the police, a sequence that was included in the final broadcast.

Faced with the kind of circumstances just described, journalists should recognise a moral or professional responsibility to provide the authorities with information. Such duties will be more pressing the closer one is to an imminent terrorist attack, and less pressing when there appears to be no immediate threat. This is not, however, the same as saying that it is appropriate that journalists should operate under a *legal* obligation to pass on information to the state, which will result in their being prosecuted if they do not do so. That said, there are indeed many legal burdens imposed on journalists to reveal information to the authorities, some of which have criminal sanctions for non-compliance (see Chapter 4). But, importantly, these duties almost always arise after the state has sought information. The duties under sections 19 and 38B of the Terrorism Act (2000) are anomalous because they arise regardless of whether the state actually asks for any material, or even knows about its existence. As such, they are proactive legal duties to inform, rather than reactive legal duties.

Such proactive legal duties to report information, failure to comply with which could lead to criminal sanctions, are unusual in modern English law (Cousens, 2013: vol 84, §43). Historically, it is true, they were more common and can be traced back to mediaeval times, when the absence of a paid professional police force meant that the responsibility for law enforcement fell on members of the public. Hence, for example, from the mid-thirteenth century, there was a common law obligation to prevent criminal violence (Heyman, 1994: 685). But over time such duties were largely abandoned, and by 1967 the last significant example was eradicated with the abolition of a common law offence called 'misprision of felony' (Lloyd, 1996: 14.23, and see below).[2] That said, there remained some provisions relating to Northern Ireland, a fact that will also be discussed later, but by 1996, the government report into terrorism legislation, written by Lord Lloyd of Berwick, recommended that even these be abandoned, as a matter of principle and practice (Lloyd, 1996: Chapter 14).

However, in recent years, these older approaches seem to be creeping back, and not only with respect to terrorism. They also seem to be emerging in areas such as immigration law (Aliverti, 2015), and the law regulating financial conduct (for a U.S. perspective, see Guerra Thompson, 2002). A 'partnership approach' to policing seeks to impose duties on both the public and the professions, so that they can pass on information and help enforce the law.

Why might such legal duties be objectionable, and particularly so within those areas of journalism dedicated to the investigation of terrorism? (They may also of course be offensive to other professions.)[3] One reason is that what some interpret as a partnership, others may see as the creation of an atmosphere in which individuals are encouraged to denounce their neighbours (Docs Not Cops, 2014; Together Against Prevent, 2015; Anderson, 2016). Surely, however, a serious journalist, or indeed any responsible citizen, should have no objection to helping the police prevent terrorism? As Charles Clarke MP (then a Home Office minister), said when the provision that would become section 19 was being debated in Parliament:

> Journalists, too, have an obligation to their profession, just like the other professions that we have mentioned, but that should not excuse

them from their responsibilities to society. For example, a journalist may become aware that Canary Wharf is about to be blown up but decides not to tell anyone in order to protect his sources. That would be unacceptable.

(House of Commons, 1999–2000: 4th sitting, 25 January 2000, 9.30pm)

Few would argue with this statement. But what is less clear is whether such duties arise, the further removed we get from Clarke's example.[4] Do they arise when we are not dealing with a ticking bomb, which might kill thousands of people, but when we are dealing with people who have breached the terrorism acts on a technicality? This is a particular problem given the breadth and scope of the UK's anti-terror laws. Should the duty arise when journalists are dealing with people who have merely sent clothing to their children, an apparently innocuous act, but one that is likely to breach the provisions of the Terrorism Act, 2000 (see below for further elucidation of this example). Even if journalists operate under a duty in such circumstances, should the duty to report the issue be a legal duty, which leads to a criminal conviction if it is breached? Lord Lloyd thought not, at least in the context of Northern Ireland, as he recommended in his review of Northern Irish terrorism laws that such laws be abolished. He argued that 'there is the point of principle that, while every citizen has a moral obligation to help the police, the state should be reluctant to transform this into a legal duty'. He also wrote, and this is a point to which this chapter will return, 'I do not regard it as satisfactory to create a wide-ranging offence, and then circumscribe it by an [administrative provision]' (Lloyd, 1996: 14.21–14.23).

There are practical reasons why these duties may not be appropriate. One arises when it is widely known that these duties exist, as this very awareness may suggest that journalists are now considered an 'ancillary investigative arm of the state' (Cram, 2009: 108), or as 'virtual collaborators, or tools for police investigation or judicial prosecution' (Voorhoof, 2002, cited in Cram, 2009: 108) This may place journalists in danger because their contacts might suspect that any material gathered will be handed to the authorities. Alternatively, contacts may simply refuse to talk, resulting in the loss of sources of information that might have benefitted society as a whole.

At the time, when we at the 'Newsnight' team discussed these curious provisions of English law amongst ourselves, Richard Watson raised a further intriguing concern. He felt that the existences of these duties might make him think twice about investigating a story. Although this had not been a major concern in this particular case, it was easy to imagine it being a problem in other circumstances. What if a source had entirely legitimate objections to having their details given to the police? It would be difficult to honour our obligations to protect the source's identity, as sections 19 and/or 38B may well have already been invoked, and we would be under a duty to share this information with the authorities.

We would then have a difficult decision about whether to protect our source and risk prosecution, or to reveal our source and thereby break a professional and ethical code. It might well be better, all things considered, to prevent this situation arising, by avoiding this type of investigation. The provisions, in other words, might operate as a 'chill' on investigative work (the notion of speech actions being chilled by the law is a well established facet of free speech law and policy: see, for example, Barendt, 1997).

While the impact of the terrorism laws on journalism has been widely discussed, these particular issues do not seem to have attracted much attention. True, as mentioned earlier, they were raised by Lord Lloyd (1996: 14.19), were subject to discussion again when the law went before Parliament (House of Commons, 1999–2000; House of Lords, 1999–2000), and have also been re-visited a little in recent times (Forward Thinking, 2016a, 2016b). But these provisions merit much more detailed discussion, which is essentially the purpose of this chapter.

The law

To return to the laws themselves: these can be summarised relatively briefly. Section 19 (Terrorism Act, 2000) creates, as has been mentioned, a duty to report. This duty is placed on various people, including journalists, who come across certain information in the course of their trade, profession, business, or employment. The duty is that the persons concerned must tell the police when they believe or suspect an offence has been committed in relation to terrorist financing, based on information that they have come across in the course of their trade, profession, business, or employment. The section 19 duty is broad, not only because of the breadth of 'terrorism' as defined by the Act (*R (Miranda) v Home Secretary* [2016] EWCA Civ 6: [38]–[56]), but also because the Act defines 'terrorist financing' itself very broadly. This means that the section 19 duty is triggered when investigators find information that many non-lawyers would not normally expect to find in this category.

For example, the section 19 duty is triggered by an offence under section 17, which is in turn triggered where a person arranges for property to be made available to another, where that property may be used for the purposes of terrorism. That means that an offence under section 17 can be committed, for example, by a parent sending clothes to their offspring, who may have become involved activities that the Act considers to be a form of terrorism. This means, in turn, that a journalist who *interviews* a parent who has posted socks to their child is under a section 19 duty to relay this information to the police. It may be considered appropriate to impose such a duty on a journalist, but the rationale for so doing is a long way from a justification based on what many would consider to be 'terrorist financing'. If the journalist fails to report the incident, then he or she will have committed an offence. There is a defence that can be made to a charge under section 19, namely that a person had a reasonable excuse not to report the information to the police, but unfortunately the Act does not define what constitutes a 'reasonable excuse'.

Section 38B TA 2000 also creates a duty to report. This duty, though, has a much wider application than the section 19 duty. In the first place, it is not confined to those who discover information in the course of their employment, or other specified circumstances: it applies to everyone, whatever their activity. Secondly, it is not restricted to information that relates to terrorism finance, but rather applies to information that a person knows or believes might be of material assistance in preventing the commission of an act of terrorism, or that might help the police arrest, prosecute or convict someone for terrorism. It does not matter where the offence was committed, or indeed where exactly in the world the person to be arrested might be found. Again, it is clear that this provision is very broad. As is the case with section 19, it is a defence to argue that a person had a reasonable excuse not to report the information to the police. Again, the Act does not say what constitutes a 'reasonable excuse'. Nor does it explain – and given the importance of these words in the section this is unhelpful – what 'material assistance' means.

Another similar provision is also worth mentioning. This is section 26 of the Counter-Terrorism and Security Act, 2015. This section places a duty on certain bodies (which are listed in Schedule 6 of the Act) to have 'due regard to the need to prevent people from being drawn into terrorism'. This has been interpreted by guidance issued by the British government (HM Government, 2015b) as including a duty to refer those at risk of radicalisation to the 'Channel' programme (HM Government, 2015a). Hence, the section creates a similar proactive duty as those found in sections 19 and 38B of the TA 2000, to report both information and people to the authorities. This has been subjected to sustained criticism, not least because it is seen as alienating sections of the community, and outsourcing policing duties to professionals like doctors and educators who are ill-suited for the task. It has also been seen as creating an informer culture, as noted earlier (Docs Not Cops, 2014; Anderson, 2016). However, section 26 is different from the other sections described, not least because the list in Schedule 6 of bodies on whom this duty is imposed does not include journalistic institutions, or individual journalists. As a result, it is less relevant to the present discussion.

Sections 19 and 38B TA 2000 and European human rights law

One preliminary question is whether sections 19 and 38B comply with the European Convention on Human Rights' article 10, which protects freedom of speech. The answer is not clear, but it is likely that they do not. In broad-brush terms, the sections might be seen as breaching the right to free speech, under article 10 of the Convention, enjoyed by everyone, and therefore by investigative journalists. Indeed, the European Court of Human Rights (ECoHR) has recognised that journalists operating as watchdogs have *heightened* article 10 rights, and held that interference with this right is met with stricter scrutiny than in other cases (see, for example *Telegraaf Media Nederland v The Netherlands* Appplication no 39315/06. 22 November 2012; and Nicol et al., 2009: 5.32–5.49). Article 8, the right to a private life, may also be undermined, where sections 19 and 38B entail that a journalist must reveal the identity of a source, and thereby breach both the source's and the journalist's right to privacy. (This is discussed in Chapter 4.) Furthermore, article 2, the right to life, may be involved, where (as in our case study, earlier) a source's safety and life may be placed in jeopardy.

There is, of course, another side to the human rights coin. That is the state's obligation under article 2 of the Convention to protect life, which provides a strong justification for sections 19 and 38B, as the provisions are designed to help investigate and prevent acts of terrorism that deprive people of their lives. Indeed, article 10(2), the article in the Convention that protects speech, is expressly limited, and some of the limitations relate to this: 10(2) provides that freedom of speech may be subject to any restrictions imposed in the interests of national security and public safety.

Studying the debates that were held in Parliament about these provisions might help resolve the issue. When the Terrorism Bill was debated at the Standing Committee, Simon Hughes MP asked Charles Clarke MP, then a minister of state at the Home Office, how the government would 'get round the argument that the provision might contravene the European convention on human rights' (House of Commons, 1999–2000: 4th sitting, 25 January 2000, 9.30pm) Unfortunately, Clarke did not engage with the point in any detail, merely asserting that the government had legal advice and believed the provision was compliant with the European Convention.

Despite the absence of any significant argument from Clarke, such a position is not implausible. Cram, for example, has argued that it is possible that both the provisions of the Terrorism Act (2000) being discussed may indeed be compliant with article 10, because of the defence of 'reasonable excuse' is found in both sections. This is because, although the Act does not make it clear what a reasonable excuse is, a court is likely to interpret the defence in such a way that article 10 is given effect (Cram, 2009: 117–118). Such, after all, is its duty under sections 3 and 6 of the Human Rights Act 1998.

However, as Cram recognises, this outcome is not certain. Moreover, there is a cogent argument that even if the defence was interpreted by a court as complying with article 10, this would not be enough to resolve the difficulties presented by the relevant sections in the Terrorism Act (2000), at least where disclosing information would reveal the identity of a journalist's source. The reason for this derives from the proactive nature of the duties – the fact that the duty to inform the authorities arises as soon as the information is known, and the relevant belief crystallises. This seems to be at odds with a major thread of European Convention case law concerning the protection of journalists' sources. Such a thread suggests that, for a state to seek disclosure of a journalist's source without breaching article 10, a *prior* review is required by a judge or other independent and impartial decision-making body (*Sanoma Uitgevers BV v The Netherlands* Application no 38224/03 Grand Chamber, 14 September 2010 [2010] ECHR 38224/03: [88] – [100]).

The problem is the nature of the duties created by section 19 and section 38B. These duties arise at the point when information becomes available, and a person believes or suspects that someone else has committed a terrorism financing offence. That timing means that a *prior* review is impossible. Similarly, the existence of the 'reasonable excuse' defence will not resolve this situation, as it can only come into play *after* the duties have arisen. Furthermore, the European Court of Human Rights has held that a subsequent review does not resolve article 10-related problems, as it would 'undermine the very essence of the right of confidentiality' (*Sanoma Uitgevers BV*: [91]).

In addition, sections 19 and 38B seem to breach other requirements of European Convention source protection law. The central relevant idea is that of proportionality. While lawyers and scholars argue over the exact nature of this doctrine, for present purposes it is sufficient to say that it requires that when a state seeks information about a journalists' source, this must be necessary for the attainment of a particular, specified purpose, and there must be no reasonably alternative way of obtaining this information (*Sanoma Uitgevers BV; Telegraaf Media Nederland; Voskuil v The Netherlands* Application no 64752/01, 22 November 2007). Sections 19 and 38B are, however, broad and sweeping, and there is insufficient scope in applying them to consider whether they are proportionate.

These arguments are likely to be important, if or when a journalist is prosecuted under section 19 and 38B. But they may not convince non-lawyers that the provisions are deficient. One reason this is so, is because a basic question arises – whether or not this matters much in practice. After all, it seems that the provisions have not been much used against journalists, so perhaps it cannot be said that they are deficient (Forward Thinking, 2016a, 2016b). However, as will be shown below, this is not a convincing argument.

The application of the law

There are two reported cases in the main legal databases, relating to the sections of the Terrorism Act (2000) mentioned previously, neither of which deal with journalists. They deal with the attempted bombing of the London transport system on 21 July 2005, and relate to defendants who either failed to provide information to prevent it, or who assisted the escape of the perpetrators (*R v Sherif* [2008] EWCA Crim 2653; *R v Girma* [2009] EWCA Crim 912). The defendants in these cases were charged, amongst other things, with breaching section 38B.

One reason that there have been so few prosecutions of journalists under these sections is likely to be because of a procedural requirement in English criminal law. Even if a journalist fails to report information to the authorities, a prosecution under sections 19 or 38B is not inevitable. This is because, before they bring any case, the Crown Prosecution Service applies a two-fold test: first, whether there is sufficient evidence to provide a realistic prospect of conviction, and second whether a prosecution is in the public interest. It is the second limb of this test that will be particularly important when considering whether or not to bring an action against investigative journalists under the Terrorism Act (2000).

The Director of Public Prosecutions has issued Guidance on how to apply this limb in cases affecting the media. The Guidance does not mention sections 19 and 38B as such (Crown Prosecution Service, 2012: Annex A), but the content of the Guidance makes it clear that it should apply to these provisions. It starts by noting that 'neither journalists nor those who interact with them are afforded special status under the criminal law', but goes on to specify that 'prosecutors are required to apply a number of specific principles' in cases affecting the media (Crown Prosecution Service, 2012: §12). It also stipulates that, when considering whether to bring an action against a journalist, a prosecutor should consider 'whether the public interest served by the conduct in question outweighs the overall criminality'. That means, the Guidance explains, that to assess whether a prosecution is in the public interest, the prosecutor should take into account (amongst other things) matters such as whether the journalist's conduct is likely to reveal a criminal offence, a failure to comply with a legal obligation, a miscarriage of justice, or which is capable of raising or contributing to an important matter of public debate (Crown Prosecution Service, 2012: §31).

It is the existence of this guidance that can lead to the argument that sections 19 and 38B are not deficient: they have not led to journalists being prosecuted, and so do not result in much real impediment to investigative journalism. The Terrorism Act, 2000, the argument goes, may have created proactive legal duties to report information, backed up by criminal penalties, but the guidelines mean that if a journalist is acting in the public interest, there is only a low risk of prosecution.

However, this argument is unconvincing, for four reasons. In the first place, as Lord Lloyd argued in respect of similar provisions affecting Northern Ireland (see earlier) the mischief created by a wide-ranging criminal offence is not removed by an administrative instruction that its application should be restrained (Lloyd, 1996: 14.23). As a point of principle, a legal provision that is narrowly tailored is preferable to one that is broad, because a wider provision is likely to criminalise conduct that law-makers did not intend to criminalise. The second issue is the fact that the recorded cases may be incomplete – there may have been prosecutions that are not available in the legal databases.

Third, even if the record is not incomplete, there remains the problem that the existence of the sections can be used as a means of coercing or persuading journalists to reveal information. Indeed, there is empirical evidence that this happened in Northern Ireland, with a similar provision that existed under section 18 of the Prevention of Terrorism Act 1989 (Walker, 1992: 141–144).[5] In more recent times, the police used Terrorism Act powers to seize the laptop of the 'Newsnight' journalist Secunder Kermani in 2015 (BBC, 2015). The eminent media law expert, Gavin Millar QC (Queen's Counsel), was reported to have 'heard of three cases in [2015] in which forces [had] threatened – but not used – to use [sic] the Terrorism Act . . . in stories involving young men who have travelled to fight in Syria and Iraq before returning to Europe and the UK' (Turvill, 2015).

Fourth, and perhaps most importantly, is Richard Watson's point made earlier, to the effect that provisions may chill investigations, dissuading journalists from undertaking investigations that they might otherwise have pursued. This is because journalists may feel it is better not to place themselves under the threat of criminal penalty, or reveal their sources or information. The point has been noted by other commentators. Cram, for instance, notes that:

> [a]t its most severe, the existence of the offence . . . would seem to constitute a substantial disincentive to engage in serious investigative journalism . . . although, as is the case with any 'chill' on freedom of expression, the extent of any inhibitory effect can never be known.
> (Cram, 2009: 117)

Do sections 19 and 38B of the Terrorism Act, 2000 'chill' investigative journalism?

Whether sections 19 and 38B do or do not chill investigative journalism is difficult to prove. One reason is because the decisions that might show that an investigation *has not* been undertaken are seldom recorded. They are manifested in the rapid responses of news executives making commissioning decisions under pressure, or in the musings of journalists who decide whether or not a particular story is worth pursuing. Only a fraction of these decisions will leave a trace, in the form of a rejection email, a spiked piece, or a story that will never be broadcast or published.

One approach to this problem is to ask investigative journalists and media lawyers for their subjective impressions of the impact of the Act, and ask whether it has had any effect on their actions (Barendt, 1997; for another methodology, see Penney, 2016). This will seldom resolve the issue finally, as memories are faulty, and subjective biases will influence recollections. Nevertheless, it can be useful approach, and a short survey of eminent investigative journalists and practicing media lawyers has been undertaken for this chapter. The sample was not extensive or representative, but is indicative, as it comprised a carefully selected number of specialists. Senior lawyers for three major international journalistic institutions responded, and four eminent practicing investigative journalists with experience of terrorism work. One further contribution was made from a lawyer who formerly worked for a large European organisation, and the comments of one of the journalists were relayed through an intermediary. The interviews took place in December 2016 and January 2017, and response was by telephone, email and social media. The results were not unanimous, but there was strong evidence that at least in a number of cases, the provisions have 'chilled' some instances of investigative journalism.

Nonetheless, some of the views obtained for this chapter were quite sceptical about the existence of a 'chilling' effect. One journalist said that he had called the police to report that 'dozens of Brits of mainly Pakistan background had gone to training camps in Pakistan and had now returned to UK' (Participant A, 21 December 2016). However, he did not feel that the provisions had impeded his other investigations. Another felt that 'this seems like a recondite area of possible press restriction, and although I have had many interactions in the area, I don't recall that particular chill' (Participant B, 22 December 2016). He went on to note that 'unless there are actual verified cases to consider, looking back, I'd say this bears mostly on lazy journalists and uncourageous lawyers, which is pretty usual. I might not have said that in 1999, if asked' (Participant B, 23 December 2016). In a similar vein, a highly experienced media lawyer responded to the question by saying:

> We would probably take careful advice from an experienced QC about how to negotiate our way regarding the legislation. I think it would often come down to what information you actually recover as a journalist. For example the provisions regarding training and glorification are obviously quite tricky to deal with but I don't think the existence of the legislation per se would chill our journalists.
> (Participant F, 21 December 2016)

Two other media lawyers agreed that the chilling effect is difficult to prove. One said 'I think my feeling would be that it probably does act as a chill, more so than some other stuff in respect of certain aspects of it', but went on to add 'can I point to a story where journalists said "I want to do this and editor said no, because of this legislation"? It's difficult to find that example' (Participant G, 23 December 2016, a point also emphasised by Participant C, 21 December 2016).

Nevertheless, there was evidence that some journalists had experienced the chill. One journalist who was interviewed provided a concrete example:

> I was interested to see how . . . undercover techniques could be used in terrorism stories. I had a tip about a centre where fundraising went on

for jihadists in Syria. . . . I even found a chap who agreed to infiltrate the place. I then began taking advice about our disclosure obligations, which as you point out were incredibly heavy. I even talked to some official sources – in general terms – to find out if they recognised that it was in the public interest for us to have the 'space' to proceed, without giving details of course. Even they recognised it would be stupid to chill this kind of investigative journalism . . . but it wasn't definitive!

(Participant D, 8 January 2017)

This participant went on to explain that the whole process was:

incredibly difficult and did have a chilling effect on those potentially commissioning a story. On the one hand, investigating it undercover was very clearly in the public interest. But the law would imply that disclosure in real time would be necessary before broadcast. The idea of disclosing at every step of the way before broadcast made it virtually impossible. In the end, I sought out some informal advice from a prominent QC . . . who's done a lot of terrorism cases. He basically thought we'd get away with it – but it was a fudge. His judgment was that assuming we would, ethically, report any imminent threat to life (as we would), and if we kept good records with a view to disclosing after broadcast, then the risk of prosecution was very low. But not impossible.

(Participant D, 8 January 2017)

This is a view that is shared by others. One journalist wrote that section 38B made asking certain questions more difficult:

is a potential problem, as we know, when journalists are talking to people who have a terrorist background, including people to whom we might want to talk about matters of a slightly historical nature. I think it's quite important that we make an attempt to understand why people turn to terrorism. Journalists should be able to say to individuals: 'Why on earth did you do that?'

(Participant E, relayed on 21 December 2016)

Moreover, that journalist went on to observe that the absence of a statute of limitations exacerbates the problem. The journalist observed that this presents problems not only for journalists, but also for academics and historians (see also Lord Desai on this point, in House of Lords, 1999–2000: col 651, earlier). This source went on to say:

This is not merely a theoretical problem. I've had someone talk to me in some detail about everything that happened to him from the moment of his arrest for possession of explosives in Manchester in the early 90s, but refuse to discuss his reasons for turning to terrorism in Belfast in the mid 70s, on the grounds that he's never been convicted of

Investigative journalism and terrorism 49

membership of the IRA. He could be jailed for two years, and fears that even if he is not prosecuted, his arrest would jeopardise his job. There's lots of people in this position.

(Participant E, relayed on 21 December 2016)

One senior lawyer with many years of experience in a large journalistic institution identified certain features of section 38B that were problematic. He said:

> the main part of the section 38B creates a disincentive to do something that is barmy to do in the first place. It stops you failing to report a planned terrorist attack, when if you did report it, that would help the authorities prevent it happening. But when it moves into different territory, which is not the normal set up, that's more difficult. For example, when you have one faction which is fighting another, and they are all classed as terrorists under the legislation. That's a strange situation.
>
> (Participant G, 23 December 2016)

In these situations, he felt the provision raises significant difficulties:

> The definition of terrorism is so broad that activity that lots of people don't consider terrorism is caught. If a journalist is following warring factions, they may say: 'we'll go alongside and seeing what they're up to'. But these fighters are technically terrorists. That can mean the journalist is going to be find it very difficult to say to potential contributors and sources 'we'll protect you from subsequent inquiry'.
>
> (Participant G, 23 December 2016)

This lawyer went on to emphasise the ambiguous nature of the provisions as a source of difficulty. He observed that:

> there's a lack of certainty in these things. When you're thrown back on arguments of what one word means in statutory interpretation, on pain of being sent to prison for five years, that's where I think the criminal penalty and the uncertainty of language becomes unattractive. I suspect it does stop people doing things they otherwise might do. There will be sources who'll expect confidentiality, when that's not deliverable without personal exposure to prosecution.
>
> (Participant G, 23 December 2016)

Another problem for those advising journalists, this participant observed, is the breadth of the provisions:

> As a matter of common sense, it will chill what you might do. Then the secondary bit of the section – securing the apprehension and prosecution of a person in the UK – that will include a terrorist offence

anywhere in the world. So those returning from Syria can be prosecuted here, as can journalists researching stories about those sorts of people. Anyone back in the UK is liable who was involved in assisting or had knowledge of preparations in travel. Those are stories which are I suspect more likely to be jeopardized, than other ones. Those and stories where the interviewee says: 'I'm a good guy I'm fed up with fighting'. Those stories are potentially more attractive, and ones you'd be likely to do, but then you've got the difficulty of the expectation of what you're doing with the information.

(Participant G, 23 December 2016)

So there is evidence that the provisions do exert a chill on investigative work. However, the participant also observed that this was not necessarily always negative. He felt that any chill exerted by the provisions:

may be a useful chill, as it prevents bad stories coming out . . . the way it has worked has changed over time. You can't divorce way the world is changing from the attitude of the authorities. When the act was passed, it was seen as a hammer to crack a nut. Fast forward 10 to 15 years and the world is different. . . . It is difficult to make a good argument that this is not something the authorities need to have in place. You can't really attack legalisation with the ferocity you'd like to. Most people would say 'given what they have to deal with and consequences, it's the least worst option'. It interferes with other rights, but it's difficult to see what else to do.

(Participant G, 23 December 2016)

International comparisons

A further way of evaluating the question of whether the laws under discussion are appropriate is to look at other jurisdictions. While not a complete answer to the question, and perhaps not even a convincing one – as every state, perhaps, might be committing the same error – the existence of similar laws in other countries that face similar threats, would provide some succour to those who *seek to defend* section 19 and 38B. It appears that, while comparable laws exist in some other countries, they are rare. A senior lawyer, who until recently held a senior position in a large European organisation (Participant H, 23 December 2016), indicated that he was aware of discussions in several European Parliaments about introducing similar rules, but nothing has been approved to introduce such explicit provisions.

Nonetheless, it is fair to say that they do exist in some countries. In Ireland, for example, there is section 9 of the Offences Against the State (Amendment) Act 1998. This creates a general duty on everyone – including journalists – to report information that a person knows or believes may be of material assistance in preventing the commission of a serious offence, or securing the arrest of someone for a serious offence. The provision was reportedly adopted as a result of the Omagh bombing (Oireachtas Library & Research Service, 2011). Where a person has such information, the section says that they need to disclose the information to the Garda as soon as practicable. In a similar way to sections 19 and 38B of the TA 2000, there is a statutory defence of 'reasonable excuse'.

In America, a similar duty to inform authorities can arise, from the old common law offence of 'misprision of felony'. As was mentioned earlier, this was abolished in the UK in 1967, but it continues to exist in the United States. The U.S. doctrine of misprision of felony provides that a person who has knowledge of the actual commission of a felony is under a legal obligation to tell the authorities about this as soon as possible (8 U.S. Code § 4 – Misprision of felony; Cornell University Law School, nd). It is likely that it can be used against journalists (*Branzburg v Hayes* 408 US 665: 697 (1972); also see the analysis in Cram, 2009: 108–109). Yet, while there have been discussions about using this provision to prosecute the family members of those who commit acts of terrorism (Alvarado, 2016), in researching this chapter, no examples of its being used against journalists who are investigating terrorism were found.

Despite these examples, however, it does seem – though more research is needed on this point – that the existence of sections 19 and 38B is somewhat of an anomaly, at least with regard to the wider international context. This might suggest that the fight against terrorism can safety proceed without such proactive legal duties, or at least without their potential application to investigative journalists. And if they did not exist, more useful public interest journalism might be undertaken. Indeed, the existence of similar provisions in some other countries can be a double-edged sword for those who try to defend sections 19 and 38B. This is because the existence of such legal duties has been used as a convenient justification by some repressive regimes in the world, in order to implement similar laws, which are then used to restrict legitimate journalism. A notorious example can be found in Ethiopia. Under Proclamation 652/2009, section 12, it is an offence for someone who has evidence that may prevent a terrorist act, or may assist in the arrest of a terrorist, to fail to tell the authorities. This provision seems to be a legal transplant – legislation based on one jurisdiction, transferred to another without sufficient evaluation of whether it is appropriate. This Proclamation has been criticised by some NGOs who see it as a tool of repression (Article 19, 2010). The precedent of the UK law may well have contributed to the adoption of indefensible legislation in other countries.

Conclusion

This chapter has provided reasons to *argue* that sections 19 and 38B ought to repealed or amended in order *i*) to increase certainty in those who apply or encounter it, to *ii*) comply with ECoHR source protection laws, and *iii*) to provide an improved defence for public interest journalism. It has argued that there are problems with the provisions, from a number of points of view: as a law and policy that affects freedom of speech, because of its breadth and ambiguity, and, of course, with regard to the chilling effect it can have on investigative journalism. But, as one participant conceded (an individual who accepted the notion that it could have a dampening effect on investigations), these problems do not necessarily lead to a conclusion that the provisions *should* be repealed or amended. We live in a dangerous world, and strong legal tools are needed to alleviate this danger.

On balance, however, the deficiencies of the sections are such that reform is needed. The question is what kind of reform? Repeal is probably ill advised; and amendment is unlikely, as there is neither the political will, nor the Parliamentary time. This is unsatisfactory: the provisions are too broad, and are having a detrimental effect on at least some journalists who wish to investigate, understand and explain terrorism. So, while amendment ought to remain a long-term aspiration, there is room to suggest other improvements that are more easily attainable. One, useful though deficient for reasons already discussed, would be to issue specific guidance for prosecutors on the application of the public interest test for sections 19 and 38B, in respect of journalism as a particular practice. Indeed, as mentioned earlier, these sections are not even cited in the Guidance that currently exists. Mentioning them explicitly, and setting out in terms what a journalist could expect to do *safely*, would be a great step forward.

Indeed, it would also be helpful to clarify what the 'reasonable excuse' defences mean, without necessarily having to initiate a court case to find out. Bringing such a case might appear to lawyers an acceptable way of clarifying the ambit of this defence, but it would mean that some journalist somewhere would have to be investigated, arrested, charged, and prosecuted under the Terrorism Act (2000). That, of course, is the problem: only those who had the stomach, time and resources for the fight would take that course of action. For every journalist of that stripe, there are likely to be dozens of others who will shy away from investigating a story that – ultimately – could be of great value to society. And that, ironically enough, is likely to deprive society of a tool – information – that could be valuably employed in the fight against terrorism, or in evaluating the state's response to it.

Notes

1 The author wishes to acknowledge his debt to Richard Watson, who first drew his attention to this subject. This chapter draws on a presentation the author made at a conference organised by the Respekt Institute, New York University in Prague, Forum 2000, at the New York University in Prague, Czech Republic, in November 2007, called *Media Freedom and Responsibility in the Age of Terrorism of Global Reach*. He also greatly appreciates the time spared to him by his interviewees, who spoke on condition of anonymity. He also wishes to thank Dr Judith Townend for

her invaluable comments on earlier drafts of the chapter, who bears no responsibility for errors herein.
2 The history of the offence and its continued viability in some countries is described in Ciociola, 2003.
3 Lord Desai raised this in the House of Lords debate on the provision (House of Lords 1999–2000: col 651).
4 This point was made in the House of Lords debate on the provision by Lords Marlesford and Goodhart. Moreover, Lord Goodhart also observed that Clarke's example is misleading, as the clause he was discussing (which resulted in section 19) was 'limited to disclosure of information relating to the commission of an offence . . . [dealing] with fundraising and property'. Not mere knowledge of an imminent attack. (House of Lords (1999–2000): col 652).
5 At page 142, Walker describes a failure by a BBC 'Panorama' crew to inform the authorities, until after the trail went cold, about an Irish National Liberation Army (INLA) roadblock set up in October 1979. This prompted the Attorney General to consider prosecuting the BBC, a course of action he decided against. But he did send a furious letter to the Chairman of the BBC, a section of which Walker reproduces. The 'Panorama' reporter was Jeremy Paxman, who describes his experiences of the incident, and the visit to the police that followed, and the uncertainty as to whether they would be prosecuted, in terms that give an insight into how journalists can be chilled by such laws. (Paxman, 2016: 102–109).

References

Aliverti, Ana (2015) 'Enlisting the public in the policing of immigration', in *British Journal of Criminology*, Vol. 55, Issue: 2, p. 215.
Alvarado, Francisco (2016) 'What will the feds do with the Orlando shooter's widow?' *Vice News*, online, 16 June, www.vice.com/en_us/article/what-will-the-feds-do-with-the-orlando-shooters-widow [accessed 8 January 2017].
Anderson QC, David. (2016) 'Supplementary written evidence submitted by David Anderson QC, independent reviewer of terrorism legislation', online, http://data.parliament.uk/writtenevidence/committeeevidence.svc/evidencedocument/home-affairs-committee/countering-extremism/written/27920.pdf [Accessed 8 January 2017].
Article 19 (2010) 'Comment on anti-terrorism proclamation, 2009, of Ethiopia', Article 19, online, www.article19.org/data/files/pdfs/analysis/ethiopia-comment-on-anti-terrorism-proclamation-2009.pdf [accessed 1 February 2017].
Barendt, Eric, Lustgarten, Lawrence, Norrie, Kenneth and Stephenson, Hugh (1997) *Libel and the Media: The Chilling Effect*, Oxford: Oxford University Press.
BBC (2015) 'Newsnight editor "Concerned" over seizure of BBC journalist's laptop', 29 October, online, www.bbc.co.uk/news/uk-34666281 [accessed 8 January 2017].
Branzburg v Hayes 408 US 665 (1972) (United States of America).
Ciociola, Gabriel (2003) 'Misprision of felony and its progeny', *Brandeis Law Journal*, Vol. 41, p. 697.
Cornell University Law School, nd, online, www.law.cornell.edu/uscode/text/18/4 [accessed 8 January 2017].
Counter-Terrorism and Security Act (2015) London: The Stationery Office.
Cousens, Michael [editor] (2013) *Halsbury's Laws of England*, Volume 83 [5th edition], London: LexisNexis.

Cram, Ian (2009) *Terror and the War on Dissent*, Dordrecht: Springer.
Crown Prosecution Service (2012) 'Guidelines for prosecutors on assessing the public interest in cases affecting the media', online, www.cps.gov.uk/legal/d_to_g/guidance_for_prosecutors_on_assessing_the_public_interest_in_cases_affecting_the_media_/ [accessed 8 January 2017].
Docs Not Cops (2014) 'Docs not cops', online, www.docsnotcops.co.uk/ [Accessed 8 January 2017].
Forward Thinking (2016a) 'Forward thinking host David Anderson QC, the independent reviewer of terrorism legislation, to discuss the effect of section 19 and 38B, of the terrorism act 2000, on the British media', 20 April, online, www.forward-thinking.org/?p=3149 [Accessed 8 January 2017].
Forward Thinking (2016b) 'Forward thinking facilitate meeting with Peter Oborne to discuss sections 19 and 38B of the terrorism act 2000', Monday 26 September, online, www.forward-thinking.org/?p=3480 [accessed 8 January 2017].
Guerra Thompson, Sandra (2002) 'The white-collar police force: "Duty to Report" statutes in criminal law theory', *William and Mary Bill of Rights Journal*, Vol. 11, p. 3.
Heyman, Steven (1994) 'Foundations of the duty to rescue', *Vanderbilt Law Review*, Vol. 47, p. 673.
HM Government (2015a) 'Channel duty guidance: Protecting vulnerable people from being drawn into terrorism: Statutory guidance for channel panel members and partners of local panels', online, HM Government, www.gov.uk/government/uploads/system/uploads/attachment_data/file/425189/Channel_Duty_Guidance_April_2015.pdf [Accessed 8 January 2017].
HM Government (2015b) 'Prevent duty guidance', online, HM Government, www.legislation.gov.uk/ukdsi/2015/9780111133309/pdfs/ukdsiod_9780111133309_en.pdf [accessed 8 January 2017].
House of Commons (1999–2000) 'Standing committee debates, standing committee D, terrorism bill', 25 January, online, www.publications.parliament.uk/pa/cm199900/cmstand/d/st000125/pm/pt2/00125s05.htm [accessed 8 January 2017].
House of Lords (1999–2000) 'HL debs vol 23 May, online, www.publications.parliament.uk/pa/ld199900/ldhansrd/vo000523/text/00523-06.htm [accessed 8 January 2017].
Lloyd, Anthony [Baron Lloyd of Berwick] (1996) *Inquiry into Legislation Against Terrorism.* Cm 3420 London: HMSO.
Nicol, Andrew, Millar, Gavin and Sharland, Andrew (2009). *Media Law & Human Rights.* Oxford: Oxford University Press.
Offences against the State (Amendment) Act 1998 (Ireland).
Oireachtas Library & Research Service (2011) 'Disclosure of information: Duty to inform and whistleblowing', online, www.oireachtas.ie/parliament/media/housesoftheoireachtas/libraryresearch/spotlights/2011_Spotlight_duty_to_inform_173444%5B1%5D.pdf [accessed 8 January 2017].
Participant A – interview by email 21 December 2016.
Participant B – interview by email and telephone, 22 December 2016, 23 December 2016 and 4 January 2017.
Participant C – interview by email 21 December 2016.
Participant D – interview by email, 8 January 2017.
Participant E – information relayed on 21 December 2016.
Participant F – interview by email 21 December 2016.
Participant G – interview by telephone 23 December 2016.

Participant H – interview by Facebook 23 December 2016.
Paxman, Jeremy (2016) *A Life in Questions*. London: William Collins.
Penney, Jon (2016) 'Chilling effects: Online surveillance and wikipedia use', *Berkley Technology Law Journal*, Vol. 31, Issue: 1, p. 117.
Proclamation 652/2009 (Ethiopia).
R v Girma (2009) EWCA Crim 912. (UK).
R (Miranda) v Home Secretary (2016) EWCA Civ 6. (UK).
R v Sherif (2008) EWCA Crim 2653. (UK).
Sanoma Uitgevers BV v The Netherlands Application no. 38224/03, Grand Chamber, 14 Sepember 2010 (2010) ECHR 38224/03 (European Court of Human Rights).
Telegraaf Media Nederland v Netherlands Application no. 39315/06, 22 November 2012 (European Court of Human Rights).
Terrorism Act (2000) London: The Stationery Office.
Together Against Prevent (2015) 'Together against prevent', online, http://togetheragainstprevent.org/ [accessed 8 January 2017].
Turvill, William (2015) 'Police force behind newsnight laptop seizure reveals BBC did not contest terrorism act application', *PressGazette*, 29 October.
Voorhoof, Dirk (2002) Paper presented at conference, 'The media in a democratic society: Reconciling freedom of expression with the protection of human rights', 30 September–1 October, Luxemborg.
Voskuil v The Netherlands Application no 64752/01, 22 November 2007.
Walker, Clive (1992) *The Prevention of Terrorism in British Law*, Manchester: Manchester University Press.

2 Researching the deep state
Surveillance, politics, and dissent

Ben Harbisher

Introduction

The purpose of this chapter is to develop a working methodology for the use of those academics, investigative journalists, and political activists who wish to conduct credible research into that nexus of forces known as the 'deep state'. While it is possible to identify a number of viable techniques for use in this field, it is also important to consider both the risks, and the inherent limitations, of conducting this type of research.

First, in terms of risk, the analyst has to be sensitive to the particular types of information that he or she might disclose, since the potential consequences of disseminating state secrets within the public domain (deliberately or otherwise) can be considerable. This risk has to be balanced against the possible benefits to the 'public interest', but the precise repercussions of conducting (and then publishing) research into the practices of the intelligence community might not be apparent for many years. The limitations, meanwhile, of investigating the deep state might include the existence of powerful barriers such as official secrecy, which forces the researcher to pursue creative responses to bureaucratic red-tape. Another major ordeal is having to work with rescinded or redacted data sets, which means having to identify useful material where state censorship has left only minor hints in the text.

These issues do not exhaust the practical challenges posed by this type of research, which extend to the basic ability to interact productively and respectfully with one's sources. In essence, the risks that might be faced are usually proportionate to the scope of the research being done. This chapter, therefore, elaborates on some of the popular approaches used in this field, in addition to describing what is perceived to be good journalistic and academic practice, based upon the insights of those working in this area. Within the course of this exploration, I examine the methods of deep state research undertaken by academics such as Monahan (2009), Newkirk (2010), and Monaghan and Walby (2012), while also considering the techniques used by journalists such as Campbell (1976), Greenwald (2013), and

Evans et al. (2009), and the risks faced by whistleblowers such as Edward Snowden and Julian Assange.

The contemporary deep state

In terms of popular culture, the notion of the deep state has often been typified as a separate entity existing alongside the visible, conventional state; as a shadow government that operates behind the facade of everyday politics; or as a clandestine group of political and commercial interests that seek to manipulate public opinion, trade and commerce. Most recently it has been identified as an international consortium of agencies whose ubiquitous use of surveillance now forms *i)* one of the largest growth enterprises in the world (as an 'intelligence-industrial' complex), and *ii)* controls the flow of digital information and thus the machinations of contemporary power (Wilson, 2009).

In an international context, news headlines regarding the activities of the deep state have in recent years been dominated by coverage of the secret intelligence programmes exposed by Edward Snowden in 2013. On 7 July 2013, the *Guardian* newspaper revealed that the United States had been conducting mass surveillance of the American population, which included the interception of internet streams and the monitoring of private telephone calls (Greenwald, 2013). The National Security Agency (NSA) was largely responsible for what many citizens have since considered to be a flagrant disregard for personal privacy, and a gross misuse of state powers, in which emails, conventional and online/video calls, instant messaging services, and internet searches were all accessed by NSA operatives without any legal warrant (Shubber, 2013). The clandestine intelligence programme known as PRISM was revealed when Snowden (a former NSA contractor) leaked confidential documents to international press agencies, thus blowing the whistle on the unrestrained (and unregulated) use of mass surveillance. The implications of Snowden's revelations were indeed wide-ranging. In addition to the unrestrained surveillance of the American population, Snowden's documents also disclosed that a number of other agencies had been operating under the same *modus operandi* on behalf of other Western powers.

In the UK, an equivalent programme known as TEMPORA was revealed by Snowden via the *Guardian* newspaper (MacAskill et al., 2013). The British signals intelligence agency – Government Communications Headquarters (GCHQ) – had plugged itself into the fibre optic cables that carry internet communications between the United States and continental Europe, under a secret agreement made with the NSA (Shubber, 2013). The purpose of this covert programme was to gather signals intelligence from every connected part of the world. This included the surveillance of military, political, commercial, and domestic targets on a massive scale, since practically the whole of the world's internet usage passes through America. Yet, spying on the world's population is in itself nothing new.

Investigative journalist Duncan Campbell first drew public attention to the activities of GCHQ in 1976 and, during 1988, exposed a programme codenamed ECHELON in which British, Commonwealth, and American security allies had been intercepting telecommunications signals for nearly 30 years (Campbell, 1976, 1988). The ECHELON programme was a joint venture between British, Australian, Canadian, New Zealand, and American security services, which were working under an initiative known as FIVE EYES (a reference to the initial five stakeholders). The point here is that contemporary surveillance projects such as TEMPORA and PRISM represent part of a hidden history of the deep state that the general population is seldom in a position to observe. At first glance the intelligence programmes discussed in this chapter appear less grandiose in scale than those exposed by Snowden or Campbell but they do, however, form part of a wider surveillance strategy in the West that attempts to detect and monitor all forms of terrorism (or terrorist-type activity). Many such programmes are now commonplace throughout Europe, as well as appearing in the United States and the Commonwealth. They are enacted principally through organisations such as the Department for Homeland Security in America, by Europol, and by British intelligence (Jones, 2014).

Surveillance, politics, and dissent

In 2009, Monahan and Palmer published the first of a series of scholarly articles on the emerging surveillance networks of the United States (2009: 617–636). These sites were later defined as forming a 'fusion intelligence complex', in which the Department of Homeland Security (DHS) had commissioned a series of new facilities to monitor risks posed by terrorist organisations and other threats from far-Left or extreme Right-wing political groups (Newkirk, 2010). In what became known as DHS Fusion Intelligence Centres, public and private sector interests were represented by a number of hybrid surveillance hubs that were composed of both federal and corporate employees. In addition to their conventional role (i.e., to detect and prevent serious crimes such as international or domestic terrorism), these fusion centres were also concerned with protecting sites of critical national importance – including telecommunications and utilities providers. It was believed that such facilities represented key terrorist targets, and unless they were protected, would render vital public services useless during a Federal emergency. However, the problem for a number of social movements was that the operation of power stations, the expansion of public transportation and aviation networks, and global economics, are contentious issues that have been the cause of numerous public disputes.

As a result of this joint security venture, the fusion centre initiative crept into the domain of 'public order' affairs, in addition to countering the threat posed by terrorism. To problematise the issue of fusion-led intelligence, a number of scholars have observed that the commercial and public concerns monitored by such facilities, have led to a conflict of interests between state and corporate surveillance on the one hand, and Western 'civil liberties' on the other. In effect, the encroachment of fusion centre surveillance into the public order domain has led these new hybrid intelligence agencies to conflate political activism with terrorism. According to Monahan:

> Fusion centre threat assessments lend themselves to profiling along lines of race, religion, and political affiliation. Their products are not impartial assessments of terrorist threats, but rather betray biases against individuals or groups who deviate from – or challenge – the status quo.
>
> (2010: 90)

Further issues are typified by the limited executive oversight (where it exists at all) of fusion centre surveillance, and the routine dissemination of sensitive personal data to third party organisations (Monahan and Palmer, 2009: 631). An equivalent concern has been the profound lack of transparency and public awareness of the operational procedures of these joint security ventures, for 'the details of these relationships are shrouded in secrecy' (ibid.: 619). Moreover, the way in which the designated targets of these institutions have been depicted, poses an even greater question for privacy advocates and campaigners alike. To put this into context, by 2015 there were over seventy-eight DHS fusion centres operating in the United States alone, with significant interest being shown in the model by America's overseas allies (DHS, 2016; Jones, 2014). With regards to the mission creep of fusion centre surveillance and the comparative profiling of both terrorists and activists under an equivalent threat matrix, the spread of these institutions equates to the criminalisation of social movements in the West.

In terms of the legitimacy of fusion centre surveillance, the role of these institutions within civil contingencies and risk aversion doctrine has aligned cause-led activism and legitimate public protest, with domestic and international forms of terrorism. By way of theorising this affiliation, Monaghan and Walby have used the term 'multi-issue extremism' (MIE) which is widely used by Canada's equivalent to the DHS (the Canadian Security Intelligence Service) and by its comparative fusion centre complex (2012: 113). The use of multi-issue extremism serves as an all-purpose term, through which law enforcement agencies are able to conduct counter-terrorism-style operations against ordinary campaign groups. In terms of fusion centre surveillance, this has led to the interception of domestic communications, and to other forms of clandestine oversight. Consequently, the said intelligence also provides a justification for law enforcement agencies to run covert infiltration operations within such groups, which provides officials with an additional insight into the activities of social movements (Monahan, 2010: 89).

Although the paradigm outlined above differs from one territory to the next, there is an equivalent 'multi-issue extremism' (MIE) discourse being touted by fusion centres throughout the West (Harbisher, 2015). In Canada, this has been investigated by Monaghan and Walby in relation to the nation's Integrated Security Units (ISUs) and the Integrated Threat Assessment Centre (ITAC). In one example, cited by Monaghan and Walby, opposition to the Vancouver 2010 Olympic and Paralympic Games (offered by the Olympic resistance movement) resulted in a number of agencies attempting to police the threat as a case of MIE:

> On the ground, the diverse Olympic resistance movement began mobilising popular opposition to the Games. This opposition began to result in intelligence material gathered from various local policing agencies. ITAC began to re-code the diverse branches of the emerging movement against the Olympic Games in the discursive framework of 'extremism' and then 'terrorism'.
>
> (2012: 148)

In the Unites States, Monahan's research into the fusion centre complex has revealed similar findings. In the second instance of MIE discourse, both race-orientated and student protest groups were depicted, in 2009, as posing an extremist threat to the state of Virginia. In citing the risk as an MIE, Virginia's threat assessment centre reported that many of these organisations were 'recognized as a radicalization node for almost every type of extremist group' (Monahan, 2010: 48). Between 2008 and 2009, the official response to this particular type of threat was further underlined by the treatment of the American Civil Liberties Union (ALCU) by the Maryland Coordination and Analysis [fusion] Centre (MCAC). During an ALCU lawsuit over a Freedom of Information request, 'the Maryland State Police had conducted covert investigations of at least 53 peace activists and anti-death penalty activists for a period of 14 months', despite admissions by covert operatives of there being 'no indication of violent activities or violent intentions on the part of group members' (89).

In the UK, significant research has been conducted into this issue by investigative journalists Rob Evans, Paul Lewis, and Matthew Taylor from the *Guardian* newspaper (2009, 2013). The British equivalent of an MIE is the term 'domestic extremism', which has been widely used by HM Constabulary as a means of shaping the public's perception of social movements, and of controlling demonstrations. As with the UK's overseas allies, the deployment of MIE classifications by intelligence agencies and law enforcement officials has been used to define campaign groups within civil contingencies doctrine as posing a threat equivalent to organisations such as al Qaeda. Although the UK is alleged to have only one official fusion intelligence centre, the Joint Threat Assessment Centre (which is a subdivision of GCHQ), local government authorities operate regional risk assessment centres, which also comply with Monahan and Palmer's earlier paradigm. In this respect, the UK's Local Resilience Forums (LRFs) coordinate different intelligence streams between regional contingency stakeholders. These include the police and emergency services, representatives from the private sector (often including their own in-house intelligence experts and security employees), and Local Government Authorities. Good evidence exists to suggest that the LRFs are equally accountable for disseminating MIE discourse into the public domain – as has been the case elsewhere in the West.

In 2006 for example, Local Government Authorities and emergency services attended a mass environmental protest at the Drax Power Station in Selby (North Yorkshire), which is one of the UK's largest coal-powered electricity providers. Activists from the Camp for Climate Action group descended on the site which, on 31 August 2006, was attended by over 3,000 police officers (Brown, 2006). During an otherwise peaceful demonstration, 39 people, intent on closing the facility and disrupting its activities, were arrested for trying to break into the power station. North Yorkshire Police later claimed it was the 'first time that domestic extremism had ever taken place in the county', thus issuing an MIE categorisation for the event (North Yorkshire Local Resilience Forum, 2006). However, the bigger picture of political policing in the UK reveals not only that the notion of domestic extremism is a 'common currency' within the force, but that a number of dedicated police units had been commissioned to attend to such matters (Evans et al., 2009: 6).

Under the operational aegis of the (now-defunct) Association of Chief Police Officers' 'Terrorism and Allied Matters' group (ACPO-TAM), further divisions were created to police public protests including the National Public Order Intelligence Unit (NPOIU), the National Extremism Tactical Coordination Unit (NETCU), and the National Domestic Extremism Unit (NDEU). Many of these departments later merged into a new task force entitled the National Domestic Extremism and Disorder Intelligence Unit (NDEDIU) following a public scandal over the failed convictions of environmental activists in Nottingham (Jones, 2011). As a result of flawed intelligence provided by an undercover operative embedded in the environmental movement, calls were made for a public enquiry into the use of Covert Human Intelligence Sources. After two consecutive inquiries into the affair, the Rose report (2011: 5), and an investigation by the Independent Police Complaints Commission (IPCC, 2011: 5), it was revealed that two Operations (codenamed Pegasus and Aeroscope) had employed NPOIU officers to infiltrate environmental groups in the region. Operation Pegasus (circa 2008) involved a number of agents who had been ordered to infiltrate groups of domestic extremists throughout the UK. Operation Aeroscope was a localised investigation into campaign groups operating within the Nottinghamshire region, which resulted in over 100 campaigners being arrested at the Iona Independent School in Nottingham, based upon intelligence that campaigners were planning to assault a nearby power station in 2009 (IPCC, 2011: 5). The resulting public scandal, the press coverage, and the inquiries all 'related to the infiltration of various domestic extremist groups' by undercover police (5). The nefarious practice of maintaining a covert identity was also brought into question following allegations by journalists, to the effect that, as part of their ruse, undercover agents had maintained personal relationships with campaigners for a number of years.

Further use of MIE discourse in the UK can be found in the depiction of the Occupy movement by City of London Police in 2011. In a letter distributed to companies within London's business district, numerous organisations were warned of the ongoing threat posed by terrorists and extremists. However, the memorandum made limited differentiation between the two categories of individuals, and financial workers were asked to remain vigilant for any signs of the 'suspected reconnaissance' of empty buildings by anti-capitalist demonstrators (City of London Police, 2011). The letter depicted further risks to the business community such as a planned electrician's strike by Balfour Beatty employees, and advised of potential direct action campaigns by the Stop Huntingdon Animal Cruelty animal rights group (SHAC). The letter framed these organisations as posing an equivalent threat to businesses as the Revolutionary Forces of Colombia, and al Qaeda, and even detailed a forthcoming demonstration by the Climate Justice Collective as posing a severe risk to trade and commerce (City of London Police, 2011).

Key research methods for investigating the deep state

So far, this chapter has outlined what a notional 'deep state' might consist of, in terms of its appearance in a number of intelligence agencies and secretive organisations, as well as the way in which they have framed public dissent as a manifestation of 'multi-issue extremism' (MIE). In order to gain a sense of how MIE discourse and fusion centre surveillance try to shape the world, or rather, how they present one account of the world according to the political objectives of the deep state, both MIE discourse and the institutions that disseminate it need to be identified and examined. The purpose of this part of the chapter is to consider how a number of investigative journalists and academics have arrived at particular conclusions, and to determine which techniques were used in their research.

The background research for Monahan and Palmer's 'The Emerging Politics of DHS Fusion Centers' (2009: 617–636) was pieced together using material gathered from a range of sources – as these articles often tend to be. In reality, not only does a wider search for empirical evidence often yield surprising results, but it can also be thought of as good academic and journalistic practice. The belief that one should always attempt to verify the sources that have been used, and cross-reference them wherever possible, is generally sound advice. For their 2009 publication, Monahan and Palmer examined a number of newspaper articles that were written between 2002 and 2008. They used the LexisNexis search engine to identify specific key words from newspapers and other such publications that existed during this period. Using this approach, they were able to perform a qualitative analysis of news reports containing references to fusion centre surveillance in the United States. The criteria of the dates for examination were based on the year that the DHS was first commissioned, following which the DHS fusions centres started to emerge.

> We conducted a LexisNexis search for articles mentioning both 'homeland' and 'fusion center', or those mentioning both 'terrorism' and 'fusion center', published between November 2002 and December 2008. November 2002 was chosen as a start date because the Department of Homeland Security was created then. The search returned 90 newspaper and magazine articles, 56 of which were deemed relevant, 49 of which were unique.
>
> (620)

Following the initial hits returned by their LexisNexis research (and the articles to which they corresponded), a wider Google search was undertaken as a means to discover key government documents from the same period. In terms of making a comparative analysis of the evidence that their initial research revealed, this was a good technique to employ – working on the premise that open governments make some of their activities public knowledge. This kind of data generally relates to the organisation of a nation's security infrastructure and to the institutions involved, if nothing else.

During this type of investigation, one of the main issues faced by both academics and reporters is the impenetrable language used by intelligence agencies and security providers. But of course this is one of the ways in which secret agendas or clandestine organisations remain hidden from public scrutiny and avoid demands for executive oversight. However, as clandestine programmes are usually referred to by their codenames within official publications (as are the key agencies, actors, or initiatives involved), a simple lesson to be learned from this investigative strategy is that one can identify the organisations based on the specific aliases that are in use. For instance, following Monahan and Palmer's preliminary research into the DHS, the fusion centre programme was also exposed. Yet, to problematise the investigation of the fusion centre complex throughout the West, a big part of the problem facing scholars and journalists alike, is that all these organisations (while they hold relatively true to Monahan and Palmer's initial paradigm) have different operational names and inter-agency relationships. In this respect, the research strategy of triangulating one's findings is an essential technique for gathering future data.

In Monaghan and Walby's later investigation into Canada's fusion intelligence complex (and the use of MIE discourse to demonise opposition to the 2010 Vancouver Games), an altogether different approach was used. The article employed Monahan and Palmer's earlier qualitative methods, but in addition to examining news reports, it also used Freedom of Information requests to gather empirical data from official sources. In their examination of how Canada's Integrated Threat Assessment Centre deployed MIE classifications to defame social movements, Monaghan and Walby explained how 'Access to Information Act (ATIA) requests' were used to reveal how 'policing and surveillance projects developed in preparation for three mega events that recently took place in Canada' (2012: 133).

From their findings, it was determined that Canada's fusion intelligence complex operates in much the same way as its continental and international allies. It consists of a number of regional surveillance hubs that coordinate streams of intelligence between different municipal, state, corporate, and law enforcement agencies. These include the Canadian Security and Intelligence Service (CSIS), the Integrated Threat Assessment Centre (ITAC), Integrated Security Units and Joint Intelligence Groups (ISU-JIG), and the Royal Canadian Mounted Police (RCMP). In 2003, the RCMP established the ISUs as a cross border, multi-agency task force designed to provide intelligence for mega events such as the Olympic Games and the G8/G20 political and economic summits. The ISUs were initially designed to collaborate with international partners such as the United States, by aligning military and domestic intelligence resources. The RCMP later amalgamated the ISUs with Canada's Joint Intelligence Group, combining municipal and provincial police authorities, the CSIS, and the armed forces, under one operational framework. According to Monaghan and Walby, the ISU-JIG collaboration was later reincarnated as the ITAC, which continued much the same role in relation to the policing of mega events:

> JIG issued its first 'preliminary' Threat Assessment related to the 2010 mega-events on 12 May 2005. Later, in a report from 1 April 2007, the JIG's function is described as follows: 'The JIG plans to develop a comprehensive public order portfolio to monitor and access high risk groups, individuals, and potential threats to Olympic-related events'. From its inception in 2005 until the 2010 mega-events, the JIG played a central role in coordinating security intelligence practices. Notably, however, after meetings in late 2006, it was decided that the editorial control of 'Threat Assessments' would be undertaken by a CSIS agency, known as the Integrated Threat Assessment Centre.
>
> (136)

From their investigation into fused corporate, military, and domestic policing resources, Monaghan and Walby were able to determine how these institutions, the ITAC in particular, used MIE categorisations to manage public order threats to mega events. Although these institutions still played their unique individual roles, from coordinating intelligence resources to conducting actual covert operations, the ITAC's editorial control of risk categorisations presented a consistent discourse to security and business partners, and of course to the Canadian public.

In addition to the research gleaned from official reports into the activities of groups such as ITAC, the aforementioned strategy of analysing media coverage of public order operations was used to determine 'how intelligence agencies have blurred the categories of terrorism, extremism and activism into an aggregate threat matrix' (133). To further their concerns regarding the reclassification of legitimate social movements and grassroots organisations as 'extremist', it was concluded that the CSIS had deliberately blurred 'the protection of private property, especially the property of Olympic corporate sponsors within the rubric of national security' as a means to justify the surveillance of protest groups (144). According to Monaghan and Walby's research, the mainstream media reported that ISU officers had used tactics such as infiltration against campaign organisations, that they had visited specific activists at their private homes to serve as a warning not to interfere with the Olympic games, and had even 'posed as bus drivers, inviting activists into their bus apparently headed to Olympic Torch Relay disruptions' (149). The latter of these propositions frames covert ISU operations as COINTELPROs, as Counter-Intelligence Programmes designed to misdirect, misinform or simply interrupt any planned campaign actions. It was therefore observed that:

> ISU officers [had] made numerous house-calls to prominent activists and critics before the Olympics. Between 3 and 5 June 2009, approximately 15 anti-Olympics activists were visited by approximately eight ISU members. The ISU also had covert officers that spent several years undercover with groups in British Columbia and Ontario.
>
> (137)

Notwithstanding, one of the main issues faced by those wishing to undertake deep state research is the limits placed on access to Freedom of Information requests, which are often denied by intelligence agencies, on the grounds of national security. Monaghan and Walby readily admit that their own ATIA requests were limited by various renditions of official secrecy, even to the extent that the ISU (et al.) had lobbied the Canadian government to place restrictions on public access to documents regarding its operations. The belief was that wider knowledge surrounding its operational practices would have *i)* severely hampered its capacity to police the Olympic games, and *ii)* that 'such information [could] be put to nefarious counter-intelligence use by terrorist or protest groups' (139).

In terms of investigating the UK's fusion intelligence complex, research published by journalists such as Rob Evans, Paul Lewis, and Matthew Taylor, and work conducted by scholars in this field, has framed much of the debate surrounding the fusion centre/MIE affair. Research strategies have included requests made under the *Freedom of Information Act 2000* (HMSO 2000) to civil contingency and police partnerships, the use of official publications, the analysis of media publications, attendance at international conferences on policing and surveillance, and networking with authors and activists in this field. Of course, leaked intelligence reports, and the use of additional materials disclosed by whistleblowers such as Edward Snowden, also provides invaluable background into deep state organisations such as the NSA and GCHQ.

The British version of a fusion intelligence complex has been presented so far in terms of the public and private sector networks that were commissioned post-9/11 to protect the UK's Critical National Infrastructure. But, of course, any investigation into the deep state must venture further than this. Under laws such as the *Civil Contingencies Act 2004* and the UK's counter terrorism strategy (known as CONTEST), a gradual blurring of lines 'between terrorism, subversion and legitimate dissent and protest' has taken place during the last decade (Home Office, 2009: 78). In an administrative context, Local Government Authorities, the police, and private sector interests have been aligned under the Civil Contingencies programme to form Local Resilience Forums, which coordinate regional efforts to prevent serious incidents. The possible events cited as having a detrimental impact on vital public services, commercial businesses, or on the general population, include industrial accidents, outbreaks of human or animal-borne disease, and even severe weather. While, arguably, the LRFs are contingency planning centres for predicting and managing risks to each catchment of the UK, they are neither intelligence agencies (on the scale of the DHS), nor do they undertake covert infiltration operations. As civil contingency partnerships, they do however, coordinate with the police (and by extension, with organisations such as the security service MI5, and GCHQ), and they do list public protests as posing threat to public safety. In this respect, the LRFs disseminate MIE discourse into the public domain in relation to the specific sites under their protection (such as power stations and airports). These risks are openly published in Regional Risk Registers and contribute to a National Risk Register which is accessible online.

Evidence to corroborate the allegations outlined above, was first highlighted in an article entitled 'How police rebranded lawful protest as "domestic extremism"', by journalists from the *Guardian* newspaper (Evans et al., 2009: 6). Here, Evans, Lewis, and Taylor reported that MIE descriptors had become one of the Constabulary's main techniques for legitimising surveillance during public order actions. They noted that MIE terms including domestic extremism were being used in an attempt to undermine public support for causes such as environmentalism, and had led to the details of several thousand suspected extremists being stored on a secret police database (6). According to the *Guardian*, evidence that official sources were using domestic extremism as a means to defame campaigners, had been found in an operational review of the public order action at Drax Power Station in 2006. Although initial requests to police sources offered limited results, a Freedom of Information request, targeted at North Yorkshire's LRF, provided evidence of an MIE being used during the police operation. In this respect, a good working knowledge of the systems, policies, and agencies that one is trying to research, will often lead to creative alternatives if the direct approach does not work. In this instance, an FOI request could have been submitted to the fire brigade, the ambulance service, or to North Yorkshire County Council, where police or state censorship might have been less obstructive. The problem for academics and journalists is that when legitimate protests become aligned with mass-casualty terrorism, they become a matter of national security and not domestic policing. It is the alignment of national security matters with those of domestic policing that makes researching the deep state even more problematic.

While the UK's LRFs represent contingency planning forums, intelligence-led activities are more conventionally conducted by the police, sometimes by private security firms or by corporate spies (Lubbers, 2012), or by the UK's security services. Overall, the British equivalent of a fusion intelligence complex is just as adverse to public scrutiny, and is equally as difficult to research as its overseas allies. Nonetheless, the intelligence infrastructure of the UK can really be broken down into three parts. One of these can be thought of in terms of conventional policing (via HM Constabulary); the second as Britain's intelligence agencies (GCHQ, MI5, and MI6); while the third is military intelligence. Whereas MI6 (the Secret Intelligence Service) is largely responsible for conducting overseas operations, MI5 directs intelligence operations at home. GCHQ is the UK's signals intelligence (SIGINT) provider, and, alongside its fusion intelligence complex (the Joint Threat Analysis Centre), distributes various information streams to more conventional partners such as the Counter Terrorism Command unit at London's Metropolitan Police.

> Within the Metropolitan Police Service, Counter Terrorism Command (also known also as Special Operations Group 15, or SO15), forms part of the Nation's wider network of similar organisations. SO15 is the lead branch on counter-terrorism duties in the UK and, according to the sub-divisional North East Counter Terrorism Network (2015), represents just one in a federation of five such institutions. . . . Overall the Counter Terrorism Network is responsible for intelligence gathering activities and preventing 'incidents of terrorism and domestic extremism'. . . . The five partners report their findings back to Counter Terrorism Command, and thereafter to the Joint Terrorism Analysis Centre, thus forming a network of major regional forces.
>
> (Harbisher, 2015: 478)

Although the paradigm set out previously demonstrates how the British fusion intelligence complex is currently comprised, as is the case with Monahan et al.'s work in this field, it is worth considering the development of these institutions and the rise of an MIE discourse in the UK as an attempt to justify public order surveillance. In actuality, the majority of information presented so far has been attained by networking with journalists, by submitting Freedom of Information requests, and also by consulting official publications. Wider approaches to deconstructing the intelligence apparatuses of the British deep state can be found by undertaking an analysis of publications from other government departments, which may work with these organisations. In terms of the alignment of political activism with international terrorism, a good starting point for any investigation is to look at the multitude of official publications on terrorism, and then by cross-referencing the institutions involved (including those cited as contributors).

In terms of understanding the origins of MIE discourse in the UK, a number of initial publications made reference to an organisation known as the RICU. The Research Information and Communications Unit at Whitehall is essentially a think tank that operates between three separate departments. These are the Foreign and Commonwealth Affairs Office, the UK Home Office, and the Department for Communities and Local Government. The RICU was established in 2007 and promotes consistent communication strategies between CONTEST stakeholders and the general public. Under the PREVENT strand of CONTEST (designed to tackle the causes of terrorism and radicalisation at their roots), the RICU aimed to create an alternative narrative to 'brands' such as al Qaeda. Instead of disseminating messages into the public domain that legitimise radicalisation, the RICU encourages all public-facing agencies to use a strategic dialogue in their communications (RICU, 2010). For example, the RICU urges all CONTEST partners not to use terms such as 'Jihad' in their communications, as this 'feeds the idea that there is a religious war between "Muslims and the West"' (58). It claims that using terms such as 'violent extremism' offers credible alternatives to depicting terrorists as promoting a specific cause, and in this way, aims to challenge the language of terrorism (66).

However, there is limited differentiation in the popular imaginary between a violent extremist and a domestic one. This later proposition illustrates the potency of MIE discourse in the West, especially when used as a political vehicle to restrict freedom of speech and freedom of assembly. The problem is that organisations, such as ACPO-TAM and the police, use an equivalent MIE discourse to define campaigners, as that used to describe acts of mass-casualty terrorism. Again, knowing the institutions involved, a wider internet search for key terms such as 'ACPO', 'terrorism', and 'language table', revealed a publication disclosed under the Levenson enquiry entitled *Guidance on Media Handling and Communication Activity at Major Incidents (Including Counter Terrorism)*, authored by ACPO in 2008 for British Transport Police. The document contains precisely the same language table as issued by the RICU, and (knowing that the acronym of 'TAM' stands for terrorism and allied matters), it is therefore possible to understand how ACPO subsidiary the NPOIU would have depicted campaign groups as domestic extremists.

Conclusion: issues and problems in researching the deep state

The biggest issue facing journalists or academics conducting research into the politics and practices of the deep state are generally all access-related. On the one hand, FOI requests offer a legitimate way to conduct research in this field yet, comparatively, significant proportions of the material which may (or may not) be returned will be suppressed as a result of national security censorship. In fact, the UK *Freedom of Information Act* makes explicit reference to materials that will be redacted for the purposes of national security (HMSO 2000, Part 2: S24). Often researchers will be faced with several pages that are completely redacted. However, conducting shrewd investigations into the subject-matter of interest, allows researchers to read between the lines and to be more selective in their choice of evidence. For example, a public disclosure into the activities of the Special Demonstration Squad (an earlier incarnation of the NPOIU), revealed that undercover officers were advised to have 'fleeting, disastrous relationships with individuals who are not important to your sources of information' (Metropolitan Police, 2015: 8). While Operation Hearne (HM Constabulary's own investigation into allegations that undercover officers had maintained personal relationships as part of their cover), was considered a breakthrough in terms of open government access, no less than 42 pages out of the 52-page disclosure were redacted. With the exception of the previous citation (which was of substantial interest to journalists), the rest of the material was unusable.

But there are other problems presented in using FOI/ATIA data sets. Previous searches for evidence (that may have produced usable results), can also be rescinded and removed from public access entirely. Fortunately, online campaign groups (and research foundations), such as Powerbase and the Undercover Research Group, now store previously accessed materials, formerly used by journalists, academics, and activists, that are no longer available in the public domain. Many such documents are today released by the authorities for a limited time only (perhaps due to storage issues), but frequently to limit general public access. In other respects, where criminal cases have been reopened or an inquiry has been called for, evidence may become unavailable in relation to forthcoming trials or police investigations. Nevertheless, as noted by Monaghan and Walby:

> The depths of information accessed through the ATIA can be remarkable, yet researchers continue to encounter stonewalling. . . . Due to redactions, delays, as well as problems such as chronic under-funding

of ATI branches. . . . ATIA users are aware that these requests rarely lead to full-picture explanations. However, disclosures can be combined to reveal policing and intelligence trends.

(2012: 138)

There are of course further limitations in using FOI data requests in the UK. In terms of stonewalling, HM Constabulary operates a Neither Confirm Nor Deny (NCND) policy for sensitive issues or publications. As noted previously, FOI requests can be delayed if the appropriate operational codename is not used in the first place. In fact, it is always advisable to seek an alternative method (such as an LRF request), to provide the basic outline and parameters for your research. Even knowing the key times, dates, operational names, etc. of the event in question can be beneficial to this process. Other barriers to legitimate FOI research can include fees being charged by public authorities to pay for the administrative time that an FOI will allegedly take. However, policies that do not even provide an opportunity for further research, like the 'Neither Confirm Nor Deny' approach applied to crucial policing events, are just as obstructive as they sound.

There are, of course, other avenues for research. The use of data sets provided by whistleblowers sometimes fills in many of the areas left blank by FOI censorship, although these sites are allegedly monitored by GCHQ and its subsidiaries (Greenwald and Gallagher, 2014). Furthermore, many influential figures involved with investigating the deep state, Duncan Campbell and Glen Greenwald especially, have themselves been the subject of police intimidation on a number of occasions. Campbell for instance has stated that:

> In my 40 years of reporting on mass surveillance, I have been raided three times; jailed once; had television programs I made or assisted making banned from airing under government pressure five times; seen tapes seized; faced being shoved out of a helicopter; had my phone tapped for at least a decade; and . . . been lined up to face up to 30 years imprisonment for alleged violations of secrecy laws.
>
> (2015)

For figures such as Edward Snowden and Julian Assange, whose leaks have revolutionised the way in which the general public now understands its relationship with the state, the price paid for investigating, or for disclosing deep state secrets, has been even higher. Snowden, for example, is currently in asylum in Russia, and has been there since 2013, for fear that his return to the United States would not result in a fair trial. Julian Assange (founder of the WikiLeaks project) is currently under asylum in the Ecuadorian Embassy in London, where he has been since 2012. Journalist Glenn Greenwald and documentary filmmaker Laura Poitras have either been held at airports during terrorism-related investigations, or have had their immediate family/partners intimidated in this manner for their respective roles in the Snowden affair (Maas, 2013).

It could be suggested, then, that conducting investigations at a local or regional level generates less interest from the authorities than stirring the metaphorical hornet's nest of multinational and government concerns. That said, without the tireless efforts of journalists such as Duncan Campbell, Glenn Greenwald, Rob Evans, Paul Lewis, and Matthew Taylor, both civil liberties and contemporary reportage in this area would fare much less well. Comparatively, significant amounts of data regarding the techniques and technologies of the deep state would remain entirely hidden without whistleblowers as they play a precarious game of cat and mouse, caught between their own ethical challenges, and the contentious practices of the state.

References

ACPO [Association of Chief Police Officers] (2008) *Guidance on Media Handling and Communication Activity at Major Incidents (Including Counter Terrorism)*. London: ACPO.
Brown, Jonathan (2006) 'The battle of drax: 38 held as protest fails to close plant', *The Independent*, 1 September.
Campbell, Duncan (1976) 'The eavesdroppers', *Time Out*, 21–27 May, 8–9.
—— (1988) 'Somebody's listening', *New Statesman*, 12 August, pp. 10–12.
—— (2015) 'GCHQ and me: My life unmasking British eavesdroppers', *The Intercept*, https://thcintercept.com/2015/08/03/life-unmasking-british-eavesdroppers/ [accessed 10 December 2016].
City of London Police. 2011. *Terrorism/Extremism Update for the City of London Business Community: 2 December 2011*, London: City of London Police.
DHS [Department of Homeland Security, US] (2016) 'Fusion center locations and contact information', *Department for Homeland Security*, www.dhs.gov/fusion-center-locations-and-contact-information. [accessed 10 December 2016].
Evans, Rob and Lewis, Paul (2013) *Undercover*. London: Guardian Books.
Evans, Rob, Lewis, Paul and Taylor, Matthew (2009) 'How police rebranded lawful protest as "domestic extremism"', the *Guardian*, 26 October, 6.
Greenwald, Glenn (2013) 'NSA prism program taps in to user data of Apple, Google and others', the *Guardian*, www.theguardian.com/world/2013/jun/06/us-tech-giants-nsa-data [accessed 5 September 2010].
Greenwald, Glenn and Gallagher, Ryan (2014) 'Snowden documents reveal covert surveillance and pressure tactics aimed at WikiLeaks and its supporters', *The Intercept*, https://theintercept.com/2014/02/18/snowden-docs-reveal-covert-surveillance-and-pressure-tactics-aimed-at-wikileaks-and-its-supporters/ [accessed 5 September 2010].
Harbisher, Ben (2015) 'Unthinking extremism: Radicalising narratives that legitimise surveillance', in *Surveillance and Society*, Vol. 13, Issue: 3–), pp. 474–486.
HMSO (2000) *Freedom of Information Act 2000*. London: Her Majesty's Stationery Office.
Home Office (2009) *Security for the Next Generation*, London: The Stationery Office.

IPCC [Independent Police Complaints Commission] (2011) *Ratcliffe-on-Soar Power Station (Operation Aeroscope) Disclosure: Nottinghamshire Police*. Sale: Independent Police Complaints Commission.

Jones, Chris (2014) '"Call it intercontinental collaboration": Radicalisation, violent extremism and fusion centres', in *Statewatch*, London: Statewatch.

Jones, Meirion (2011) 'Trial collapses after undercover officer changes sides', *BBC Newsnight*, www.bbc.co.uk/news/uk-12148753 [accessed 10 October 2016].

Lubbers, Eveline (2012) *Secret Manoeuvres in the Dark: Corporate and Police Spying on Activists*. London: Pluto Press.

Maas, Peter (2013) 'How Laura Poitra helped Snowden spill his secrets', *New York Times*, www.nytimes.com/2013/08/18/magazine/laura-poitras-snowden.html?pagewanted=all&_r=0 [accessed 10 October 2016].

MacAskill, Ewen, Borger, Julian, Hopkins, Nick, Davies, Nick and Ball, James (2013) 'GCHQ taps fibre-optic cables for secret access to world's communications', the *Guardian*, www.theguardian.com/uk/2013/jun/21/gchq-cables-secret-world-communications-nsa [accessed 5 September 2010].

Metropolitan Police (2015) *Operation Hearne – SDS Tradecraft Manual*. London: Metropolitan Police.

Monaghan, Jeffrey and Walby, Kevin (2012) 'Making up "Terror Identities": Security intelligence, Canada's integrated threat assessment centre and social movement suppression', *Policing and Society: An International Journal of Research and Policy*, Vol. 22, Issue: 2, pp. 133–151.

Monahan, Torin (2009) 'The murky world of "Fusion Centres"'. *Criminal Justice Matters*, Vol. 75, Issue: 1, pp. 20–21.

——— (2010) 'The future of security? Surveillance operations at homeland security fusion centres', *Social Justice*, Vol. 37, Issue: 2–3, pp. 84–98.

Monahan, Torin and Palmer, Neal (2009) 'The emerging politics of DHS fusion centres', *Security Dialogue*, Vol. 40, Issue: 6, pp. 617–636.

Newkirk, Anthony (2010) 'The rise of the fusion-intelligence complex: A critique of political surveillance after 9/11', *Surveillance & Society*, Vol. 8, Issue: 1, pp. 43–60.

North East Counter Terrorism Unit (2015) 'Background', www.northeastctu.police.uk/about/background [accessed 1 April 2015].

North Yorkshire Local Resilience Forum (2006) *North Yorkshire Local Resilience Forum: Notes of the Joint Operations Group*, Northallerton: North Yorkshire Local Resilience Forum.

RICU [Research Information and Communications Unit] (2010) *Prevent: A Communications Guide*, London: Home Office.

Rose, Christopher (2011) *Ratcliffe-on-Soar Power Station Protest Inquiry into Disclosure*, London: Crown Prosecution Service.

Shubber, Kadhim (2013) 'A simple guide to the prism controversy', *Wired*, www.wired.co.uk/article/simple-guide-to-prism [accessed 5 September 2010].

Wilson, Eric (2009) *Government of the Shadows: Parapolitics and Criminal Sovereignty*, London: Pluto Press.

3 State, hierarchy, and executive power
Journalists under duress

Stuart Price

Introduction: power, journalism, and investigative work

Drawing on theories of power and the role of journalism in the reproduction of public life, this chapter provides an insight into the nexus of *opportunity and constraint* that confronts all reporters,[1] not just those whose sense of vocation drives them beyond the limited procedures associated with 'administrative journalism' (Kreiss, in Alexander et al., 2016) or the negative attitude exemplified by Lloyd when he attacked 'Greenwald and others' for '[taking] investigative journalism and going beyond a discipline of checking, to an assumption of bad faith' (2017: 135). Despite the differences between the principles that inspire investigative work, and those that underpin the creation of more generic material, both can be interpreted as expressions of the same 'ideal' public function, characterised by its independence from officialdom and an interest in the timely dissemination of factual information about recent events (McQuail, 2013).

This tradition, though never entirely pure in spirit or execution, offers an obvious contrast to modes of communication that are designed to 'spin' incidents for the benefit of elite social groups (see below), suggesting that the most immediate task facing those who identify themselves as serious journalists, is to maintain the principles (public service and autonomous enquiry) within which a continuum of practices (from the 'descriptive' to the 'interrogative') can continue to exist. If this is achieved, then 'journalism as a moral enterprise' (Seib, 2002: xi) will also remain a viable proposition.

The success of this venture depends, however, on how claims to ethical commitment are interpreted within a 'globalised' political culture, one that is driven by commercial imperatives yet also affected by national, regional, and local conditions. The 'moral enterprise' may survive, but under less than ideal circumstances, and it is often difficult to align a rhetorical attachment to high standards with the actual content encountered in news stories. A great deal of journalistic discourse, for example, might be couched in the language of freedom and self-determination, but may actually reinforce crude myths about national identity: the unscrupulous media agitation that helped to produce the Brexit vote is a case in point (Cadwalladr, 2018).

Since so many news organisations and individual practitioners fail to meet even the most basic standards of veracity, it is hard to assign socially progressive values to journalism as a whole. This does not mean, however, that the problem is solved simply by assigning the higher purpose to investigative work: although this form of journalism may provide a more inspiring example, such an act would be to confuse procedure with principle. A more measured approach would be to acknowledge the contradictory nature of the normative framework – at once 'principled' and corporate – that provides the context for the production of news, and to recognise the fact that public culture as a whole is absorbed and reproduced through the mutually constitutive forces of institutional discipline and independent enquiry.

At the same time, there is no doubt that a 'radical imaginary' (one that offers an alternative to the dominance of patriarchal capitalism), has not disappeared from view, although the majority of even the most censorious journalistic interventions are not necessarily meant as fundamental attacks on the rationale that underpins the social order. Investigations may, for example, interrogate the more outrageous excesses of political or corporate leaders, to such an extent that these critiques might, inadvertently, shake the foundations of particular regimes, but the intention of such enquiries is usually confined to complaints about the lack of integrity in public life.

The investigative journalist R. Nadeswaran (known by his nom de plume Citizen Nades), provides an example of this attitude. Based in Malaysia, he described his main focus as 'bread and butter issues' (Hicks, 2016), declared that his quarrel was 'not with politicians', and said he was pleased that his criticism of the 'abuse or misuse' of 'public funds or power' was greeted with approval by the upper echelons of the Malaysian government (2016). Aligning themselves with a watchdog that barks at dishonest bureaucrats can provide a useful alibi for dominant social actors, as they pursue their own, more sophisticated forms of corruption, but there is no guarantee that this implicit agreement between investigator and state power will benefit the individual journalist.

This was certainly the case with the Chinese investigative reporter Liu Jianqiang who, believing that he was operating within a system that allowed him to expose local corruption or regional injustices – but not the iniquities of the system or the authoritarian behaviour of its national leadership – wrote a piece that seemed to conform to this approach (Barnett, in Schiffrin, 2014: 165). Liu Jianqiang described a murder committed by a provincial official (the victim was the man's wife), but the article was 'banned from publication by the central authorities' (165). The use of outright censorship draws attention to the authoritarian paranoia common in many nations, but there are other more covert methods of obstruction that reduce the chance that powerful regimes ('democratic' or otherwise) will be held responsible for specific forms of injustice or coercion.

Identifying, for instance, the 'digital threats' directed against journalists, Deibert drew attention to 'the global proliferation of so-called lawful interception malware *sold exclusively to governments*' so that their operatives are able to 'remotely and secretly access and monitor the computers and phones of their targets' (2017: 248, my emphasis). Deibert, a Canadian academic who runs an organisation called Citizen's Lab, also revealed how the Mexican state used the Israeli-made spy software Pegasus, to monitor the phones of international human rights advocates who were investigating 'the high-profile disappearance of 43 students at the Ayotzinapa teachers' college in Guerrero in 2014' (Democracy Now!, 2017). State hostility was, in other words, directed at those seeking the truth, and not at the suspected malefactors – a situation familiar to many investigative journalists. In some countries, even the pretence of legality is discarded: reporting from Gaddafi's Libya in 2011, the BBC journalist Rana Jawad called a friend to ask about the political situation and heard 'a pre-recorded message effectively saying the call was not allowed', which meant that 'the line had been monitored by the regime' because the owner of the phone was suspected of dissent (Jawad, 2011: 132–133).

In the light of this kind of surveillance, Lloyd's remark accusing journalists of 'bad faith' (see earlier) is less than convincing. The spectacular exposés produced by lone journalists or whistleblowers are remarkable exactly because they have to break through a barrier of silence and hostility, not because they are irrational. As suggested at the beginning of this chapter, the root of the clash between those who break news stories, and those public and private bodies that place institutional preservation above all other considerations, lies in the fact that most journalists retain at least a formal attachment to the concepts of balance and technical accuracy. The pursuit of these principles, however flawed, distorted, or poorly applied, offers an alternative paradigm to the routine products of the promotional culture controlled by elite social groups.

Journalism: intrusive practices and structural antagonism

Seib provides a well-known reference to moral purpose when he repeats the adage that the 'long-standing mandate' of journalism is to 'comfort the afflicted and afflict the comfortable' (2002: 2). Yet, even where it falls below the highest professional standards, one factor above all appears to unsettle powerful states and secretive corporations – the unavoidably *intrusive* nature of newsgathering.

It is not just the ethical quality of a specific enquiry, or the strength of individual news conglomerates, or the reputation of particular journalists, that upsets established interests, but the simple fact that reporters do not necessarily seek advance approval for their activities. Driven by deadlines, they encounter resistance, not because they adopt, unfailingly, a rigorous investigative stance (or adhere to precepts that would increase the reputation of their profession), but because *they follow established journalistic procedures*. This is the key to understanding why serious journalism, regardless of its political affiliation, is so contentious, and why it has such a significant international impact.

The various confrontations between journalists and executive power (produced, for example, by the latter's invocation of the 'national interest' to stifle or restrict debate),[2] can be attributed, therefore, to a *structural antagonism* between the interrogative principle (primarily but not exclusively associated with investigative journalism) and the defensive generation of official public discourse (the routine production of a rationale designed to provide a broadly plausible, but not necessarily accurate, explanation of events). It is perfectly possible, therefore, for states to pay lip service to an exalted but essentially meaningless set of principles, and to conduct 'business as usual'. When the African National Congress came to power in South Africa, freedom of expression was enshrined in the Constitution, and 'formal censorship of the press' came to an end: new forms of restriction, however, came into play, which produced a regulated, essentially ideological account of life in the country (Geertsema-Sligh, in Byerly, 2016: 96).[3]

In Uganda, to take another example, despite the supposed existence of a liberal media environment, journalists still 'have to haggle to get public information' (Kaija, in Byerly, 2016: 318). The gulf between the claims made by governments that they work on behalf of the public, and the deplorable conduct driven by adherence to abstractions like the 'national interest', are not however confined to 'developing' or supposedly dysfunctional democracies. Many nations subscribe to progressive, *trans-national* codes of media and governmental conduct yet, once again, formal commitment to freedom of expression, found in documents like the Universal Declaration of Human Rights, do not necessarily result in practical support for determined enquiry (317). Discussing the Snowden case, Greenwald noted that 'while [Edward Snowden] was on the plane from Hong Kong, the U.S. government . . . revoked his passport . . . many of us did not even know [it] had that power . . . no hearing, no charges, no due process' (in Bell and Taylor, 2017: 37).

The essential question (touched on previously) is whether, in responding to these challenges, the strategies adopted by investigative reporters go further than the exposure of the foibles and weaknesses of individuals or institutions, to provide an accurate account of underlying systemic problems, such as social and economic inequality. Where this is the goal, even the most ferocious methods used by determined investigators are usually regarded as justified. It is only when the same techniques are applied to 'ordinary' people, that some practitioners are accused of harassment and bullying. If the victimisation of individual citizens by journalists is clearly unacceptable, we should also distinguish between those enquiries conducted *on behalf of* the powerful, and those directed *against the interests* of dominant groups. All such activity, however, takes place in an environment that is created and maintained by forces that even the most determined social actors cannot control. Once again, this brings us back to the issue raised at the beginning of this chapter – the forces that both enable and constrain the production of news.

Journalism and authority: institutional pressures

A useful insight into the institutional pressures that affect all practitioners was provided by Marc-François Bernier and Marsha Barber. Having interviewed a sample of Canadian reporters, they found that these professionals adhered 'in more or less the same proportion' to identical journalistic values (in Weaver and Willnat, 2012: 339). They were, to varying degrees, prevented from staying true to their ideals because of the 'ownership characteristics, management practices, and convergence strategies' of the organisations to which they belonged (339). Since all reporters, irrespective of their location, work and live 'in a climate of intense competitive pressures' (Gerbner, 1965: 205), they will encounter not only the 'impersonal' condition of state sovereignty (Gerstenberger, 2007), and the autocratic behaviour of influential figures, but also a series of internal institutional hurdles. In confronting these challenges, a major problem facing qualified reporters (and many other bodies of accredited personnel) is that, though they exercise 'technical autonomy' or the 'right to use discretion and judgement in the performance of their work' (Rottwilm, 2014: 10), this does not extend to meaningful control over their immediate working environment, let alone the normative standards that are meant to govern their efforts.

The mismatch between an apparently desirable, yet vaguely paradoxical condition (certified status and independent agency), and the realities of everyday labour (subordination to various forms of authority), is not confined to one occupation. Journalism, however, benefits from advantages that some other careers lack, including the fact that the workforce is supposed to make contributions (albeit limited in scope), to public debate. Most employees, if their opinions are sought at all, are not meant to do much more than echo the 'values' espoused by their managers, though opportunities for dissent are provided by social media platforms and phenomena like 'citizen journalism' which – though treated by many established correspondents as a peripheral or even dangerous development (Podger, 2009) – may help maintain the endlessly renewable principle of autonomous commentary and investigation.[4]

Journalism and authority: ten fields of influence

Despite the widespread tendency to downplay the influence of formal authority, this chapter emphasises the continued importance of the state as an 'ultimate' power broker, certainly with regard to mass media systems. This stance is supported by the recent work of academics like Meyen, who identify states' 'natural interest in guiding, steering, and controlling' the 'public information and opinion-forming stages' of the communication process (2018: 1). The institutional picture sketched out earlier, and expanded in the argument that follows, is complicated by the fact that, although *some* of the dominant formations associated with state power are seen as essentially repressive, others (such as the legal system), can support the dissemination of public information, and thus by extension the relative 'health' of democratic systems. Equally, commercial news conglomerates (dedicated, in theory, to the unfettered circulation of timely reports), can play a major part in the suppression of useful knowledge. The common factor in all situations is the permanent subsistence of 'legitimate' authority: whatever form it takes, benign or otherwise, the intransigent existence of a 'command structure' creates a mental apprehension of power that (counterintuitively) obviates the need for direct instructions. As a result, hierarchies are replicated through the behaviour and actions of their willing or unwilling subjects, all of whom attempt to advance, through a cost/benefit analysis, what they believe to be their individual interests.

The question of individual complicity is an important element of any study of power, but although the emphasis of this chapter is on the (sometimes murky) institutional origins of executive influence, this position should not be confused with the 'dominance/control' paradigm, encountered in McNair's caricature of critical approaches to power and ideology. He identifies a model in which 'capitalist culture, and *journalism in particular*' (my emphasis), is seen as a 'monstrous apparatus bearing down on passive populations of deluded, misguided or manipulated people' (McNair, 2006: vii). No reference to an academic source that supports this position is actually provided, and it is worth noting that, as early as 1980, Abercrombie et al. debunked the notion that the purpose of ideology is to try to control subordinate classes through the imposition of 'dominant' beliefs (for a more nuanced analysis of the 'ideological', see below).

In the meantime, if those conceptions of 'the public' that go to the other extreme (imagining it as a unitary social force capable of independent action), are also excluded from the equation, we are left with ten distinct but interdependent fields of influence that can either augment or degrade the journalistic function. These categories can be enumerated as *i)* the 'ensemble of power centres' (Jessop, 2008: 37) that constitute the contemporary patriarchal *state*,[5] including its legal and regulatory apparatus (see the conclusion for a commentary); *ii)* a *trans-national corporate* sector dominated by *managerialism* (see below) and driven by the need to accumulate capital, impose 'efficiency savings', maximise shareholder dividends, and in some cases monopolise resources; *iii)* 'mainstream' *news institutions*, considered both as forms of managerial authority and as commercial 'hubs' that follow specific (often 'flexible' or precarious) practices; *iv)* international bodies, like the UN, devoted to the oversight of moral/political issues; *v)* formal *political parties concerned with obtaining electoral approval*; *vi)* organisations with a limited oppositional remit, like mainstream *trade unions and charities*; *vii)* criminal organisations that can intervene to prevent, often violently, particular lines of enquiry; *viii)* a *socioeconomic elite*, composed of individuals who may belong to, or associate with, one or more of the first seven domains of activity; *ix) independent* bodies set up by, or on behalf of journalists critical of established systems (such as the International Association of Independent Journalists, and the International Consortium of Investigative Journalists); and *x)* the growth of new or 'unorthodox' political/communicative practices that resemble some aspects of standard journalism, but which emerge from popular initiatives (or even 'astroturf'[6] campaigns), and which may go on to become identifiable centres of influence.[7] The last item here recognises the importance of affective sites, but maintains a distinction between established institutions, and emergent entities that have yet to coalesce into a fully coherent form.

Although this catalogue covers the major fields of power, it is often hard to determine the origin of a specific initiative, or to decide which centre exercises most sway in any one situation. This is not only because there are multiple sites of influence at work, but also because not all social forces seek publicity for the functions they perform.[8] This discretionary, rather than overt, exercise of power, makes it harder still to determine the *relative strength* exerted by any single element. In addition, external and internal forces can in certain circumstances be closely aligned. For example, some of the edicts that appear to emerge from senior members of news organisations have their origin in the depths of state[9] or corporate bureaucracy, both of which act as centres of executive authority.

Journalists, the economy, and austerity

Arguing, therefore, that journalists are affected by a number of variables (some of which actually work in their favour) is only the first step in getting to grips with the question of power. In pursuit of this goal, two of the most significant contextual circumstances that govern journalistic activity should be mentioned. The first is the simple fact that journalists have to operate in an environment that is not only ideologically hostile to many of their basic assumptions, but also physically hazardous. Between 1992 and 2018, for example, 844 journalists were murdered, and a further 462 were killed covering wars or other dangerous assignments (Committee to Protect Journalists, 2018). Jawad, who reported for the BBC on the Libyan revolution (see earlier), testified to the extreme fear and confusion she felt when her husband warned her that the reports she filed from Tripoli might result in a visit from Gaddafi's 'death brigades' (2011: 135). Besides the fatal hazards produced by state and non-state terror, wars, and other perilous situations, a second major challenge faced by journalists is the need to endure the vagaries of a competitive marketplace.[10] It is this reality that requires a closer focus on the economic milieu within which journalists operate.

A study conducted by Meyen examined no less than 46 mass media systems across the globe, and demonstrated that media freedom and 'journalists' autonomy' depend on 'not only the governmental system', but on 'economic realities' (2018: 2). These realities are often made evident through the apparently unremarkable characteristics of contemporary working practices, such as the long-standing distinction between permanent and temporary (or precarious) staff. This condition is, however, only one symptom of a larger problem – the use of an 'economic' rationale to maintain the imbalance of power between the executive leadership of organisations, and the rank and file. Wage earners are kept in a state of insecurity, since any expansion of the numbers of those in the labour force can also mean the erosion of 'regular' employment and the growth of casual or zero-hours labour. While full-time workers are usually aware that they might undergo a change in status (advancing in their careers or, conversely, becoming less secure), those who have only tenuous institutional links cannot exercise the (albeit circumscribed) privileges that even 'entry level' salaried staff take for granted.

In journalism, the compensation for institutional and economic insecurity is supposed to be the independence associated with working as a freelancer. This benefit, according to some sources, is overplayed. Journalists in permanent employment are, according to recent research, actually 'more *independent*' than might be expected, while those on casual or temporary contracts turn out to be 'more *restricted*' than supposed (Rottwilm, 2014: 10, my emphasis). Besides this sobering assessment of divergent roles there are qualitative, seemingly 'extra-economic' divisions between individual employees – differences, in other words, that emerge from characteristics that should have no bearing on the status of workers.

The experience of female reporters is a case in point, where major disparities in pay and progression (Byerly, 2016), and widespread instances of sexual harassment (Bradley, 1999) mean that the career expectations of women are demonstrably inferior to those of men (Urwin, 2017). In addition, journalists from minority ethnic backgrounds and those whose expressions of gendered identity and sexual orientation differ from the dominant paradigm, suffer from multiple forms of discrimination.[11]

Oppressive and exploitative behaviour can prevent the fulfilment of even the most routine tasks and, in a culture that exonerates the perpetrator, results on occasion in the expulsion of the victims from their posts, rather than the censure of the organisation itself. The problem appears to be global in scope. One newly appointed employee in a Chinese news agency, Sophia Huang Xueqin, suffered the unwelcome attentions of a senior male colleague. The victim went on to run a nationwide poll to gauge the extent of the crisis, discovering that, from a total of 200 responses, only 16.1% had never experienced harassment. In her immediate circle of friends, Huang Xueqin discovered that five had left their jobs as the result of this behaviour. The few men who indicated that they agreed with her campaign, qualified their stance, saying that 'they could not support her publicly, as speaking out about sexual harassment would negatively impact the media industry's image' (Lai, 2017).

Within, therefore, the ever-present threat of precarious work, redundancy, 'voluntary' severance, and unemployment, there are more particular examples of injustice. If the fortunes of the precariously employed are determined by their partial exclusion from the workforce, the price paid by full-time workers for their integration into the system, includes their subjection to authority.[12] Those who are *removed from the economy altogether* will either encounter the disciplinary system once known as social security (Seabrook, 2016) or, in many countries, face utter destitution.[13] Ultimately, socioeconomic factors cannot be separated from the political sphere: when individuals are made redundant, the rights lost are not merely 'industrial', but civil.

In the current period, governments and corporations present austerity as the inevitable consequence of economic necessity, yet the political interventions made by executive cabals allow some groups to experience the full force of this 'universal' condition, while others are protected.[14] The question, then, is how it is possible for economic and psychological discipline to be applied to selected groups, while the governing rhetoric of the period continues to speak of a collective fate in which all have to bear some form of hardship. The answer lies in the use by dominant groups of an approach to organisation that weakens traditional forms of solidarity, replacing them with a form of power that makes the individual bear the weight of institutional indebtedness and failure.

Managerialism: a universal practice

In the last few decades, one particular cross-sectoral ideological practice, known as *managerialism* (Enteman, 1993), has been used to organise the conditions of service that both state and corporate employees must observe. The first requirement for the successful application of this 'new' technique, is already found in those workplaces that conform to patriarchal-capitalist precepts – the existence of a hierarchical structure that can oversee the division of labour and the successful pursuit of specialist functions. Hibou suggests that 'the painless and . . . invisible character of constraint may be made possible by the *routinization of the exercise of power*' (Hibou, 2011: 13, my emphasis), while McGuiness argued that the creation of a 'managerial hierarchy' inevitably 'sacrifices equality' while at the same time failing to compensate workers sufficiently 'for their loss of autonomy in controlling the work process' (in Thompson et al., 1991: 79).[15] If the covert goal is, however, to maintain the existence of ailing institutions so they can act as *clearing houses for capital*, benefitting exploitative groups of corporate raiders and their internal allies (who collect inflated salaries and multiple payoffs), then the decline or 'downsizing' of particular organisations is seen as a natural part of the economic order.

Promoted by 'open-sector' careerists[16] who feel no particular allegiance to individual owners or enterprises, managerialist precepts are, as suggested earlier, embedded in the hierarchical structures of major organisations,[17] and are used to increase the power of executive officers while creating a hazardous, insecure, impermanent, and competitive 'career path' for their subordinates. As a trans-national attempt to discipline workers[18] through a combination of material threat (precarity), labour discipline, and the white noise produced by 'management-speak', managerialism requires a form of behavioural re-alignment (Sennett, 1999).

This type of oversight and control[19] is not, however, confined to professional spheres, but is widely replicated within the 'basic social units' (Ahrne, 1994: 3) that underpin contemporary life. These forms of association, among which Ahrne counts 'enterprises, clubs or states' (3), will not necessarily employ the same degree of control to synchronise the efforts of their members,[20] yet they are all involved in the reproduction of material and ideational outcomes, the successful attainment of which usually depends on the ability of leading elements to persuade or compel individual members to follow a general line. In the case of managerialism, a nervous obsession with authority and the endless maintenance of a professional 'self' spills over from the workplace into the lifeworld, supporting the notion that the practice has become, quite apart from its use as an industrial technique, a major instrument of socialisation (Duménil and Lévy, 2018).

Attacks on professional standards: 'internal' pressures

The attempt to exercise control over journalistic activity is, therefore, more complex than the outright repression of internal dissent. Even seemingly mundane processes like the prevalence of 'rules and budgets' are also used as subtle 'instruments of control' (Benveniste, 1977: 27).[21] From a journalist's point of view, therefore, managerialism is the general *regime of productivity* that replaces older approaches, generating the quasi-economic conditions within which news, as a facet of public communication, is produced.

Since Gerbner (1965) described the frenetic world in which 'mass communicators' worked, the form of the news business is supposed to have changed, from large industrial conglomerates that manufactured a product intended for a national (though nonetheless segmented) audience, to an insecure state of affairs in which the workforce is atomised and the output supposedly tailored for a 'niche' market. Although the advocates of 'entrepreneurial journalism' present this development as a form of empowerment (allowing reporters to become self-sufficient and flexible), critics of the process believe that it 'emerges at a time of institutional crisis for journalism', using the growth of digital technology to 'promote an ideology that masks the precarious nature of contemporary media work' (Cohen, 2015: 513).

The 'professional ideology' (Deuze, 2005) embraced by working journalists is therefore a useful, though imperfect, basis for forms of resistance, in the face of an essentially disciplinary imposition of authority (one that, nonetheless, individual careerists can 'buy into'). If an ideology is conceived, not as a pure or absolute worldview designed to hoodwink the oppressed (see the earlier reference to McNair), but as *a reasonably coherent collective perspective* animated in response to rival positions or external events, then any attempt to analyse the 'hidden' processes of news production (the tension between opportunity and constraint mentioned at the beginning of this chapter), should pay attention to those accounts that describe the conflict between an 'ideal' journalistic function and everyday practices. The point is that it would be difficult to appreciate the challenges reporters face without referring to the ways in which they explain and categorise their experience.

An ideological stance in this case is thus imagined as a *defensive collective mindset* that is the natural consequence of unequal power relations: groups of 'professionals', though often divided by their own ambitions and attachment to managerialist precepts, recognise some basic commonality, if not of status, then of purpose. In the traditional newsroom (or contemporary 'hub'), those who regard themselves as genuine journalists – as opposed, for example, to a managerial group that issues edicts – reproduce their ideational position through the (sometimes ironic) articulation of the difference between their own practical activity and supposed common sense, and the spurious values and outlandish goals advocated by their institutional leaders. As noted earlier, a central aspect of this clash is economic, as management attempts to 'downsize' operations.

One anonymous worker, operating in a highly pressured environment in South London, described exactly this situation, when he drew attention to 'the constant battle between the editorial staff, who are pushing to produce quality journalism even though everyone is overstretched, and the management, who have openly said that we will need to cut corners' (Mayhew, 2016). According to this informant, the types of activity that managers were prepared to sacrifice included 'investigating local stories and holding local government to account' (2016). The portrayal of the journalists as the standard bearers for a laudable ideal ('quality journalism'), is contrasted with the attitude attributed to their bosses, consistent with the articulation of 'oppositional' or critical positions.

In this instance, as is usually the case during periods of industrial strife, management did not engage with the moral criteria used to frame the debate, preferring instead to issue statements that described 'the need to revisit [the company's] cost base to ensure a sustainable future', and to create 'a workable structure' within this form of fiscal restraint (Mayhew, 2016). 'Sustainability', with its positive ecological overtones, actually meant a number of staff redundancies, in a business that, in 2014, had apparently made '£60 million profits before tax' (2016).

'External' resistance to investigative work

The internal suppression of journalistic activity is not the only mode of control encountered by established correspondents. On occasion, they might be supported by their employer, but find themselves in confrontation with state agencies. In 2015, award-winning UK investigative journalist Jeanette Oldham was informed that she could no longer put direct questions to Birmingham's Office of the Police and Crime Commissioner (OPCC), after she had run stories questioning the fairness of contracts awarded by the OPCC to a company that employed the Deputy Commissioner's daughter. In this case, Oldham was supported by her employer, the *Birmingham Mail*. Her editor declared that 'Jeanette is one of the foremost investigative reporters in the UK who has simply been carrying out her job, holding the powerful to account and reporting on the spending of public money' (Ponsford, 2015).

The spokesperson for the OPCC had apparently objected to 'the huge amount of time and public resources spent on often speculative inquiries' (2015). In response to this explanation, the editor of the *Birmingham Mail* declared that 'we believe the OPCC may have banned her because her line of questioning has riled them, which would be funny if the consequences to a free press weren't so serious' (2015). Both the excuses used by the OPCC, and the defence offered by the newspaper, draw upon references to the normative expectations of their audiences, namely, to the waste of 'public' resource, but only the news organisation referred to the dangers such behaviour posed to the existence of a 'free press'.

Although the general expectation is that democratic systems will display certain types of political virtue, and that 'Western' democracies are particularly attentive to the wishes of their citizens, much depends on the concrete political form assumed by each polity, and the attitude of its government to the role of public media. In 2018, Spanish TV reporters employed by the state broadcaster RTVE appeared on screen in black clothes 'to protest against political interference, gender bias and unequal pay' (Jones, 2018). The action was known as *Viernes Negro* (black Friday), because that was the day chosen to draw attention to the refusal of the Spanish state to use a reasonably transparent process to appoint the Chair of the RTVE.

Control and 'voluntary' obedience

From the examples in this chapter, it seems clear that the exercise of control need not resemble the old caricature of an editor barking orders at nervous underlings (though this still occurs). This is in part because many contemporary bosses often avoid any meaningful contact with employees, while ensuring that managers also escape responsibility for the consequences of bad decisions: the *diffusion of responsibility*, a tactic that makes it is difficult to trace the origin of an attack on working conditions, has become common in many workplaces. However, because authority is recognised as an inevitable and 'natural' part of working life, this situation is not always felt as an absolute imposition. Even before their entry into the profession, journalists are imbued with certain attitudes, through their participation in training regimes, University courses, professional accreditation schemes, and as a result of contact with established practitioners: ultimately, their early socialisation as members of a particular culture (Therborn, 1980) remains of primary significance, reinforced by the managerialist developments already described.

All such influences help individuals acclimatise to the ideological atmosphere produced within mainstream news organisations, although this does not mean that they will necessarily conform to, or agree with, the often deliberately disruptive positions adopted by executive cabals.[22] The essential condition, however, that governs the day to day reproduction of institutional life, is the fact that 'actors tend to reproduce institutions in a given field of activity without requiring either repeated authoritative intervention or collective mobilisation' (Battilana and D'Aunno, in Lawrence et al., 2009: 31).

In other words, it is the habitual repetition of routine actions that, in a 'post-ideological' environment, keeps institutional life on track (Price, 2011). Power, therefore, *subsists* in formal institutions (Price, in Fishwick and Connolly, 2018) and, because it is embedded in hierarchical relationships and processes, does not need constant, dramatic activation. What matters, then, is not a crude display of domination, but the existence of structures that are able to issue routine orders/requests that will be recognised both as legitimate, and of some benefit to those who have to demonstrate compliance.

As a consequence, it is the willing investment of effort in tasks that individuals believe will advance their personal ambitions, that reproduces what I have called the '*hierarchical* organisation of "consensual" rule' (Price, in Price and Sanz Sabido, 2016: 18, emphasis in original). In other words, workers take 'voluntary' actions within a *permanent structure* that they know is governed by a core executive. This form of organisation will embrace a rationale (often in the form of a 'mission statement') to justify its control of people and resources, and will in addition institute a training regime that provides workers with a set of skills and discourses that are supposed to guarantee professional standards.[23]

A structural contradiction within the information economy

The Introduction to this chapter suggested that there is a basic commonality between all forms of journalism, provided they are devoted to the production of accurate and independent accounts of recent events.[24] This means that the observation made by Weaver and Willnat, which notes that there has been 'a blurring between journalism and other forms of public communication' (2012: 529) is less important than the difference between the professional and/or moral disposition to provide an account of social reality that is useful, not just to 'key stakeholders', but to 'the public' as a whole, and on the other hand, the more *restrictive communicative behaviour* of many 'complex organisations' (Etzioni, 1975), in which the central concern is reputation management (Aula, 2010; Coletti, 2017). The exponential growth of internal PR or 'communication' departments, embedded within most public, private and hybrid institutions, is a testament to this condition.

Although the two forms of communicative behaviour identified here, are imagined as distinct, this does not mean that journalists and PR operatives do not collaborate, nor that they never share some of the same values (Sallot and Johnson, 2006; Mellado and Hanusch, 2011). Just as those who occupy positions of authority are not invariably corrupt, and their critics (i.e., journalists, academics, and activists) are not necessarily unwavering in their commitment to 'truth and justice',[25] the devotees of PR can on occasion follow more rigorous principles (depending in part on the position adopted by their clients). News stories, meanwhile, may well bear the contradictory traces of both practices.[26]

The more substantial point is that the conflict between an attachment to 'truthfulness', and the promotional agenda generated by an overbearing Establishment, is actually an expression of a *structural contradiction* within the information or 'knowledge' economy. Put another way, this is not just a moral issue or a question of scale (the David vs. Goliath scenario), but also an inevitable product of the system known as liberal democracy, which relies both upon the dissemination of 'reliable' information (which can be acted upon for instrumental purposes), and of more general *social myths* (that promote a sense of communal purpose and cohesion).[27] In both cases, institutional communication is central to the 'coordination of social life' (Thompson et al., 1991) and helps determine the exact discursive form taken by the various stories, myths, 'social narratives' (Price, 1996: 7), and 'selective imaginaries' that are supposed to describe 'the lived experience of an inordinately complex world' (Jessop, 2008: 239).

The exact difference between the two modes described here is not always evident, because (as suggested earlier) the two impulses can appear within the same source, despite the time-honoured distinctions between specific genres (like financial news and entertainment), and between the publications that address the interests of particular audiences (such as *Bloomberg Business* and vehicles like *Hello!*). The real reason that journalists, and the public relations operatives used by public bodies and major conglomerates, sometimes find it difficult to work in harmony, is because an often 'disorderly' public function (represented by journalistic practices), is bound to clash with the products of a judiciously crafted and essentially propagandistic exercise.

As noted, this chapter examines the complex institutional framework that oversees the production of 'journalistic' work as a mode of public communication, so that more light can be shed on the interrogative/critical interventions that are the subject of this book. My argument here is that the drive to disseminate information is an essential part of the 'democratic' management of the social order. This approach is less concerned with the 'abuse' of power, than with its form and character, meaning that exchanges between journalists and authority, whether positive or negative, are seen as the consequence – in line with the observations made earlier – of *structural inequalities* and the hierarchical management of people, resources, and information.

Journalists can certainly take advantage of existing structures – some of which are governed by a liberal ethos – or can strive to create an alternative 'space' for enquiry, but neither tactic will remove the pressures created by external intervention, nor alter the reproduction of the normative sociopolitical assumptions that circulate within the profession itself. Investigative work faces a similar challenge, as it struggles for attention within an economic system that generates large volumes of 'generic' and seemingly inconsequential material.[28]

Conclusion: state, power, and journalism

Despite major revisions to models of power, in which the concept of the state has been demoted from a dominant unitary force, to a site where an assortment of interests compete or collaborate, it is still posited, in formal terms, as the overarching influence within a national territory. In this sense, certain practical effects are attributed to particular states, and we still expect that entity known as the state to bear ultimate responsibility for the 'sociospatial organisation of capitalist society' (Clark and Dear, 1984: 1). Part of the reason that the state is often, in recent years, presented as a loose configuration of powers, rather than a directive authority, is precisely because it has, in the period that followed the Second World War, escaped its more 'contentious political responsibilities', not only by devolving certain functions to lower echelons (1), but by treating its duties as liabilities and going on to privatise them.

This, in turn, is a symptom of the malaise that afflicts the higher echelons of state and corporate authority. Journalists, therefore, should not be disparaged because their enquiries annoy the professional sophists who maintain the rhetorical veneer of public or private institutions. In a political climate dominated by the precepts of 'reputation management' *any narratives* that describe political or economic activity (not just those produced through the long-term interrogation associated with investigative work), have the potential to disrupt the synthetic identity[29] assumed by state entities and industrial conglomerates.

It is worth repeating the point made previously, to the effect that the source of the tension between journalists and those in positions of authority, can be found, not in the supposedly transgressive behaviour of reporters, but in the morbid sensitivity of secretive cabals, to any form of searching, rational enquiry. The real commitment of dominant groups is, I would argue, to the appearance of integrity and civic virtue, rather than the public good as such, and it is this fiction that can be undermined by the unauthorised exposure of political machination or financial irregularity.

Where the active and determined pursuit of the truth brings journalists into conflict with powerful groups[30] (however truth is construed, as a local, provisional, or 'universal' goal), then there is a further implication that must be addressed – not only that many prominent bodies have invested excessive effort in the management of external perception, but that this is only a symptom of the fact that they remain *entirely untouched by the responsive flexibility* that is supposed to characterise modern structures of governance.

As it becomes apparent that the factions involved in the direction of public life have adopted the hierarchical principle employed by executive power (replicating, within every workplace, the same modes of internal surveillance and control), the popular notion that multiple sites of influence enhance the democratic process begins to look overly optimistic. This is not to deny the contribution of non-state actors and third-sector bodies to the general management of political culture, nor to question the growth (augmented by social media) of progressive social collectives (many of which provide journalists with information and support), but rather to take issue with perspectives that insist that the appearance of 'horizontal' formations has led to the thoroughgoing diffusion of socio-political influence. If this process was as substantial as some claim, then there might, for example, be less recourse to Freedom of Information requests, and journalists might not find it necessary to create their own trans-national investigative groups.

A serious 'reality check' may therefore be overdue. Quite besides the fact that the contributions to governance made by commercial stakeholders are unlikely to encourage the development of radical economic initiatives, it is often the case that 'alternative' centres of authority do not grow from grassroots agitation, but owe their existence to the efforts of a 'core' regime that 'creates multiple channels of overlapping jurisdictional authority' so that approved agents can monitor one another's activities (Cooley, 2005: 61).

Rather than imagine, therefore, that executive power is being eroded by the appearance of numerous sites of influence, this chapter maintains that the hierarchical principle, enabled by the philosophy and practice of managerialism (Clarke and Newman, 1997; Parker, 2002; Duménil and Lévy, 2018), has been disseminated throughout the social order. If this is an accurate assumption (in which top-down decision-making, hermetically sealed from popular influence, occurs in both centralised and 'devolved' forms of authority), then the determined enquiries of investigative journalists will continue to provide a corrective to the dubious, multi-agency exercise of 'discretion' on matters that should never have been hidden from public view.

Notes

1 The model outlined here is one that regards conflict between journalists and various manifestations of authority as inevitable, founded on the claim that power is afforded to, yet exerted over, all correspondents, including full-time reporters, 'citizen journalists', and those who operate as freelancers.

2 See, for example, Prime Minister Theresa May's attempt to justify the bombing of Syria, in which she described the airstrikes as conducted in the UK's 'national interest' (Stewart, 2018).
3 Institutions and/or individuals operating inside a specific territory, or working within a field of activity over which a particular state formation exercises (or tries to exercise) control, are bound to share a collective perception of how far they can exercise their supposed independence.
4 This situation has been complicated by the emergence of non-professional online news sources (see, for example, Singer, 2003).
5 By state patriarchy I mean the political manifestation of capitalist power, in which profits are maintained by treating women as an easily designated 'class' of workers that can be paid less than their male counterparts: this convenient ploy was used in apartheid South Africa when the vast majority (some 80%) of the population was identified as 'black', and kept in a state of absolute poverty.
6 Applied to campaign groups, 'astroturf' refers to artificial, top-down initiatives that disguise themselves as grassroots operations, drawn from the name for the material used to create artificial lawns.
7 All these forms of agency try to manipulate prominent socio-political concepts (such as the public, the economy, the national interest, democracy, professional standards, citizenship, and so on), in an attempt to gain an advantage during conflicts over resource or principle.
8 The more direct form of interference associated with the discretionary exercise of power can take a number of forms, from the refusal of senior public figures to engage with their critics, to deliberate attempts at social control, associated with censorship and outright repression.
9 References to the larger issues of state power will inevitably inform any discussion that covers the 'impersonal' structures described by authors like Jessop (2008) and Gerstenberger (2007), the collusion between governments and covert political forces (Bonini and D'Avanzo, 2007), and the role of public authority in managing austerity (Lorey, 2015).
10 Another long-term economic factor is the overall place of journalists (as 'irregular professionals') within the class system. Employers' preference for a university-educated workforce does not mean that reporters will automatically enter the ranks of the middle classes. Although journalism was once deemed suitable for upwardly mobile individuals from the working class, attempts to turn it into, alternatively, a haven for 'privileged' graduates, or a 'neo-liberal' hub for the regurgitation of corporate messages, has reduced its usefulness in this respect.
11 One group that is never usually identified as the target of institutional prejudice (though it often overlaps with members of the categories described here) is composed of those motivated by Leftist political beliefs: there is a whole study that could be written on the fate of this tendency.
12 Although most of those working in middle-class occupations might be offended by the thought that they have, ultimately, to demonstrate obedience, the fact remains that no institution can function without the ability to ensure *practical* expressions of 'agreement' from its subordinates, whatever the individual operative may think about the quality or relevance of the task in hand.
13 These facts cannot be removed from the study of journalism, since its personnel have a duty to understand the wider environment that gives meaning to their work.
14 While the rich are cushioned by their wealth, and protected through the use of tax breaks, the (politically atomised) working classes do not have the independent clout to exert decisive influence, nor the ability to produce a 'master narrative' that can advance their own interests. The continuing relevance of class analysis can be observed in the fashioning of 'austerity' as a calculated response

to the economic crisis of 2008, during which the core executive of Western governments, unable to conceive of any system other than the one that had just failed (since the alternative would mean relinquishing their own power), chose to defer the crisis of capital by shoring up the banking system.
15 Although dependence on hierarchical systems (where each rank issues directives to the one below it), is not unique to journalism, it is the nature of the profession – its notional commitment to the maintenance of unrestricted public communication – that makes any executive suppression of investigative enquiry particularly objectionable.
16 See Benveniste (1977).
17 The culture we (in the 'advanced nations') inhabit, with its emphasis on citizenship, consumer choice, electoral participation, and more particularly the separation of a 'democratic' private life from our expectations of workplace organisation, allows managerialism, as a mode of control, to thrive.
18 In the current period, given the prevalence of neo-liberal business principles and the structural and psychological atomisation of the workforce, it seems as though the 'major and recurrent conflicts over the organisation of work' associated with earlier periods of capitalist development (Rueschmeyer, 1986: 71), are largely absent. While this view can be substantiated by the apparent decline in traditional forms of activity, like the fall in the incidence of strikes, this does not mean that industrial conflict itself has ceased to exist.
19 Within contemporary institutions, employees are provided with the technological means for 'self-monitoring' as an addition to the standard modes of discipline and self-control they are encouraged to develop.
20 It would not be accurate to characterise all organisations as hierarchical: some groups may follow the principles of egalitarianism. My overall intention, however, is to do more than just distinguish between the generic category in each case (opposing, for instance, the qualities of 'enterprises' to 'clubs'), by suggesting that, in practice, control is exercised variably within particular *examples* of each category (e.g., 'club x' as opposed to 'club y'), according to the pressures of time and circumstance.
21 The general notion of profitability is also therefore an ideological mechanism that can be employed as a disciplinary measure: the true state of a company's finances is usually a closely guarded secret.
22 In practical terms, it is often less dangerous to make a show of complying with management initiatives, than to resist them.
23 This need not preclude the formation of consensus, but this goal is achieved on the understanding that all participants in the process understand their place in the production of the version decided upon by core management. Within this mode of 'agreement', people engage in strategic displays of deference, while covertly embracing 'deviant' practices.
24 This, by definition, excludes traditions like 'yellow' journalism, the removal of which would help preserve a vision of the profession as a rational undertaking.
25 This simple description of the ultimate goal of journalism was uttered by Dorothy Byrne, Head of Channel Four News and Current Affairs, during her address to the Leicester Media School, De Montfort University, 25 January 2017.
26 There are many collectives that are not primarily concerned with the production of news (see Chapters 5 and 14), yet which replicate, or even exceed, the principles associated with 'good' journalism.
27 This is, for example, evident in the distinction between the concepts of 'market intelligence' and the notion of 'market confidence', where the first is supposed to refer to reliable, 'actionable' information, and where the second draws attention to a general condition that only obliquely relates to the buoyancy of economic growth.

28 Although the uncomfortable truths unearthed by investigative reporters may stand a greater chance of disturbing the unspoken consensus that underpins public debate, the form of commitment it represents is in a sense *depoliticised*, in line with the expectation that the best practices draw their strength from their political neutrality.
29 By 'synthetic' identity, I refer to the tendency to create positive but unreliable narratives that describe the supposed virtues of state and corporate institutions.
30 In the case of enterprises, like newsrooms, that are supposedly governed by ethical standards, and which are staffed by professional operatives, the question is first what forms of antagonism actually occur within, and beyond, the confines of the institution. The second issue is whether or not, considering the apparent scarcity of 'militant' behaviour, these conflicts qualify as evidence of a struggle between executive authority and a 'rank and file' that has a distinct sense of its own collective identity.

References

Abercrombie, Nicholas, Hill, Stephen and Turner, Bryan S. (1980) *The Dominant Ideology Thesis*, London: Allen St Unwin.
Ahrne, Göran (1994) *Social Organizations: Interaction Inside, Outside and Between Organizations*, London: Sage Publications.
Aula, Pekka (2010) 'Social media, reputation risk and ambient publicity management', in *Strategy & Leadership*, Vol. 38, Issue: 6, pp. 43–49.
Barnett, Robert (2014) 'Introduction to: Liu Jianqiang and Ceng Gong, "Tiger Leaping Gorge Under Threat" in *Southern Weekend*', in Schiffrin, Anya [editor], *Global Muckraking: 100 Years of Investigative Journalism from Around the World*, New York: The New Press.
Battilana, Julie and D'Aunno, Thomas (2009) 'Institutional work and the paradox of embedded agency', in Lawrence, Thomas B., Suddaby, Roy and Leca, Bernard [editors], *Institutional Work: Actors and Agency in Institutional Studies of Organizations*, Cambridge: Cambridge University Press.
Bell, Emily, Owen, Taylor, Khorana, Smitha and Henrichsen, Jenn [editors] (2017) *Journalism after Snowden: The Future of the Free Press in the Surveillance State*, New York and Chichester, West Sussex: Columbia University Press.
Benveniste, Guy (1977) *Bureaucracy*, San Francisco: Boyd and Fraser Publishing Company.
Bernier, Marc-François and Barber, Marsha (2012) 'The professional creed of Quebec's journalists in Canada', in Weaver, David H., and Willnat, Lars [editors], *The Global Journalist in the 21st Century*, London and New York: Routledge.
Bonini, Carlo and D'Avanzo, Giuseppe (2007) *Collusion: International Espionage and the War on Terror*, Hoboken: Melville House Publishing.
Bradley, Harriet (1999) *Gender and Power in the Workplace: Analysing the Impact of Economic Change*, Houndmills and New York: Palgrave Macmillan and St Martin's Press.
Byerly, Carolyn M. [editor] (2016) *The Palgrave International Handbook of Women in Journalism*, Houndmills: Palgrave Macmillan.
Byrne, Dorothy (2017) Address to the Leicester Media School, De Montfort University, 25 January.
Cadwalladr, Carole (2018) 'Arron banks, Brexit and the Russia connection', *the Guardian*, Focus Section, 17 June, 35–37.

Clark, Gordon, and Dear, Michael (1984) *State apparatus*, London: Allen Unwin.

Clarke, John and Newman, Janet (1997) *The Managerial State: Power, Politics and Ideology in the Remaking of Social Welfare*, London, Thousand Oaks, CA and New Delhi: Sage Publications.

Cohen, Nicole S. (2015) 'Entrepreneurial journalism and the precarious state of media work', in the *South Atlantic Quarterly*, Vol. 114, Issue: 3, pp. 513–533.

Coletti, Bill (2017) *Critical Moments: The New Mindset of Reputation Management*, New York: Lioncrest Publishing.

Committee to Protect Journalists (2018) '844 journalists killed', *CPJ*, https://cpj.org/data/killed/murdered/?status=Killed&motiveConfirmed%5B%5D=Confirmed&type%5B%5D=Journalist&typeOfDeath%5B%5D=Murder&start_year=1992&end_year=2018&group_by=year [accessed 30 June 2018].

Cooley, Alexander (2005) *Logics of hierarchy: The organization of empires, states, and military occupation*, Ithaca: Cornell University Press.

Deibert, Ron (2017) 'Digital threats against journalists', in Bell, Emily and Owen, Taylor [editors], *Journalism after Snowden*, New York: Columbia University Press.

Democracy Now! (2017) 'NYT: Mexican government surveilled international investigators probing ayotzinapa case', 10 July, www.democracynow.org/2017/7/10/headlines/nyt_mexican_govt_surveilled_international_investigators_probing_ayotzinapa_case [accessed 4 August 2017].

Deuze, Mark (2005) 'What is journalism? Professional identity and ideology of journalists reconsidered', in *Journalism*, Vol. 6, Issue: 4, pp. 442–464.

Duménil, Gérard and Lévy, Dominique (2018) *Managerial Capitalism: Ownership, Management and the Coming New Mode of Production*, London: Pluto Press.

Enteman, Willard F. (1993) *Managerialism: The Emergence of a New Ideology*, Madison: University of Wisconsin Press.

Etzioni, Amitai (1975) *A Comparative Analysis of Complex Organizations*, New York: The Free Press, Palgrave Macmillan.

Geertsema-Sligh, Margaretha (2016) 'South Africa: Newsrooms in transition', in Byerly, Carolyn M. [editor], *The Palgrave International Handbook of Women and Journalism*, Houndmills and New York: Palgrave Macmillan.

Gerbner, George (1965) 'Institutional pressures upon mass communicators', in *The Sociological Review*, Vol. 13, Issue: 1_suppl, pp. 205–248.

Gerstenberger, Heide (2007) *Impersonal Power: History and Theory of the Bourgeois State*, Leiden: Brill, Academic Publishers.

Greenwald, Glenn (2017) 'The surveillance state', in Bell, Emily, Owen, Taylor, Khorana, Smitha and Henrichsen, Jenn [editors], *Journalism after Snowden: The Future of the Free Press in the Surveillance State*, New York and Chichester, West Sussex: Columbia University Press.

Hibou, Béatrice (2011) *The Force of Obedience: The Political Economy of Repression in Tunisia*, Cambridge and Malden, MA: Polity Press.

Hicks, Robin (2016) 'Q&A with Malaysian investigative journalist R. Nadeswaran: My quarrel is not with politicians', *Mumbrella Asia*, 21 January, www.mumbrella.asia/2016/01/nadeswaran-malaysian-investigative-journalist [accessed 15 July 2018].

Jawad, Rana (2011) *Tripoli Witness*, London: Gilgamesh Publishing.

Jessop, Bob (2008) *State Power*, Cambridge and Malden, MA: Polity Press.

Jones, Sam (2018) 'Spanish newsreaders wear black in protest against "political interference"', *The Guardian*, online, www.theguardian.com/world/2018/

may/11/spanish-newsreaders-wear-black-in-protest-against-political-interference [accessed 21 July 2018].

Kaija, Barbara (2016) 'Uganda: Women near parity but still leaving newsrooms', in Byerly, Carolyn M. [editor], *The Palgrave International Handbook of Women and Journalism*, Houndmills and New York: Palgrave Macmillan.

Kreiss, Daniel (2016) 'Beyond administrative journalism: Civic skepticism and the crisis in journalism', in Alexander, Jeffrey C., Breese, Elizabeth Butler and Luengo, María [editors], *The Crisis of Journalism Reconsidered*, New York: Cambridge University Press.

Lai, Catherine (2017) 'No #MeToo in China? Female journalists face sexual harassment, but remain silent', 5 December, HKFP online, www.hongkongfp.com/2017/12/05/no-metoo-china-female-journalists-face-sexual-harassment-remain-silent/ [accessed 23 April 2018].

Lloyd, John (2017) *Journalism in an Age of Terror: Covering and Uncovering the Secret State*, London and New York: I.B. Tauris.

Lorey, Isabell (2015) *State of Insecurity: Government of the Precarious*, London and New York: Verso.

Mayhew, Freddy (2016) '"The entire newsroom is at breaking point": Newsquest journalists speak out on eve of London newspapers strike', *Press Gazette*, 12 October, online, www.pressgazette.co.uk/the-entire-newsroom-is-at-breaking-point-newsquest-journalists-speak-out-on-eve-of-14-day-london-newspapers-strike/ [accessed 23 April 2018].

McGuiness, Anthony (1991) 'Markets and managerial hierarchies', in Thompson, Grahame, Frances, Jennifer, Levačić, Rosalind and Mitchell, Jeremy [editors], *Markets, Hierarchies and Networks: The Coordination of Social Life*, London and New York: Sage Publications.

McNair, Brian (2006) *Cultural Chaos: Journalism and Power in a Globalised World*, London and New York: Routledge.

McQuail, Denis (2013) *Journalism and Society*, Los Angeles, London, New Delhi, Singapore and Washington, DC: Sage Publications.

Mellado, Claudia and Hanusch, Folker (2011) 'Comparing professional identities, attitudes, and views in public communication: A study of Chilean journalists and public relations practitioners', in *Public Relations Review*, Vol. 37, Issue: 4, pp. 384–391.

Meyen, Michael (2018) 'Journalists' autonomy around the globe: A typology of 46 mass media systems', in *Global Media Journal*, German Edition, Vol. 8, Issue: 1, Spring/Summer, pp. 1–23.

Parker, Martin (2002) *Against Management: Organization in the Age of Managerialism*, Cambridge: Polity Press in association with Blackwell.

Podger, Pamela J. (2009) 'The limits of control: With journalists and their employers increasingly active on social media sites like Facebook and Twitter, news organizations are struggling to respond to a host of new ethics challenges', in *American Journalism Review*, Vol. 31, Issue: 4, pp. 32–38.

Ponsford, Dominic (2015) 'Award-winning investigative journalist "banned" from putting questions to Birmingham crime commissioner', *Press Gazette*, online, 19 June, www.pressgazette.co.uk/award-winning-investigative-journalist-banned-putting-questinos-birmingham-crime-commisioner [accessed 12 May 2018].

Price, Stuart (1996) *Communication Studies*, London and New York: Longman.

——— (2011) *Worst-Case Scenario? Governance, Mediation and the Security Regime*, London and New York: Zed Books.

——— (2016) 'The "Borderless State": ISIS, hierarchy and trans-spatial politics', in Price, Stuart and Sanz Sabido, Ruth [editors], *Sites of Protest*, London: Rowman and Littlefield International.

——— (2018) 'Resistance and revolution: Working-class intransigence, the libertarian tradition, and the Catalan crisis', in Fishwick, Adam and Connolly, Heather [editors], *From Protest to Resistance: Fighting Back in Hard Times*, London: Rowman and Littlefield International.

Rottwilm, Philipp (2014) *The Future of Journalistic Work: Its Changing Nature and Implications*, Report, Oxford: Reuters Institute for the Study of Journalism.

Rueschemeyer, Dietrich (1986) *Power and the Division of Labour*, Stanford: Stanford University Press.

Sallot, Lynne M. and Johnson, Elizabeth A. (2006) 'Investigating relationships between journalists and public relations practitioners: Working together to set, frame and build the public agenda, 1991–2004', *Public Relations Review*, Vol. 32, Issue: 2, pp. 151–159.

Seabrook, Jeremy (2016) *Cut Out: Living without Welfare*, London: Penguin and the Left Book Club.

Seib, Philip (2002) *The Global Journalist: News and Conscience in a World of Conflict*, Lanham, MD: Rowman and Littlefield International.

Sennett, Richard (1999) *The Corrosion of Character: The Personal Consequences of Work in the New Capitalism*, New York: WW Norton & Company.

Singer, Jane B. (2003) 'Who are these guys? The online challenge to the notion of journalistic professionalism', in *Journalism*, Vol. 4, Issue: 2, pp. 139–163, SAGE.

Stewart, Heather (2018) 'May hits back at critics: bombing Syria was in our national interest', *The Guardian*, 16 April, 1.

Therborn, Goran (1980) *The Ideology of Power and the Power of Ideology*, London and New York: Verso.

Thompson, Grahame, Frances, Jennifer, Levačić, Rosalind and Mitchell, Jeremy [editors] (1991) *Markets, Hierarchies and Networks: The Coordination of Social Life*, London and New York: Sage Publications.

Urwin, Rosamund (2017) 'Why I'm building a sisterhood: Female journalists set up network to fight sexual harassment in the media', *Evening Standard*, online, 3 November, www.standard.co.uk/lifestyle/london-life/female-journalists-set-up-network-to-fight-sexual-harassment-a3675716.html [accessed 2 July 2018].

Weaver, David H. and Willnat, Lars [editors] (2012) *The Global Journalist in the 21st Century*, London and New York: Routledge.

4 Can you keep a secret? Legal and technological obstacles to protecting journalistic sources[1]

Richard Danbury and Judith Townend

Introduction

Journalists should protect their sources. They should, above all, protect those sources (including whistleblowers), that have provided them with information in confidence. This principle is included in journalistic codes of ethics around the world. It is a precept that is frequently interpreted rigidly, and at times so rigidly that it can put journalists in direct conflict with legal requirements to disclose information. Should a journalist comply with the law but break the ethical rule, the journalistic community will frequently condemn such an act.

In the UK, for example, the seventh principle of the National Union of Journalists' Code is that a journalist '[p]rotects the identity of sources who supply information in confidence and material gathered in the course of her/his work' (NUJ, 2011). In 2003, the NUJ expelled a young journalist for disclosing the identity of a source, even though he did so because that source had confessed to murder (Wallace, 2003). Similarly controversial was *The Times*' decision to obey a court order to assist police in their prosecution of former Liberal Democrat minister Chris Huhne. In 2012, Huhne was charged with perverting the course of justice in a speeding points case: the newspaper eventually provided the police with information that identified its informant, although the newspaper and the reporter defended their actions (Lewis, 2013). The prevailing assumption, then, is that journalists should protect a source that has been afforded confidentiality, whatever the personal and organisational cost.

This chapter considers whether this assumption is realistic. It surveys some of the contemporary legal and technological obstacles that journalists face in protecting their sources. It uses the UK as a case study, but similar concerns arise in other places in the world, as reflected by current discussions within the European Parliament (Lambert, 2017). Although the legal and technological obstacles are integrally connected, we will consider each category separately. The analysis is grounded in a round-table discussion that the authors organised at the University of London's Institute of Advanced Legal Studies in September 2016, with the support of Guardian

News and Media, at which the issue of source protection in a digital age was discussed by 25 experienced investigative journalists, lawyers, and representatives from NGOs (ILPC, 2017).

We conclude that, whatever a journalist's intentions, these obstacles now make protecting a source – their identity, and the confidential information they communicate – extremely difficult. In the Huhne case, for example, police used powers under the Regulation of Investigatory Powers Act, 2000 (RIPA, 2000) to access mobile and landline phone records which identified the source used by a second newspaper (the *Mail on Sunday*). In doing so, they bypassed the need for judicial authorisation, and acted without the knowledge of the media organisation and journalist concerned (Craven, 2014). In such an environment, how can the NUJ's seventh principle – and other similar ethical rules – be maintained? Given the difficulties of protecting a source, what should a journalist do? In this chapter, we offer some legal, practical, and technological suggestions.

The law: balancing interests

Before we demonstrate how source protection laws in the UK are becoming increasingly ineffective, it is first useful to consider briefly why laws of this type exist, and what they seek to do. The laws that govern when, and under what circumstances, journalists can be compelled to reveal the identity of their sources arise from a need to balance competing societal interests. On the one hand, there are the interests of a source seeking anonymity because of the potential damage caused by the revelation of their identity; and the interests of a journalist seeking to protect his or her source, because this facilitates the flow of useful information provided by the source. On the other hand, there are the interests of the state in – for example – seeking information for the purposes of policing, national security, or administrating justice.

It is appropriate to *balance* these interests because they are frequently instrumental interests, not absolute ones. There is no absolute value in protecting the identity of a journalists' source: sources are protected because this helps – amongst other things – journalists perform their 'watchdog' function. Such activity by journalists is necessary to a thriving democracy, as the European Court of Human Rights (amongst other international and national courts) has frequently recognised (see the discussion below). Equally, however, there is no absolute value in, for example, protecting national security in itself, or the administration of justice in itself. Society, we would argue, protects these interests appropriately only because they are instrumental in the protection of higher order interests – such as, for example, the right to life, the capacity of humans to flourish, or the imperative to treat individuals equally.

The fact that the societal interests commonly involved in source protection are frequently instrumental, not absolute, means they can be traded off against one another. Such trading off, however, needs to be predictable yet flexible, and normatively convincing. It is this that the laws that protect sources seek to achieve. It is a difficult task because it is difficult to formulate a set of rules with these qualities. But, generally speaking, this has been achieved over the past decades in the UK, and a relatively effective balance has evolved in response to the judgements of the European Court of Human Rights.

An example of balancing

A prominent example of this balance evolving over time can be seen in the application of the general statute that governs the protection of sources in UK law – the Contempt of Court Act, 1981 (CCA, 1981). Section 10 CCA, 1981 says that:

> [n]o court may require a person to disclose, nor is any person guilty of contempt of court for refusing to disclose, the source of information contained in a publication for which he is responsible, unless it be established to the satisfaction of the court that disclosure is necessary in the interests of justice or national security or for the prevention of disorder or crime.

This, it can be seen, creates a basic rule that protects journalists' sources. It does this both by imposing a restriction on the ability of courts to order journalists to reveal their sources, but also by restricting the ability of the court to find a journalist, who is protecting their source, in contempt. The provision is wide in its range and application. For one thing, it does not only apply to journalists, because section 10 CCA, 1981 is worded in such a way that bloggers and citizen journalists can use it: the section has been described as 'indiscriminate in the ambit of its protection' (Blom-Cooper, 2008: 269).[2] For another, sources can be protected even where the information they communicate is of little value to society. In the words of a senior judge, Lord Justice Laws, concurring with the judgement of the rest of the Court of Appeal in a case in 2001:

> It is in my judgment of the first importance to recognise that the potential vice – the 'chilling effect' – of court orders requiring the disclosure of press sources is in no way lessened, and certainly not abrogated, simply because the case is one in which the information actually published is of no legitimate, objective public interest. Nor is it to the least degree lessened or abrogated by the fact (where it is so) that the source is a disloyal and greedy individual, prepared for money to betray his employer's confidences. The public interest in the non-disclosure of press sources is constant, whatever the merits of the particular publication, and the particular source.
> (*Ashworth Hospital Authority v Mirror Group Newspapers Ltd*, Court of Appeal, 2001: 101)

But, as part of the balancing of interests, what the section gives with one hand, it takes away with another. The protection afforded by the first phrase in section 10 is lessened by the provision's second phrase. One problem for those who wish to protect journalists and their sources is that this is also very wide. Consider, as an example, what may be 'in the interests of justice', and leave aside for present purposes the references in section 10 to national security, and the prevention of disorder or crime. It is likely, on the face value of these words at least, that it is in the *interests of justice* for a court to order a journalist to reveal the identity of a source, where that source has broken a duty of confidentiality. Duties of confidentiality will frequently be owed by sources to their employers, and a source will frequently breach such a duty by talking to a journalist. An employer who has had their confidentiality breached in such a way may well have a legal action against the source, and also the journalist.

Because both aspects of section 10 are wide, and competing interests are embodied in the provision, the courts have wrestled with how it should be applied. They have, to adopt the phrase used earlier, sought a balance that is predictable yet flexible, and normatively convincing. It has not been an easy process. A more complete survey of the evolution of the case law is beyond the scope of this chapter, and can be found elsewhere (for example, in Cram, 2009; Millar and Scott, 2016; Phillips, 2014), but one recurrent issue was that English law was frequently found to be out of kilter with European human rights law, in that it paid insufficient regard to the protection of sources (*Ashworth HA v MGN Ltd*, Court of Appeal: [97]; Nicol et al., 2009: 1.18).

This led to the UK courts aligning their interpretation of section 10 of the CCA, to the interpretation made by the European Court of Human Rights (ECoHR) of article 10 of the European Convention on Human Rights (ECoHR) (see *Mersey Care v Akroyd [No2]*, Court of Appeal, 2007). Article 10 protects freedom of expression.[3] This is engaged, because journalists employ their article 10 rights when communicating to the public, and an essential part of such communication can be that they receive information from sources. Being able to protect their sources helps maintain that flow of information. (Article 8,[4] the provision that protects privacy, can also be engaged, and this – as well as article 10 – will be discussed in more detail later.) The upshot of this is that section 10 CCA, 1981, interpreted in the light of article 10, has evolved into a reasonably coherent and effective means of protecting sources, which balances such protection against other societal interests.[5]

But this protection is being undermined, and it is contemporary legal and technological change that has had this effect. Legal issues have arisen because there are other more specific laws that deal with particular instances where information is sought from journalists, and these can be less protective of journalistic sources than section 10 CCA, 1981. Overuse, or inappropriate use of these laws, upsets the delicate balance. These laws can generally be divided into two categories – those that apply when individuals are seeking information from journalists, and those that apply when it is the state that is seeking information. The latter are more important for present purposes. Technological issues have arisen because of changes in communication technology, and in particular from data analytic techniques that can be applied to meta-data. We will discuss each in turn.

Upsetting the balance: legal issues

The statute of central importance to consider where the state is seeking information from a journalist is the Police and Criminal Evidence Act, 1984 (PACE, 1984). This established a regime that differentiates journalistic material from other information (section 13), which is further classified into either 'special procedure material' (section 14) or 'excluded material' (section 11), depending on whether it is held under a duty of confidence. If the authorities are seeking disclosure of special procedure material, the protections afforded to journalists are lesser, and it is easier to convince a court to order the release of such material. The criteria that have to be applied – the 'access conditions' – can be found in schedule 1 to the Act. It is more difficult for the authorities to gain access to excluded material.

A senior media lawyer at our round-table said that protections under PACE, 1984 for journalistic material – whether special procedure or excluded – have proved to be effective. Too effective, in fact, in the opinion of some, and there have been suggestions that the protections that are afforded by PACE, 1984 should be narrowed. Lord Justice Leveson, in his investigation into the culture, practice and ethics of the press in 2011–2012, explored this possibility, eventually recommending that the Home Office should consider amending specific protections contained within PACE (Leveson, 2012: 42; discussed, for example, in Phillips, 2014).

But this effective protection provided by PACE, 1984 can already be reduced or evaded. One way this can happen is where another law provides a route by which the state can apply to the court to gain access to journalistic material, and this other route has weaker protections. There is a wide range of other laws that are available to the authorities for such a purpose. These include the Terrorism Act, 2000 (section 37 and schedule 5, paragraph 5 and 6), the Criminal Justice Act, 1987 (section 2), the Inquiries Act, 2005 (section 21) and the Financial Services and Markets Act, 2000 (section 13). Each of these statutes sets out the circumstances in which a state authority can obtain information, and they can overlap. This means that there can be multiple legal avenues through which the state can seek the same journalistic material.

It is here that our research indicated there can be a problem. Where, for example, the state is seeking journalistic material that deals with terrorism, the Terrorism Act, 2000 applies. Access to material that is protected under PACE, 1984 as special procedure material, and as excluded material, is gained much more easily under paragraphs 5 and 6 of Schedule 5 of the Terrorism Act, 2000. A result of this is that the balance that attempts to protect conflicting societal interests has been disturbed. Participants at our round-table reported that this a problem because the terrorism laws in question are very broadly framed, and that upsets the appropriate balance of competing societal interests described earlier in this chapter. (This point is also examined by Danbury in Chapter 1.) Support for such a view can be found in the fact that the courts have decided that the police have used terrorism laws to gain access to journalistic material in situations where they should not have done so. (To be more precise, the Court of Appeal has found that the powers under schedule 7 of the Terrorism Act, 2000 to stop and question people, if used in respect of journalistic information, is incompatible with the ECoHR because it is not 'prescribed by law': *R (Miranda) v Home Secretary* (Court of Appeal, 2016: 94–117.) The net effect of this is that protections that should have been afforded to sources have been evaded. We have focused here on the example of terrorism and the Terrorism Act, 2000, but other examples of this 'legislative arbitrage' could have been highlighted. It also results in the upsetting of a carefully balanced system in areas other than terrorism.

Upsetting the balance: technological issues

The second problem with the legal structures that protect sources, beyond this legislative arbitrage, results from technological innovation. It also arises because PACE, 1984 focuses on protecting content, not the protection of sources and their identities as such. That this is a weakness can be demonstrated by considering the Regulation of Investigatory Powers Act, 2000, and how the police have used this act to seek journalistic information. RIPA, 2000, until recently, provided the main legal framework governing the acquisition and disclosure of content and communications data. It has been supplemented and replaced in many areas by the Investigatory Powers Act, 2016 (IPA, 2016). But it is worth considering here, because there has been extensive experience of how it operates in practice. This experience not only illustrates the point we wish to make, but also offers a guide to some of the potential weaknesses of the IPA, 2016. It also helps inform our suggestion of how these can be ameliorated.

RIPA, 2000 enables intelligence and security agencies, police, customs, and other public agencies to access communications data from telecoms companies for a variety of purposes. Part I chapter I allows for the interception of communications – in other words, the content. Part I chapter II allows for access to communications data through service providers. Part II creates (amongst other things) an authorisation defence for covert surveillance by public authorities (this includes following targeted people, and filming in public places). Intrusive surveillance (placing probes in houses or cars, and similar activities) requires prior judicial authorisation, and is only available for the investigation of serious crime, which the Act defines. State interference with property, such as planting a bug or installing wireless telegraphy, is dealt with by Part III of the Police Act, 1997.

There is no specific mention made or protection in RIPA, 2000 itself for confidential journalistic material, which may immediately seem to be a problem. This was, however, addressed by the *Acquisition and Disclosure of Communications Data Code of Practice*, a document that became effective from 25 March 2015. The Code introduced 'enhanced safeguards' to protect the article 10 ECoHR rights of journalists (Home Office, 2015: 3.78–3.79). Effectively, this provided that where confidential journalistic material was likely to be obtained, the processes under PACE, 1984 should be used. That meant that prior judicial approval would normally be required.

However, and this is the point, it subsequently became apparent that a number of police forces had used the communications data route under Part I chapter II of RIPA, 2000, and applied directly to telecommunications companies for source-related data. In doing so, they had effectively circumvented the protections of PACE, 1984 (see, for example, *News Group Newspapers v Metropolitan Police Commissioner*, UK Investigatory Powers Tribunal, 2015). Indeed, in February 2015, the Interception of Communications Commissioner Sir Anthony May found the Code to be deficient. He recommended that it be altered, to 'provide adequate safeguards to protect journalistic sources' (Interception of Communications Commissioner's Office, 2015: 37). Consequently, a revised *Code of Practice for the Interception of Communications Data* was issued in January 2016 (Home Office, 2016).

This highlights the weakness of PACE, 1984 from the point of view of journalistic source protection. Meta-data – information about communication, rather than the contents of the communication itself – can be used by the authorities to identify journalistic sources. This can happen when information about who spoke to whom, on what machine, and on which account and when, is cross-referenced with other information. Moreover, more sophisticated data analytic techniques can be applied to reveal even more sensitive information. This is true in areas beyond journalistic source protection. A striking and disturbing example of such techniques being used in the 2016 American election is described by Grassegger and Krogerus (2017). Yet this meta-data is obtained more easily by authorities under RIPA, 2000 than PACE, 1984, and that means that authorities can evade the carefully balanced protections afforded by PACE, 1984.

Here, we have just considered the UK, and in particular the provisions under PACE, 1984 and RIPA, 2000, but it is clear that this problem is likely to be more widespread. For one thing, it is likely to affect the implementation of the new IPA, 2016, and measures of similar ambit – for example, the Digital Economy Bill, currently being considered by Parliament. It will also be relevant in other countries. As the academic lawyer Andrew Scott explained at the workshop that forms the basis of this chapter (ILPC, 2017), '[l]egal protection against disclosure/delivery up orders [is] irrelevant if surveillance, retention of/access to communications data, or interception of communications allows investigating authorities an easy route to information'. Under such circumstances, it is very difficult – if not impossible – for a journalist to protect the anonymity of their sources. The answer to the question posed at the beginning of the chapter – 'can you keep a secret?' – is, from a legal point of view, 'frequently no'.

Practical legal responses

What to do?[6] Legally, one way of redressing the balance is to look to the European Court of Human Rights. As has been described, the decisions of the ECoHR on article 10 has deeply influenced decisions of domestic courts on section 10 CCA, 1981, and it also influences (amongst other things) court interpretations of other laws that relate to source protection. This is because the UK has signed up to the European Convention on Human Rights, and incorporated the Convention into UK law by the Human Rights Act, 1998 (HRA, 1998). Section 3 of the HRA, 1998 says that UK courts must interpret domestic legislation in a way that is compatible with the Convention, and section 6 indicates that courts themselves must act in ways that are compliant with the Convention.

There are two main articles in the ECoHR that are relevant – article 10, already mentioned, which protects rights of free speech, and has special application to watchdog journalism (see, for example, Millar and Scott, 2016; Nicolaou, 2012; Phillips, 2014 and the case law following *Goodwin v The United Kingdom* (European Court of Human Rights, 1996), and article 8, which protects rights to privacy. These provide a standard against which contemporary laws, and the application of them, should be judged. It provides a way of assessing whether the balance between the competing societal interests, laid out earlier in this chapter, is achieved.

Article 10

As indicated earlier, article 10 protects freedom of speech. The leading ECoHR case on article 10 relating to source protection in this context is *Goodwin* (1996). In this case the Strasbourg Court found, amongst other things, that:

> protection of journalistic sources is one of the basic conditions for press freedom . . . without such protection, sources may be deterred from assisting the press in informing the public on matters of public interest . . . the vital public-watchdog role of the press may be undermined and the ability of the press to provide accurate and reliable information may be adversely affected . . . such a measure cannot be compatible with Article 10 of the Convention unless it is justified by an overriding requirement in the public interest.

The jurisprudence of the court has laid out a series of tests against which specific laws on source protection should be judged. These are based around the ECoHR's three-fold test, that to be permissible, any infringement of article 10 should be prescribed by law, pursuant to a legitimate aim, and necessary in a democratic society – which includes a requirement that it should be proportionate. This means in *substantive* terms that any law – or its interpretation by the courts – needs to embody a variety of factors. These include the need to limit any interference with freedom of speech; to balance the public interests at stake between the dissemination of the source's information and the public interest in revealing their identity (or other relevant information); and the motives, objectives, and conduct of any journalist and their source.

The court also sets out some *procedural* factors that need to be built in to any law. These derive significantly from the case of *Sanoma Uitgevers BV v The Netherlands* (European Court of Human Rights, 2010), and include the requirement that any law that interferes with article 10 in relation to source protection must have effective legal procedural guarantees for a journalist. In practical terms, this means that there must be the guarantee of review by a judge or other independent and impartial decision-making body, of a decision that results in the revelation of a source's identity. Importantly, any review of such a decision must be made *in advance* of access to the information sought. Such a view was reinforced by the decision of *Telegraaf Media v The Netherlands*, European Court of Human Rights, 2012).

Article 8

As well as article 10, the other jurisprudence of the ECoHR that is relevant relates to article 8 – the right to a private life. Both the privacy of a journalist and their source can be interfered with when the state seeks to identify a journalist's source. Moreover, article 8 and article 10 can combine together where state surveillance is undertaken specifically to identify sources. (This is not always the case, and does not occur, for example, where the procurement of journalistic information is incidental to the purposes of an investigation).

Early guidance from the European court on how to apply article 8 came in *Klass v Germany* (European Court of Human Rights, 1978). This case confirmed the view that state interception or surveillance could be legitimate under article 8(2), but only where it is in accordance with the law, necessary in a democratic society, and proportionate (the usual test that the ECoHR applies). In interpreting this, the court noted that where the state is acting covertly, the individual will necessarily be prevented from seeking an effective remedy of his or her own accord, or from taking a direct part in any review proceedings. This is because such a person will not know that he or she is under surveillance, and will not know that there are any review proceedings in which they can take part. That means that, for any interception or surveillance to be compliant with article 8, the supervision of state powers in this context must be adequate to compensate for the absence of court oversight. In particular, the court subsequently explained in *Telegraaf Media* (European Court of Human Rights, 2012), this means that any review must take place before, rather than after covert interception or surveillance. This is because, a 'review post factum . . . cannot restore the confidentiality of journalistic sources once it is destroyed' (*Telegraaf Media*, European Court of Human Rights, 2012: 101).

Implications for source protection laws

What do these considerations mean for any evaluation of the law of source protection in the UK? They set out minimum standards, against which laws that seek to afford access to journalistic sources should be judged. They mean, for example, that the recently passed IPA, 2016 needs to be applied in such a way that it sufficiently protects journalists' sources, and provisions on disclosure of public authority information in the Digital Economy Bill ought to be drafted with such protection built-in. In respect of the IPA, 2016, we recommend that this can be achieved by the drafting and adoption of Codes of Practice in ways that comply with the ECoHR's jurisprudence, although we are concerned by the lack of an obligation to notify media parties of judicial authorisation requests in the legislation itself. In particular, such Codes should ensure that there is independent and impartial – and as far as can be achieved, transparent – oversight of any investigation that may reveal a journalist's sources. Where it is proposed that there should be surveillance for the purposes of identifying a source, this oversight ought to take place before any surveillance is undertaken. And, more generally, the Code should also be alive to, and prohibit, the abuse – or overuse – by the authorities of laws that permit access to meta-data and data analytics, to reveal journalistic information that is otherwise protected by law.

Nonetheless, we recognise that this may not be sufficient. A practical obstacle still stands in the way of ensuring these minimum standards in law. As Tom Hickman has argued cogently on the limitations of public law, judicial review is beyond the capability of most people (Hickman, 2017). If protection is only afforded to the rich, it cannot be fair and efficient protection. The point can be extended to the difficulty of bringing other types of legal challenges too: the costs and complexity of mounting a defence or challenging a court order are often prohibitive, especially to individuals and small media organisations.

Technology

This chapter has thus far concentrated on the legal risks to sources and journalists, and has discussed technological change in that context. However, rapid technological development in the twentieth and twenty-first centuries has had an impact on source protection beyond the law. It is to this that we now turn. The appearance and widespread use of digital communication technologies, including internet-based services, have been great enablers for freedom of expression – an individual wishing to reach a large audience no longer needs the financial resource to buy a printing press.[7] At the same time, however, digital communication methods have also allowed increased state and corporate capacity for surveillance. The technological protections for sources have not kept pace with the ability of states and other actors to use technology to intercept or monitor communications. Increasingly, journalists have become aware that any digital or other direct contact with a source who wishes to remain anonymous can make keeping a promise of confidentiality very difficult (see, for example, Posetti, 2015; Pearson, 2015). These difficulties have been brought into stark focus during contemporary debates about surveillance in the UK. Journalistic sources, and journalists, are increasingly vulnerable to being identified by state agencies and other actors.

Practical responses

However, technology – as well as presenting challenges for those who wish to protect their sources – also offers opportunities. There are a number of potential technological tools available to facilitate the protection of sources, and anonymous whistleblowing. A full survey of these is, again, beyond the scope of this chapter, but recommended resources can be found elsewhere (see Carlo and Kamphuis, 2016). Suffice to say that for present purposes, the resources available to journalists and their sources include tools such as SecureDrop, the secure deletion of information, the encryption of communication, and the encryption of internet browsing. These afford a response to the legal and technological difficulties that make it difficult for journalists to protect their sources.

Yet, at our meeting, practitioner journalists raised concerns about how these tools work in practice. For example, in respect of secure online submission systems, it was said that use of these was tricky to achieve without leaving digital footprints. These footprints can lead to the revelation of the identity of a source. Moreover, the difficulties in avoiding or minimising such a trail are enhanced where inexperienced or vulnerable sources are communicating with journalists, or where communication takes place through an intermediary. Even in situations where this is not the case, participants noted that jigsaw identification of sources via several pieces of information was a possibility. These, it was said, are not resolved by secure online deposit box technology.

Moreover, there are problems that arise from the very nature of anonymous secure online deposit systems. Anonymity is clearly one way of protecting source identity, and can be built into such tools. However, anonymity raises problems of its own. It makes it impossible, or very difficult, to assess the motivations and provenance of material provided to journalists. That means it is difficult for a responsible investigative journalist to use the material delivered by them, because they cannot be sure of its provenance, veracity, context, and the motive of the source. Knowledge of such information can be crucial in an evaluation of whether it is in the public interest to investigate and report. That said, it was observed that there might be other tools that could be used to overcome this difficulty, and OnionShare, an anonymous and secure filesharing tool, was mentioned as one.

Turning to secure means of communication, there are valuable tools available, such as the encryption programmes Pretty Good Privacy (PGP) and GNU Privacy Guard (GPG). PGP was essential to Glenn Greenwald's reporting of the Snowden revelations. However, the appropriateness of information security methods will vary in different circumstances, and not least because even the experts can find it difficult to use them correctly. Indeed, Glenn Greenwald very nearly missed his scoop, because he did not use encryption. In the words of Micah Lee, security engineer and journalist at *The Intercept*: 'Greenwald didn't use encryption and didn't have the time to get up to speed, so Snowden moved on' after making initial anonymous contact with the journalist (Lee, 2014). Luckily for Greenwald, the story found him via another route, through the filmmaker Laura Poitras, who did use GPG.

But even this route was not easy. To get in touch with Poitras initially, Snowden had first to contact Micah Lee, to obtain her GPG key. Moreover, Lee's account of his crucial role in the process exposes the potential for source identification even with a source as technologically competent as Snowden. In his first email to Lee, Snowden (writing anonymously) had forgotten to attach his key, which meant that Lee could not encrypt his response. Therefore, Lee was forced to send him an unencrypted email requesting his key. Lee comments: 'His oversight was of no security consequence – it didn't compromise his identity in any way – but it goes to show how an encryption system that requires users to take specific and frequent actions almost guarantees mistakes will be made, even by the best users' (Lee, 2014).

If it is difficult for professionals to protect themselves using these technical tools, it is even more difficult for non-professionals. A participant directly working with whistleblowers emphasised this point, when observing that many people do not think about encryption; sources with Edward Snowden's mindset and technical background are rare. For many sources, the main concern is going public; and when they are dealing with the media, to what extent they trust the journalist. Encryption, and similar ways of covering their digital tracks, is a secondary consideration for such people.

Given these opportunities to slip up, some of our participants wondered if old-fashioned and pre-digital methods could still serve a purpose; for example, receiving information by post, fax or hand-delivery. Another suggested that reporters could advertise online when they will be in the office, so an individual could find them in person. While this could be useful in some situations, another participant – a freelancer – observed that this would not necessarily help those journalists who operated without an office base. And, in any event, any contact between a source and a journalist could still be vulnerable to surveillance, by tracking smartphone locations, for example. In addition, as Smyth and O'Brien argue:

> the capability to tap your computer or phone has been decentralized and privatized . . . to minimise risks of state and private interference investigative journalists should always adopt appropriate data security protocols.
> (Committee to Protect Journalists, 2012: 17)

Risk assessment, in the end, will be essential, and this requires thinking about who the target of the information is, what resources are available to them, whether they have the motive to seek to identify a source, and whether they have the opportunity to do so. Thinking through this process is of central importance *before* any communication takes place. In practice of course, as the Snowden-Greenwald example shows, this is not always possible, and even when it is, it is not always the complete answer. Ultimately, therefore, we feel there is no technological solution to the threats to source protection for journalists. These are questions of human interaction, and the ideal protection of sources comes from the behaviour of sources and journalists. Technology is a tool: but more important than the tool, is the way it is used by human beings.

Conclusion

These legal and technological threats to the protection of anonymous sources' identity and communications return us to our original question. Given these legal and practical difficulties of protecting a source evident from both our discussions with practitioners and a review of the literature, what should a journalist do? In our report of February 2017, we make recommendations, divided into actions for different actors. We have mentioned some specific suggestions on current law and policy (namely, the Investigatory Powers Act and the Digital Economy Bill, passing through Parliament at the time of writing), that we feel should sufficiently protect journalists and their anonymous sources in ways that are compliant with the UK's international human rights obligation, particularly those under the ECoHR. Essential to this is the provision of independent judicial oversight regimes to safeguard legitimate protection. Comparable points, though obviously transposed to different doctrinal contexts, can be made in other jurisdictions.

For journalists and news organisations, our recommendations also apply more broadly than the UK. We focus on the care journalists should show for sources, and suggest they and their organisations should review and strengthen policies on secure technology, source care, and protection. We suggest that they consider how journalists engage with sources that wish to remain anonymous, and offer and participate in training on working with confidential sources to make journalists and sources aware of the practicalities and limitations of source care and protection. We also identify a number of research questions that need further study. It was evident from our discussion that we needed to draw on better empirical evidence on the extent to which different jurisdictions offer protection for whistleblowers and journalists, and whether lessons can be learned from legislation in other territories. It is clear that we need to interrogate definitions of journalism and evaluate whether this can help the drafting of source protection laws.

Against this background, we also see the need to revisit international journalists' ethical codes. We feel there should be additional provisions for journalists to warn their sources of the vulnerabilities of their communication before offering assurances of anonymity. The Society of Professional Journalists in the United States, for example, says that anonymity should be reserved 'for sources who may face danger, retribution or other harm, and have information that cannot be obtained elsewhere' (Society of Professional Journalists, 2014). We feel this limitation – and similar limitations – is not enough, nor are the general provisions on harm avoidance sufficient. There is scope for ensuring that additional information about a source's vulnerability is provided before proceeding with the contact.

In sum, we conclude that a journalist should continue to strive for confidentiality, but needs to be alert to the legal and technological dangers that might reveal their sources. They should consider when it would be appropriate to share their concerns with a source. Not all anonymous sources will anticipate the potential for interception as Edward Snowden did, or take such extreme steps to protect their identity. There may be an ethical obligation to inform them of their vulnerability before offering confidentiality and proceeding with the investigation. These obligations arise because it is very difficult for modern journalists truthfully to answer 'yes', when asked the question: 'can you keep a secret?'

Notes

1 Material in this chapter is drawn from a research project undertaken by the authors in autumn 2016 at the Institute of Advanced Legal Studies with the support of Guardian News and Media, and published as a working report (Townend and Danbury, 2017). The authors offer their thanks to all who contributed to this initiative and in particular, Dr Andrew Scott (LSE) and Gillian Phillips (*The Guardian*) for their assistance with building an overview of the relevant law. Of course, all errors and commissions remain the authors' own.
2 It is important to note a point that follows from this. In this chapter, we discuss the issue of *journalistic* source protection, and protecting *journalists'* sources. However,

we do not necessarily mean to confine the arguments we advance to institutional journalists. They can apply to what can be called functional journalists too – those undertaking journalistic activity, without being members of an institution of journalism. Whether they do or not is a complex and important area, but depends on a discussion beyond the scope of this chapter. We touch on it briefly in the conclusion.
3 (1) Everyone has the right to freedom of expression. This right shall include freedom to hold opinions and to receive and impart information and ideas without interference by public authority and regardless of frontiers. This Article shall not prevent States from requiring the licencing of broadcasting, television or cinema enterprises. (2) The exercise of these freedoms, since it carries with it duties and responsibilities, may be subject to such formalities, conditions, restrictions or penalties as are prescribed by law and are necessary in a democratic society, in the interests of national security, territorial integrity or public safety, for the prevention of disorder or crime, for the protection of health or morals, for the protection of the reputation or rights of others, for preventing the disclosure of information received in confidence, or for maintaining the authority and impartiality of the judiciary.
4 (1) Everyone has the right to respect for his private and family life, his home and his correspondence. (2) There shall be no interference by a public authority with the exercise of this right except such as is in accordance with the law and is necessary in a democratic society in the interests of national security, public safety or the economic well-being of the country, for the prevention of disorder or crime, for the protection of health or morals, or for the protection of the rights and freedoms of others.
5 Although it is not perfect. A significant problem, which we return to at the end of this chapter, results from the transaction costs involved in defending a legal action that seeks a source, and the chill those costs entail. It may well be cheaper and easier for a journalist or a journalistic organisation – particularly smaller operations and freelancers – to release source-related information that is requested of them by a lower court, than to appeal such an order.
6 This section derives from Dr Andrew Scott's presentation at the ILPC workshop (ILPC, 2017).
7 In 1960, AJ Liebling famously noted that 'Freedom of the press is guaranteed only to those who own one' (Liebling, 1964; and see Breiner, 2014).

References

Blom-Cooper, Louis (2008) 'Press freedom: A constitutional right or cultural assumption?' in *Public Law*, Issue: 2, Summer, pp. 203–204.
Breiner, James (2014) 'What freedom of the press means for those who own one', *MediaShift*, http://mediashift.org/2014/12/what-freedom-of-the-press-means-for-those-who-own-one/ [accessed 12 March 2017].
Carlo, Silke and Kamphuis, Arjen (2016) *Information Security for Journalists*, [3rd edition], online, London: The Centre for Investigative Journalism, www.tcij.org/resources/handbooks/infosec [accessed 20 March 2017].
Committee to Protect Journalists (2012) *CPJ Journalist Security Guide: Covering the News in a Dangerous and Changing World*, New York: CPJ.
Contempt of Court Act 1981 (1981) London: The Stationery Office.
Court of Appeal (2001) *Ashworth Hospital Authority v Mirror Group Newspapers Ltd*, [2001] 1 WLR 515: CA.
────── (2007) *Mersey Care v Akroyd (No2)*, 94 BMLR 84.

——— (2016) *R (Miranda) v Home Secretary*, [2016] EWCA Civ 6.
Cram, Ian (2009) *Terror and the War on Dissent*, Dordrecht: Springer.
Craven, Nick (2014) 'How police hacked the mail on Sunday', *Mail Online*, www.dailymail.co.uk/news/article-2780809/How-police-hacked-Mail-Sunday-Officers-used-anti-terror-laws-seize-phone-records-identify-source-exposed-Chris-Huhne-s-speeding-points-fraud.html [accessed 12 March 2017].
Criminal Justice Act 1987 (1987) London: The Stationery Office.
European Court of Human Rights (1996) *Goodwin v The United Kingdom* [1996] 22 EHRR 12.
——— (2010) *Sanoma Uitgevers BV v The Netherlands*, Application No. 38224/03 [2010] ECHR 38224/03.
——— (2012) *Telegraaf Media v The Netherlands*, Application No. 39315/06 [2012] 34 BHRC 193.
Financial Services and Markets Act 2000 (2000) London: The Stationery Office.
Grassegger, Hannes and Krogerus, Mikael (2017) 'The data that turned the world upside down', *Motherboard.vice.com*, https://motherboard.vice.com/en_us/article/big-data-cambridge-analytica-brexit-trump?utm_source=vicefbusads&utm_campaign=interest [accessed 21 March 2017].
Hickman, Tom (2017) 'Public law's disgrace', *UK Constitutional Law Association*, online, https://ukconstitutionallaw.org/2017/02/09/tom-hickman-public-laws-disgrace/ [accessed 12 March 2017].
Home Office (2015) 'Acquisition and disclosure of communications data code of practice', www.gov.uk/government/publications/code-of-practice-for-the-acquisition-and-disclosure-of-communications-data [accessed 12 March 2017].
——— (2016) 'Code of practice for the interception of communications data', www.gov.uk/government/publications/interception-of-communications-code-of-practice-2016 [accessed 12 March 2017].
Human Rights Act 1998 (1998) London: The Stationery Office.
ILPC (2017) 'Source protection report and resources', *Information Law & Policy Centre Blog*, https://infolawcentre.blogs.sas.ac.uk/source-protection-report-2017/ [accessed 12 March 2017].
Inquiries Act 2005 (2005) London: The Stationery Office.
Interception of Communications Commissioner's Office (2015) 'IOCCO inquiry into the use of Chapter 2 of Part 1 of the Regulation of Investigatory Powers Act (RIPA) to identify journalistic sources', http://iocco-uk.info/docs/IOCCO%20Communications%20Data%20Journalist%20Inquiry%20Report%204Feb15.pdf [accessed 17 March 2017].
Investigatory Powers Act (2016) London: The Stationery Office.
European Court of Human Rights (1978) '*Klass and others v. Germany*', https://hudoc.echr.coe.int/eng#{"itemid":["001-57510"]} Strasbourg [accessed 11 July 2018].
Lambert, Jean (2017) 'While the UK attacks whistleblowers, the EU is defending them – that is, until Brexit happens', *Independent.co.uk*, www.independent.co.uk/voices/brexit-eu-britain-whistleblowers-european-parliament-defending-them-a7589581.html [accessed 12 March 2017].
Lee, Micah (2014) 'Ed Snowden taught me to smuggle secrets past incredible danger: Now I teach you', *The Intercept*, https://theintercept.com/2014/10/28/smuggling-snowden-secrets/ [accessed 12 March 2017].

Leveson, Brian (2012) *An Inquiry into the Culture, Practices and Ethics of the Press: Executive Summary and Recommendations*, London: The Stationery Office.
Lewis, Helen (2013) 'Isabel Oakeshott: Vicky Pryce double-crossed me', *New Statesman*, www.newstatesman.com/staggers/2013/03/isabel-oakeshott-vicky-pryce-double-crossed-me [accessed 12 March 2017].
Liebling, Abbot (1964) *The Press*, New York: Ballantine Books.
Millar, Gavin and Scott, Andrew (2016) *Newsgathering: Law, Regulation, and the Public Interest*. Oxford and New York: Oxford University Press.
National Union of Journalists (2011) 'NUJ code of conduct', www.nuj.org.uk/about/nuj-code/ [accessed 21 March 2017].
Nicol, Andrew, Millar, Gavin and Sharland, Andrew (2009) *Media Law and Human Rights*, Oxford: Oxford University Press.
Nicolaou, George (2012) 'The protection of journalists' sources', in Casadevall, Josep, Myjer, Egbert, O'Boyle, Michael and Austin, Anna [editors], *Freedom of Expression: Essays in Honour of Nicolas Bratza*, Oisterwijk: Wolf Legal Publishers.
Pearson, Mark (2015) 'How surveillance is wrecking journalist-source confidentiality', *The Conversation*, http://theconversation.com/how-surveillance-is-wrecking-journalist-source-confidentiality-43228 [accessed 12 March 2017].
Phillips, Gillian (2014) 'On protection of journalistic sources', Centre for Media Pluralism and Media Freedom, http://journalism.cmpf.eui.eu/discussions/on-protection-of-journalistic-sources/ [accessed 12 March 2017].
Police Act 1997 (1997) London: The Stationery Office.
Police and Criminal Evidence Act 1984 (1984) London: The Stationery Office.
Posetti, Julie (2015) 'Protecting journalism sources in the digital age', in Ichou, Rachel Pollack [editor], *World Trends in Freedom of Expression and Media Development: Special Digital Focus*. Paris: UNESCO.
Regulation of Investigatory Powers Act 2000 (2000) London: The Stationery Office.
Society of Professional Journalists (2014) 'SPJ code of ethics', www.spj.org/ethicscode.asp [accessed 11 April 2017].
Terrorism Act 2000 (2000) London: The Stationery Office.
Townend, Judith and Danbury, Richard (2017) *Protecting Sources and Whistleblowers in a Digital Age*, London: Institute of Advanced Legal Studies, https://infolawcentre.blogs.sas.ac.uk/source-protection-report-2017/ [accessed 12 March 2017].
UK Investigatory Powers Tribunal (2015) *News Group Newspapers v Metropolitan Police Commissioner*, UKIPTrib 14_176-H.
Wallace, Ashleigh (2003) 'Union kicks out journalist', *BelfastTelegraph.co.uk*, www.belfasttelegraph.co.uk/imported/union-kicks-out-journalist-28154342.html [accessed 12 March 2017].

Part II
Activism, investigation, and the quest for social justice

This section delves further into some of the hidden controversies that demonstrate the nature of the contest between, on the one hand, state systems and corporate interests, and on the other their dedicated critics, made up of journalists, academics, popular movements, and individual campaigners. The emphasis of the three pieces, published for the first time here, is on NGO and citizen-led investigations and initiatives, with particular reference to the techniques used to establish reliable accounts of contemporary and historical injustices. The investigative work of the radical charity Global Witness, the social media strategies adapted by community activists in the Brazilian favelas, and the struggles of Spain's Memory Movements to reveal the hidden abuses of the past, all feature in this section. Each one of the authors has had direct experience of a form of research that can be arduous, unpredictable, and on occasion dangerous. In this respect, it prefigures Part III, where the physical hazards of working in a 'hostile environment' are even more evident.

The first contribution, Chapter 5, is by Ruth Sanz Sabido. In 2015, Sanz Sabido began work on a documentary called *Herencias del '36* (Legacies of '36), which examined popular recollections of the Spanish Civil War (1936–1939) and of the decades-long dictatorship that followed Franco's victory over the elected Republican government. This project created a thematic parallel to her ethnographic study *Memories of the Spanish Civil War* (2016), but also forms the background to the analysis offered here of the 'Memory Movements', groups of citizens dedicated to discovering the truth about the many extra-judicial executions carried out in Spain during the years of war and repression. Until the replacement in 2018 of Partido Popular (the governing party, which had become mired in corruption scandals) by Pedro Sánchez's PSOE, the process of recovering the past and investigating the various crimes committed in the 1930s, was made exceptionally difficult by the neglect or outright hostility shown by successive governments. The 'pact of silence' in Spain, in which the offences committed during the Franco era were obscured, was especially traumatic for the defeated Republicans, and the author recognises 'the use of new media to circumvent a national system that seems to oppose, or ignore, popular demands for social reform'.

Sanz Sabido's account is particularly notable for the fact that she toured the sites (often roadside graves) where the victims of fascism were buried, conducted interviews with grieving families, and followed the work of the volunteers who strove to find the remains of the 'disappeared'.

Chapter 6 presents Ali Hines' in-depth study of Global Witness, a radical NGO that campaigns to end all those 'environmental and human rights abuses' produced by 'the exploitation of natural resources and corruption in the global political and economic system' (Global Witness website, nd). Its website carries the banner 'Find the Facts, Expose the Story, Change the System', and it is these edicts that reveal its commitment to social justice, and which hint at the use of methods that will be familiar to investigative journalists. The chapter, which is based on interviews with leading campaigners from the organisation, begins with extended references to the undercover work conducted in the mid-1990s on the Thai-Cambodian border, when three activists tried to gather reliable information on the illegal timber trade. Much in the spirit of 'long-form' journalism, the goal of the NGO is to produce reliable reports that are based upon 'detailed evidence-based arguments', which can be 'months and sometimes years in the making'. In July 2018, an even more explicit connection was made with established investigative formats, when the *Guardian Weekend* magazine collaborated with Global Witness to produce a colour supplement called 'The thin green line' (21 July 2018), which focused on the people across the globe who fight to protect vulnerable swathes of land from poachers, big business, those who pollute the environment, and other threats. The core of the current chapter, however, is made up of three case studies: the 'Mansions' campaign, which was designed to alert the public to the purchase of London properties by corrupt overseas politicians; the 'Rubber Barons' investigation from 2013, which was Global Witness' first investigation on land grabs in Vietnam; and a study of corruption at the highest levels of the Cambodian government.

The attempt by the poor residents of the Brazilian favelas to address the negligence of the mainstream media, and to overcome the fear and brutality faced in their daily lives, forms the subject-matter of Chapter 7. Fernanda Amaral, a Brazilian national, focuses on the social media forms employed to reinvigorate community life, exemplified by this piece, which describes a project that required direct access to some of the most dangerous urban sites in Brazil. 'For several days', Amaral writes, 'I tried to gain access to the favelas of the Complexo do Alemão and the Complexo da Maré' (two of the poorest neighbourhoods). 'Time and again', she writes, 'I was prevented by violent events'. Both the neighbourhood gangs and the police constituted a serious threat to life in these neglected communities. The chapter identifies two forms of intervention that helped to break the cycle of misrepresentation, within which the residents of the favelas felt they were trapped. One was the work of those investigative journalists who had joined organisations like ABRAJI (the Associação Brasileira de Jornalismo Investigativo, or the

Brazilian Association of Investigative Journalism), and the other was 'the self-activity of young residents, who decided to cover their own neighbourhoods by creating material online' gathered on their smartphones. During some of the most brutal police incursions, these young people, some of whom were not yet teenagers, used the Twitter profile of a community newspaper to circulate real-time footage of police activity, the reaction of the drug dealers, and the sheer panic of the residents.

5 Citizens' investigations

Recovering the past in contemporary Spain

Ruth Sanz Sabido

Introduction

In the summer of 2015, on the outskirts of a village in the north-western province of Léon, Spain, a group of forensic experts and researchers, from the nearby city of Ponferrada, stood by an unmarked roadside grave. At this place, during the Civil War of 1936, a number of unarmed men had been executed by Nationalist insurgents, and their bodies left in full view of anyone passing in the street. The volunteers who had gathered at this spot belonged to one of Spain's Memory Associations, which are dedicated to the collection of any evidence that can help the descendants of the 'disappeared' find out what had happened to their relatives. I had accompanied the Ponferrada activists as part of a documentary project called *Herencias del '36* (Legacies of '36), which eventually carried the testimonies of some 40 people whose families had suffered during the War and its aftermath. As we examined the grass verge that concealed the graves, an elderly man passed by. When I asked him if he had been living in the area at the time, he denied being present: then, however, he turned back to say that he had been 6 years old in 1936, and had been among the local children who had stood around looking at the bodies of the victims. Wherever I went, memories of the War would emerge in ordinary conversation. On a separate occasion, in a different part of the country, I made contact with an activist who worked with another section of the Memory Movement. He, too, was interested in investigating extra-judicial executions. As we walked along the street, he passed a man he knew, and the two exchanged a brief greeting. Then, as we moved out of earshot, my informant told me that the father of the man to whom he had spoken 'was one of the killers' – in other words, one of those who had participated in politically motivated murders during the war, or the dictatorship that followed.

These two incidents illustrate an ever-present feature of life in contemporary Spain – the constant and unavoidable intrusion of the traumas of the past into the political and cultural fabric of the present. My own reasons for visiting the country grew from this awareness, as I began to gather material for a book on the Civil War (Sanz Sabido, 2016) and the *Herencias del*

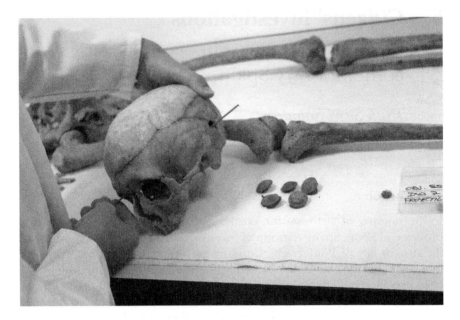

Figure 5.1 A technician in the Ponferrada laboratory tracks the bullet wound that killed an unknown victim of Francoist repression.
Photograph: Stuart Price, 15 May 2015.

'*36* documentary. My visit to Ponferrada was therefore just one stage in an investigative trip that encompassed multiple sites across Spain. The success of these projects depended, as noted earlier, on conducting interviews with families that had experienced the loss of relatives, and who had endured the long years of dictatorship that followed the victory of the Nationalists in 1939. Besides visits to execution sites, cemeteries, private homes, the laboratory in Ponferrada (see the photograph in Figure 5.1), and seats of local government, my investigations required archival research and, as already mentioned, the creation of a close relationship with Spain's Memory Associations, which are dedicated to investigating the crimes of the Franco era.

The Spanish context

In recent years, Spain is supposed to have undergone a gradual but steady transformation from totalitarian rule to democracy, and to have 'moved on' from a period of suffering which is meant to have ended, variously, at the close of the War, at Franco's death, during the official 'Transition' to a constitutional/monarchical democracy in 1978, or after the failure of the 1981 coup led by elements of the Civil Guard and armed forces. This perception pervades many contemporary accounts of political renewal, while the appearance of a new wave of street protests, from 2011 on, seemed to provide fresh hope of a new direction.

Writing about the 15M protest movement, which (among other things) objected to corruption, the political dominance of the two main bourgeois parties, and rampant unemployment, Russell describes the rejection of 'old systems' and the appearance of alternative modes of social organisation (2016: 68). She draws attention to the creation of 'new style collaborative spaces' and the appearance of 'de facto news services like Sol TV' which live-streamed the occupation of Madrid's Puerta del Sol (68–69). Other authors have drawn attention to the supposed renewal of Spanish political culture: Gerbaudo, for example, contributes to this optimism, which he identifies with an unexpected revival of inclusive 'popular identities' that were used to make a successful appeal to the 'virtual totality of the political community' (2017: 90).

These developments have certainly helped to create a more positive atmosphere in Spain, at least until the response to Catalan separatism revived nationalistic sentiment and caused some considerable fractures on the Left (Price, in Fishwick and Connolly, 2018). The modest triumphs of the present must, therefore, be understood in the context of a long historical gestation. The *Indignados* movement and 15M, for example, were not the originators of a counter-culture: these movements were instead the latest in a tradition of resistance that had always had to improvise forms of protest in the face of official neglect or hostility. This is true, for example, of the PAH (the Plataforma de Afectados por la Hipoteca, or Platform for People Affected by Mortgages) which, following the financial crisis, was set up (in 2009) to defend those whose properties were threatened with repossession. Organised as a non-hierarchical, non-violent movement dedicated to direct action, it was one of the precursors of the models used by 15M. The same spirit of co-operation and working-class solidarity can be seen in events like the recent 8M Women's Strike, which took place on International Women's Day in 2018 and saw some five million workers take action across Spain (Jones, 2018). Once again, however, it would be impossible to appreciate the truly radical quality of this action without referring to historical precedents, like the Mujeres Libres movement of the 1930s (Ackelsberg, 2000).

In Spain, as suggested earlier, the two main political parties, the Partido Socialista Obrero Español (PSOE), the Spanish Socialist Workers' Party; and Partido Popular (PP), a conservative party, have dominated the media coverage of politics. Their position, recently challenged by political insurgencies on the Right (Ciudadanos, the Citizens' Party), and on the Left (Unidos Podemos, or 'United We Can'), remains powerful enough to grant them 'an omnipresent locus in political events, a greater ability to determine the agenda in the Spanish media, and a strong, centralised role in political debate' (Casero-Ripollés et al., 2015: 98). Faced with the difficulty of gaining traction in the mainstream press and TV, trade unions, Leftist political tendencies, and activist movements in Spain have come to rely on social media to coordinate their campaigns, which are then given some visibility by the online contributions of local news organisations like the *Diario de Léon* (Fidalgo, 2016), news agencies such as the Inter Press Service (Benítez, 2013) and investigative sites like Civio (part of the Global Investigative Journalism Network).

The use of new media to circumvent a national system that seems to oppose, or ignore, popular demands for social reform, can be traced back to the remarkable events of 2004, when the government of José María Aznar blamed the Madrid train bombing (which killed 192 people) on Basque separatist militants of the ETA (Euskadi Ta Askatasuna), although the evidence pointed towards Islamist terrorists belonging to al Qaeda. The ruling party, Partido Popular, lost the General Election, which followed three days after the attacks. Its defeat was attributed in part to the conviction that the government had lied about the perpetrators of the bombing. During this crisis 'online sites and mobile phones acted as peripheral public spheres, enabling a horizontal 'quick deliberation' that questioned the vertical official truth' (Pérez, 2006: 221). These 'counterinformation sites' acted as '"mass mobilizers", receiving about 1.5 million visits the day of the protests' (221), but it appeared that they were still dependent on traditional media, both in terms of information and with regard to the agenda-setting function of mainstream forms (Doval-Avendaño, 2010).

The Memory Movement

This chapter contends that current political developments in Spain cannot be understood without the determined efforts of those organisations (like the ones that make up the Memory Movement), which have devoted themselves to the pursuit of an uncomfortable truth. It examines some of the ways in which Spanish 'Memory Associations' operate both as distinct (yet internally diverse) social movements, and as 'investigative' bodies that must delve into shadowy events that the mainstream media and the state are determined to ignore. The material that follows is drawn from findings that emerged during an ethnographic study of 2015, conducted with the members of six Memory Associations: these were the Asociación para la Recuperación de la Memoria Histórica (ARMH), the Associació per a la Recuperació de la Memòria Històrica de Catalunya, the Asociación Salamanca Memoria y Justicia, Memoria y Libertad, Mesa de Catalunya d'Entitats Memorialistes, and Todos los Nombres. The chapter discusses the ways in which these Associations coordinate their work, the challenges that they encounter in their day-to-day activities, and the strategies that they deploy in order to counteract the systemic opposition and neglect that they encounter within Spain. It compares the characteristics of the different collectives, and argues that, despite their shared goal (broadly, to redress the grievances caused by Franco's repression), the Memory Movement is typified by a number of divisions. These, I argue, are produced *i)* by ideological and historical rifts, *ii)* by the ways in which the 'associative fabric' of individual organisations is created, or *iii)* by a combination of the first two factors.

Making sense of the past

Despite their differences, all the Memory Movements in Spain share a broad objective: the desire to recover and disseminate the memories that have been repressed since the end of the Spanish Civil War (1936–1939). This means in effect the narratives produced by Republicans, Communists, Socialists, Anarchists, and Libertarian Communists, all of whom were not only defeated during the conflict itself, but who were also subjected to continuing forms of repression for several decades, during and even after the dictatorship of Francisco Franco (1939–1975). In short, it is the ongoing state-sponsored obliteration of the memories of *the defeated* that gives the Memory Movement a reason to exist.

According to the Associations, over 114,000 people died as a result of Franco's extra-judicial executions, although Beevor (2006) claimed that the total is closer to 200,000. It is worth pointing out that, even though the number of deaths attributable to the war was ultimately a consequence of the military coup of 1936, these figures refer specifically to the victims of repressive practices that were directed at civilians, and which took place 'behind the lines' (Preston, 2012). Huge numbers of casualties were caused, not in conflict between armed combatants, but because of localised processes that involved the targeting of individual 'enemies' in areas where there had, technically speaking, been no war, or in places where it had already ended. Escudero (2014) points out that, according to Article 7 of the Rome Statute of the International Criminal Court (Rome Statute), the crimes committed by the Francoist authorities qualify as crimes against humanity, as they constitute multiple systemic acts, such as murder, imprisonment in violation of fundamental rules of international law, torture, persecution of specific political groups, and enforced disappearances, all of which were committed against a civilian population as a key element of Franco's desire to annihilate any political opposition.

The Memory Associations devoted to recalling the crimes of the period are third-sector, not-for-profit organisations that function, on the whole, through a large network of volunteers. The project I conducted followed an ethnographic approach (Gobo, 2008; Madison, 2012; Thomas, 1993), which included observations; shadowing; interviews, both individually and in groups; and discussions amongst members and collaborators. The Associations, which operate in different locations across the country, granted me access to their facilities and their collaborators, who could provide details about the type of work conducted by each group. The material gathered throughout the course of these interactions provides rich data about what the Memory Movement means in practice, and sheds light on their achievements and the obstructions they have encountered.

To begin with, the Asociación para la Recuperación de la Memoria Histórica (ARMH, Association for the Recuperation of Historical Memory), the largest Memory Association in Spain, opened the doors of their exhumation laboratory, and provided an insight into their resources and working patterns, not only of the individuals who work at the core of the collective, but also of the volunteers who play a central role in the activities conducted in several Spanish regions. Nevertheless, in order to gain a more rounded view of the principles that define the movement, and a more thorough awareness of the nature and volume of the work, exchanges were conducted with five additional organisations: Associació per a la Recuperació de la Memòria Històrica de Catalunya, Asociación Salamanca Memoria y Justicia, Memoria y Libertad, Mesa de Catalunya d'Entitats Memorialistes, and Todos los Nombres. In the interest of anonymity, participants have been given pseudonyms, despite the fact that all members are perfectly open about the work that they do. Despite the shared goal of redressing the legacy of Franco's repression, the variety of stances towards the work that is conducted, and towards the methods that are espoused, make for a fragmented programme of political and cultural initiatives.

Truth, justice, and reparation

On the last Saturday of every month, representatives of various Memory Associations in Seville – ordinary citizens who lost relatives as a consequence of Franco's repression since 1936 – meet in the central Plaza de la Gavidia in Seville to discuss the latest developments concerning their plight. For eight years, they have made plans for future actions, while reviewing the state of their cause in its local, national and international contexts. Their objectives are clear – to expose the truth, to work for justice, and to demand reparation (for a typical memorial referring to these concepts, see the photograph in Figure 5.2).

As a necessary first step in attaining these goals, they believe that the Spanish state should acknowledge the real character of the events that followed the military uprising of 18 July 1936: in other words, the *truth* must gain official and public recognition. The perpetrators of repression should consequently be brought to *justice* (rather than praised for their actions), and the damage inflicted to the victims should be *repaired* in any way possible. Some of these offences, such as the execution of thousands of people, are in fact irreparable, but 'reparation' should be understood in terms of an acknowledgement and willingness to investigate these and other crimes committed during this period, such as, for example, the expropriation of houses and other private properties, which were taken over by Franco's supporters and have never been returned. These property 'transfers' represent, together with the purging of those who had remained faithful to the legitimate Republican government (such as teachers, civil servants and soldiers), a form of socioeconomic repression that forced thousands

Figure 5.2 The Republican flag flies above a memorial to the '17 Roses of Guillena'. The 17 women were from a small village some 14 miles from Seville, who were murdered by Falangists in 1937. The inscription below the flag reads 'Truth Justice Reparation'.

Photograph: Ruth Sanz Sabido, 29 May 2016.

of families to re-start their lives, elsewhere and in different professions, in order to survive.

The first time I attended this meeting in Seville, in 2014, David, one of those who had gathered in the square, declared that 'we may not be a mass social movement, but we *are* a social movement' (David, 2014). David's remark, and his emphasis on the fact that his group is part of a social movement, is best understood by considering the emergence and increased visibility of other social movements in Spain since 2011 (see above). To a large extent, the 15M occupations in May 2011 had brought about images of crowded streets and frequent media attention (Díaz and Requena, 2011; Elola, 2011). Although subsequent 15M demonstrations were arguably less populous and also received less coverage – while successive initiatives, such as the *mareas* (tides) of protestors, experienced a drop in numbers – David's emphatic statement sought to reclaim, for his own collective, some of the space that seemed to have been taken over (or, indeed, opened up) by anti-austerity movements. This is not to argue that the Memory Movement is at odds with these initiatives, since its adherents feel that they have much in common with contemporary socioeconomic struggles. They explain their position by drawing upon history: 'We are in the streets also with the tides, the green tide, the orange tide . . . making the same demands that *they* made 75 years ago' (Carballar, 2013, my translation and emphasis). The reference to '*they*' means those who, in the 1930s, fought against fascism and for freedom and social rights, and who were subsequently punished for doing so (for the images of the 'disappeared' set up by the Seville Association, see Figure 5.3).

In this gathering of fewer than 40 people in a small square in Seville, we witness the convergence of past and present, as the memories of 'historical' violence re-animate old struggles in a contemporary setting. The effects of repression are passed down through the generations, as the relatives of those who were executed find that there is no resolution to their demands. Under the motto '*Verdad, Justicia y Reparación*', they are engaged in a constant struggle to develop mechanisms against the invisibility that is imposed upon them by the state and other agents while, of the same time, they are denied the resources and support that they require. For David, the problem is not so much whether Spain's *memoria histórica* (historical memory)[1] is technically defined as a social movement, but more crucially, whether its very existence is acknowledged in the first place. Such a recognition would challenge the erasure of everything that is related to the memories of 'the defeated' in the Civil War.

Figure 5.3 Images of the 'disappeared', Plaza de la Gavidia in Seville.
Photograph: Ruth Sanz Sabido, May 2014.

Following his victory in 1939, Franco was the first to manage the official memory of what had happened in Spain during the previous three years: according to this myth, his troops had saved the country from the Left-induced chaos of the Second Republic (1931–1936), eventually managing to establish a 'good' National-Catholic order that brought restitution, morality, and stability to a society which the 'Marxist hordes' had nearly destroyed. From the moment that Franco assumed power, the formal legitimacy of the Second Republic was ignored, and was further obliterated under the continuing inflexibility of the dictatorship (1939–1975). Against this backdrop, Franco's dead were, from 1939, recognised as *victims*, while those he had killed were consigned to an endless state of oblivion. So, for example, properties that were requisitioned by those who supported Franco's regime were never returned to their rightful owners, and bureaucratic processes such as claiming for widow's pensions required the claimant to state that their spouse had simply died, without noting that the cause of death was extra-judicial execution.

After Franco's death, the pact of silence agreed during the 'Transition to democracy' served to acquit the culprits and to ensure the historical erasure of the victims. Despite its focus on individual victims, the Memory Movement is not focussed solely on the resolution of personal issues. In fact, the relatives of victims want to fulfil objectives that not only pertain to the private sphere, but that also transcend it: in essence, this means challenging Franco's myths and the narrative that promotes a 'model' transition to democracy. This process involves, amongst other things, the outright rejection of the 1977 Amnesty Act (the legal expression of the 'pact of silence', through which the crimes of Francoism are not to be investigated) and the ambiguous or even negative response to the 2007 Historical Memory Act.

Even though the latter was supposed to facilitate the recovery of memory by enabling the exhumation of victims, the elimination of any public symbols that glorify Francoism, and the extension of assistance to the victims, the fact remains that the Historical Memory Act does not revoke the 1977 Amnesty Act in any effective way. Essentially, the Historical Memory Act has, for the most part, facilitated a number of conversations regarding the revision of street names and the removal of other Francoist symbols, although these local debates do not always bear fruit. As a collection of guidelines, it contains no actual mechanisms to enforce the ideas that it advocates, hence failing in addition to establish an investigation into the crimes themselves (Escudero, 2014). Consequently, judges continue, as a matter of rule, to refuse to attend any sites where the remains of Franco's victims are found. As noted by Escudero (2014), 'by preventing investigation and accountability, the Act has become a permit for impunity and a symbol of the triumph of dictatorship over democracy', even though it claims to do exactly the opposite. This is the context that defines the movement as a whole and (broadly) determines its objectives.

A fragmented movement

The Memory Movement comprises a number of Associations that work on redressing various aspects of Franco's repression: the tortures experienced by political prisoners, the use of forced labour, detentions in concentration camps, extra-judicial executions and burials in mass graves, the existence of a child trafficking network, and so on.[2] Due to the lack of resources, each Association tends to specialise in, or focus on, one of these issues. Nevertheless, the variety of approaches and working methods evident within each group is not the main factor in creating the 'fragmentation' that I analyse in this section. In one sense, the diversity of concerns and working methods speaks to a willingness to redress the variety of unresolved issues that arise from Franco's repression (see above). An awareness of limited resource also reinforces the tendency to distribute the large number of outstanding cases amongst different collectives. Despite the differences in focus and practice, the interconnections that exist between the Associations provide, together with the shared historical context through which they have all developed, the common ground that enables us to amalgamate them under the umbrella of the Memory Movement.

Although it is perhaps inevitable that some division of labour should occur, the more substantial divisions that exist between the Associations are mainly associated with two broad challenges. On the one hand, fragmentation may occur due to the residual politico-historical differences that exist between some of the groups. On the other hand, rifts may be identified when considering some of the key elements of social movement organisation in general (such as resourcing and performance), irrespective of their particular focus. These dimensions are useful because they provide us with a framework for understanding the working processes of the movement, beyond the limited significance afforded to them in political and media discourse. Nonetheless, as I will point out later, these dimensions are deeply interconnected in practice and cannot be easily separated.

Politico-historical divergences

This dimension, which is rooted in the history of the Spanish conflict, and the political, economic, and social nature of the clashes that characterised the 1930s, reflects an ideological difference that existed not only between Left and Right, but also within the Left itself. Despite the frequent reference to the existence of 'two Spains', it is necessary to challenge what has become a chronic oversimplification of the Civil War: the conflation of communists, socialists, anarchists, and libertarian communists as if they were all part of one homogenous 'Republican' camp. On the one hand, the recognition of the variety of stances that motivated different people to fight helps to recover the memory of the 'forgotten among the forgotten', namely, those who fought against fascism but also rejected the oppressive control of the state as such (Sanz Sabido, 2016; Price, in Fishwick and Connolly, 2018). With this recognition comes a deeper historical understanding of the development of the war and its outcomes.

On the other hand, this complex ideological background, albeit frequently overlooked, is still an inherent part of the contemporary movement. A clear illustration of the enduring socio-political rifts is found, for instance, in the fact that certain groups within the Memory Movement are explicitly connected to specific political parties, such as Izquierda Unida (the United Left). Nevertheless, other collectives clarify that, even though each member may have a more or less formal political affiliation, the constitution of the Associations do not use any known political acronym. So, for example, one of the board members of the Asociación Salamanca Memoria y Justicia explained:

> Every one of us belongs to a party. I am Izquierda Unida, and some of my colleagues are too, but others are PSOE [Partido Socialista Obrero Español]. We know which parties we vote for as citizens, but what we do in the association is not connected to that. It is connected . . . in a way, because we believe that these issues should be resolved . . . you know? But we do not do anything on behalf of the parties, or to advance their campaigns, and they don't fund us anyway.
>
> (Leonor, 2015, my translation)

Of course, any initiatives that promote the objectives of the Memory Movement are either officially independent, or are supported, in one form or another, by trade unions or parties that sit within some faction of the Left (but never, unsurprisingly, within the parties of the Right).

The degree of commitment to the cause of 'memory' is, therefore, often (though not always) underpinned by ideological stances, at either individual or collective levels, and frequently manifests itself in explicit ways. However, on other occasions, these indicators may be more tacit, albeit still deeply rooted in history. I would argue that this is precisely one of the factors that explain the stance taken by several Memory Associations in relation to the exhumation of victims. It is useful at this point to note that the number of Associations concerned with conducting exhumations of the dead are, in fact, a minority. Although it is not possible to know exactly how many Associations there are in total at local, regional, and national levels, according to Gordillo (2014), only 20% of these collectives work on this area, while the majority choose to focus on other aspects, either because members have been more severely affected by other forms of repression, or because they do not believe that exhumations should be performed in the first place.

It is this latter point that, I contend, provides us with an additional insight into the enduring politico-historical divisions within the movement. The dismissal of this activity is not, from this particular perspective, related to the denial of the *existence* of thousands of mass graves that have yet to be exhumed, although this argument is sometimes advanced by conservative politicians and their associates.[3] Rather, 'pro-memory' arguments against the performance of exhumations are varied and include references to the importance of preserving the original evidence of genocide by leaving the graves intact, as well as the categorical assertion that it must be the state – and no any other agent – that must take responsibility for the graves and must conduct the exhumations as a mark of public recognition.

Collectives that are in favour of exhumations agree that the state should certainly take responsibility, but argue that, while the state fails to do so, it is important to advance the work. On behalf of the ARMH (Asociación para la Recuperación de la Memoria Histórica), my informant Silva pointed out that:

> right now we have a list of 1,539 people who disappeared and are being sought by their relatives. They meet the requirements of the protocol established by the United Nations. We know where they may be and, if we had the resources, we would be able to find them.
>
> (Silva, 2015, my translation)

The figure of 1,539 refers to the number of applications that the ARMH has received to exhume graves, although the grand estimated total of disappeared is approximately 114,000, placing Spain (according to the United Nations) in the second position – after Cambodia – in the rank of countries with the highest number of disappeared victims in a conflict.

Whether certain seemingly pro-memory collectives are in fact attempting to delay the resolution of these outstanding matters, is not entirely clear, but it can be argued that some Associations may oppose exhumations because they fear that specific and uncomfortable accusations may arise from the evidence that is unearthed. There may be ideological motivations, or at least a desire to protect certain factions within the Left, based on the concern that the exhumed remains may belong to victims of Left-wing factions that opposed the state system *per se*, or which resulted from the clashes that developed between different groups. In addition, it is important to consider the stance of these pro-memory, but 'anti-exhumation', groups towards the modern Spanish state, and whether the ideological allegiance of some to the 'democratic' system plays a part in their conception of how (and by whom) those exhumations that do take place, should be conducted.

Organising, resourcing, and performing the movement

Most individuals involved in the Associations collaborate on a voluntary basis, and carry out a variety of undertakings, from activities that are crucial to the advancement of the cause, such as painstaking archival searches, legal assistance, and the donation of scientific resources and labour, to more mundane but equally important tasks, such as helping to tidy up a laboratory or taking stock of the merchandise that is available to raise funds. In the collectives with which I have worked, there are only four people – individuals who work at the core of the ARMH – who receive a salary for their work in the Association, and even this is not always the case:

> The thing to understand here is that we don't do this as a job, to get paid. We only get paid enough to live. . . . We barely have any money to do what needs to be done, with the graves and all, so we prioritise the work over our own personal needs. . . . In fact, when the funds dried up, we spent several months working as volunteers, for free, because we care about getting this done.
> (Diego, 2015, my translation)

His colleague, Aida (2015), explained this point in further detail:

> When the government stopped the funds, we had two options. We thought, either we continue working without any resources, or . . . we have to draw the curtains and wait until the money returns, *if* it returns . . . because . . . you can't be sure it will. And, well, we decided that we needed to continue. It could take months or years before we get money again, and we can't . . . we can't allow that. People are dying without knowing where their fathers or brothers or sisters are.
> (Aida, 2015, my translation)

Associations that conduct exhumations, such as the ARMH, take responsibility for their cases from the very moment a relative contacts them with information about the location of the grave, and what they might know about the events surrounding the execution. The process followed by the ARMH and other pro-exhumation collectives is, in principle, rather similar. The first step is to complete an investigation of any legal documents that may shed further light on the circumstances of the death, in order to contrast the data with the details provided by witness accounts. Any information that can assist the team with the precise location of the graves could potentially save them days of conducting excavations in the wrong places. In addition, any details about other individuals who were killed at the same time or buried in the same place can help in the production of an increasingly accurate map of graves that are yet to be exhumed.

Volunteers across the country carry out the task of looking through relevant archives in different locations, depending on the courts and civil registers that need to be visited. Indeed, the ARMH has a significant number of contacts that they rely upon when something needs to be done in other provinces and regions. Once the information is gathered and compared, the exhumation works can begin, at least in principle. The problem arises at this point, as the Association does not have enough financial resources to attend to all the applications that they receive from victims' relatives seeking assistance. The objective of the ARMH is to find all the victims and return their remains to their families, but the general lack of support means that most of these applications have become part of a backlog that continues to increase.

Despite their drive to clear this backlog, pro-exhumation collectives are very mindful of the ways in which the evidence is handled (see earlier, regarding the need to retain evidence of genocide). For this reason, their task is not solely concerned with locating and exhuming the graves, but also with treating the site very much as the murder scene that it was. These 'scientific' exhumations, as they are often described, therefore comprise a number of analyses, from anthropological studies to DNA tests, that record all the details about the location, how the remains were found, the position of the bodies, any evidence of violence, and any other details that, from legal and scientific perspectives, contribute to the overall mapping of Franco's extra-judicial executions and repressive practices. Their hope is that, one day, they may be able to present this large amount of evidence in court. In the meantime, however, it helps to denounce the situation in awareness-raising exercises, using as an audience anyone who may want to listen, in the knowledge that the truth had previously been repressed. As one of my respondents noted:

> Bones can talk, you see? They don't want us to find out what the bones have to say. What they want is for us not to do anything, because the longer it takes to complete the work, the less evidence we will find, and maybe less people might be interested later on. That's what they would want us to do . . . wait, wait, and wait.
>
> (Roberto, 2015, my translation)

Scientific exhumations are, however, different from those that were conducted privately in the late 1970s, after Franco's death, and roughly up until 1981, when the failed coup of 23 February took place. Álvaro, who was actively involved in helping families to exhume their relatives during that period in the province of Salamanca, recalls how he initially started by looking for his own relatives, but when the word spread, other individuals contacted him and he began to assist others. 'It all stopped', he recalls, 'with 23F. People got scared and exhumations came to a halt' (Álvaro, 2015, my translation). More recently, Álvaro, who is now in his 80s, collaborates closely with the Asociación Salamanca Memoria y Justicia, lending his knowledge and support to the executive board. He explains, however, that those exhumations sought to return the victims' remains to their relatives, and were not as thorough as the ones that have been conducted since 2001, when a mass grave containing 13 bodies was exhumed in Priaranza del Bierzo (León). One of those bodies belonged to Emilio

Silva's grandfather. Silva, who organised the exhumation, is the founding President of the ARMH.

While the ARMH, with its focused intention to attend to all the relatives' requests, struggles to keep up with the amount of work, other Associations do not even attempt to complete the cycle that begins with the receipt of an application and ends with an *entrega* ceremony, in which the remains are publicly returned to the relatives and given burial according to their wishes. Asociación Salamanca Memoria y Justicia, for example, has only conducted one exhumation because they managed to gather enough resources to do so, and normally only go as far as to conduct the preliminary archival investigation:

> Our work translates into a growing list of victims of the repression in the province [of Salamanca]. It is at least a way of documenting it, so they are not forgotten ... but we send the details to Ponferrada [to the ARMH] as they have better resources. We cannot cope with that type of work.
>
> (Cinta, 2015, my translation)

The Asociación Salamanca Memoria y Justicia firmly believes that exhumations have to be conducted, so that all the victims are buried with dignity and their relatives can 'close a cycle that has remained open for them and should not have' (Cinta, 2015, my translation). However, as Cinta points out, the work that they manage to complete is mainly an investigatory exercise of tracing the victims and what happened to them, by searching legal files.

Although one of the key findings of the ethnographic encounter was that each Association works as an independent unit that follows its own principles and modes of organisation, there are instances of collaborations between some of the collectives, thanks to the good rapport that exists between them. Another example of this is the Andalusia-based initiative Todos los Nombres, which acts as the main point of contact for the ARMH when they have queries about southern Spain.

The Asociación Salamanca Memoria y Justicia also built a memorial in the cemetery of Salamanca, where the names of the victims are engraved in the walls for the sake of public awareness and recognition.[4] They think that, since they do not have their remains to bury (many cemeteries in Spain tend to consist of walls with deep recesses that are used as tombs), this is at least a symbolic way of giving them some 'wall space'. Álvaro (2015) noted, in a mode of reflection, that 'there are more. There are many more. But where are we going to put them?', in reference to the fact that, having updated the original memorial with an additional set of names, they had already run out of space (see photograph in Figure 5.4).

For the Associació per a la Recuperació de la Memòria Històrica de Catalunya, the process is different because the administrative context in which

Figure 5.4 The names of some of the thousands of people executed by the Nationalists, inscribed on the memorial wall in the cemetery, Salamanca, Spain.
Photograph: Stuart Price, 19 May 2015.

they operate – within the regional government of Catalonia – provides them with an official route to conduct the exhumations:

> We receive requests from the families. We do the investigation, but the exhumations are conducted by the Generalitat. We give them the information we find out, and the details of the relatives who applied, so we act as liaison between the family and the administration.
> (Sergi, 2015, my translation)

The difference between the Associations in Salamanca and Catalonia lies in the existence (or lack of) an institutional dimension, which is best understood in the context of Spain's division into semi-autonomous regions or communities (*Comunidades Autónomas*). Individual regions have unequal degrees of power to make decisions independently from the central government (which may or may not be led by the same party as the one governing each region).

As with the organisation and resourcing of the movement, the performance element also provides a varied picture. For example, Mesa de Catalunya d'Entitats Memorialistes organises a gathering, similar to the one in

Seville (see above), on the last Saturday of every month in Plaça de Sant Jaume in Barcelona, opposite the Generalitat (the government of Catalonia). There is, however, no communication between the two events, and the activities that they carry out are different. While in Seville the group meets to have a discussion about the latest developments, focusing primarily on the disappeared and executed, in Barcelona there are a wider variety of issues represented (prisoners, torture, forced labour, and so on). The objective of these meetings is two-fold: to disseminate information through the display of stands, photographs, and posters, and to collect signatures to demand that Franco's crimes are investigated. The variety of approaches to non-institutional collective action is explained by the independence of each group, which allows for organic forms of organisation. However, there seems to be no formal way of communication and co-operation between most Associations, with some of them choosing to collaborate as and when required. Beyond those occasions when direct collaborations develop, communication typically consists of receiving updates on what other Associations are doing elsewhere, primarily through following one another's social media sites.

Much in the same way as some collectives maintain a good relationship and collaborate when required, there are also cases when there is a decision *not* to work with a specific group. I do not argue that members of an Association would vote not to have any dealings with another (I did not encounter this within the parameters of this study). However, on some occasions, some members may have personal (political) views that interfere with their role of representing the wider collective. This form of fragmentation became obvious when, having contacted one of the Associations and arranged meetings with its board and other members, these plans came to a halt when they learned that one of the other collectives was also involved in the project. Although this was no secret, it had not seemed necessary to inform any of the Associations of this fact. The collective withdrew from the meeting we had previously agreed upon, but failed to offer any explanation for their reaction beyond one request: if any of the members decided to meet us on an individual basis, they hoped that they would not be 'conflated under the same organisation' which 'seems to have taken the monopoly of the memory movement' (Anonymised, 2015). The meetings that had been arranged with three individual members were kept, and none of them could offer an explanation about what had happened, as they claimed not to understand it either. Paco, one of these members, stated that 'sometimes there are clashes. I think it's silly. Don't we already have enough problems to deal with, to be creating more issues amongst ourselves?' (Paco, 2015). Paco's words point at the fragmentation that exists between different organisations, which seems, in this case, to be the result of a political conflict. It is therefore not possible to understand the organisation and performance aspects of the movement as separate elements from the politico-historical dimension discussed earlier.

Conclusion

Eighty years after the beginning of the Civil War, and 40 years after Franco's death, the Spanish state still has much unfinished business to deal with, particularly with regard to the victims of Francoism (Christie, 2011). The lack of mechanisms to guarantee a successful transitional justice after 1975 meant that no truth commissions were established. Instead, procedures were established in order to ensure that investigations into Franco's crimes would never take place. Any change to these mechanisms, as demanded by the Memory Movement, would require a reconfiguration of the Spanish system, that have to go deeper than just an official acknowledgement and apology for these crimes, because questions would also need to be answered about how the 'Transition' was conducted: for example, why these investigations have been postponed for so long (when they should have taken place in the 1970s), and why has Spain systematically failed to comply with international human rights laws?

Underpinning these questions is a challenge to the myth of the 'model' Transition that was transmitted to the public. Arguably, the Transition would not have been successful had it not been based on the approach taken by the 1977 Amnesty Act. However, this does not deny – or justify – the fact that those who suffered repression were forced to endure the condition of victimhood. Neither does it explain why the decisions that seemed necessary in the later 1970s have not yet been revised in any substantial way.

Under these circumstances, the Memory Movement continues to develop strategies to meet old and new challenges. As noted by Lorena, a collaborator of the ARMH in Galicia, 'our objective is to disappear. It is not to be necessary anymore. Then there will be no reason for the Association to exist. That's what we want' (Lorena, 2015). Lorena's perspective is that, once the state accepts its responsibility and commits to the completion of all exhumations, her work, and the work of the Association, would no longer be required. This position illustrates what seems to be the default perspective on what the role of the state should be. However, there is some divergence of opinions about this point. Gordillo (2015), for instance, contends that exhumations should be, in fact, a combined effort: 'the state needs to take responsibility, but I think associations should be in charge of the exhumations with the support of the state'. I would argue in favour of this position, since the modern state must take responsibility, yet cannot be trusted to resolve the crimes committed by Franco's regime.

Notes

1 The notion 'historical memory' (*memoria histórica*) describes the need to remember an aspect of the past before it is thrown into oblivion, so that the identity of the community is based on a reconciled knowledge of the past and of the ways in which that past is relevant to the present.

2 Some of the human rights violations that occurred during the dictatorship include: more than 130,000 people were executed extrajudicially; 700,000 people were held in concentration camps from 1936 to 1942; 400,000 people became political prisoners and were subjected to torture or forced labour; and 500,000 people were exiled for their political beliefs (Escudero, 2014).
3 See, for example, José Joaquín Peñarrubia's intervention in the Senate on 8 October 2015, when he claimed that 'there are no more mass graves to find, unless they insist on finding Federico García Lorca in all four cardinal points in Spain. Right now there is nowhere else to go' (Torres Reyes, 2015, my translation).
4 In addition to the wall, the Association has an online database that records the victims of Franco's repression (executions, imprisonment, fines, and so on) in the province of Salamanca (including individuals from other parts of the country who died or were imprisoned there). As of January 2016, the database had 11,624 names of victims. The Association points out that the details provided are based on the data that is available through oral testimonies, archived documents, and books, so the list may not be complete (AMJS, 2016).

References

Ackelsberg, Martha A. (2000) *Mujeres libres: el anarquismo y la lucha por la emancipación de las mujeres*, Barcelona: Virus.
Aida (2015) Interview, 17 May.
Álvaro (2015) Interview, 20 May.
AMJS (2016) 'Base de datos de víctimas', *Salamanca Memoria y Justicia*, http://salamancamemoriayjusticia.org/vic.asp [accessed 14 June 2017].
Anonymised (2015) Email Correspondence, 19 May.
Beevor, Anthony (2006) *The Battle for Spain: The Spanish Civil War 1936–1939*, London: Phoenix.
Benítez, Inés (2013) 'Victims memorial in Spain awaits names of the dead', *Inter Press Service*, online, www.ipsnews.net/2013/09/victims-memorial-in-spain-awaits-names-of-the-dead/ [accessed 27 March 2018].
Carballar, O. (2013) 'Esto no es memoria histórica, es historia. Y vamos a contar la historia de verdad de este país de una puñetera vez', *Andaluces.es*, 24 September, www.andalucesdiario.es/gente/la-gavidia-la-plaza-de-mayo-de-andalucia [accessed 14 May 2016].
Casero-Ripollés, Andreu, García Santamaría, José Vicente and Fernández-Beaumont, José (2015) 'Thee politicisation of journalism in Spain: Three obstacles to the professional autonomy of journalists', in *Anàlisi. Quaderns de Comunicació i Cultura*, Vol. 53, pp. 95–109.
Christie, Stuart (2011) 'Introduction to 1st edition by Stuart Christie: The Spanish war that never died', *The Aftermath: 75th Anniversary of Spanish Civil War (1936–2011)*, 4–5. Commemorative booklet of the Spanish Civil War by Trade Unionists in North West of England.
Cinta (2015) Interview, 19 May.
CIVIO (nd) 'Spanish investigative journalism site', https://civio.es [accessed 26 March 2018].
David (2014) Interview, 28 May.
Díaz, Paula and Requena, Ana (2011) 'El movimiento 15-M se hace más grande', in *Público*, 19 June, www.publico.es/espana/movimiento-15-m-mas-grande.html [accessed 14 May 2016].

Diego (2015) Interview, 17 May.

Doval-Avendaño, Maria Montserrat (2010) 'Information sources in the Spanish social media during the "Three Days of March"(11–13 March 2004)', in *Revista Latina de Comunicación Social*, Vol. 65, p. 325.

Elola, Joseba (2011). 'El 15-M sacude el sistema', *El País*, 22 May, http://politica.elpais.com/politica/2011/05/21/actualidad/1305999838_462379.html

Escudero, Rafael Baena (2014) 'Road to impunity: The absence of transitional justice programs in Spain', *Human Rights Quarterly*, Vol. 36, Issue: 1, pp. 123–146.

Fidalgo, Carlos (2016) 'La ARMH quiere que el cementerio del Carmen recuerde a 200 fusilados', *Diario de Léon*, www.diariodeleon.es/noticias/bierzo/armh-quiere-cementerio-carmen-recuerde-200-fusilados_1102645.html [accessed 25 March 2018].

Gerbaudo, Paolo (2017) *The Mask and the Flag: Populism, Citizenship, and Global Protest*, Oxford: Oxford University Press.

Gobo, Giampietro (2008) *Doing Ethnography*, London: Sage Publications.

Gordillo, C. (2014). Interview, 28 May.

——— (2015). Interview, 27 June.

Jones, Sam (2018) 'More than 5m join Spain's "feminist strike", unions say', *The Guardian*, online, 8 March, www.theguardian.com/world/2018/mar/08/spanish-women-give-up-work-for-a-day-in-first-feminist-strike [accessed 18 March 2018].

Leonor (2015) Interview, 19 May.

Lorena (2015) Interview, 12 May.

Madison, D. S. (2012) *Critical Ethnography: Method, Ethics and Performance*, London: Sage Publications.

Paco (2015) Interview, 24 May.

Pérez, Francisco Seoane (2006) 'Book review of *13-M: Multitudes on line*', in Sampedro, Víctor F. [editor], *Journal of Communication*, Vol. 56, pp. 218–234, International Communication Association.

Preston, Paul (2012) *The Spanish Holocaust*, London: Harper Press.

Price, Stuart (2018) 'Resistance and revolution: Working-class intransigence, the libertarian tradition, and the Catalan crisis', in Fishwick, Adam and Connolly, Heather [editors], *From Protest to Resistance: Fighting Back in Hard Times*, London: Rowman and Littlefield International.

Roberto (2015). Interview, 17 May.

Russell, Adrienne (2016) *Journalism as Activism: Recoding Media Power*, Cambridge and Malden, MA: Polity Press.

Sanz Sabido, Ruth (2016) *Memories of the Spanish Civil War: Conflict and Community in Rural Spain*, London: Rowman and Littlefield International.

Silva (2015) Interview, 19 May.

Sergi (2015) Interview, 29 May.

Thomas, Jim (1993) *Doing Critical Ethnography*, London: Sage Publications.

Torres Reyes, A. (2015). 'Un senador del PP asegura que 'ya no hay más fosas que descubrir', *El País*, 8 October, http://politica.elpais.com/politica/2015/10/08/actualidad/1444329004_489460.html [accessed 9 June 2017].

6 Global Witness and investigative journalism

Ali Hines

Introduction

On 7 July 2016, the Cambodian pro-government *Fresh News* website published an anonymous letter and an accompanying cartoon. The drawing was a doctored version of Nazi propaganda from 1943, showing Roosevelt and Churchill helping Stalin to execute a woman – who symbolised Peace – on a 'Jewish chopping block'. In the new version, the wartime leaders were replaced with logos of London-based NGO Global Witness, the *Phnom Penh Post* and the *Cambodia Daily*, with the Star of David substituted for the Cambodian flag. The accompanying letter threatened to kick both media outlets out of Cambodia (Fresh News Asia, 2016). Meanwhile on Facebook, Cambodian Prime Minister Hun Sen posted a set of photos of himself and his children raising a glass in his office – a message interpreted by many to mean, 'We don't care, we're still in power' (Global Witness, 2016a).

The production of these bizarre media gestures was in retaliation to a Global Witness report released that morning. The report, *Hostile Takeover* (Global Witness, 2016b, see below), was the result of a major investigation into the corruption that underpins Cambodia's economy. It provided the evidence for what most Cambodians suspected but could never prove – that family members of Prime Minister Hun Sen are amassing vast personal fortunes in the country's private sector. The report showed how members of the Hun family wield significant control across most of Cambodia's lucrative industries, with links to major global brands. Some of the domestic companies to which they are affiliated have been accused of a litany of abuses, including land grabbing, and violence and intimidation against local populations.

The Cambodian government is no stranger to Global Witness' campaigning – the NGO targeted the country for its very first investigation back in 1995, on the illegal timber trade. Its three Founding Directors, Patrick Alley, Charmian Gooch, and Simon Taylor, were all friends working at the Environmental Investigation Agency (EIA). The EIA pioneered investigative conservation on subjects such as the ivory trade, but it was whilst working here that it occurred to the three environmentalists that there was something missing in the international 'marketplace' of NGOs: the link between exploitation of natural resources, conflict, and corruption. It was through that prism that Global Witness came about. As co-founder Patrick explained:

> The Paris Peace Accords had been signed in 1991 and the U.N. was brokering elections in Cambodia. It was the most expensive U.N. intervention ever... Cambodia had been in a state of war for 30 odd years so it was quite a big news story. We read that timber from areas controlled by the Khmer Rouge was being traded along the border. There was very scant information.
>
> We thought, well, the rain forest is being cut down, which is bad. And the money is being used to fund possibly one of the nastiest rebel organizations ever, and a war. Why doesn't somebody stop that? And we said, 'Hell, why don't we?'
>
> (Connell, 2007)

After a short fundraising stint and eventually a grant from Oxfam Novib (Netherlands), Simon and Patrick embarked on Global Witness' very first investigation. Making an initial trip to Washington, D.C. at the recommendation of a former colleague, they followed up with contacts there and got the names of people who could help them on Cambodia. They flew to Thailand and Cambodia in January 1995 and over five weeks drove 3,500 kilometres on the Thai side of the 700-kilometer border, following every kind of road. The Khmer Rouge were just on the other side of the border. They later went to Cambodia itself, avoiding the Khmer Rouge-occupied territory. In this way, they built up a picture of how the trade worked. By posing as timber buyers they hoped that in this way people would talk to them (Connell, 2007). They did:

> The Thai loggers were amazingly talkative. It was an interesting atmosphere. They didn't seem to think they were doing anything wrong. What we managed to do was talk to the people in the Thai logging camps along the border who were directly connected by road to the Khmer Rouge operations on the other side. We got hold of documentation and managed build up a picture that showed, in the dry season, between $10 million and $20 million a month was being generated by the Khmer Rouge sale of timber to Thailand. That was the first time anybody had been able to put a figure on it.
>
> (Connell, 2007)

Aware that NGOs can often suffer reputational risk due to exaggeration or sensationalising issues, the three decided right from the start that they weren't going to do this. As Patrick explained:

> We based our figures on the minimum firm information that we knew. Where we got the information from was actual documentation that

showed a particular deal. More than anything, we talked to the Thai truck drivers who drove the logs across the border. They knew where they'd been, they knew how much timber they were bringing, and they knew how often they did it. We tried to get every piece of information verified from three independent sources. We wouldn't talk to one truck driver and believe everything he said, but if we talked to three different truck drivers, or two truck drivers and a manager, and the information coincided, then we felt pretty safe to go with what we had.

(Connell, 2007)

Working with local fixers and interpreters was crucial to their investigation, but Patrick and Simon hired translators who were either journalists or NGO people, not straightforward translators. As Patrick noted:

They were all Thai people. What you needed was not just someone to translate the language, but to give you a sense of how things were. If a situation was going to turn ugly or people were getting suspicious, we wouldn't necessarily know it, like we'd know it with a fellow Brit or an American. So it's quite useful, in fact, crucial, to have a sense of the situation.

(Connell, 2007)

Two investigations were carried out, in January and May 1995. Global Witness held press conferences both in Phnom Penh and Bangkok on 24–25 May. The border was closed on 26 May 1995, cutting off a vital source of funding to the Khmer Rouge which eventually defected to the government 18 months later when around 500 military rebel fighters joined the government army after negotiations between rebels and senior army commanders (BBC News, 1998; Connell, 2007).

Global Witness today

Over 20 years later, Global Witness has expanded its geographical reach but its mission remains the same, which is to end both the exploitation of the environment and offences against human rights, crimes that are driven by the exploitation of natural resources and corruption in the global political and economic system (Global Witness, 2016c). As Tong (2011: 5) states in her research on investigative journalism in China, the 'paradoxical nature embodied in the practices of investigative journalism comes from . . . the authoritarian nature of the regime that tames and controls the media and the adversarial nature of investigative journalism that rivals the power'. It should be noted here that the majority of states in which Global Witness carries out its investigations are either dictatorships or quasi-democracies. The organisation has therefore positioned itself as a 'public watchdog' and is increasingly focused on what is known as the 'shadow system'; that is, when deals involving natural resources are typically done behind the scenes through illegitimate means. Its main methods typically follow that of any investigative journalist, stated by de Burgh (2008: 6) as 'reporting, whistle-blowing and protection of sources, researching (or "digging") establishing proof and self-protection in an age of very sophisticated surveillance'.

In order to expose the system, the organisation often takes a 'follow the money' approach – knowing who is financing a project, who is buying the product or raw material, and who else is making the project possible. This tactic exposes who is really profiting from these deals and opens up opportunities to enact change. Global Witness believes that the only way to protect peoples' rights to land, livelihoods and a fair share of their national wealth is to demand total transparency in the resources sector, to pursue sustainable and equitable resources management, and to stop the international financial system from propping up resource-related corruption. De Burgh (2008: 5) argues that the 'boldness and brazenness of investigative journalism is to be interpreted as a function of the decline of authority of politicians and institutions'. I would also, however, argue that it is actually a challenge to effective *governance* – one that exists to serve the interest of its citizens. As Ettema and Glasser stated (1988, 1989, cited in Tong, 2011: 13), Global Witness aims to 'contribute to civic betterment by catching the attention of the public and arousing their anger through media exposure of wrongdoings or social pitfalls' and to 'inspire civil consciousness and challenge the boundaries of civil morals in order to improve society' (Tong, 2011: 14).

One frequently asked question is how the organisation decides which countries to investigate. There are a number of factors used to ensure that the most productive strategic choices are made. They include questions such as: where does Global Witness already have some leverage? Which countries and regions do key international players, such as major governments, donors, and influential companies actually care about? What is the political and strategic importance of the country? Where is the greatest opportunity to make an impact? There may be countries where, for example, a major shift in government provides an opportunity to change resource policies from the ground up. However, before moving into a country, it is also necessary to consider what the costs and risks might be, since for example starting work in a new, difficult political environment, may mean that gains are hard-won and small, compared to the benefits of continuing to work in countries that are already well known. It is also important to take account of the costs and risks of engaging in a country or region where there is a fundamental lack of stability.

On a more practical level, the ability to carry out investigations 'in-country' is crucial to any decision. Security risks have to be considered, as well as relative ease of travel, the legal environment, whether there is a story to be told and, of most importance, the needs of civil society. This last point is crucial: Global Witness's entire model of working depends on strong civil society partnerships. These can take various forms, from short-term research projects to long-term advocacy coalitions, but whatever the circumstances, it is vital to think beyond a single exposé: if abuse is to be stopped, and a healthier political environment sustained, local civil society must be involved. With no local staff or offices in-country, local people – from confidential sources to lobbyists – are essential to Global Witness' work.

The Global Witness team draws on a wide range of skills, from undercover investigations and painstaking financial research, to information gathering on the ground, and close co-operation with partners and activists all over the world. The techniques used to gather evidence include interviews, secret filming, photography, document research, and often just dogged physical presence – for example, investigators monitoring illegal timber trades sometime spend days counting logging trucks as they move across borders and through checkpoints. The final reports produced by this NGO are months and sometimes years in the making, and detailed evidence-based arguments will always provide the essential foundation for extended enquiry. This supports de Burgh's approach to investigative journalism, which he describes as:

> attempt(ing) to get at the truth where the truth is obscure because it suits others that it be so; they choose their topics from a sense of right or wrong which can only be called a moral sense, but in the manner of their research they attempt to be dispassionately evidential. They are doing more than disagreeing how society runs; they are pointing out that it is failing by its own standards. They expose, but they expose in the public interest which they define. Their efforts, if successful, alert to failures in the system and lead to politicians, lawmakers and others taking action even as they fulminate; action that may lead to regulation or legislation.
>
> (2008: 19–20)

In this sense, Global Witness goes beyond traditional journalism by not just challenging power but also strategically advocating change. As journalist Bill Moyers told the organisation:

> Global Witness is the backbone of hope for journalism. I mean fearless journalism, tough and independent journalism, journalism that in a world of increasing oligarchy will tell us the truth about money and power and the corruption that is robbing everyday people of their rights and resources. Just as importantly, Global Witness goes beyond traditional journalism by advocating and helping to deliver systems changing solutions and accountability for injustice around the world. So, yes, the backbone of hope for journalism – and our spine for the future.
>
> (Global Witness, 2016c)

Open data-gathering

The last ten years have seen huge advances in online data, and learning how to interrogate these data sets effectively is crucial to a robust investigation. One of the most commonly used data sets is company registers. Company registers and services that aggregate them, such as Open Corporates, can be used to ask conduct more powerful queries than just name searches. Questions such as, 'Who are the shareholders of all companies within a specific group?', or 'Which are the addresses at which the greatest number of companies are registered', and (if the registry has shareholder data) 'Which companies from this group have offshore shareholders?', are all useful starting-points for a serious investigation.

For example, in January 2014, the Open Knowledge Foundation and Global Witness undertook a joint investigation of company registries and tax avoidance. Using data from Companies House, they searched for Ugland House equivalents in the UK. Ugland House is a building located in the Cayman Islands to which 18,857 companies are registered which, in 2008, caused U.S. President Barack Obama to call it 'either the biggest building or the biggest tax scam on record' (Leary, 2008). Global Witness looked for contemporary equivalents to Ugland house by searching for the postcodes at which the greatest number of companies were registered. As can be seen in Table 6.1 there is one particular address (just down the road from the Global Witness office at the time, in fact) to which more companies are registered than had been the case with Ugland house.

One huge obstacle to extending this form of enquiry, however, is that many countries do not have their company records digitised. In highly corrupt societies, records are often kept in disarray and left 'un-digitised' on purpose. Digital records are much easier to monitor and audit, and it is much harder to 'lose' or alter documents for political purposes or for the right price. There is therefore a general push from campaigning groups to computerise corporate registers (including historical data) and to put these online. Meanwhile, actions taken to prevent corporate digitisation include bureaucratic foot dragging, flat refusals to turn over the information, and even (if rumours are to be believed) the covert destruction of internet IT cables.

Data from company registers can also be used to create compelling and informative visualisations of complex corporate networks, helping gain

Table 6.1 Postal codes of registered companies

Rank	Postcode	Number of companies registered at postcode
1	EC1V 4PW	28,172
2	N12 0DR	11,331
3	B18 6EW	9,301
4	WA1 1RG	8,598
5	SW1Y 5EA	7,709

insight into how different individuals and groups connect. Of course, this also raises the questions as to the real meaning of open data. Due to the multifarious uses and abuses of the term 'open', it can sometimes be difficult to understand precisely what a government means when it says that it will 'open' a given piece of information. The Open Definition states that data is open when it fulfils the requirements of *legal*[1] and *technical*[2] openness (Open Definition, 2016; my emphasis).

Data- and text-mining

Text mining is now used regularly by journalists to explore and analyse large collections of documents. In fact, it is hard to imagine how some of the big scoops over the last few years would even have broken without text mining. The WikiLeaks diplomatic cables, for instance, consisted of 251,287 files (WikiLeaks, 2013) and the MPs expenses scandal involved 700,000 documents (*The Guardian*, 2009). Without the help of computational tools for identifying significant bits of information, it would have been impossible for the major news outlets to carry any meaningful analysis of these stories. In the past, text mining was primarily used by geneticists and by those sometimes disparagingly referred to as 'techies' and 'geeks'. However, there are now some simple online and offline tools for performing powerful analysis into the affairs of large corporations. Text mining can be especially useful, for example, when looking for specific entities over large collections of documents; identifying specific types of data within large volumes of text (e.g., places, people, and organisations); and looking for trends and patterns in data sets (e.g., the output of the social media accounts of a network of investigative targets).

The extraction of data from interactive maps published by governments and other organisations – also known as data-scraping – can also be a useful tool. Global Witness' Democratic Republic of Congo (DRC) Conflict Minerals teams were able to scrape data from government maps that contained a huge amount of information on artisanal mines in Eastern DR Congo. The organisation was able to pull the data into simple spreadsheets that could be saved and applied on the ground by the campaign team in question. They also found useful information on the relative frequency of armed groups at the mining sites. This process has another advantage, allowing the user to keep a snapshot of information at a particular time so that later changes can be noted.

Case study: 'No Safe Haven'

The 'No Safe Haven' campaign, or 'Mansions' campaign as it was known internally, was launched during the summer of 2015 and is one of the few UK-focused campaigns that Global Witness has undertaken. It emerged as a result of the work the organisation had carried out in countries such as Libya, Cambodia, and Afghanistan. Teams in-country had realised that most of the people being investigated (officials, and their associates and families) all had links to the West, usually via the possession of a house, bank accounts, or other assets. An interview was conducted with the lead campaigner, specifically for this chapter, in order fully to understand the rationale for the campaign and how it was carried out.

> It was a consistent constant element that all the campaigns we worked on at some point – whoever the kleptocratic group was in charge – they would create these havens for themselves in the West. And the point of creating the havens in the West, buying up property and buying up assets, as well as finding ways to get visas or passports – part of the reason for that was to launder money, but the other part was to create this better life for them and their family which could also often result in the laundering of a reputation, so you could, for example, pitch yourself as an international business person in some way.
> (Mansions Campaigner, interview with author, 2016)

The majority of places that were being used as these so-called safe havens were typically property targets or holiday destinations for the elite – cities such as London, New York, Sydney, and Miami. The rationale for focusing on London was for both legal and practical reasons. Not only is Global Witness physically located there, but a large number of the necessary contacts with available leads were also based in the capital. Global Witness was familiar with the legal and governance systems, and the UK government had already started begun to recognise this problem. This was due in part to a substantial amount of work on the beneficial ownership of companies – since the existence of anonymous companies was an inherent part of the 'safe havens' problem – which Global Witness had undertaken in 2013. As the Mansions campaigner explains, it also brought home the problem of a corrupt global network to a new domestic audience:

> There were quite a few Global Witness campaigns where people knew about this (problem) but it wasn't quite relevant enough to incorporate into the campaign. And also importantly, where it came from was a recognition that there are only so many pressure points in-country, and you come in as an outsider and try and campaign for change, but if you come across consistent blocks you have difficulty making the same argument. Meanwhile if you set the premise that people are only going to steal if they have somewhere to hide it, then your target of the West of being a safe haven is a really strong one and somewhere we can get a lot of traction . . . you know that corruption is a huge issue that affects everyone and is ruining lives but is seen as quite a technical issue that's far away, and so this is really saying that corruption is something that affects people here day to day.
> (Mansions Campaigner, 2016)

Global Witness was initially approached by a source who had access to a database of some of the most expensive properties in London. Whilst it was decided not to use that particular database, it demonstrated that it was possible to buy up enough records to start an investigation. The first step was therefore to buy up a land registry database containing 2,600 of the most expensive properties in London, in the areas that are known to be popular with corrupt officials, such as Knightsbridge and Chelsea, and subsequently to reach out to particular sources. Global Witness came across a technical challenge with the land registry titles: having initially thought that the focus would be on these most expensive properties in London, it turned out that land registry titles were held by a company which classified them as commercial – often simply office buildings – rather than residential property. Working with the communications team, the campaign honed in on one specific type of property.

> From a messaging point of view, we decided it was really important, if we wanted to get the British public and politicians to care, it was easier if we focused on things like mansions, luxury houses, because that's what gets people excited in a way that a big office building in the centre of town doesn't.
>
> (Mansions Campaigner, 2016)

It was also known from previous investigations that most corrupt individuals own property through a company rather than in their own name, so leads had to be combined. As the Mansions campaigner explained:

> You couldn't just buy the most expensive [property records] – you had to buy some expensive [property records] and then just go around identifying which were residences and buy up that address. It was a lot of footwork – we used a team of five volunteers to go out to very specific areas and buy up the records of really posh squares but make sure that it was actually a home, it would make a good story, we could find the links.
>
> (2016)

This presented some serious challenges – the most suspect properties were owned by anonymous companies, which made it very difficult to produce any kind of statistical analysis based on the database. To overcome this, all the details held on any property including specific individuals involved were run through the LexisNexis database Worldcheck. As the Mansions campaigner noted:

> So if you're taking on any crime you would use Worldcheck as due diligence, and we negotiated a free trial of Worldcheck for two weeks, and narrowed these 2600 properties down to 129 red-flag hits based on

what we could see from this superficial information, then from these 129 we used a team of five volunteers to start looking online for other links between these properties and other dodgy people, figuring out which regions they're associated with and anything else you could find out about them.

(2016)

One of the most effective ways to gain further information was through pertinent public documents such as council planning documents and the electoral roll. This information was triangulated through compiling knowledge of the community through discussions with other NGOs, journalists, and other sources, as well as physical footwork in the relevant areas. What became clear was that this was an issue that a large number of people knew about and were incensed about, but the information had never been pulled together, creating a backlog of data to compile and investigate.

Due to very limited resources, Global Witness decided to work in a coalition with other organisations interested in the same issue. Transparency International took the lead in compiling statistics and developing a policy. Global Witness led on the investigation and regularly shared information on case studies. The two organisations coordinated to release a final report. For both organisations, it was not only the research that had proved to be challenging, but the 'messaging' also:

> From our point of view, the reason that we focused on London property – our ultimate aim is to stop people from physically entering but we knew again that from a story perspective, that if we talked about houses and mansions that people get interested and understand it immediately, and then we hoped to transition to a conversation about visas and passports and asylum, but treading very, very carefully, because we don't want – especially as the world is tending towards more right-wing approach – you don't want to stoke any kind of xenophobic attitude towards foreigners, so that was probably the biggest challenge for us. There was a real opportunity for us, in terms of the fact that this campaign draws on a lot of the kind of Brexity, *Daily Mail* [type stories], and so one of the biggest challenges has been finding a way to use that responsibly, and to illustrate that there's almost two sets of rules – if you're a princeling, if your Dad was a President and he murders people and he oppressed and he stole millions from the state budget, you could still have access to the UK – you can fly in, in your private jet, get access to this mansion, hire fancy lawyers, hire a fancy real estate agent, find yourself a good bank, and you get treated pretty well, you're almost untouchable. Meanwhile, for someone who comes in who's been persecuted by a regime like that, you run up against all these kinds of legal hurdles, so whilst we're not saying foreigners are bad, we're trying to say that there seems to be one set of rules for this corrupt elite because

they've got money and pensions, and meanwhile we're persecuting a set of people who really deserve to be given a safe haven.

(Mansions Campaigner, 2016)

Channel 4 was also involved in its own undercover investigation into the issue of corrupt money and real estate, but it lacked the research bases. Global Witness was therefore able to negotiate with the channel, exchanging libel-checked research for a certain amount of air-time within the Channel 4 documentary. Transparency International released its report, 'Corruption on Your Doorstep' in March 2015, which outlined the problem, followed by the Global Witness investigative report, 'Mystery on Baker Street' in July 2015. Channel 4 followed up by airing its programme a week later (Channel 4, 2015). Then, on 28 July 2015, Prime Minister David Cameron announced a policy that Global Witness had been be calling for, stating that the UK government would take specific steps to stop corrupt money from entering the UK's property market (Wintour, 2015). As the Mansions campaigner stated, 'It was a combination of luck, the media stories all being coordinated, public attitude being ready, political appetite being ready, but being really strategic about who we worked with' (2016). The campaign also supported what de Burgh (2000: 9) recognised as 'one of the most important fields for inquiry . . . public administration at the local level, where huge amounts of money are expended, all citizens are involved and opportunities for corruption frequent, in no matter what society'.

Case study: 'Rubber Barons'

The 'Rubber Barons' (2013) investigation was Global Witness' first investigation on land grabs and focused on two of Vietnam's largest rubber companies: the state-owned Vietnam Rubber Group (VRG) and the private Hoang Anh Gia Lai (HAGL). Large-scale rubber plantations are the biggest driver of land grabs and deforestation across the Mekong region, and the investigation was a natural progression from the organisation's historic work on illegal logging in Cambodia and Myanmar (Burma).

Both VRG and HAGL have established rubber plantations in Vietnam, but due to a lack of available land had, over the last ten years, expanded into neighbouring Cambodia and Laos. Their impact is great: each company and their affiliates were believed to own, respectively, a total of 362,000 hectares (ha) and 81,000 ha of rubber alone in Cambodia and Laos (Global Witness, 2013: 42–43). Both Cambodia and Laos have strong laws protecting indigenous land and forests, but these laws are routinely flouted by both companies and corrupt government officials. VRG and HAGL are no exception – their subsidiary companies operating in various provinces have routinely stolen farming land from ethnic communities and have cleared previously untouched forest (see the image of a villager resting in the shade of a felled tree in Figure 6.1). These land grab cases were not new and had

Figure 6.1 A villager rests in the shade of a felled tree inside a HAGL subsidiary company's rubber concession in Cambodia in 2013. Communities often know nothing about the deals struck for their land until the bulldozers arrive to start clearing.

Photograph: Global Witness (2013).

been well publicised by the domestic media, but what had not been realised was that all these case studies and companies were linked via the ownership of Vietnam's two rubber company giants. This approach also highlights an issue recognised by de Burgh (2008: 9) whereby 'investigative journalism is very much needed out in the provinces where state power in particular is hardly regulated'.

Unlike many other developing countries, Cambodia has extensive open data on its land investments. This has been compiled as part of the Open Definition website which describes itself as 'an online hub compiling freely available data in a 'one-stop shop' . . . [providing] the public with up-to-date, accurate information about Cambodia and its economic and social development' (Open Definition, 2016). Twelve subsidiary companies in total belonging to VRG and HAGL, which were known to be problematic plantations, were selected for field research. Global Witness has built up a network of trusted field researchers over the years, most of whom have journalistic or investigative backgrounds. All field research is conducted undercover due to the security risk, with researchers often working under the guise of research students or journalists. This is particularly the case in Cambodia, where we are officially banned from entering the country. A qualitative social science methodology was used to assess the impacts of the plantations (both positive and negative) and a list of guiding interview questions provided to, and discussed with the field researcher, who also made other suggestions based on his local knowledge. It was also important that ethical standards were followed and to ensure that women and minorities were also interviewed separately and given an individual voice.

In the case of 'Rubber Barons', the field researcher not only interviewed the affected communities but also spoke to local government officials, and current and previous company staff, including individuals who had worked on the sawmills inside the company concession. Many of these interviews strongly indicated links between VRG in particular and Cambodia's premier logging syndicate, through alleged signed contracts with companies and individuals well-known by communities to be involved in the prolific logging of rare wood species. In addition to interviews and eyewitness accounts, the researcher also took aesthetically compelling photographs of deforestation and illegal logging, as well as more evidence-based photographs of, for example, complaint letters sent to the local authorities, stamped logs stacked inside concessions, and trucks of timber leaving the concession. GPS points of the concession boundaries were also taken, which were used both as evidence of the location, but also for mapping purposes. In order to assess the extent of protected forest clearance, as well as other types of illegal logging, Global Witness created a number of maps. The first maps for both VRG and HAGL were created through layering the concession boundaries over LANDSAT 7 imagery and government-produced forest cover of evergreen, semi-evergreen and deciduous forest (Global Witness, 2013: 17). This showed how the concessions had been allocated from what should be legally protected forest. A second set of maps was created by layering concession boundaries over satellite imagery, both prior to the concessions being allocated, and afterwards: this showed forest clearance both in and outside the concession boundaries in a compelling format (Global Witness, 2013: 18).

For VRG, research on the company address, and the addresses of where the subsidiary companies were registered, unearthed a web of relationships with the Cambodian government. Research showed, for example, that the company was operating out of a prestigious Phnom Penh property owned by Land Management Minister Im Chhun Lim. Nineteen companies were registered at this address, eight of which belonged to VRG (Global Witness, 2013: 30). This was ascertained through an analysis of Ministry of Commerce registration information and the Ministry of Agriculture, Forestry and Fisheries Economic Land Concession database. As an end note, it should be noted here that Global Witness' previous and in-depth research of illegal logging and the timber syndicate in Cambodia provided an extensive evidence base from which to conduct this part of the research.

Research on the financial backing of companies

As well as conducting field research on the social, environmental, and governance impacts of VRG and HAGL's rubber plantations, Global Witness also wanted to uncover who was financing these companies. The campaign was, in fact, designed as a segue into a wider China/Asia-focused campaign and it was suspected that the majority of investors would be Vietnamese and Chinese private equity funds. The research, however, told a different story. Most of the finance research was nothing more sophisticated than a deep Google search, starting with HAGL's annual company report, broker reports, and the stock exchanges on which HAGL and VRG's equitised subsidiary companies were listed. Using a trusted contact who works in the finance sector, Global Witness was also able to acquire the shareholder registries for both HAGL and VRG, although this was still limited as it only showed those investors who were required to disclose their shares under certain financial standards. The Global Witness Land Campaigner (Rubber) revealed that:

> Trying to get a full list of all the companies' shareholders was probably the most time-consuming piece of the research. It proved almost impossible to get a fully comprehensive list of 100% of the investors, in part due to Vietnamese law which only requires investors investing in over 5% of a company's shares to be disclosed. . . . And once we knew which stock exchange the companies were listed on – so in this case the Professional Securities Market, which is like the unregulated little brother of the main London Stock Exchange – we hired some pro-bono lawyers to look at the type of equity listing and what it meant from a regulatory and disclosure oversight and what that could mean for us in terms of leverage. Worryingly, there are so few requirements for companies listed on the Professional Securities Market, which meant that HAGL wasn't actually in breach of anything. Which is shocking.
>
> (2016)

The research on the financial investors turned up not only a number of Vietnamese equity funds, but also some more familiar global names, with the likes of Deutsche Bank, Credit Suisse, Goldman Sachs, and the International Finance Corporation (IFC) – the private lending arm of the World Bank.

> When we found all these Western links through the investors, it was great in terms of the potential for capturing people's attention, but it also made the story really complicated as we had so many actors involved, so many big names, which both the field research and the desk research had thrown up. So with the investors we decided to focus both on Deutsche Bank – in part because it had already had its wrist slapped for financing land grabs in the past, but also because it attaches certain

standards to its lending – and the International Finance Corporation, as it also has pretty rigorous environmental and social standards. Because of course its mandate is to help alleviate poverty, and this investment was in direct contravention to that as well as its own standards.

(Land Campaigner [Rubber], 2016)

One advantage of conducting lengthy desktop searches is that the research often brings up unexpected finds. In this case, Global Witness came across HAGL's Confidential Circular Offering (a type of company prospectus for a bond or other type of security) as part of its Initial Public Offering on the London Stock Exchange. In this document HAGL admitted that a number of its operations were illegal, stating that, 'Certain of our existing projects are being developed without necessary government approvals, permits or licenses and development and operation of certain projects are not fully in compliance with applicable laws and regulations' (Global Witness, 2013: 35). As the Land Campaigner (Rubber) explained:

> This was a gem of a find as it not only served as formal written admittance directly from the company itself of its illegal wrongdoings, but it meant we could also use it in our meetings with HAGL investors in discussions after the report and say to them, 'This went out to all investors prior to HAGL listing – did you read it? If not, why not?' And to really press them on their due diligence processes on the companies they were financing.
>
> (2016)

Global Witness also looked at other actors involved such as the service providers, researching as to whether, for example, HAGL's auditor, Ernst & Young, was in contravention of any relevant laws such as the UK Bribery Act, through HAGL potentially profiting from illegal logging. Other commercial pressure points were also explored such as HAGL's partnership with Arsenal Football Club. HAGL Chairman Nguyen Duc had set up his own football club – HAGL FC – and had made a partnership with Arsenal FC on a joint academy and advertising deals (Arsenal Football Club, 2007): HAGL was given the official merchandising rights for Arsenal in Vietnam. 'We looked at FIFA and FA standards and regulations to see if Arsenal was in breach of any of them through its partnership with HAGL but concluded that the links were too tenuous with little chance of a positive outcome' (Land Campaigner [Rubber], November 2016).

The final report placed VRG and HAGL's operations in Cambodia and Laos within the context of the legal frameworks designed to protect indigenous land rights and forests, and its discourse focused on the risk for investors, diverting from the moral and ethical arguments often made by NGOs. As de Burgh (2008: 6) states, 'law shapes both the methods employed (and the editorial agenda) pursued by investigative journalists', and in this case

152 *Ali Hines*

Figure 6.2 Villagers walk through recently cleared forest inside a HAGL rubber plantation in Cambodia in 2013.

Photograph: Global Witness (2013).

the key concept of 'public interest' was promoted both through the use of persuasive and accurate, but also legally admissible evidence.

The impact was significant, with HAGL's share price dropping 6% on the day of the report (although the cause and effect of this outcome cannot be certain) (Lewis, 2013). Following subsequent meetings with the companies' investors, and little progress made by the companies to improve their operations, a number of investors divested from HAGL and VRG. This included Deutsche Bank, which was investing via Duxton Asset Management, a third-party fund. Our Land Campaigner (Rubber) noted that:

> We praised Deutsche Bank for doing the right thing and put out a press release saying as much. However, what we didn't check – and this was a mistake on our behalf – was its other investments, and in fact whilst the bank was divesting from HAGL through one branch, it was actually investing even more in the company through one of its passive investment funds.
>
> (2016)

Global Witness continues to work with civil society in Cambodia to try to get redress for the communities affected by the HAGL and VRG's rubber plantations and has managed to stop significant loans being given to HAGL through confidential work with investors, whilst HAGL itself continues to operate under the rubric of 'business-as-usual'.

Optimising desk research

The 'Rubber Barons' case study as outlined previously is a good example of simple but effective desktop research. Google Advanced Search is an easy-to-use but often overlooked method of finding information online that is difficult to find through websites. The following represent a number of generic practical examples used by Global Witness in its investigations:

site: this allows the user to restrict their search to a given domain, e.g., site:http://sec.gov. This will not only show pages that are listed on the website itself, but any files and pages that have been left up on the servers on the domain (intentionally or unintentionally). It is also very helpful when searching sites that don't have site search functionality or where it has been poorly implemented.

filetype: this enables the user to restrict their search to particular kind of files, e.g., filetype:pdf. This can be useful when used in combination with 'site' as companies sometimes upload presentations or PDFs to their web servers which are not intended for public consumption and are not linked from their main website. It is also a technique for finding archived press releases and documents.

inurl: allows the user to search for sites where specific terms appear in the URL, e.g., inurl:pub. This is especially useful for LinkedIn, as it lets you return only results that contain publicly accessible information.

Case study: 'Hostile Takeover'

In 2015, a Global Witness source in Cambodia approached the organisation saying that they had scraped the Cambodian corporate registry and were currently holding – in spreadsheet form – all the data for all the companies in Cambodia. The Cambodian corporate registry was already publicly available and had recently been updated by the Ministry of Commerce. However, the upgrade had involved the creation of a secure log-in where the user had to register an email address. This was highly problematic in the context of civil society repression, and cyber-surveillance, and meant that the government was able to monitor who was using it and for what purposes. The result of this was that activists and journalists deemed it too dangerous to use. Having access to the full dataset therefore provided an opportunity for Global Witness. In an interview conducted with the Land Campaigner (Cambodia) for the purpose of this chapter, they explained how the investigation evolved:

> The original idea was to take that data and turn it into something that we (Global Witness) hosted, fully secure and that added some really

good search functions so that the information was a lot more useable, so that's where it began and then we began building the database from the spreadsheets. The reason for wanting to produce a story was to drive traffic to the Cambodia corporates database, you know, we thought 'GW launches database' is not going to get covered by anyone but if we could tell a really compelling story with the database, not only would it get media coverage and drive traffic but it would also be an example to civil society and journalists of what can be done with data which initially looks very dry.

(Land Campaigner, 2016)

Options for two different stories were discussed, the first being an investigation into Prime Minister Hun Sen and his family, and all the companies they had interests in either directorships or chairmanships or shareholdings. The second considered was a broader story looking at the Council of Ministers (the Cambodian Cabinet) and investigating how many business holdings they had between them. It soon became clear which story would have the most impact.

In Cambodia they obviously don't declare all of their business interests but the impunity level is so high they do declare a lot of them, so it was very easy to open those original spreadsheets, for example, and search for the word 'Hun' or 'Hun Mana' [Hun Sen's eldest daughter] and then you could immediately see in seconds that she came up 20–30 times. So it was quite obvious quite quickly that that could have been a good story. We ended up hiring a freelance journalist to do the work and within the first day he was meant to do an initial shallow sweep looking at the potential for those two stories and it became clear very quickly that the better story was going to be on Hun Sen and his family.

(Land Campaigner, 2016)

The broader human rights situation in Cambodia, as well as Global Witness' status in-country, made this a particularly high-risk investigation. Hun Sen's ruling party was thought to have lost the election in 2013, but alleged electoral fraud meant they scraped through to victory (The Economist, 2013). An increase in the crackdown on civil society and anti-state sentiment online was described as 'a cyber-war team trawling online to see what people are saying and then they take law suits and defamation suits and arrest people' (Land Campaigner [Cambodia], 2016), who went on to explain the risk for Global Witness and its partners undertook this particular investigation:

Obviously being GW it adds a whole new level of risk because we were thrown out of Cambodia in 2007 and have a persona non grata status there, so, for example, we never communicate with people in Cambodia from a Global Witness email address, we take a lot of security concerns, so in terms of this investigation, the only person that was involved was the source, and then when we were doing (the report) we were really careful not to even use a graphic designer or a printer in Cambodia. When we released Family Trees in 2007 even the graphic designer got death threats, so we went to the Khmer diaspora in (Washington) DC and did all the translation there and design.

(2016)

Hours after the 'Hostile Takeover' report was launched, three of Hun Sen's children came out on Facebook and criticised the report, accusing Global Witness of being politically motivated and trying to influence an election, despite local elections being 11 months away from the launch of the report and the national election still two years away. The online 'Nazi' propaganda, noted at the start of this chapter, soon followed.

Three days later, at 9 a.m. on Saturday 9 July in a petrol station in Phnom Penh, Khem Lay – a well-known Cambodian political commentator and activist – was murdered. According to Dara et al. (2016), the suspected gunman claimed the killing was a dispute over money but others have labelled it a political assassination. Calling the killing 'highly alarming', the UN Special Rapporteur on the Rights to Freedom and Assembly Maina Kiai also hinted at the possibility of state involvement. Ley had recently made comments to the local media about the Hun family's business interests as exposed by Global Witness. 'Circumstances are plainly suspicious given his standing as a critic of the government and his recent comments in the media about the Global Witness report on the Prime Minister's family's business empire', Kiai said. 'There needs to be an urgent, thorough and independent investigation into the murder' (Dara et al., 2016). Global Witness (2016d) also released a statement calling for an investigation, but noted murderers in Cambodia's 'long history' of killings of political, human rights and labour activists were 'rarely brought to justice'.

As Shultz (1998, cited in Tong, 2011: 5) argues, investigative journalism in the West is thought to be a major contribution of the press to democracy and the cornerstone of democracy. The situation, however, is different in countries such as Cambodia, as it is above all an authoritarian country, rather than a democratic one. Waisbord states that investigative journalism is crucial to democracy, not only because it is connected to the 'logic of checks and balances' in democratic societies, monitoring powerful individuals and institutions such as government bodies and corporations, but also because it helps nurture an informed citizenry, which enables to public to hold government accountable through political participation such as voting (2001, cited in Tong, 2011: 11).

Despite the continued levels of impunity of Hun Sen and his cronies in the authoritarian state of Cambodia, such reporting is crucial in challenging authority and to expose cracks in a landscape of censorship. As a non-Cambodian organisation, Global Witness' reporting also contributes to notions of the 'public sphere'. As de Burgh (2008): 106) points out, as investigative journalism 'upholds people's right to know about controversial issues and events through media exposure, it is central to debates about the public sphere'. In the wider context of media censorship in Cambodia, any public interest reporting contributes to the public sphere as a 'stage', that is 'international in its reach, in which profound (economic and) ideological struggles are played out about who controls and decides to expose information' and 'who the information speaks on behalf of' (de Burgh, 2008: 106).

Conclusion: investigative journalism in a corrupt democracy

These are interesting and challenging times for investigative journalism. Both the ways in which news is being gathered and the ways in which it is being reported and communicated is changing rapidly. As Bradley (2016) argues, in the UK, the state of investigative journalism is fairly strong but its form is changing. On the one hand, traditional media outlets such as *The Telegraph* and Channel 4 are committing resource to the work of investigation. On the other hand, the *Guardian* has just cut its entire investigative journalism team in order to cut costs, while 'traditional heavyweights' such as 'Panorama' and 'Dispatches' are moving towards more consumer, issue-based documentaries rather than hard-hitting investigations (Bradley, 2016). These are often cheaper, less risky and guarantee strong audience figures. One advantage of this, however, is that it leaves a gap for organisations such as Global Witness and Greenpeace, particularly when it comes to environmental investigations and the typical 'follow the money' approach. In the United States, investigative journalism has become a sector in itself: as Oldroyd (2016) states, at the last count, there were 150 non-for-profit investigative journalistic organisations operating there, compared to less than half a dozen in the UK, due to the difference in philanthropic attitudes in the two countries.

A more imminent challenge is the landscape in which investigative journalists now have to operate. At the time of writing this chapter, Donald Trump had recently been voted President-Elect of the United States following one of the most bitter elections in U.S. history. Trump had just appointed climate change denier and attorney general of the oil- and gas-intensive state of Oklahoma, Scott Pruett, as head of the Environmental Protection Agency and Exxon CEO Rex Tillerson to be Secretary of State. Under Tillerson, Exxon deliberately misled the public over the threats of climate change and is under investigation by the New York Attorney General (Barrett and Philips, 2016). Meanwhile, in North Dakota, months-long protests continue around the controversial Dakota Access oil pipeline scheduled to pass by sacred Native American land belonging to the Standing Rock Sioux tribe. As Levin (2016) states, the protests have become an international rallying cry for indigenous rights and climate change activism. A small victory had just been won – on 4 December 2016 it was reported that the U.S. Army Corps of Engineers was denied a permit for the construction of a key section of the Dakota Access Pipeline (Rott and Peralta, 2016). Yet the Trump administration has given the project the go-ahead. The pipeline is just one amongst dozens of conflicts of interest and personal affiliations associated with Trump's presidency which have made the headlines. Herein lies the problem: as Chayes (2016) states, 'networks that weave together public officials and business magnates have rewritten our legislation to serve their own interests', whilst quasi-independent institutions such as oversight organisations and courts have been 'deliberately disabled – starved of operating funds or left understaffed'. Whilst these are not practices which can be defined as illegal, they 'clearly cross the line to the unethical, the inappropriate, or the objectively corrupt have been defended by those who cast themselves as bulwarks of reason and integrity' (Chayes, 2016).

The problem does not just lie in the United States: a recent report from Counter Balance (2016: 4) states that one of the principal issues to have emerged from their collective analysis on European public financing institutions is that 'many practices that enable institutional capture and that the public has historically viewed as "corrupt" are actually fully legal under current legislative frameworks in Europe'. They go on to argue that 'such "legal corruption" is the subject of extensive analysis within academic and activist circles, particularly in the global South, but is rarely discussed within mainstream policy circles in the North'. The challenge, therefore, is to push the definition of corruption beyond the officially acknowledged and legally defined crimes of bribes, money-laundering and fraud and to expose the deterioration of our democratic societies undertaken through other legal means which promote the anti-social gains of a few.

Notes

1 Legal openness requires that there is no legal restriction on how you used a piece of information beyond the need to attribute the source. Open data will generally have an open licence applied to it.
2 Technical openness requires that the information is made available in a machine-readable form. Data is machine-readable if your machine can process it. For example, Excel files are machine readable, and so are CSV files. However, a PDF is not technically open despite this fact that governments and companies regularly release transparency data in this form.

References

Arsenal Football Club (2007) 'Gunners announce deal with Vietnamese football club', March, www.arsenal.com/news/ news-archive/gunners-announce-deal-with-vietnamese-club.

Barrett, Paul and Philips, Matthew (2016) 'Can ExxonMobil be found liable for misleading the public on climate change?' Bloomberg, 7 September, www.bloomberg.

com/news/articles/2016-09-07/will-exxonmobil-have-to-pay-for-misleading-the-public-on-climate-change.

BBC News (1998) 'World: Asia-Pacific Khmer Rouge guerrillas surrender', *BBC News*, 5 December, http://news.bbc.co.uk/1/hi/world/asia-pacific/228447.stm.

Bradley, Jane (2016) *New Kids on the Block in Investigative Journalism*, Event held at the Frontline Club, London, 13 October, Recording, https://soundcloud.com/greenpeace-energydesk/event-new-kids-on-the-block-in-investigative-journalism.

Chayes, Sarah (2016) 'It was a corrupt election: It's time we realized it', *Foreign Policy*, 6 December, https://foreignpolicy.com/2016/12/06/it-was-a-corruption-election-its-time-we-realized-it-trump-united-states.

Connell, Christopher (2007) 'Q&A with Patrick Alley, co-founder of global witness, winner of the 2007 commitment to development ideas in action award', Center for Global Development, 17 December, www.cgdev.org/article/qa-patrick-alley-co-founder-global-witness-winner-2007-commitment-development-ideas-action.

Counter Balance (2016) 'Corrupt but legal: Institutionalised corruption and development finance', December.

Dara, Mech, Chheng, Niem, Samean, Lay and Turton, Shaun (2016) 'Longtime rights champion Kem Ley gunned down in broad daylight', *Phnom Penh Post*, 10 July, www.phnompenhpost.com/national/longtime-rights-champion-kem-ley-gunned-down-broad-daylight.

De Burgh, Hugo (2008) *Investigative Journalism: Context and Practice*, London and New York: Routledge.

The Economist (2013) 'Feeling cheated', 29 July, www.economist.com/blogs/banyan/2013/07/cambodias-election.

Fresh News Asia website (Khmer language version), 7 July 2016, http://m.freshnewsasia.com/index.php/en/28418-2016-07-08-00-23-50.html.

Global Witness (2013) *Rubber Barons: How Vietnamese Companies and International Financiers Are Driving a Land-Grabbing Crisis in Cambodia and Laos*, London: Global Witness.

—— (2015) *Mystery on Baker Street*, London: Global Witness.

—— (2016a) 'We don't care, we're still in power', *Global Witness Blog*, 31 August, www.globalwitness.org/en/blog/we-dont-care-we-are-still-power/.

—— (2016b) *Hostile Takeover: How Cambodia's Ruling Family Are Pulling the Strings on the Economy and Amassing Vast Personal Fortunes with Extreme Consequences for the Population*, London: Global Witness.

—— (2016c) 'Global witness: About us', www.globalwitness.org/en/about-us/.

—— (2016d) 'Global witness strongly condemns today's murder of a Cambodian political activist', *Global Witness*, press release, 10 July, www.globalwitness.org/en/press-releases/global-witness-strongly-condemns-todays-murder-cambodian-political-activist/.

The Guardian (2009) 'MPs' expenses: The Guardian launches major crowdsourcing experiment'. 23 June, www.theguardian.com/gnm-press-office/crowdsourcing-mps-expenses.

Land Campaigner (Cambodia) (2016) Interview with the author, 18 November.

Land Campaigner (Rubber) (2016) Interview with the author, 18 November.

Leary, Alex (2008) 'Obama targets Cayman "Tax Scam"', *Politifact*, 9 January, www.politifact.com/truth-o-meter/article/2008/jan/09/obama-targets-cayman-islands-tax-scam/.

Levin, Sam (2016) 'Dakota access pipeline: The who, what and why of the standing rock protests', *The Guardian*, 3 November, www.theguardian.com/us-news/2016/nov/03/north-dakota-access-oil-pipeline-protests-explainer.

Lewis, Simon (2013) '"Rubber Baron" rejects global witness report', *Cambodia Daily*, 16 May, www.cambodiadaily.com/archives/vietnams-rubber-baron-rejects-global-witness-report-24471/.

Mansions Campaigner (2016) Interview with the author, 18 November.

Oldroyd, Rachel (2016) *New Kids on the Block in Investigative Journalism*, Event held at the Frontline Club, London, 13 October, Recording, https://soundcloud.com/greenpeace-energydesk/event-new-kids-on-the-block-in-investigative-journalism.

Open Definition (2016) http://opendefinition.org/Open Development Cambodia, http://archive.opendevelopmentcambodia.net/about/background/.

Rott, Nathan and Peralta, Eyder (2016) 'In victory for protesters, army halts construction on Dakota pipeline', *National Public Radio*, 4 December, www.npr.org/sections/thetwo-way/2016/12/04/504354503/army-corps-denies-easement-for-dakota-access-pipeline-says-tribal-organization.

Tong, Jingrong (2011) *Investigative Journalism in China: Journalism, Power and Society*, London: Bloomsbury Publishing.

Transparency International (2015) *Corruption on Your Doorstep: How Corrupt Capital Is Used to Buy Property in the UK*, London: Transparency International.

WikiLeaks (2013) 'Full set of cables to be released over months', 15 November, https://wikileaks.org/gifiles/docs/10/1045448_wikileaks-full-set-of-cables-to-be-released-over-months-.html.

Wintour, Patrick (2015) 'David Cameron vows to fight against "dirty money" in UK property market', 28 July, www.theguardian.com/politics/2015/jul/28/david-cameron-fight-dirty-money-uk-property-market-corruption.

7 Violence and impunity in Rio de Janeiro's favelas
Citizens, smartphones, and police malpractice

Fernanda Amaral

Introduction: mediating the Brazilian favelas

In November 2010, a series of violent acts, coordinated by criminal factions in several parts of Rio de Janeiro, Brazil, left more than 37 people dead and over 100 burnt-out vehicles in the streets. The gangsters' ability to maintain their income from drugs and extortion, had been challenged by the appearance of the Police Pacification Units (in Portuguese, the UPPs), a force that, since 2008, had regularly carried out raids on the favelas (districts known for their extreme poverty and deprivation). In this case, the State Security Department had decided to takeover the notorious Complexo do Alemão – a neighbourhood in the north of Rio, and supposedly the epicentre of the criminal underworld – in a mega-operation supported by the Army and Navy.

This action attracted attention because the Complexo do Alemão was known as one of the strongest bastions of drug dealing. As Abreu explained (2013) the explosion of violence in this district in the 1990s, confirmed its reputation in the mainstream media as a place of ill repute:

> magazines and television shows demonstrate the gradual deterioration of the territory, which was called, for example, 'the city of trafficking' and a 'complex of favelas known for explosions of violence' (Veja, 1994), and four years later, as a 'bunker of organized crime', (Istoé, 1998); then as the 'most violent place in Rio . . . with the largest amount of illegal weaponry in the city' (Rede Record, 2008); and finally, at the time of its retaking by the Police, an 'area dominated by fear' (Rede Globo), 'heart of the carioca evils [the] most violent place in the world' and even 'hell'.
>
> (Epoca) (Abreu, 2013: 35, my translation)

Historically, the favelas have always suffered from poverty and abandonment. Since the early days of their emergence, the extensive urban space they occupy, and their population density, are inversely proportionate to the attention they receive from the government, the mainstream media and

Brazilian society as a whole. Lack of interest in the fate of their fellow citizens is, perhaps, the natural consequence of the first two forms of neglect in the political and media spheres. The fact is that for more than a century, the favela, although a vibrant centre of public life, has had no place in politics – except during elections, when candidates step into the slums promising improvements in exchange for votes and then disappear, returning in four years to garner votes for new elections (Ribeiro, 2014). Media coverage of community developments is similarly superficial – except when it is time to amplify violence and other problems (Abreu, 2013; see also Ramalho, 2007).

This legacy of neglect and misunderstanding forms the background to the incursion of the police into the Complexo do Alemão in 2010. Although the eyes of the entire population were on one of the city's largest slum complexes, journalists found it difficult to report what was happening within the favela, even providing misleading information (Lopes and Alves, 2011). Unable to enter the complex itself, reporters huddled together in Grota, an area outside the favelas, and had to rely on the scant information provided by the police and the images captured by the helicopters flying overhead.

Journalists and residents: alternative perspectives

At the end of 2016, I travelled to Rio de Janeiro to conduct field research, and encountered these limitations first hand. For several days, I tried to gain access to the favelas of the Complexo do Alemão and the Complexo da Maré. Time and again, I was prevented by violent events, many of which occurred while I was already on my way to these sites. In fact, as soon as I arrived in the city, a police helicopter crashed, and three police officers were killed. This incident aggravated the wave of violence that the residents of the favelas still have to endure to this day.

In the past, news reports about the slums and their residents, whether through design or inadequate information, framed them as almost beyond redemption. Two developments helped to offset the negative coverage: one was the work of investigative journalists, grouped together in organisations like ABRAJI[1] (the Associação Brasileira de Jornalismo Investigativo, or the Brazilian Association of Investigative Journalism), and the other was the self-activity of young residents, who decided to cover their own neighbourhoods by creating material online that had been gathered on their own smartphones. It was in this context that the tweets of a group of young people from 11 to 17 years gained national attention.

The favela residents Rene Silva (17 years old), Igor Santos (15), Débora (11), Gabi (12) and Jackson Alves (13), used the Twitter profile of a community newspaper, that had been created years before, to narrate real-time footage of the police entry into the favela, the reaction of the drug dealers, and the panic among the residents, all recorded through the windows of their homes. With the mainstream media struggling to cover the facts (since they lacked access to the local area that the young people inhabited) the youths' profile on Twitter (@vozdacomunidade) became the main source of information about the police movements in the favela on that morning. Followers of this group account on Twitter grew from some 180 before the occupation to over 30,000 in just three days, creating an extensive impact, affecting even the traditional media (Lopes and Alves, 2011).

The *Voz da Comunidade* was created by Rene when he was only 11 years old, with the intention of making a newspaper especially designed for the locals, highlighting the good side of the favela, since the Complexo do Alemão, dominated by violence, only ever made the news 'when the content referred to drug dealing and trafficking wars' (Abreu, 2013: 26, my translation). Rene did not know it at the time, but on that November morning in 2010, his real-time broadcast would change the course of community journalism in Rio's favelas. After the *Voz da Comunidade* case gained prominence, other initiatives emerged, and became trusted sources of news for the favela residents, and a space for the promotion of their rights.

The development of the Brazilian favelas: ethnicity and poverty

In discussing the impoverished slums and the struggle to represent the lives of their inhabitants, it is important to understand the origins and history of the favelas, so that it is possible to glimpse the complex human relations that take place within these communities. Currently, there are over 11 million Brazilians living in slums, equivalent to 6% of the country's population. In the Complexo do Alemão alone, there are 70,000 residents. The inhabitants of these areas face shortages of essential public services such as sanitation and garbage collection, and in addition are not guaranteed the forms of public safety that should be the basic right of citizens. In São Paulo, the largest city in the country, 20% of the population lives in slums, followed by Rio de Janeiro, where the favelas are home to 19% of the population (IBGE, 2010).

In the early years of the twentieth century, Rio de Janeiro was known for its violence, open sewers, licentiousness, unhealthy housing, and epidemic diseases (Zaluar and Alvito, 2006). In 1900, mail exchanges between the Head of the 10th Police District and the Police Chief (available at the National Archives in Rio de Janeiro), dated November 4, makes the attitude of the authorities quite clear:

> Obeying the request for information which Your Excellency, in document No. 7.071. . . . I have said that the Morro da Providência is infested with vagabonds and criminals . . . the complete extinction of the malefactors will be necessary, which must be achieved using a considerable siege, that to take effect will need at least the assistance of 80 fully armed soldiers.
>
> (Zaluar and Alvito, 2006: 8, my translation)

Also according to Zaluar and Alvito (2006: 9), the document is important because it shows that only three years after the appearance of the first Rio slum, it was already perceived as a 'focus of deserters and thieves' and yet it is first mentioned as a double problem: one sanitary, due to the unhealthy conditions of the places of residence, and the other concerning law enforcement, as it was allegedly occupied by vagabonds and bandits. The two perspectives seem to reinforce each other.

Yet a radical redevelopment of the city began to take place, promoted by Mayor Pereira Passos (who was in power from 1902 to 1906). According to Abreu (1997), such urban changes suffered by the centre of Rio in the following years also created major waves of displaced people who crowded into the favelas in search of housing. The favelas then began to prosper. Even with unsanitary conditions, the slums attracted more and more people who could not find any viable housing next to the centre. According to Lessa (2005), 'in the former quilombos, tenements and favelas, the search for proximity to the subsistence market and the reduction of time spent travelling, prevailed at the expense of space and sanitation' (Lessa, 2005: 291, my translation).

The Complexo do Alemão, the scene of the events mentioned at the beginning of the text, came to prominence in the 1920s when the region was a major industrial centre. The site was a large farmhouse, owned by a Polish man named Leonard Kaczmarkiewicz who went on to sell land to northeastern Brazil migrants who came to the city in search of employment. Due to his Polish accent and surname, the area was mistakenly given the epithet 'German', giving the name of what was originally one particular hill, to the whole complex of favelas (Complexo do Alemão – the German's Complex).

In 1948, the first census of the favelas of Rio de Janeiro was conducted. It is both surprising and shocking to discover that an official public document states that 'the "black and brown" prevailed in the favelas because they are "hereditarily backward", lacking ambition and maladjusted to modern social needs' (Zaluar and Alvito, 2006: 13, my translation). This form of prejudice against the black population in post-slavery Brazil has been transferred to the slum dwellers, since the vast majority of them were black or brown.

The relationship between the presence of these former black slaves increases in poverty, and the growth of the favelas remains a significant factor, since today the black population in Brazil, although a majority (50.7%, IBGE, 2010), suffers from prejudice and forms a disproportionately large part of the poor population in the country. In the Brazilian favelas, 67% of the population is black (Meirelles and Athayde, 2014):

> If today 67% of slum inhabitants are black, it is certain that they are part of a long line of people excluded from the economic system ... the human brother from Africa was, for most of Brazil's history, considered a 'thing', a tool or asset, not a person, and even less a citizen.
> (Meirelles and Athayde, 2014: 42, my translation)

From dictatorship to narcocracy?

Meanwhile in the 1970s, during the military dictatorship, strong economic growth in Brazil generated a great exodus of workers from the poorer regions of the country to the richest and most developed areas, especially in the southeast. During these 30 years (1940–1970), it is possible to explain the growth of the slums by relating it to the attraction of the cities that were developing at this time. Lessa (2005) explains that the Brazilian cities, especially Rio, had an enormous power of attraction for the poor population because, despite the insecurity, the metropolis:

> raises the welfare standard and accessibility to social services. The metropolis, when it grows, is a construction site and a space of possibilities that continually attracts poor labour power from the smaller cities and the countryside.
> (Lessa, 2005: 293, my translation)

The flood of workers that came to the city settled in the slums when they found they could not find popular housing options. Spaces that had been neglected during the formal process of urbanisation, such as steep slopes and mangroves, were occupied by this poor group as they sought places to live. This movement has, over the years, generated densely populated slums and has expanded the settlements beyond urban areas and the metropolitan peripheries. In the late 1970s and early 1980s, drug trafficking gangs had spread through the Rio de Janeiro favelas. These gangs discovered that the slums were the perfect environment in which to carry on their drug trafficking schemes, since these areas could not rely on a significant security or police presence (Leeds, 1996).

It was at this time that the Complexo do Alemão began to gain notoriety as a dangerous place, with the rise of bank robbery, car theft, and, eventually, drug trafficking gangs. These drug dealers established a relationship with the wider community: in exchange for its silence regarding their activities, the gangs provided some essential services within the slum, such as internal security, medicine, money for emergencies, food for the poorest, etc. However, these criminal groups also never hesitated to warn and compel people not to cooperate with the police, at the risk of imperilling the residents' lives:

> In fact, whoever the dealers suspect of being an informer is punished harshly – expelled from the community or even exterminated [yet] the inhabitants have little or no respect for the police, who always treated them with contempt and violence simply because they are *favelados*.
> (Leeds, 1996: 243, my translation)

Another important point to highlight is that the lack of respect for the police is also a result of its essential corruption, and is thus a factor in the success of organised crime and a real hinderance to the government when it tries to address the violent situation in the favelas. The police benefit from criminal activities through the so called 'arrego' – bribes paid by drug dealers to the police so that they do not 'disturb' their business arrangements – while treating the residents in an abusive and disrespectful manner. Sage, cited in Leeds (1996: 246, my translation) argues 'in the favelas at least, democracy has been replaced by the creation of a narcocracy . . . wherein the economic structures and policies are the result of the general involvement, direct or indirect, in drug trafficking'.

Nowadays, the Rio slums experience not only wars for dominance between drug dealers from different factions, but also a war between a parallel power and public security forces which, besides having to deal with the problems of corrupt and poorly trained officers, decided to 'occupy' some of Rio's favelas in order to expel the criminals, using the so-called UPPs (Police Pacification Units). This constant war between the security forces and the drug dealers reflects the idea that the slums have become 'synonymous with disregard for law and order, a space that requires police raids' (Meirelles and Athayde, 2014: 9, my translation).

News agendas and negative representation

As we have seen, the Brazilian favelas were already imagined as a location of social pathology and a health problem, from their emergence more than a century ago; nowadays, this discourse is extended to point that the slum is also seen as the 'epicenter of urban violence' (Baroni et al., 2011: 313, my translation). Thus, the representation of the favela in the media can be seen as a direct product of the slum's reputation within society, especially so in the case of the government, which always saw it as the 'place par excellence of disorder' (Zaluar and Alvito, 2006: 14, my translation). The mainstream media must have recognised its role in the diffusion and crystallisation of such representation in the collective imagination, which for over 100 years has created a 'specific cognitive universe from which we interpret the events linked to it (the favela) . . . a universe of violence, deprivation and segregation from the rest of the city' (Vaz and Baiense, 2011: 2, my translation). It is therefore important to consider the stigma endured by the slums' inhabitants themselves, the 'favelados', since their negative media representation bears a great responsibility for the way in which they are perceived by both within and beyond the borders of Brazil. The image of criminality really took root in the popular imagination from the 2000s on (Vaz and Baiense, 2011), virtually decreeing that every *favelado* is or is about to become a thug (Rinaldi, 2006).

Although the predominant idea of the favela, in different periods, is that of a violent place, this way of portraying the favela has actually fluctuated greatly over the years. Initially, as noted earlier, it was seen as a place of great danger due to the presence of vagabonds and rascals, as well as a health problem and a place of extreme poverty (Zaluar and Alvito, 2006). With its growth and expansion to other areas of the city, the slum has been seen as a blot on the landscape, an argument used to justify the programmes of removal, both of housing and of residents (Vaz and Baiense, 2011). Yet in the early 1980s, the typical representation of the favela was of poverty and deprivation, with little emphasis on crime or violence in general. Indeed, a survey, conducted by Vaz and Baiense (2011), shows that violence was not the main image perpetuated by the media at that time. Even as the notion of violence began to gain importance in the end of that decade, less than the half of the news (43%) analysed at that time fell into the subjects crime/violence (Vaz and Baiense, 2011).

During the 1990s, however, a gradual transition can be perceived, moving from the image of the favela as a territory associated with poverty, to a representation of the favela as a place connected to crime, and a source of violence responsible for the chaos in the city. During the 2000s, poverty ceases to occupy space on the public agenda, being replaced by security. In the statistical collection of the *O Globo* newspaper in 2010, 67% of the news related to the favelas addressed issues of violence/crime, demonstrating that this kind of framing 'has become hegemonic' (Vaz and Baiense, 2011).

But the dominant framework of violence is not the only problem in the journalistic coverage of the favelas. In a survey conducted between 2004 and 2006, it was found that the press tends to explore topics related to 'drug dealing, police brutality, violence and crime, but the voices and perspectives of slum dwellers are rarely represented' (Baroni et al., 2011: 310, my translation). In the book *Media and Violence* (2007), Ramos and Paiva present the abovementioned survey results and discuss another fact revealed by it – that media coverage contributes to the criminal culture in the favelas and reinforces the negative stereotype of the place and its inhabitants:

> Most of the professionals . . . recognize that their media vehicles bear a great responsibility in the characterisation of popular territories as exclusive spaces of violence. At the same time they admit that the population of these communities rarely have any coverage of issues not related to drug trafficking and crime.
> (Ramos and Paiva, 2007: 77, my translation)

The journalists justify this partial and negative coverage by citing the difficulty of speaking with the locals who – either for fear of reprisals from the drug lords or because of the negative relationship they have with the press – are rarely willing to talk to them and often associate the arrival of journalists in the favelas with the arrival of the police (Ramos and Paiva, 2007). In addition, the relationship of the favela with the media has always been distant, and the residents often see the journalist's perspective as an 'alien view' (Baroni et al., 2011: 318, my translation).

The growth of internet use: residents as witnesses to murder

However, the uptake of the internet in these communities (Meirelles and Athayde, 2014), allows the slum to find ways to be seen and heard. At a time when the online audience in the world now exceeds that for the written press and broadcasting audience, and when in Brazil both audiences are already equivalent in size (Lopes and Alves, 2011: 117), this empowerment of the poor through technology is highly relevant. In Custodio's opinion, 'the residents have increasingly dominated communication channels and platforms to make their own voices and demands heard' (2014). Walking around the favelas these days, you can see people on their smartphones all the time – more than a tool for leisure, these smartphones are also an instrument of communication used to give voice and space for the *favelados* through their own reports of the events. The rise of so-called citizen journalism, 'a range of web-based practices whereby "ordinary" users engage in journalistic practices' (Goode, 2009: 1288), is favouring the dialogue of the favela with the rest of society, helping to contribute to the increased visibility of the poorest population, and to a more nuanced cultural profile in the media. As one commentator notes:

> The familiar dynamics of top-down, one-way message distribution associated with the mass media are being effectively, albeit unevenly, pluralised. Ordinary citizens are [building] their own networked communities.
>
> (Allan, 2007: 2)

It is in this context that young people who are 'connected' (like the creators of the *Voz da Comunidade*), gain extreme importance. This type of initiative allows the inhabitants of the favela to feel that they can be heard. During police operations, for example, even when there is no-one present from the community newspapers, the residents themselves are in charge of filming all the action and can send footage and comments to communal news sources to be released through social media (usually on a Facebook page or group). The police, accustomed to working without having to worry about the word of eyewitnesses, began to be aware of the constant possibility that they might be filmed.

In 2015, for example, an unidentified resident of Morro da Providência, through the window of his house, filmed the police shooting dead a man suspected of drug dealing. The young man, running, was unarmed. The policemen, however, placed a spare pistol in the hand of the deceased and discharged the weapon, with the intention of transferring remnants of gunpowder to the victim. They left the gun close to the body in order to claim that it had been found at the scene of the crime, and that they had only fired in self-defense. The video provoked a real scandal in relation to the usual police reports of 'resistance followed by death'.

When the Brazilian public authorities learn that someone has been killed as a result of police action, an incident report is drawn up describing a 'killing resulting from police intervention', which may also be referred to as 'resistance followed by death'. In Rio, only 3.7% of the incidents registered as 'resistance followed by death' produce a lawsuit (Cardoso et al., 2016). Out of a total of 220 investigations of police killings opened in 2011 in Rio, after four years, only one case led to a police officer being charged (Amnesty International, 2015). This helped reinforce an atmosphere where the police felt that they could shoot first and ask questions later. But the video mentioned previously – produced because now the residents understood the power of social media – started a big debate on police violence in Rio. What was once mentioned only within the favelas began to be discussed in the newspapers, investigations were ordered, and the matter was highlighted throughout the country. These police officers were arrested, which might be considered a victory, but in the overall circumstances is unfortunately only a small triumph.

Eduardo de Jesus, for example, was only 10 years old when he was killed with a rifle shot to the head, while sitting at his front door and playing with his mobile phone. The shot was fired of a maximum distance of only 5 metres. According to the residents, no shot had been heard before the one that killed Eduardo. The police, however, claimed that they were involved in a confrontation with drug traffickers and that Eduardo had been accidentally hit during an exchange of fire. The police also attempted, according to Amnesty International, to modify the crime scene by removing Eduardo's body before the forensics team arrived.

This interference was prevented due to the mobilisation of residents, including local media activists. Eduardo's case could stand for the experience of so many other boys dying in the favelas: only the police version is usually reported by the media, which generally portrays the boys as 'involved in drug dealing activities' (Abreu, 2013). However, through residents' reports and videos on social networks, this particular case has gained the attention of the wider society and even of members of international human rights organisations. In November of 2016, however, the case against the policeman who killed Eduardo was shelved and no one was arrested, showing that there is still a long way for the favela residents to change how the media, society and politicians treat the people who live in these neighbourhoods.

With the popularisation of smartphones as recording devices, cases in which the police deliberately prevent people recording their actions have also arisen. Although every Brazilian citizen has the right to film the police using public roads, Rene Silva (founder of *Voz da Comunidade*) was recently arrested for contempt when filming a removal action in a settlement in Complexo do Alemão. The police were removing residents and ordered Rene and his brother Renato to stop filming. According to Rene, one of the policemen, realising that he was still taking pictures, removed the smartphone from his hand. When he tried to retrieve the device, he was arrested.

Renato, who also refused to surrender his camera, was also taken into custody (Cannabrava, 2016).

The *Viva Favela* portal

Stories like that of Rene and Renato are the result of a new generation of residents who, with the popularisation of the internet, started to use social networks to talk freely about the favela. It also shows how the use of these media has placed strong pressure on the official bodies, and slowly brought some changes to conditions in the slums. The residents' response to neglect has created a new community of individuals dedicated to providing timely and relevant accounts of life in their districts. Yet this was prefigured in 1995, when the desire for 'a more precise and less prejudiced approach' to life in the favelas was voiced (Ramalho, 2007: 15, my translation). A group of community leaders asked for the help of an NGO (Viva Rio)[2] in an attempt to launch an initiative. It was only, however, in 2001, that the *Viva Favela*[3] portal would become a reality, bringing 'a broader vision of these communities and, to the surprise of many, interfering with traditional media' (Ramalho, 2007: 15, my translation).

The *Viva Favela* portal worked through the concept of 'community correspondents': slum dwellers were recruited through a sort of selective process by professional editors, and worked together with journalists on the portal team. The community correspondents were the ones going to the streets and alleys of the favelas to investigate the stories, decided in advance in a staff meeting with the whole team. Professional journalists had the hard work of editing the texts so that they could be published. According to Bete (one of the community correspondents at the time of the creation of the initiative), these reporters were not welcomed in the favelas, so the project would not have worked if the journalists themselves were to investigate the news stories. In Ramalho's words, 'the reporter does not care who is there, but is more concerned with his story [which] can lead to sensationalism and a distorted view' (Ramalho, 2007: 34, my translation).

The 'community correspondents' approach was working well – with the help of the traditional journalists working in the project to transform their material into proper stories – but there was a major concern not to represent a favela in a way that did not correspond to reality. Unlike the mainstream media, which only printed stories about violence and poverty in the favelas (Abreu, 2013), the community correspondents avoided addressing these issues, and any matters that could place them in conflict with the community. They refused to talk about drug dealing and the gangs, and did not like to address matters that involved violence in general. In practice, 'everyone always preferred . . . to show the "good favela"' (Ramalho, 2007: 35, my translation). Within this scenario, the journalists worried that someone looking at the material produced by *Viva Favela* in 2020 would come across an 'unreal' account that completely excised the drug dealing and violence, which was not the intention of the project.

The murder of Tim Lopes and the problems of community journalism

Tim Lopes was an investigative journalist working undercover for *Rede Globo* with the intention of revealing how young girls were forced into prostitution at the 'baile funks' (dance parties) in the Complexo do Alemão, when he was captured by a gang run by Elias Pereira da Silva, known as Elias Maluco (or Crazy Elias). At this time, in 2002, da Silva controlled drug dealing in the area. Lopes was recognised because of another undercover job he had previously undertaken, an expose of the drugs trade, the footage of which had achieved wide public circulation. He was brutally tortured: his eyes were burned with cigarettes, his limbs were severed with a ninja sword, and his body was placed within several tyres, covered in fuel and burned – a practice known as the 'microwave', used by the most violent gangs within Rio.

Lopes's death demonstrated the failure of most newsrooms to protect their employees who worked in the favelas. Lopes' co-worker, who had assisted him on previous missions, said that no employer with a conscience would have let an undercover reporter return to a dangerous place, where his face was already known (Ortiz, 2011). Reporters had, in the past, felt fairly secure in the slums, since they knew that the gangs calculated that the media presence would make the police think twice about kidnapping and killing their members (Ramalho, 2007).

After Lopes' death, which shocked the whole city, severe security measures began to be applied to any journalistic activities involving the favelas. *Rede Globo*, where Lopes worked, expressly forebade journalists to visit them, and implemented the use of bulletproof vests and armoured cars whenever teams were sent to work close to those areas. SBT (TV station), and *EXTRA* and *Folha* (newspapers), also adopted strict security measures. All the media outlets followed suit, allowing their journalists to enter the favelas only with police escorts or on police operations. Lopes himself had been raised in a favela and struggled to force such places onto the agenda of mainstream media: ironically, his death made the media coverage of the favelas even more precarious (Ramalho, 2007).

At this critical juncture, the *Viva Favela* project faced two opposing realities: at the moment it had become virtually the only source of news from within the favelas, it found that many of its community correspondents abandoned the project for fear of retaliation. As Ramalho noted, the portal was unique in that it could call upon 'reporters and photographers 24 hours a day inside the favelas', yet at the same time, 'practically none of them wanted to talk about issues that did not convey a positive view of the community' (2007: 132, my translation).

The Borel massacre and media attitudes

In 2003, in a further intensification of the violence, four young people were murdered in Borel favela. Their families and local residents claimed that those responsible for the killings were Military Police officers, but this claim received no attention from the mainstream media. Outraged, the residents, supported by various NGOs, decided to write a detailed denouncement, addressed to then President Lula. The letter was also passed to the *Viva Favela* team, which checked its veracity and then enquired whether the Cabinet of the President and the Minister of Justice had received it: apparently, they had not. After learning about the contents of the letter (prompted by the contact made by the *Viva Favela* team), the authorities promised to take action. The *Viva Favela* team then started a run of interviews with relatives of the dead, and with Borel residents, and published the first material on the subject, thus obtaining the attention of the mainstream media. After all this publicity, the case was thoroughly investigated and became 'one of the ... human rights violations with the greatest repercussion in the country' (Ramalho, 2007: 123, my translation). Representatives of Amnesty International and the UN came to Borel to investigate the murders.

The importance of the joint work of residents and professional journalists, developed by *Viva Favela*, was increasingly seen as an alternative to the established modus operandi of the press. For Marcelo Beraba, editor of *Folha de São Paulo* newspaper, although the media had some interest in covering the favelas, they knew neither the intricate network of narrow streets, nor the delicate relationships that existed between residents and the gangs. Consequently, he wrote,

> this coverage oscillates between an excessive emphasis on violence (with reports almost always from a single source, the police, since entering the favelas became too dangerous for the press) and unusual reports of exceptional cases, like the girl from a favela who gained a place at a dance school in Germany. . . . The typical resident, who is neither criminal nor a rare case of virtuosity, goes unnoticed.
> (Ramalho, 2007: 131, my translation)

The problem, however, goes deeper than that. The Brazilian media tends to give greater emphasis to the misfortunes that have occurred in the middle- and upper-class areas of the city, and ignores the deaths of the poor and the favelados victimised by the daily violence they encounter. In 2012, when a young white man was murdered by the police in one of São Paulo's richest neighbourhoods after he crossed a police checkpoint, the street protests of friends and family members received massive media coverage. In the same month, another young man was murdered by police, but this time in a poor part of the city. In this case, there was also a protest held by friends and family, but without press attention. 'Protests at the murder of poor people', wrote Capriglione 'do not appear in the newspaper' (2015: 57, my translation).

In addition to the often negative media agenda itself, the difficulty of gaining access to the favelas, combined with the residents' lack of trust in traditional news media, means that poor communities will still suffer neglect. For Denise Ribeiro, editor of the *Extra* newspaper in 2004, 'we face the difficulty of not being able, in many cases, to enter the communities . . . the fact that we have to ask permission to enter a favela shows that these places are restricted areas' (in Ramalho, 2007: 193, my translation). 'It is much easier', she said, 'to cover the views of the Police officer because they talk to us and the residents do not' (193). This is where projects such as *Viva Favela* can help to secure admission to the favela, promoting collaboration between professional journalists, residents, and community correspondents.

This success, however, did not come without risk. These first inhabitants who began using social networks to report events in the favelas challenged the so-called 'law of silence' that often prevailed within communities, and which created so many problems for the *Viva Favela* project. Professor Fernanda, an employee of a former school attended by Rene (the young man who created the *Voz da Comunidade*), was horrified when she saw that the boy was narrating the events in real time. '"They're going to kill Rene" she said, really kill him, in the woods, in a tyre, in a very horrible way, as the residents of the community know only too well' (Abreu, 2013: 21, my translation).

Warned by professional journalists about the risk of exposing themselves in this way – after all, at that moment no one knew what the future held for the favela's residents – the teenagers used the *Voz da Comunidade* Twitter account to declare that 'WE DID NOT MAKE ANY COMPLAINTS ABOUT aggressions in the Alemão!', arguing that the '*Voz da Comunidade* team does not comment on drug dealers or police' (Abreu, 2013: 24). Once again, the fear of retaliation hampered the free communication of the favela residents but, perhaps protected by the considerable impact achieved by their Twitter coverage of the police operation in the Complexo do Alemão (see the beginning of the chapter), the *Voz da Comunidade* staff continued to report what was happening in the favela. In addition, the success of the group stimulated similar initiatives in other favelas. In the same period, 'collectives' of residents were also created, that specialised in the production of news content and started to produce more complex and high-quality material, often being taken up by major international newspapers, such as the *Coletivo Papo Reto*. With all this mobilisation of the residents, violent events that take place inside the slums of Rio de Janeiro rarely pass without the appearance of comments, alerts, photos, and also videos made by the inhabitants. These videos often become essential evidence to show what actually occurred in the streets.

In 2015, for example, Alan Lima and Chauan Cezario were shot by police inside the Palmeirinha favela. One of them died and the other was injured and later arrested. The police alleged that the youths were armed and shot in their car. A video recorded before Alan died, however, shows a group of unarmed adolescents playing in the street when the police hit both youths with gunfire. Only with the release of this video on social media was the family able to prove that the version disseminated by the authorities was not true, leading to the arrest of the police officer responsible for the shooting.

Also in 2015, the video showing police officers creating a crime scene after murdering an unarmed young man (see earlier), stimulated a great deal of debate about the police action in the Rio de Janeiro favelas and led to the arrest of the police officers involved. If it had not been for the popularisation of social networks and smartphones by slum dwellers, situations like these would remain known only to the residents themselves, and would not alter society's perception of the favela. The work of groups like the *Voz da Comunidade* makes life in the favelas a little more safe. These days, the inhabitants know that if something happens, there will be people filming the events and challenging the authorities. These 'citizen journalists', who usually risk their own well-being to publish the truth, are not only helping to change the way the mainstream media reports on the favela, but also the way in which the police work within these districts. Most important of all, these actions help to empower the favela residents to stand up for themselves and to fight for better living conditions for all.

Notes

1 For Associação Brasileira de Jornalismo Investigativo, or the Brazilian Association of Investigative Journalism, see www.abraji.org.br/
2 NGO Viva Rio http://vivario.org.br/
3 *Viva Favela* project [http://vivafavela.com.br/]. The author gratefully acknowledges the CAPES Foundation, Ministry of Education of Brazil, Brasília – DF 70040–020, for its financial support. Process Number 13689–13–4.

References

Abreu, Mauricio de Almeida (1997) *Evolução Urbana do Rio de Janeiro* [3rd edition], Rio de Janeiro: IPLANRIO.
Abreu, Sabrina (2013) *A Voz Do Alemão: como Rene Silva e outros jovens ajudaram a mudar a imagem da comunidade/Sabrina Abreu e Rene Silva*, São Paulo: nVersos.
Allan, Stuart (2007) 'Citizen journalism and the rise of "mass self-communication": Reporting the London bombings', *Global Media Journal*, Vol. 1, Issue: 1, pp. 1–20.
Amnesty International (2015) 'Você Matou meu Filho!' *Anistia internacional*, www.anistia.org.br/direitos-humanos/publicacoes/voce-matou-meu-filho/ [accessed 22 March 2017].
Baroni, Alice, Aguiar, Leonel, and Rodrigues, Felipe (2011) 'Novas configurações discursivas no jornalismo: narrativas digitais nas favelas, do Rio de Janeiro', in *Estudos em Comunicação*, Vol. 9, May, pp. 309–327.

Cannabrava, Melissa (2016) 'Rene Silva e Renato Moura são detidos enquanto faziam cobertura de remoção no Alemão', *Voz das Comunidades*, www.vozdascomunidades.com.br/geral/rene-silva-e-renato-moura-sao-detidos-enquanto-faziam-cobertura-de-invasao-no-alemao/ [accessed 29 March 2017].

Capriglione, Laura (2015) 'Os mecanismos midiáticos que livram a cara dos crimes das polícias militares no Brasil', in *Bala Perdida – A violência policial no Brasil e os desafios para sua superação*, São Paulo: Boitempo, pp. 55–60.

Cardoso, Francisca Letícia Miranda Gadelha, Cecchetto, Fátima Regina, Corrêa, Juliana Silva, et al. (2016) 'Homicídios no Rio de Janeiro, Brasil: uma análise da violência letal', in *Ciência & Saúde Coletiva*, Vol. 21, Issue: 4, pp. 1277–1288.

Custodio, Leonardo (2014) 'Tipos de midiativismo de favela', *Favelas at LSE*, www.blogs.lse.ac.uk/favelasatlse/2014/09/18/tipos-de-midiativismo-de-favela/ [accessed 26 January 2017].

Goode, Luke (2009) 'Social news, citizen journalism and democracy', in *New Media & Society*, Vol. 11, Issue: 8, pp. 1287–1305.

IBGE [Instituto Brasileiro de Geografia e Estatística] (2010) '2010 population census', www.ibge.gov.br/english/estatistica/populacao/censo2010/ [accessed 20 January 2017].

Leeds, Elizabeth (1996) 'Cocaína e poderes paralelos na periferia urbana brasileira: ameaças à democratização em nível local', in Zaluar, A. and Alvito, M. [editors], *Um século de favela* [5th edition], Rio de Janeiro: Editora FGV, pp. 233–276.

Lessa, Carlos (2005) *O Rio de todos os Brasis (Uma reflexão em busca de auto-estima)*, Rio de Janeiro: Editora Record.

Lopes, Flávia Valério and Alves, Wendencley (2011) 'Discurso e redes sociais: o caso "Voz da comunidade"', *Ciberlegenda*, Vol. 25, pp. 111–123.

Meirelles, Renato and Athayde, Celso (2014) *Um país chamado favela: a maior pesquisa já feita sobre a favela brasileira*, São Paulo: Editora Gente.

Ortiz, Fabiola (2011) 'Morte de Tim Lopes foi caso anunciado, diz colega que fugiu do país após ameaça de traficantes', in *UOL Notícias*, 16 July, www.noticias.uol.com.br/cotidiano/ultimas-noticias/2011/07/16/morte-de-tim-lopes-foi-caso-anunciado-diz-colega-que-fugiu-do-pais-apos-ameaca-de-traficantes.htm [accessed 31 January 2017].

Ramalho, Cristiane (2007) *Notícias Da Favela*, Rio de Janeiro: Aeroplano.

Ramos, Silvia and Paiva, Anabela (2007) *Mídia e violência: tendências na cobertura de criminalidade e segurança pública no Brasil*, Rio de Janeiro: IUPERJ.

Ribeiro, Geraldo (2014) 'Candidato, depois de outubro, não some, não!' *Extra*, 17 July, www.extra.globo.com/noticias/brasil/eleicoes-2014/candidato-depois-de-outubro-nao-some-nao-13283117.html [accessed 27 March 2017].

Rinaldi, Alessandra de Andrade (2006) 'Marginais, delinqüentes e vítimas: um estudo sobre a representação da categoria favelado no tribunal do júri da cidade do Rio de Janeiro', in Zaluar, A. and Alvito, M. [editors], *Um século de favela* (5th edition), Rio de Janeiro: Editora Fundação Getulio Vargas, pp. 299–321.

Vaz, Paulo and Baiense, Carla (2011) 'Mídia e enquadramento: as representações da favela na virada do século XXI', in *Proceedings of the VIII Encontro Nacional de História da Mídia*, Guarapuava, PR: Unicentro, pp. 1–15.

Zaluar, Alba and Alvito, Marcos (2006) *Um século de favela*, Rio de Janeiro: Editora Fundacão Getulio Vargas.

Part III
The hazards of investigation
Journalists on assignment

The subject-matter of this section is, as before, international in scope, but focuses on the ways in which investigative journalists operate in hazardous environments, or in situations where political or social obstacles make their enquiries difficult. The practical problems of working in countries like Syria, Iraq, Southern Kurdistan, and Egypt (and, in the final chapter, the British overseas territory of Bermuda) are legion, but appear here as the strictures of bureaucracy, the misery of war, and the burden of cultural oppression. Besides their various trials and tribulations, the six authors describe the special techniques used in difficult circumstances, and reveal how dependent journalists can be on the 'fixers' and contacts that have the local knowledge needed to survive.

In some cases, however, the expert is none other than the journalist conducting the enquiry, clearly demonstrated in Chapter 8, in which Ahmed Bahiya, an Iraqi national, describes an assignment in which he had to work in the sectarian environment of a country ravaged by war. Bahiya, familiar with the dangers of operating in unstable and unpredictable situations, was tasked with finding an ex-Guantanamo detainee who had returned to Iraq: this man found that, though ostensibly free, he was not safe among his own people. 'The ultimate goal' of Bahiya's mission was to produce a story 'that revealed the dilemma faced by those who had been falsely accused, yet upon release had been rejected by their communities'. The larger political context is provided in some detail, as the author sets out the political background to the current situation, noting in particular 'the rise of ethno-sectarian violence and civil war after the American invasion', the political contest between Shia and Sunnis that followed, and how these seemingly intractable problems undermined the creation of a coherent Iraqi polity.

Chapter 9 is the collective effort of three authors: Peter Geoghegan, Billy Briggs, and Brindusa Ioana Nastasa. Geoghegan and Briggs are among the founders of *The Ferret*, a Scottish investigative network, one that is 'committed to taking a non-partisan approach' to the production of news stories. The organisation operates on a co-operative basis, encouraging its subscribers to contribute to the development of the collective as a whole. Chapter 9 begins with Geoghegan's detailed survey of the news economy (see also Chapter 14), noting that 'a slew of new digital journalism start-ups have stepped into the gaps created by the retreat of legacy media'. The chapter goes on to detail the experiences of Briggs and Nastasa as they embarked, respectively, on journeys to Northern Iraq and Turkey. Briggs, accompanied by the photographer Angie Catlin, intended 'to document the impact' of the Battle of Mosul on the civilian population. Nastasa, on the other hand, created a report called 'A Second Syria', which details 'the economic situation of Syrians in Turkey through the stories of several highly skilled refugee migrants fighting to survive on less than minimum wage'. Both accounts provide an insight, not only into the narratives that the writers sought to create, but more particularly into the practical business of working under duress and with very limited resources.

Zahera Harb is the author of Chapter 10, which examines the aftermath of the Arab revolt and the role of social media, and concentrates on 'the interface between *journalistic* activity and the political structures of the Egyptian state', in the period after the uprisings of January 2011. Citing Howard and Hussain, she notes that investigative journalism was not an established feature of mainstream media practice, but its principles were upheld and pursued by citizens. Political reform within the wider region is, according to Harb, difficult to achieve, forcing activists to create an alternative social and political sphere online. Although social media networks did not of themselves 'generate revolutions', Harb argues that 'they were able to facilitate them, helping to generate a sense of connectedness' and creating an autonomous space for sharing their grievances (see also Chapter 7 on social media use in the Brazilian favelas). Although there was a significant expansion in the number and strength of media organisations after the revolts, this increase did not, unfortunately, help create a more democratic culture, because two rival groups – the military and the Muslim Brotherhood – drew most media groups into their orbit, resulting in the polarisation of debate, the 'instrumentalisation' of Egypt's media, and the marginalisation of independent journalism.

Dana Selassie's analysis of the problems facing the British overseas territory Bermuda appears in Chapter 11, and offers a portrait of another dysfunctional social order, mired in problems created by its colonial past and current status as a dependent political entity. Besides this issue, Selassie, who is a Bermudan citizen, emphasises the legacy of Bermuda's media system, and its reliance, at various stages in its history, on both the United States and the UK. The particular case study presented in this chapter concerns the legal and procedural obstacles faced by a Canadian TV team as they tried to complete a documentary on the 1996 murder of a young compatriot, the tourist Rebecca Middleton. The film was part of the 'Murder in Paradise' series, which used an often quite sensationalist format to reveal the dark side of overseas tourism. The international coverage of the Rebecca Middleton trial, meanwhile, during which the incompetence of the authorities was made painfully evident, 'not only tarnished Bermuda's national image, but challenged the island's supposedly impeccable reputation as a safe and tranquil paradise for overseas visitors'. Canadian news media were instrumental in keeping the case in the public eye, as Middleton's family members pleaded for the case to be reopened and justice to be served.

8 Surviving the sectarian divide
Investigative journalism in the quagmire of Iraq

Ahmed Bahiya

Introduction

This chapter examines the role of investigative journalism within a 'hostile environment' – in this case, one that I know from the inside. The core of this study is divided into three thematic sections: the contemporary political situation in Iraq, the condition of the country's media, and material drawn from an investigation conducted in 2012. I have interspersed the first two narratives with elements of the third, which provides details of a story that may surprise some people: the fact that an individual released from the nightmare of detention in Guantánamo Bay found himself more at risk living as a free citizen in Iraq. After spending years in American custody, a group of newly released prisoners (who were now no longer regarded as 'enemy combatants') tried to resume a normal existence in the land of their birth. Yet many Muslim communities in Iraq, governed by cultural and religious values and norms, refused to accept these men into their midst. The very fact that these innocent victims had been imprisoned was enough to create the suspicion that they must be dangerous insurgents.

'Radio Free Iraq' and the risks of investigation

To all appearances, it was a normal working day at Radio Iraq H'ur or 'Radio Free Iraq'. Although the station was staffed by Iraqi citizens, and seemed to be an Iraqi initiative, the parent company of this organisation was none other than Radio Free Europe/Radio Liberty (RFE/RL), started in 1959 by the National Committee for a Free Europe (rferl.org). Initially, both Radio Free Europe and Radio Liberty (RFE/RL) were funded through the Board for International Broadcasting (BIB), and thereafter by the Broadcasting Board of Governors (BBG), both of which were sponsored by the U.S. Congress. On the day in question, 1 February 2012, members of staff working in the production section received a recorded message from an unknown person. The caller had used a number specially allocated for Iraqi citizens who wished to pass on sensitive information, concerning anything from everyday complaints to corrupt practices and major government failings. To the caller, it would have seemed as though he had rung a local Iraqi number, but his message was actually picked up by the Radio Free Europe station based in Prague, the capital city of the Czech Republic.

The man who left the voicemail spoke in the main about the persecution he had suffered, the loss of his rights, and his life after prison. He was particularly interested in discussing the predicament of those ex-detainees who had spent years in the Guantanamo Bay detention camp but who, he claimed, had never actually committed a crime. The only clue to the man's identity was the fact that he had mentioned the place he was calling from, which was one of the cities in the south-central part of Iraq and which lay within the Shia majority provinces. As it happened, I used to work in that province and the area around it, producing several news reports from the region over the years.

Some days after the message had been received by the station, I was directed by the department of investigative reporting in the Radio station to undertake a mission, the chief aim of which was to search for the caller, based on the reference to the city and the little information about his case that could be gleaned from the recorded message. The ultimate goal was to produce a story that revealed the dilemma faced by those who had been falsely accused, yet upon release had been rejected by their communities. It was not to be an easy task. A substantial proportion of people in the outside world, and within Iraq itself, regarded Guantanamo as a place full of dangerous terrorists, and anyone who had been detained there, as a genuine threat. Secondly, I lived in a city that was governed by several Shia Islamic parties, each of which had their own armed militias. As a result, my decision to conduct the investigation had to be considered very carefully, due to the high levels of risk that the case attracted.

Besides the brutal wars, which extended over some decades, the rise of ethno-sectarian violence and civil war after the American invasion – especially the political battles between Shia and Sunnis – undermined the integration of the Iraqi people as a coherent polity, and made them yet more dependent on their sectarian identity. If any journalist dared to produce an alternative narrative to the ones preferred by, respectively, Shia and Sunni politicians, the risk was that the armed groups might kidnap or kill the reporter concerned. A report issued in 2007 by the Communication and Media Commission (CMC) stated that 'journalists face the challenge of reporting on other parties critically . . . [those] who are too critical of other factions often have been subjected to blackmail and death threats, if not death itself' (2007). Nevertheless, journalists have taken on the responsibility of trying to enlighten the world and to play the role of watchdogs. That, of course, comes with a heavy price. In order to understand the extraordinary pressures faced by reporters, the nature of Iraqi sectarianism and the national media context needs to be understood.

The emergence of sectarianism in Iraq

Until the 2003 U.S.-led invasion and occupation, the Iraqi population had maintained a long-standing history of secularism and a strong national identity despite their ethnic and sectarian differences. The changes witnessed in Iraq after 2003 heralded the emergence of ethnic/sectarian violence and tension between the different sects of Sunnis, Shias, and Kurds who comprise the Iraqi community as a whole. Under U.S. policy, the promotion of sectarian identity became an acceptable state of affairs (Haddad, 2013). Moreover, political groups actively helped to divide the Iraqi community, since their main concern was to secure proportional representation within the governing system and state institutions, and (in both the Sunni and Shia communities) to build a communal base by mobilising notions of victimhood. As Hagan et al. argued:

> A Shia sense of victimhood followed from the brutal repression of Shia individuals and groups by Saddam [Hussein] in southern Iraq following the first Gulf War . . . while the Sunni also felt victimized by the intensifying international sanctions that followed this war.
>
> (2015: 8)

Sectarian violence erupted and escalated to the level where it started to threaten the country's fragile democracy. Iraqi political activists were locked in a contest for power, using communal fear and sectarianism as a weapon to achieve their goals and to create new constituencies. For instance, the limited official support received by Shia parties returning from exile, such as the Islamic Supreme Council of Iraq (ISCI, previously known as the Supreme Council for Islamic Revolution) and the Dawa party, led these groups to utilise a discourse that emphasised the importance of 'majority rule, de-victimization, and preventing the emergence of a new dictatorship' (Al-Qarawee, 2014: 6). Meanwhile, the failure of the Iraqi political elite to develop an inclusive system of government resulted in an intensification of internal divisions. Shia people started seeing Sunnis as terrorists supported by, and actually belonging to, specific Arab Gulf countries, such as the Kingdom of Saudi Arabia (KSA) and Qatar, while Sunnis considered Shias as de facto Iranian agents.

The modern expression of these divisions is seen in the rivalry between the different sects and the fight for power, resources, and status. According to Al-Qarawee, 'a conflict emerged about which "group" would have the biggest share of power, which community would be dominant, and which national narrative would prevail' (Al-Qarawee, 2014: 5). Communal representation has become the main factor governing political relationships, as opposed to models of citizenship. This, in turn, has resulted in the intensification rather than an easing of the existing divisions. Indeed, communal mobilisation is seen by the majority of Iraqi political parties as an effective instrument that enables them to maintain their power in the country.

The Iraqi media under Saddam Hussein

During Saddam Hussein's regime, Iraqi audiences received their news from state-controlled TV channels and print media. Hussein was described by a Reporters Without Borders/Reporters Sans Frontières (RSF) report as a 'predator of press freedom' who managed the Iraqi media with 'an iron fist and has given them the single mission of relaying his propaganda' (Al-rawi, 2010: 5). The mass media were the means through which all the social and moral values and norms were dictated to the public (Al-rawi, 2013; Cazes, 2003).

Bengio stated that the media landscape was simply 'an omnipotent propaganda machine' which 'played the role of the Ba'ath regime's watchdog, thus contributing significantly to its survival and longevity' (2004: 109–110, in Isakhan, 2007: 16). Iraqi journalists were obliged to join the Ba'ath Party. The death penalty was imposed by Saddam Hussein on any individuals who insulted or criticised the President or members of his government (Al-rawi, 2012). During the Ba'ath era there were only five state-owned dailies and a single satellite channel (Al-Marashi, 2007). Uday Hussein, the brutal eldest son of President Saddam Hussein, was actually appointed as the Head of the Iraq Journalists Union (Bengio, 1998; Daragahi, 2003). All Iraqi journalists were obliged to join the Union. In 1999, more than 1,000 writers were fired by Uday Hussein for not praising his father (Bengio, 2004).

Journalists whose writing diverged from the regime line faced arrest, torture, and execution. According to the Iraqi Press Agency, in 2001 alone, around 50 journalists fled persecution (Al-Deen, 2005). Muhammad al-Qaisi, an Iraqi freelance reporter said, 'I am caught in a game of cat and mouse. Murdering a journalist is easier than running a red light in Iraq' (Ricchiardi, 2011). But those journalists who were loyal to the regime were rewarded with generous salaries, incentives, land, and cars. Meanwhile, the Iraqi people had little or no access to information beyond that provided by the government sources. The Iraqi press acted as representative of the Ba'ath Party ideology, and was widely used by the authorities to influence the Iraqi people. This was confirmed by Latif Nessaif Jassim, the Minister of Information, who stated that 'the revolutionary press and its cultures were . . . the tools that the Ba'ath Party . . . would use to make general opinion support our main goals' (Hadhum, 2012: 44). Hashim Hassan explained that the press in Iraq:

> from 1968 until 1979 was full of the Arab Ba'ath Socialist Party's ideologies [and] the main tool for the policy to implant that ideology in the press was the ministry of information, which intervened in every subject and chose the terms which suited Ba'ath ideology.
>
> (Hassan, 2007)

According to United Nations Development Programme UNDP (2003:63), 'The Baathist state-owned media prevented journalists from writing freely and hindered the efforts to improve their skills in investigative reporting', meaning that the majority of journalists 'relied on official sources, especially from the Iraqi News Agency, which was affiliated with the Ministry of Information' (Bennani et al., 2003: 62). The only critical topics that newspapers were able to publish from time to time, were mainly about public services such as water and electricity, and these usually blamed the country's bureaucracy, not its leadership. Hadhum (2012) indicates that freedom of speech was limited and controlled, while the press served the 'revolution and its activities'. Despite the advice that Saddam had given in a meeting with a group of Iraqi journalists in January 1980, 'write without limits or hesitation or fear for the possibility that the state might like or dislike your writings' (Al Bakri, 1994, in Hadhum, 2012: 56), things were very different in practice. The Pan-Arab Cultural and Information Office held full power, through its laws and instructions, to control the topics that journalists should cover, and the way in which they were allowed to write, all in an attempt to align the views of the journalists with the ruler's perspectives.

The Iraqi media post-Saddam

Following the invasion of Iraq in 2003, media ownership ended up in the hands of competing political factions. As a result, media organisations have since been shaped to service the interests of their new owners, making them nothing more than a tool to disseminate particular ideologies. It is difficult for outsiders, who may have had little knowledge of the country before the invasion of 2003, to imagine the profound changes that have taken place in the years since the occupying forces left. Dozens of independent newspapers, radio broadcasting, and satellite stations have emerged in the country. Rugh (2004) stated that between 2003 and 2004, more than 200 independent newspapers were produced. There were also several radio stations established in the country, which exceeds 20 stations as well as more than 15 Iraqi-owned TV channels (Isakhan, 2009).

The development of broadcasting in Iraq required the establishment of a new regulatory framework for the Iraqi media. The Media Development Advisory Team (MDAT) was responsible for developing this regulatory framework (Price et al., 2007). The team started its work early in 2003, and was 'funded by the United Kingdom's Foreign and Commonwealth Office [which] took control of broadcast licensing', while 'contractors employed by the U.S. State Department and USAID began focusing on telecommunications issues' (Price et al., 2007: 22). The MDAT meanwhile 'compiled a database of broadcasters, designed an application form and produced a new license, all based on international models [which] included terms and conditions holding broadcasters accountable for violating license terms'(Price et al., 2007: 22).

There was a long consultation process involving a number of Iraqis and a wide range of independent international members (Al-rawi, 2012). In March 2004, 'Order Number 65' was signed, which established the Communications and Media Commission (Amos, 2010). It was the first independent Iraqi body to be responsible for regulating all forms of media communications, including voice and data telecommunications, radio broadcasting, and TV channels, as well as information and internet services. The CMC's main responsibilities included 'investigating any potential wrongdoing and determining whether a violation had occurred and imposing any sanctions' (Price et al., 2007). It was also tasked to provide a code of practice to establish ethical boundaries and rules regarding content restriction and freedom of speech, together with a behavioural guide for media establishments to follow during elections. According to the CMC, journalists and media bodies are obliged to follow the strict media regulations stipulated in the 'Guidelines on Accuracy and Balance' (2007) when covering any news (Al-rawi and Gunter, 2013).

In sum, the reality on the ground today is completely different from the original plans made by the U.S. government. Deborah Amos stated in her report for Harvard's Kennedy School of Government that the U.S. government spent over half a billion dollars on media development (Amos, 2010). In his ground-breaking study of Iraq's press system, Ibrahim al-Marashi (2007) warned that 'ethnosectarian media empires' were providing the psychological groundwork for bitter divisiveness and conflict. The notion of establishing good journalistic practices in Iraq by applying universal moral principles is constantly thwarted by the current political climate.

Investigative journalism in 'emerging democracies': the case of Iraq

The work of investigative reporters in developing countries and emerging democracies is likely to be different in nature to that experienced by reporters in the United States or the UK. This is due to the particular difficulties that they face. Iraq is not only a highly dangerous environment, but is also supposed to be an 'emerging', as opposed to a stable, democracy (Kim and Hama-Saeed, 2008). According to Jerry Kammer, the relative absence of investigative work is due to the lack of institutional support for journalists, the absence of laws that could protect them, and the lack of interest among Iraqi media owners (Salloum, 2009). There are therefore huge limitations on expressing any public opinions that contradict the views of the political elites. Media coverage is limited to certain sets of topics. Working against such a media environment is a massive challenge for Iraqi journalists who may even pay with their lives if their work doesn't meet the interests and expectations of the political or Islamist parties (*Al-Monitor*, 2017).

Additionally, investigative work is ideologically challenging, unearthing facts that might conflict with the ideals of the political factions and parties that rule the country. Ziad al Ajili, the Director of the Journalistic Freedom Observatory, reinforced this point, noting that 'officials don't want journalists to write about things such as security issues, violations of human rights, lack of basic services, and corruption' (Amos, 2010: 30).

According to Saman Noah, the general manager of the Network of Iraqi Reporters for Investigative Journalism (NIRIJ), 'real investigative journalism is not seen in Iraq and such stories appear rarely' (Iraqi Media House, 2017). Certainly, there are many excellent reporters in the country, but they are often unable to undertake even the most basic enquiries because of the many obstacles placed in their way. Meanwhile, the authorities were simply not used to even the simplest investigative practices. Open data journalism is the most common type of journalistic work in Iraq. Government officials are used to providing local journalists with information about projects accomplished, official visits, and decisions made. Journalistic styles that differ from this common trend are usually simply rejected.

A severe lack of training is one of the barriers that journalists face, which can be fatal in a country that is so volatile. The most recent example of this situation was the death of war photographer, Ali Resan, who worked for the Iraqi TV channel Alsumaria TV and was killed by an ISIS sniper while covering the war in Mosul province. He was looking for a good position to film the heated battle but had no body armour or helmet (Sa'adoun, 2017). Since the time that ISIS took over Mosul province in Iraq on 10 June 2014, more than 13 journalists have been killed and 44 were injured, according to the figures from the Iraqi Journalists Syndicate and the Journalist Freedoms Observatory (Sa'adoun, 2017). According to a report released by the Reporters Committee for the Freedom of the Press (RCFP), 'Iraqi journalists have faced a unique threat because they're targeted by various groups, including Sunni and Shiite militias, al-Qaida in Iraq, local police and authorities as well as U.S.-led forces' (Harder, 2008). Two Iraqi Sharqiya TV journalists, correspondent Saif Talal and his cameraman Hassan al-Anbaki, were killed by Militiamen as they returned from reporting on violence and militia attacks in eastern Iraq's Diyala province (*The New Arab*, 2016).

Many writers have noted this problem. Amos (2013: 34) argued that 'for many years the major threat to freedom of expression in Iraq was the death threat', while International Federation of Journalists (IFJ) General Secretary Aidan White stated that in Iraq 'journalists are being killed with impunity in broad daylight . . . journalism has become a deadly profession in Iraq and each new attack is not only an attack on an individual but on press freedom as well' (International Federation of Journalists, 2006). In addition, international organisations monitoring the status of journalists in Iraq have repeatedly named it as the world's most dangerous place for journalists (Kuttab, 2007). Moaid Al Lami, the President of the Iraqi Journalists Syndicate (IJS) stated that, 'since 2003, approximately 400 journalists have lost their lives in Iraq; this number is the highest in the world' (United Nations Educational, Scientific and Cultural Organization, 2015). Several programmes have been

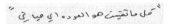

Figure 8.1 Extract from notebook.

instigated by the Iraqi government and a number of international NGOs, such as UNESCO and The International Federation of Journalists (IFJ), have cooperated with the IJS to demand increased safety for journalists in Iraq. However, their efforts have yet to bear fruit. The seemingly endless sectarian conflict still produces corpses, from both Shia and Sunni communities, dumped in the streets and bearing signs of torture.

I, too, had been in life-threatening situations. As a journalist, I was an easy target for different political parties, insurgents, criminal gangsters, or militant groups. I had to be wary of the people around me, and even of my friends, as I did not necessarily know their true affiliations, whether political, sectarian, or regional. Shia Militias, for example, control their own political entities (including intelligence agencies) and function independently of the state, attracting hundreds of young people to their ranks. They maintained several offices throughout Iraq, especially in the city where I was conducting my investigation (see extract from notebook in Figure 8.1).

The interview: 'I want to get back to my life'

Although an experienced journalist, before February 2012, I had never been involved in investigative work, nor had I even considered pursuing such a course. Despite the probable danger in this assignment, I was excited enough to accept it. I thought I might be of some assistance to people who wished to re-join their communities. Besides this, I admired the bravery of those who had faced so much danger and pain. In Iraq, there is no 'rehabilitation' programme designed to reintegrate ex-detainees into society: they are left entirely to their own devices. Although motivated by humanitarian interest, I had to exercise caution: how could I be sure that the information I received was always reliable? My quarry, AA, was one of seven Iraqi citizens (*The New York Times*, 2002), who had been held in the United States' Guantanamo Bay detention camp in Cuba. *The New York Times* has reviewed thousands of pages of government documents released in recent years as part of the project called 'The Guantánamo Docket' which 'is an interactive database of documents and analysis from *The New York Times* about the roughly 780 men who have been detained at Guantánamo as enemy combatants since January 2002' (*The New York Times*, 2002). AA was a citizen from one of the southern Iraqi provinces who, in the late 1980s, escaped the Ba'ath regime's policies by fleeing the country. In 1987, he had served as an infantry corporal in the Iraqi military before, in November 1988, he worked as a border guard. In 1989, he left Iraq for Iran, where he stayed in a refugee camp for five years. In 1994, he left Iran for Pakistan and, according to his account, began to work for a Pakistani merchant, helping him to sell various goods. It was this role, he claimed, that required him to move between Pakistan and Afghanistan.

While working in Afghanistan for his employer, AA had been arrested by the Taliban and, according to his story, thrown into jail. He said that he had a letter in his possession which was signed by a Taliban official, which noted that he should leave Afghanistan. After a short period, the Taliban administration of the prison decided to pass him on to the International Red Cross (IRC). On 15 August 2001, he had been instructed by the Taliban to leave Afghanistan within 20 days, on pain of further incarceration. His deportation documents had been received by an IRC representative who started working on his case to get him out of the country. He did not, however, possess any documents that would allow him to enter Pakistan. His situation required an official International NGO to process his case, but according to AA's account, the process was delayed because 9/11 occurred, and as a result all the International NGOs such as the Red Cross and the United Nations left Afghanistan, so that his case remained in a kind of legal limbo. He complained to me that the IRC had not really made enough of an effort to help him.

Upon his release in Afghanistan and the departure of the IRC, the detainee managed to get back to Pakistan by himself. He claimed that some people he knew helped him to enter Pakistan illegally, but he was again arrested, this time in April 2002 by the Pakistani police, who took him into custody in Khustand. He said that was arrested for two reasons: the first was that he did not have a passport, and the second that the authorities assumed that he was a spy. Pakistani police later handed the detainee to the Pakistani Inter-Service Intelligence Directorate (ISID) which eventually passed him on to the U.S. forces, which in turn sent him to the Guantanamo Bay Detention Camp. AA summarised his story as follows:

> After a short period of time Taliban decided to hand me over to the Red Cross . . . and then I went to back again to Pakistan where I was arrested and handed over to US forces. The US forces sent me to Guantanamo Bay Detention Camp.
>
> (AA, interview with author)

The Americans accused of him of two offences, the first being that he was a threat to the United States, while the second was that he had been an enemy combatant. Enemy combatant means 'an individual who . . . was a part of . . . hostile forces . . . and who engaged in an armed conflict against the United States' (Elsea and Garcia, 2010: 27). Suspicion had been aroused due to his routes of ingress and egress to and from Afghanistan and Pakistan.

He was eventually cleared of all these charges in 2006, but his detention continued for another three years because of the situation in Iraq, described by the American general Petraeus as 'lack of adequate governmental capacity, lingering sectarian mistrust, and various forms of corruption' (2007: 2). The most important of these was probably the security problem. This situation persisted for many years, when finally, on 17 January 2009, the detainee was set free from Guantanamo and transferred to Iraq. After spending more than seven years away from his family without charge or trial and knowing nothing about his future, he looked back on his experiences and said that 'the worst parts of [his] detention were knowing his family was worrying continually about him' (AA, interview with author). After arriving in Iraq, the government kept him in prison in Baghdad for a further nine months to ensure that he did not represent any threat to the security of the country. Finally, he was released from prison and sent back to his family in his own province in the South of the country.

The first meeting to interview AA was held at his parents' house. It was an old house where he lived with his mother, who was weighed down with sadness. I had the opportunity to meet her and talk to her for few minutes. During our conversation about AA's experiences, she wiped the tears from her eyes. His mother said that AA's absence had 'made me old, lose my sight' and that she had 'become sick because of his absence' (interview with author).

I had been invited to sit in a small, unfurnished guest room, which contained only a carpet and some sponge cushions. During our one-to-one interview, AA expressed himself with passion and sadness, recounting how he remembered 'that day when my family picked me up from the prison . . . it was the happiest moment to come back to the outside world and to join my family for the first time after seven years' (AA, interview with author). Despite being offered a taste of freedom, all the years he spent in prison meant that he had lost everything. As one of the former Guantanamo inmates, he was unable to secure employment, and said 'I have no work now, owing to my health situation and constant pain from the effects of my torture' (AA, interview with author). At this point, I will try to explain just how I got to the point of being able to interview the victim in the first place: in other words, I will retrace my steps in order to outline the detailed work of the investigative process.

The investigation: tactics and hazards

In an investigation that would last for several weeks, I made a series of informal enquiries in the various parts of the city mentioned by the ex-detainee. My goal was to find any leads that could take me to his place of residence or the location where he was hiding. As I eventually learned, my quarry had tried to disappear from sight for a variety of reasons: he was aware of the general mood in the city and, besides this, he was under surveillance by Iraqi intelligence agents. My goal at that time was to conduct, as Kaplan said, a ' "systematic inquiry" . . . [which] cannot be conducted over a short-term period' (Kaplan, 2013: 11). Sullivan goes on to note that 'certain truths cannot be uncovered unless you have the time to perform a . . . long-term inquiry' (11).

My quest began with my own social networks and any friends who used to work with security agencies and government departments in the province. In face-to-face meetings, I was careful to avoid raising any suspicions, avoiding the use of an insistent tone and trying to make the exchange as natural as possible. The use of indirect questions was an important ploy. I then arranged meetings with officials, using social networks, and visiting civil society institutions and government offices. I travelled to the heart of the city where the ex-prisoner's tribe used to reside. On arrival, nobody was willing to cooperate. Basic distrust of the press was a constant factor. A typical example was an official I have called 'GM'. I had been introduced to this man by another journalist who was a friend of mine. At the beginning of my enquiries, he showed a willingness to cooperate, but when I met him in his office and asked for details about my subject, I felt as though I myself was the target of an investigation.

However, I continued to persevere: the collectivist nature of Iraqi Arabic society meant that I had to place the emphasis on building trust and relationships with the different parties (such as tribe members, governmental employees and people who used to work with national and international NGOs in Iraq) before starting my report. This was an important turning point in my research mission, as a friendship with a person who was working in a humanitarian aid organisation provided me with important information and documents. The tribal nature of some areas that I visited required me in some cases to use my own family reputation as another strategy to build trust with people. I belong to a famous Iraqi tribe that is well known across wide swathes of the country, and which generates respect. This allowed a wide range of people to feel more confident in talking to me.

Once I had discovered the name of the prisoner's tribe and its location in Iraq, I made contact with several people from his community. Some weeks later, and after several research trips to the relevant villages, I was able to make contact with a member of the ex-prisoner's immediate family – in this case, his younger brother. As noted earlier, my profession put me in the path of daily threats, such as terrorist attacks in the form of vehicular attacks, suicide attacks, bombings, or threats from armed groups and militias such as Asaib Ahl al-Haq and The Badr Organization. The growth of the Shia militias was evident in the country.

I therefore had to protect myself by using a variety of tactics. I used sometimes to operate under a fake name, especially when I filed reports about sectarian conflicts in Iraq, or corruption. I knew from the very beginning that these armed groups did not tolerate criticism, so I was very careful when writing articles or dealing with topics that might displease them. Any enquiry could lead the militias to accuse someone of being a spy, and thus face the threat of kidnapping or death. My response was to treat every day as a gift. Sullivan made the sombre assessment that, according to the Committee to Protect Journalists (CPJ), 'three-quarters of all reporters that are killed, are killed because of their journalism' (Sullivan, 2013: 19).

It was, therefore, ultimately my own responsibility to protect myself and to survive whilst doing my job. The experience of investigating sensitive issues in such circumstances was really challenging. Specific examples include an email threat I received from an armed group who called themselves God's Army (Jaish Allah). I believed at first that it was a sick joke made by some of my friends. Very few people could know my private email as I worked with Radio Free Europe. However, what happened later was alarming, as I received a further warning from the group, which described me as an 'agent who violated Iraq's honour'.

I set myself several rules: the first and the most important was not to drive my own car, but instead to use a taxi. In addition, it was easy to be tracked or followed if you visited the same place more than once. During the research process I used to visit some places several times, one being the area were the tribe of the ex-detainee lived. It was a small district 15 miles from the provincial city centre, and few people lived there. An unrecognised visitor or car was a notable event. Second, I also had to use a different phone number to my usual one, giving it out only when obliged to do so. Third, I made no electronic contact with anyone using my real email address.

It was also my responsibility to protect my sources and keep their identities hidden. Keeble (2008: 33) says that informers often 'reveal something that is vital to the public interest: the sort of thing that politicians conceal. They have the right to be protected'. I decided from the very beginning to conduct meetings in protected rather than public places. Most of my contacts were happy to let me visit them at their homes or, if it was secure enough, at their place of work. Finally, after a long period of searching, I was able to meet the person I was looking for and talk to him. He was waiting on the corner of a nearly empty street. It was a short meeting in which he passed me a piece of paper that bore his address.

The next day I rented a taxi and met him at his home. He did not trust the Iraqi media as he thought it was owned by political Islamists and militias, yet was sure that international media could help carry his story to without the threat of persecution. After collecting the all data and information about his story and the people I met, I sent the report to the Radio Free Europe and Radio Liberty (RFE/RL) in Prague, which was happy to broadcast his story. The station featured the ex-detainee's voice recalling the most painful moments in Guantanamo. 'In 2009', he said 'I was fully cleared of all cases and set free from Guantanamo Bay Detention Camp' (AA, interview with Author). He ended the interview by saying 'nobody knows or can imagine what I was facing at Guantanamo – the torture and the humiliation' (AA, interview with Author).

Conclusion

The most surprising thing happened one week afterwards, when the radio station received a call from the International Red Cross (IRC) in Amman, the capital of Jordan. This source recounted what happened with AA, and how IRC people had tried their best to help him. The IRC representative who spoke to the station assured us that the ex-detainee's complaint about their lack of support on his behalf, was simply not true. The Prague station passed on my contact details and the IRC in Amman asked me to send AA a message that the organisation still wanted to offer him assistance, if he could get to the IRC HQ office in Basra province, where he could receive the medical treatment he needed. I felt that this follow-up represented a real material success for me, quite apart from the fact that the story had been aired. At the same time, this incident demonstrated very clearly that one has always to be cautious when taking the testimony of a witness at face value: although the intervention of the IRC confirmed the general accuracy of my informant's story, this detail showed that he was not necessarily reliable in all respects.

Additionally, there were two important issues that the story raised. The first point, as mentioned earlier, is that ex-prisoners trying to re-join their community suffer more than just the imprisonment itself. In this case, the victim was left jobless, and suffering severe illnesses because of the years he spent in detention. In Iraq, there was no institutional structure to offer him help. The second issue concerns journalism in Iraq and what it means to conduct an investigative enquiry in a country that is governed by such an ethno-sectarian system. Journalists and people with sensitive issues were, for the most part, simply unable to publish or broadcast their stories. Iraqi media establishments were either biassed because of their ownership or not willing to take the risk of publishing or broadcasting stories that might offend powerful groups. The challenges I encountered raised several questions in my mind and made me look at the work of journalism and the media sector in Iraq from a different angle. How, I wondered, could investigative work could be developed in such environment?

According to International Media Support (IMS), investigative journalism is, despite all the challenges, gaining ground in Iraq, and there is a huge need for good reporters (International Media Support, 2012). Hisham Hasan, the Dean of Baghdad University Media College, in an interview with IMS, said that 'the Iraqi media is like a dead body. We need to inject life into this body. By providing teaching in investigative journalism, we help . . . to confront the widespread corruption and lack of fundamental freedoms of expression in our country' (International Media Support, 2012). Yet the Iraqi media is not only restricted by the cycle of violence that has spread throughout the country. It is also often hamstrung by the many legal restrictions placed on their activities. For example, libel suits were filed in the courts against the *Al-Mashriq* and *Al-Parlaman* newspapers which had accused the Iraqi Minister of Trade of corruption (Al-rawi, 2012). In a survey conducted by Kim and Hama-Saeed (2008) regarding Iraqi journalists' attitudes, 'it was strongly pointed out that criticising the Shi'ite leader of the Mahdi Army, Muqtada Sadr, or the Prime Minister, Nouri Maliki, was "unthinkable"' (588). However, the lack of training in the field is also a significant issue and will require a great deal of effort to overcome. Hassan added that 'I would like to ask International Media Support (IMS) and the Network for Iraqi Reporters (NIRIJ) to assist in developing the curriculum. As for teaching, currently we have no qualified professors to teach investigative journalism' (International Media Support, 2012: 1). After 2003, a number of NGOs and public networks launched several projects in an attempt to enhance this branch of journalism in Iraq.

The Network of Iraqi Reporters for Investigative Journalism (NIRIJ) was the first network to help investigative journalists and support this field of journalism (The Network of Iraqi Reporters for Investigative Journalism, 2016). NIRIJ was launched in 2011 by a number of professional investigative journalists. Its aim is to:

> Improve the skills of the Iraqi investigative journalists and to work on spreading the investigative culture in Iraqi journalism, to be a regulatory service that . . . follows financial and administrative corruption cases, indicates deviations and mistakes in official and civil behaviour.
> (The Network of Iraqi Reporters for Investigative Journalism, 2016: 232)

However, work in this field still lags behind its counterparts in the rest of the world (The Network of Iraqi Reporters for Investigative Journalism, 2016). Lack of experience and training had significantly affected the development of my own personal investigation process. The little experience I had gained from being self-taught, and my own common sense, were my main guides in covering this story.

References

Al Bakri, Wail Izzat (1994) *The Development of the Press System in Iraq, 1958–1980*, Baghdad: Cultural Events Publishing House.
Al-Deen, Hana Noor (2005) 'Changes and challenges of the Iraqi media', *Global Media Journal*, online, www.globalmediajournal.com/open-access/changes-and-challenges-of-the-iraqi-media.php?aid=35090 [accessed 30 March 2018].
Al-Marashi, Ibrahim (2007) 'The dynamics of Iraq's media: Ethno-sectarian violence, political Islam, public advocacy, and globalization', in *Cardozo Arts and Entertainment Law Journal*, Vol. 25, p. 95.
Al-Monitor (2017) 'Iraqi journalists kidnapped and murdered', www.al-monitor.com/pulse/originals/2017/01/iraq-journalists-kidnapping-murderprosecution.html#ixzz4zesesjiq [accessed 20 February 2017].

Al-Qarawee, Harith Hasan (2014) *Iraq's Sectarian Crisis: A Legacy of Exclusion*, Carnegie Middle East Center, Washington DC: Carnegie Endowment for International Peace.

Al-rawi, Ahmed K. (2010) 'Iraqi women journalists' challenges and predicaments', in *Journal of Arab & Muslim Media Research*, Vol. 3, Issue: 3, pp. 223–236.

―――― (2012) *Media Practice in Iraq*, London: Palgrave Macmillan.

―――― (2013) 'The US influence in shaping Iraq's sectarian media', in *International Communication Gazette*, Vol. 75, Issue: 4, pp. 374–391.

Al-rawi, Ahmed K. and Gunter, Barrie (2013) 'Political candidates' coverage in the 2010 Iraqi general elections', in *Journal of Middle East Media*, Vol. 9, Issue: 1, pp. 69–94.

Amos, Deborah (2010) 'Confusion, contradiction and irony: The Iraqi media in 2010', Joan Shorenstein Center on the Press, Politics and Public Policy, Discussion Paper Series #D-58, June.

Bengio, Ofra (1998) *Saddam's Word: Political Discourse in Iraq*, Oxford: Oxford University Press.

―――― (2004) 'In the eyes of the beholder: Israel, Jews and Zionism in the Iraqi media', in Parfitt, Tudor and Egorova, Yulia [editors], *Jews, Muslims and Mass Media: Mediating the "Other"*, London and New York: Routledge, pp. 109–119.

Bennani, Farida, Elsadda, Hoda, Fergany, Nader, Jadaane, Fahmi and Kubursi, Atif (2003) *Arab Human Development Report: Building a Knowledge Society*, New York: The United Nations Development Programme.

Cazes, Séverine (2003) 'The Iraqi media: 25 years of relentless repression', *Reporters Without Borders*, online, www.rsf.org [accessed 22 February 2017].

Communication and Media Commission (2007) 'CMC Magazine', http://cmc.iq/en/pdfcmc/releasestawasol/pdfs/17.pdf [accessed 30 March 2018].

Daragahi, Borzou (2003) 'Rebuilding Iraq's media', in *Columbia Journalism Review*, vol. 42, no. 2, pp. 45.

Elsea, Jennifer K. and Garcia, Michael John (2010) 'Enemy combatant detainees: *Habeas Corpus* challenges in federal court', Congressional Research Service.

Global Investigative Journalism Network (nd), https://gijn.org [accessed 13 November 2018].

Haddad, Fanar (2013) 'Sectarian relations and Sunni identity in post-civil war Iraq', in Potter, Lawrence G. [editor], *Sectarian Politics in the Persian Gulf*, London: Hurst, pp. 67–116.

Hadhum, Haider S. (2012) 'The media in transition: The rise of an "independent" press in post-invasion Iraq and the American role in shaping the Iraqi press 2003–2005', unpublished thesis, City University of London.

Hagan, John, Kaiser, Joshua, Hanson, Anna and Parker, Patricia (2015) 'Neighborhood sectarian displacement and the battle for Baghdad: A self-fulfilling prophecy of fear and crimes against humanity in Iraq', in *Sociological Forum*, Vol. 30, Issue: 3, pp. 675–697.

Harder, Amy (2008) 'Report: Hundreds of Iraqi journalists forced into exile', *The Reporters Committee for Freedom of the Press*, online, www.rcfp.org/browse-media-law-resources/news/report-hundreds-iraqi-journalists-9forced-exile [accessed 19 February 2017].

Hassan, Hussein D. (2007) *Iraq: Tribal Structure, Social, and Political Activities*, Washington, DC: Library of Congress, Congressional Research Service.

International Federation of Journalists (2006) 'IFJ says Iraqi journalism is "Deadly Profession" as media death toll reaches 160', 15 November, www.ifj.org/nc/news-singleview/browse/401/backpid/33/category/news/article/ifj-says-iraqi-journalism-is-deadly-profession-as-media-death-toll-reaches-160 [accessed 18 January 2017].

International Media Support (2012) 'Investigative journalism', www.mediasupport.org/journalism-education-in-iraq-boosted-with-investigative-specialisation [accessed 2 February 2017].

Iraqi Media House (2017) http://iraqimediahouse.com [accessed 23 March 2017].

Isakhan, Benjamin (2007) 'The role of the press in Iraq's long struggle for democratic reform', in *OUR Media-NUESTROS Medios VI 2007: Sustainable Futures, Roles and Challenges for Community, Alternative and Citizens' Media in the 21st Century: Proceedings of the 2007 International Conference*, New South Wales: University of Western Sydney, p. 1.

——— (2009) 'Manufacturing consent in Iraq: Interference in the post-Saddam media sector', in *International Journal of Contemporary Iraqi Studies*, Vol. 3, Issue: 1, pp. 7–25.

Kaplan, David E. (2013) *Global Investigative Journalism: Strategies for Support*, 14 January, A Report to the Center for International Media Assistance, Washington, DC: National Endowment for Democracy.

Keeble, Richard [editor] (2008) *Communication Ethics Now*, Leicester: Troubador Publishing Ltd.

Kim, Hun Shik and Hama-Saeed, Mariwan (2008) 'Emerging media in peril: Iraqi journalism in the post-Saddam Hussein era', in *Journalism Studies*, Vol. 9, Issue: 4, pp. 578–594.

Kuttab, Daoud (2007) 'The media and Iraq: A blood bath for and gross dehumanization of Iraqis', in *International Review of the Red Cross*, Vol. 89, Issue: 868, pp. 879–891.

The Network of Iraqi Reporters for Investigative Journalism (2016) 'About us', www.nirij.org/?page_id=232 [accessed 12 February 2017].

The New Arab (2016) 'Popular mobilisation militia "kills" TV crew in Iraq's Diyala', *The New Arab*, online, www.alaraby.co.uk/english/news/2016/1/12/popular-mobilisation-militia-kills-tv-crew-in-iraqs-diyala [accessed 23 February 2017].

New York Times (2002) The Guantanamo Docket. https://www.nytimes.com/interactive/projects/guantanamo/detainees/current [accessed 17 June 2018].

Petraeus, David H. (2007) 'Report to congress on the situation in Iraq', 11 September, Assistant Secretary of Defense (Public Affairs), Washington, DC.

Price, Monroe, Griffin, Douglas and Al-Marashi, Ibrahim (2007) 'Toward an understanding of media policy and media systems in Iraq: A foreword and two reports', Departmental Papers (ASC), 1 May, 59.

Ricchiardi, Sherry (2011) *Iraq's News Media after Saddam: Liberation, Repression, and Future Prospects*, Washington, DC: Center for International Media Assistance.

Rugh, William A. (2004) *Arab Mass Media: Newspapers, Radio, and Television in Arab Politics*, CA: Greenwood Publishing Group.

Sa'adoun, Mustafa (2017) 'Looking for a suicidal job? Try Iraqi war reporter', *Global Investigative Journalism Network*, http://gijn.org/2017/02/13/looking-for-a-suicidal-job-try-iraqi-war-reporter [accessed 22 February 2017].

Salloum, Saad (2009) 'Jerry Kammer discusses investigative journalism in Iraq', niqash.org, at www.niqash.org/en/articles/society/2427/ [accessed 13 February 2017].

Sullivan, Drew (2013) *Investigative Reporting in Emerging Democracies*, Sofia, Bulgaria: Information Resource Center, U.S. Embassy.
UNDP (2003) *United Nations Arab Human Development Report: Building a Knowledge Society*, New York: Arab Fund for Economic and Social Development.
The United Nations Educational, Scientific and Cultural Organization (2015) www.unesco.org/new/en/iraq-office/about-thisoffice/singleview/news/unesco_and_iraqi_journalists_syndicate_sign_agreement_and_wi/ [accessed 29 March 2017].

9 Co-operative international coverage? *The Ferret*'s foreign reporting

Peter Geoghegan, Billy Briggs, and Brindusa Ioana Nastasa

The past decade has brought sweeping changes to established newsrooms. Many print outlets – struggling amid declines in advertising revenue and newspaper sales – have been forced to lay off staff, to reduce operating costs, and to look for new models for raising revenue (Kaye and Quinn, 2010). This retrenchment has often been particularly notable in foreign coverage. At the same time, a slew of new digital journalism start-ups have stepped into the gaps created by the retreat of legacy media. The biggest players in this emerging media market have been for-profit outfits funded predominantly by the traditional advertisement-led model supplemented by advertorial and other curated content (Carlson and Usher, 2016). As these start-ups have grown in size and scale, so too has their interest in – and backing for – hard news reporting, domains once seen as the preserve of more established media. *Buzzfeed*, for example, has assembled impressive editorial teams and dedicated significant resources to investigative journalism on both sides of the Atlantic. Online outlets have also committed resources to international reporting. *Vice* – which often relies on precariously employed freelance staff – has been responsible for some of the most prominent video journalism from in and around the frontlines of contemporary global conflicts.

The media's digital revolution has also been the harbinger of a marked growth in not-for-profit public service journalism (Jarvis, 2011; Price, 2017). This trend has been particularly discernible in the United States, where a culture of philanthropic support for journalism is relatively long-standing (Birnbauer, 2011). The 'not-for-profit newsroom' *ProPublica* has won Pulitzer prizes. New digital outlets have also emerged in Europe, Australia, and elsewhere (McChesney, 2016). A sizable number of these new ventures have chosen to organise along co-operative lines (Hunter et al., 2013). Media co-operatives can take different forms. In 2009, the *West Highland Free Press*, which is published on the Isle of Skye, became the first employee-owned newspaper in the UK, following a buy-out by workers. Other media co-operatives, such as *New Internationalist*, are 'multi-stakeholder', with both workers and readers involved in the governance and running of the magazine. Media co-operatives are not new – German daily *Die Tageszeitung* (often known as 'the Taz') has been publishing since 1978 – but the democratic structures under-pinning co-operatives are particularly attractive in an era of declining trust in the media among the general public (Geoghegan, 2017).

The Ferret – of which two of the authors are also co-directors – is a co-operative digital platform based in Scotland, focused on investigative journalism. *The Ferret* was launched in 2015 by a small group of mainly freelance journalists with the promise to deliver independent journalism that 'noses up the trousers of power'. Since then the website has carried over 100 exclusives and a number of extensive international investigations. *The Ferret* is partly a response to the struggles facing local media in Scotland and the withdrawal of resources from investigative journalism (Geoghegan, 2016). Advertiser-led models for online journalism have often struggled to provide both in-depth and local reporting due to the onus on generating 'clicks' for revenue (Picard, 2011). Mindful of this, *The Ferret* elected not to run any advertisements and instead to generate income predominantly through subscriptions. Content on the site is guarded by a porous pay wall that allows three 'free views' a month before prompting readers to subscribe at a cost of between £3 a month and £100 a year. In its first two years, *The Ferret* attracted almost three-quarters of a million page views, with turnover and subscriptions doubling in the project's second year. All content on the website is paid for, normally at a day rate of £110. *The Ferret* also reflects wider concerns about media ownership. The website is a multi-stakeholder co-operative with both readers and journalists involved in the day-to-day running of the organisation. As well as publishing stories, *The Ferret* frequently runs training programmes and workshops on various aspects of investigative journalism including Freedom of Information legislation and fact-checking. As *The Ferret*'s membership has grown, it has increased the organisation's capacity to support longer investigations and more international reporting. In this chapter, we will look in more depth at examples of *The Ferret*'s foreign work, but first it is important to place the emergence of *The Ferret* within both its specific geographical context, and wider changes in the relationships between journalism and its public in an era when news consumption is increasingly online.

The Ferret: a co-operative approach

The Ferret consciously sought to respond to a series of democratic, economic and ethical crises facing journalism – and journalists – in Scotland (Price, 2017). Over the past decade, Scotland's devolved parliament has become more powerful and the focus on specifically Scottish issues in public and political discourses has become ever more pronounced. At the same time, the financial clout of the Scottish press decreased sharply with diminishing resources available for investigative and reportage work (Geoghegan, 2017). Broadcasters, too, have struggled to cover adequately the depth of the changes in Scottish politics and society (Hassan, 2017). As a consequence,

Scottish audiences have often expressed higher levels of media distrust than elsewhere in the UK, or in comparable polities (Geoghegan, 2016). This was not always the case. Scotland used to boast one of the highest concentrations of newspaper readers in the world. In its heyday, the *Sunday Post* sold 1.7 million copies every week in a country of five million. Still published in Dundee by D.C. Thomson, which is also responsible for the *Beano*, the *Sunday Post* was selling around 142,000 by mid-2017.

The decline of the Scottish press has been most acutely felt in what were once its quality titles. In 2005, *The Scotsman* had more than 500 journalists and production staff. By 2016, that figure had fallen to just 130. Tabloids have fared little better. Sales of the Glasgow-based *Daily Record* fell by 63.5% between 1992 and 2011 (Geoghegan, 2014). Foreign reporting in the Scottish press has been badly hit. In the early 1990s, Maurice Smith (writing in *Paper Lions: The Scottish Press and National Identity*) considered the possibility of *The Herald* appointing a Moscow correspondent in the wake of the dissolution of the Soviet Union (Smith, 1994). However, both *The Herald* and *The Scotsman* have long since closed all their foreign bureaus. *The Herald* carries just a single page of foreign news each day, comprised mainly of wire copy. *The Scotsman* no longer has the financial clout or the ambition to support a pool of experienced international stringers. At the time of writing, Scotland faces Brexit – an outcome a majority of Scots voted against – without any dedicated Brussels correspondents in either its print or broadcast outlets.

Scottish journalism has gone through these democratic and economic challenges at the same time as the wider news industry has faced serious ethical questions in the wake of phone-hacking and other revelations of press malfeasance (Franklin, 2014). From its inception, *The Ferret* deliberately sought to address the perceived legitimacy gap between journalists and audiences by affording would-be readers a say in its journalism. At its launch, readers were asked to vote on their preference of three possible subjects for investigations: NHS cuts, asylum in Scotland, or fracking. Almost 800 people took part in this online poll, with fracking topping the vote. Subsequently, a crowdfunding campaign was launched in July 2015, with a target of £3,800, to fund the fracking investigation. The campaign raised almost three times its target. The money funded a lengthy investigation into fracking involving Freedom of Information (FOI) requests, document searches, and interviews. In all, around a dozen stories on fracking were published on the website. Many received widespread attention and were republished in other media outlets. The investigation was regularly cited in the ongoing policy debate on fracking in Scotland at the time. The crowdfunding campaign also 'boot strapped' *The Ferret* financially, allowing it to begin generating new stories beyond the original fracking investigation, and to begin attracting subscribers. Since then, each quarter has registered a net gain in subscribers. *The Ferret* has won a number of journalism awards and, in the spring of 2017, launched a fact service (FFS) backed by a one-year, €50,000 Google Digital News Initiative grant.

The Ferret's model reflects both distinctly contemporary demands for more open and transparent media organisations and creative approaches to production and distribution that are rooted in journalistic history (Moe, 2010). Pioneering English journalist Daniel Defoe (1660–1731) and Edinburgh's eighteenth-century pamphleteers were supported by subscriptions and patrons. *The Economist* and *The New Yorker* today rely predominantly on subscriptions, too. *The Ferret* has attempted to expand the range of reader engagement beyond the bare cash transaction by actively asking readers what subjects they would like to see investigated. *The Ferret* also seeks to build trust between audience and journalists through its institutional structures. Every subscriber is automatically a member of the co-operative with full voting rights, and readers are represented by directors elected to the project's Board. Elections take place at the annual AGM. At launch *The Ferret* published a mission statement committing the organisation to public service journalism. Since then, it has published quarterly reports of all financial activities including how much each director is paid for their journalism. Anecdotal evidence suggests *The Ferret*'s ownership structure and active commitment to transparency has played an important part in attracting subscribers. *The Ferret* also runs regular public events that frequently mix workshops and skills transfer with live debates and discussion. As such *The Ferret* fits into what Hunter and Van Wassenhove (2010) call 'stakeholder media', a form of journalism that serves communities that believe that they cannot obtain comparable quality of information or coverage of their issues of concern in mainstream media outlets.

The Ferret's international reporting

In practice, *The Ferret* is coordinated through a 'digital newsroom' with its five journalist directors – who are each paid a small monthly retainer – operating as an editorial team connected via Slack, a cloud-based software that is used for group communication by numerous media organisations including *The Washington Post*. Day-to-day editorial work is discussed online, with monthly board meetings dedicated mainly to agreeing on strategic objectives, and identifying any pressing issues that might arise, as well as discussing the progress of longer-term investigations. Although the vast majority of *The Ferret's* subscribers are based in Scotland, there is a perceptible appetite among its readers for international stories, particularly those that chime with *The Ferret*'s public service commitment. In the first six months, almost all of *The Ferret's* content was Scottish – or UK – focused, but there has been a conscious drive to support more foreign coverage. *The Ferret* operates under strict financial pressures – which will be expanded upon in the concluding comments – but it is able to choose to commit resources to the exhaustive international reporting that many established media, in Scotland and elsewhere, have increasingly pulled back from. Thus far, *The Ferret* has featured reports on environmental malpractice in Bosnia, life in refugee camps in Calais, fracking in the United States and a host of other international stories. In the case studies that follow two *Ferret* journalists – co-director Billy Briggs and Romanian documentary filmmaker and multimedia journalist Brindusa Ioana Nastasa – discuss their foreign reporting for *The Ferret* in depth.

Billy Briggs: the Battle of Mosul

In March 2017, I visited Northern Iraq (also known as Iraqi Kurdistan and/ or Southern Kurdistan) with photographer Angie Catlin to cover one of the biggest international stories of the year – the Battle of Mosul. An offensive to take back Mosul from ISIS had started on 17 October 2016, so our trip was planned in order to have a series of stories in place for *The Ferret* that coincided with the six-month mark of the battle between Iraqi forces and ISIS, their Islamic State enemies. Our aim was to document the impact of that battle on the civilian population and to look at wider related issues, including how Iraqi Kurdistan was coping with a humanitarian crisis as a result of ISIS's violence. Our time would be spent in the Kurdish cities of Erbil and Duhok and in and around Mosul, Iraq's second largest city, where ISIS was fighting Iraqi military forces. We had a small team of local fixers and conducted around 50 interviews over the period, including meetings with – among others – Kurdish and Iraqi soldiers, Yazidis, a Christian militia, politicians, academics, injured civilians, hospital patients, medical staff, and internally displaced people from Mosul and elsewhere in Iraq.

The trip to Iraqi Kurdistan would be our latest venture as a reporting team. Former staffers at *The Herald*, Catlin and I both left the newspaper in 2006 to focus on producing in-depth reportage stories for newspapers, magazines, and websites. Since then, we have visited over 20 countries together, mostly reporting from conflict zones on human rights violations and humanitarian issues in places such as Gaza, the West Bank, Lebanon, Pakistan, Syria, Guatemala, Haiti, Russia, and Nepal. We had previously been to Iraqi Kurdistan, in 2012, when we spent time in the Qandil mountains with PJAK, an armed group proscribed as a terrorist organisation by both the United States and the EU.

As freelancers, Catlin and I aim to make a couple of international trips each year, usually spending around a fortnight each time. Our last trip had been to Pakistan more than two years earlier – a frightening but exhilarating experience working undercover in Taliban strongholds – so our proverbial feet were itchy, to say the least. We had looked into visiting Yemen – our first choice – to report on its ongoing war, but this proved unfeasible for two reasons: access to the country was extremely difficult with all flights stopped for months at a time; and the cost of operating in Yemen was prohibitively expensive, with security per day costing around $500.

So, our second choice was to revisit Iraqi Kurdistan and we were particularly keen to do so in light of the incursion by ISIS and developments since that event. The Islamist terrorist group had captured the city in 2014, routing Iraqi forces, so the latter – backed by Kurdish forces fighters and an international coalition – was fighting to retake ISIS's so-called Caliphate. The date 17 April 2017 would mark six months since the offensive to retake Mosul from ISIS had begun. A relevant 'hook' – such as an anniversary – is an important journalistic consideration for any story, in order to engage both editors and readers, so we decided to go ahead, and arrive before this date to report on the start of the Battle of Mosul.

Another reason for choosing Iraqi Kurdistan was our excellent Kurdish contacts. I have cultivated a network of Kurdish connections as a result of having reported on issues surrounding Iraqi/Kurdish asylum seekers and refugees when I was a news reporter. Building a network of contacts is fundamental to investigative journalism. It takes time, but is worth the effort over the long term, and is likely to produce regular stories plus exclusive access and information. For example, our trip to the Qandil Mountains with PJAK would not have been possible without our Kurdish contacts. The key is building personal relationships – and trust – over time. If people respect you as a journalist, then they will provide you with information.

We usually fund our own international trips and recoup costs by selling articles on our return. This is our usual modus operandi as commissions in advance are, sadly, rare these days. In this instance, however, *The Ferret* was able to fund the trip to Iraq up front, which allowed us to focus our attention squarely on story-gathering in the field and logistics in the immediate run-up to our departure for Iraqi Kurdistan.

Planning

In summer 2016, we met with Kurdish contacts in the UK to talk about what kind of stories would be feasible if we made the Mosul trip. We had researched and produced a wish list, so the next step was to try to nail everything down. It is vital to plan well in advance: what stories/issues could we cover? What access would be possible on the ground? How long would it take to arrange that access? Who can help us on the ground when we were in the region? What stories could they suggest? Could we cover issues that haven't yet been reported – in other words, could we obtain genuine exclusives? We also had to think carefully about logistics, including costs, travel, insurance, accommodation, essential medical injections, security risks, and equipment. Feedback from our Kurdish contacts at the outset was positive. We were told that pretty much everything we'd asked for *may* be possible. Of course, there are *never any guarantees* and experience had taught us that best laid plans often go awry (for example, we had to work undercover in Syria in 2009 after our fixer suffered a heart attack). But, as the result of two meetings with people we trusted, we decided our trip was on.

Our next step was to get a commission. I suggested that we approach *The Ferret* because of its commitment to international human rights issues.

While the vast majority of *The Ferret*'s coverage has a Scottish focus, there is a commitment at an editorial level to covering foreign stories where possible. The Battle of Mosul was a major international news story, so we felt it would enhance *The Ferret*'s reputation to carry exclusive reports and eye-witness reporting commentary from Iraqi Kurdistan. Also, there had been little coverage of the impact of ISIS on Iraqi Kurdistan, as detailed by our Kurdish contacts, so we felt we could offer an insight into important but under-reported issues. Thankfully, *The Ferret* editorial team agreed, and we were commissioned on the basis that we offered three in-depth, multimedia reports alongside a 'Reporter's Notebook' digital diary which would include quirkier interviews to provide a unique insight into people's lives in a warzone. These daily updates of text and images from on the ground were published on the website *Medium* while we were in country.

Our next step after securing a commission was to book flights and accommodation, and to enquire about visa entry requirements. We had to monitor developments on the ground on a daily basis and work out a detailed schedule with our Kurdish fixers. A 14-day trip usually allows for 10–11 working days on the ground. That is not long, especially in a conflict zone where bureaucracy can be problematic. There's also travelling time to take into account, so time was at a premium, especially when commissioned to cover three major stories.

Reporting from the field

We arrived in Erbil, Iraqi Kurdistan, on 17 March 2017 but later than expected as our flight was delayed by some ten hours. This meant that our first day was taken up by jumping through the first of many bureaucratic hoops, but our trip eventually worked out well, although we encountered numerous problems along the way. Despite planning in advance and trying to anticipate problems we had to face – as with every international trip – a variety of challenges. We arrived in Iraqi Kurdistan at Newroz, the Kurdish New Year, which meant public offices were closed for the holiday and the region was almost at a standstill. For various reasons, the timing was unavoidable, and although we had talked at length with our fixers in advance, we were unable to secure some interviews and access. For example, we were not able to gain access to camps for Internally Displaced Peoples (IDPs) near the Kurdish city of Duhok. We also had a trip to Kirkuk cancelled at the last minute. We had planned to visit the city to document Save The Children's work to help traumatised youngsters who had lived under ISIS rule, but the authorities refused permission due to new restrictions. This story was viewed as a 'banker', as we had arranged the visit four months previously, so we were hugely disappointed at the late cancellation. We had also hoped to spend time on the frontline with the Peshmerga, but they were not fighting at that juncture.

Despite these challenges, we managed to cover five stories in total. The first was a 2,000-word reportage piece on the humanitarian crisis created by the Battle of Mosul. We focused on how Kurdish hospitals were struggling to cope with the influx of thousands of injured civilians from Mosul, as this issue had not been widely covered. After the offensive began in October 2014, soldiers, injured civilians, and ISIS fighters were taken to hospitals in Erbil, the Kurdish capital. We had been advised of the problems facing the city and arranged an interview with the man responsible for health in the region, Dr Saman Barzangy, who (together with some colleagues) talked at length about various issues along with some colleagues. Dr Barzangy is responsible for 23 hospitals in the Erbil area and 18 specialised centres, and told us that 'this [the Mosul battle] is another crisis for us. We've been receiving 150 to 200 trauma cases a day plus hundreds of non-trauma cases – including maternity cases and chronic diseases. We had 29,000 patients in the first three months [after the offensive started]'.

Of that 29,000, 14,000 were trauma cases, people who had been shot and/or injured in explosions. Dr Barzangy also talked about ISIS chemical attacks, recalling how 'we received 15 cases. All of them (patients) were burned and had shortness of breath and irritation to the skin – in the last two weeks'. He couldn't say which chemicals were used, believing that the incident needed further investigation, but mustard gas was mentioned by local media. During that interview we asked for permission to visit a local hospital, and Dr Barzangy arranged for us to visit Erbil's Emergency Medical Center (EMC), where we spent several hours interviewing staff and injured patients. Around 95% of patients were from Mosul, many with terrible injuries after being shot or caught in explosions (see photographs in Figures 9.1 and 9.2). These included women who had lost limbs and young children clearly in pain.

The hospital said it had also treated Iraqi soldiers and ISIS fighters. EMC is a not-for-profit organisation led by a surgeon called Dr Rawand Haweizy who is an expert in war surgery. He told us that 'we've had 130 trauma patients since the 1st March – 18 days in total as today is 19 March – and 170 in February'. Most people were the victims of bombs, mines and bullets.

He gave us a tour of EMC, which was filled with Mosul's maimed. In the first ward, a 5-year-old girl called Shehad lay on a bed. She was wearing pink pyjama trousers and was stripped to the waist, her left arm bandaged. She grimaced in pain, watched by her mother Layla. The family came from a small village on the outskirts of Mosul called Allela, which was under ISIS rule until the offensive started. She had suffered a fractured arm in an explosion, and although her father Abdullah also survived the blast, he lost an eye. 'They think it was a mine', Haweizy said.

Afterwards, we visited the Kurdish frontline, near Mosul, to witness injured people from the west of the city being transferred from Iraqi ambulances, to Kurdish medics who ferried them to Erbil.

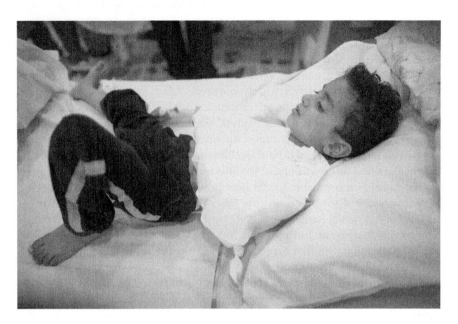

Figure 9.1 Five-year-old Husan was shot in west Mosul. He was being treated at the EMC in Erbil, Iraqi Kurdistan.

Photograph: Angela Catlin, March 2017.

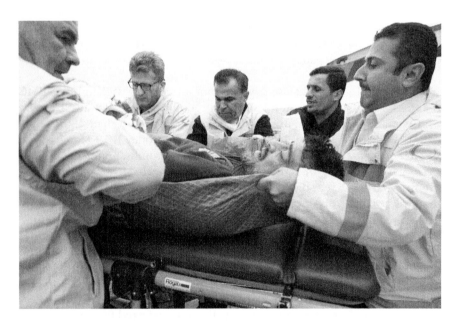

Figure 9.2 An injured Iraqi man from west Mosul being helped by Kurdish medics on the outskirts of Mosul, Iraq.

Photograph: Angela Catlin, March 2017.

Our access was negotiated by Dr Barzangy, and aided by our fixers who got us through a series of Peshmerga checkpoints before arriving about 10 miles from Mosul city centre. On arrival, we witnessed injured people arriving from Mosul and people who had fled the fighting including frightened families with children. We conducted numerous interviews, with the help of our fixers, and took photographs and video footage. Being able to witness live events first-hand complemented the earlier interviews and hospital visit. Moreover, we were able to document an important humanitarian issue.

The next story we covered was the situation facing the Yazidis, a religious minority who had been persecuted by ISIS and suffered terribly. Our aim was to conduct a series of interviews with a view to explaining the problems facing this displaced population. To do this, we relocated from Erbil to Duhok which involved almost a full day of travelling by car on roads made inaccessible by the conflict. This meant we lost a full day working which increased the pressure. In Duhok, we interviewed a doctor who runs a centre that supports Yazidi women who managed to escape ISIS captivity. It is the only specialised centre in Iraqi Kurdistan. She talked about gang rapes, broken limbs and the psychological damage that women suffered. 'Most were raped multiple times. Many were gang raped. Some had broken bones . . . broken legs . . . when they came to us. Many had genital problems'. This doctor, a pharmacist, explained that the centre was established after the first survivor arrived in Duhok on 18 September 2014 – a 15-year-old girl who had managed to escape from ISIS captivity in Mosul. 'She required urgent medical and psychological help', the doctor told us, adding that she quickly realised there would be many more victims. 'At the start our main concern was to give them medical support because they had been raped. Then we realised that most had trauma so we involved psychologists'.

We also interviewed a Yazidi couple in a Duhok market. They had met each other in an IDP camp on the outskirts of the city and married last year. We also visited Lalish, the spiritual heartland for the Yazidis, an ancient village which is the main site of pilgrimage. There, we interviewed an IDP family from Sinjar who fled to Mount Sinjar when ISIS attacked in 2014. Ali – the father – had since joined a Yazidi battalion with the Peshmerga and was due to return to the frontline.

The Lalish trip worked well, but it was a case of adapting quickly to a fast-moving situation, which you often need to do on foreign reporting trips because even the best-laid plans regularly go awry. After arriving in Duhok, we had had a run of bad luck for three full days with interviews falling through and doors closing left, right and centre. So, our fixer suggested we visit Lalish 'on spec', arguing that – at the very least – we would enjoy a fascinating afternoon. Fortunately, this worked well and we were able to obtain useful interviews and photography to weave into our Yazidi story. The rest of the report was finalised a few days later, on our return to Erbil, when we visited a Yazidi encampment in a part of the city called Dream World. This tiny community was being supported by the University of Kurdistan, whose students and staff were visiting the Yazidis to provide education and activities such as art therapy.

While staying in Duhok – we were there for five days – we also managed to get permission to visit a Christian village, close to Mosul, that had been controlled by ISIS for more than a year. Batanaya – a couple of hours drive from the city – was now under Kurdish control but in disputed territory. Most of the town had been completely destroyed and its population would not be able to return for some time, possibly several years. The destruction was jaw dropping. Christian tombs in a cemetery had been opened and desecrated as ISIS stole gold from the dead. We saw ISIS tunnels under homes and interviewed Kurdish soldiers who had fought against ISIS. The Peshmerga were preparing for the aftermath of ISIS's defeat in Mosul, and the possibility of a new conflict between Iraqi Shia militias and Kurds. We also visited the nearby town of Tellesskaff, also ruled by ISIS, albeit briefly, where we interviewed a family which had arrived in a van packed with belongings, because they intended to return to their home after two years away. These visits were granted by the Peshmerga, after we had met with their head of media on arrival in Erbil.

With the help of a different fixer from Erbil – recommended by an English journalist – we also spent a day with a Christian militia established after ISIS invaded in 2014. The Ninevah Protection Unit (NPU) has around 500 fighters who patrol Christian towns and villages burned out by ISIS. They were based in Al Hamdaniya, a place ruled by the Islamist terror group but largely destroyed and now resembling a ghost town. ISIS tried to raze Al Hamdaniya to the ground before they withdrew. Three-quarters of the houses were burned and/or destroyed, along with many Catholic churches. The town was sprayed with black graffiti and its people were scattered all over Iraqi Kurdistan. Our fixer managed to get us through various military checkpoints – both Kurdish and Iraqi – before we met with the NPU's founder and leader, who was a former soldier with the Iraqi army. He arranged for a tour of the town with his fighters, some of whom agreed to be interviewed. A former soldier with the Iraqi air defence force, the leader said he established a military force to protect Al-Hamdaniya and other Christian places in the wake of ISIS attacks. He started with just 15 soldiers, but now has around 500 men who've been trained by the Americans and armed by Iraqi forces. He told us that 'the NPU is a trial to keep our people safe. We are trying our best to protect our people and to help them. We saw what happened to the Yazidis and the big powers didn't help them. We felt the pain of the Yazidis'.

We also managed to get into Mosul for around three hours during the battle. We did this with the help of the aforementioned fixer who was highly experienced in working with the international media. This proved costly at $300 for his time, but our other fixers refused to take us to the city, due to security concerns. Local fixers were charging up to $1,000 a day to get into west Mosul where ISIS was fighting Iraqi forces. The east of the city was under Iraqi control but still unsecure. Indeed, Iraq's counter terrorism units were hunting ISIS sleeper cells. We drove close to the centre and managed to obtain some video and photography plus a short interview with staff who worked at the Al Salam hospital (see photograph in Figure 9.3) before it was bombed by the United States. People had been used as human shields by ISIS fighters, who had occupied the top three floors.

On the ground, we were in continual contact with *The Ferret* editorial team back in Scotland, talking through stories and giving updates on progress as well as supplying content for the regular diary updates. On returning to the UK, we produced five multimedia reports for *The Ferret* on various aspects of the stories we covered on the ground in Iraqi Kurdistan. These stories combined text, stills, and also video to tell the stories to *The Ferret*'s audience and members, and received a really strong response. A number of subscribers pointed out that *The Ferret* – a very recent addition to the Scottish media landscape – was able to provide coverage of a major international conflict that almost no other dedicated Scottish outlet had. Although *The Ferret*'s focus is primarily Scottish, many subscribers commented positively

Figure 9.3 Al Salam Hospital, East Mosul, Iraq.
Photo: Angela Catlin, March 2017.

on the decision to fund reportage from such an important story. The daily Reporter's Notebook diary on *Medium* (the storytelling app) also attracted significant attention. In an era of diminishing budgets for such freelance reporting – often the bedrock of foreign coverage in the past – working with *The Ferret* gave us an opportunity to tell these stories in the round.

Brindusa Ioana Nastasa: making 'A Second Syria'

I am a Romanian documentary filmmaker and multimedia journalist. In 2016, along with my German colleague Annabella Stieren, I embarked on a project to document how refugee children perceive their displacement and how parents use storytelling to explain the situation to their kids. We travelled to camps in Calais, Dunkirk, Turkey, and Greece in order to collect 'bedtime stories' from Syrian, Kurdish, and Afghan refugee families. This multimedia project was later published in *Der Spiegel*. At the same time, I researched and produced my MA dissertation project at City University based on the material we collected. This work became the multimedia project 'A Second Syria' which was published by *The Ferret* in June 2016 (see photographs in Figures 9.4 and 9.5).

Using videos, photos, sound bites and text, 'A Second Syria' describes the economic situation of Syrians in Turkey through the stories of several highly skilled refugee migrants fighting to survive on less than minimum wage. More than 90% of the estimated 2.7 million Syrians in Turkey do not have

Figure 9.4 Boys' class in Syrian school in Istanbul, Turkey.

Photograph: Brindusa Ioana Nastasa, April 2016.

Figure 9.5 Syrian restaurant in Aksaray, Istanbul, Turkey.
Source: Brindusa Ioana Nastasa, April 2016.

the status of 'refugee'. Living outside camps, they are considered 'guests'. They are not entitled to receive any support from the state. Obtaining a work permit is a complicated and cumbersome process, which pushes most Syrians into working illegally in the informal labour market. This has caused a decline in the job market which affects the poorly educated, women, and informal casual workers. The once flourishing Turkish economy has slowed markedly since the Syrian civil war began in 2011: the growth rate has fallen by more than half, unemployment has risen, and the value of the Turkish lira has dropped by around 70%. A deal between Turkey and the EU in 2016 brought hope of a solution to the refugee crisis, but barely anything has changed.

Initially, I wanted to compare the effects of the migration crisis on the economy of several European countries, but travelling to Turkey inspired and motivated me to focus on the economic situation of Syrians there. Before we left for Turkey, we did a lot of research into where the refugee communities are located, and through Facebook groups we found Syrians and journalists willing to talk to us and help us. A journalist from the Turkish daily newspaper *Milliyet* offered to take us to a family he had previously interviewed. We got along so well with this reporter that he ended up going with us everywhere and translating for us. Another person who offered his help in a Facebook group was Majd, a Syrian studying pharmacy in Istanbul. Majd also offered to translate for us. Another Syrian, Eyad, replied to our message and became one of the central characters in our story, meeting us several times in Istanbul.

Another method we used to find useful contacts was to go to Arabic restaurants in the evening, to ask waiters about their stories. Majd would ask them in Arabic if they would like to talk to us while we had a drink or ate in their restaurant. We also travelled to the coastal city of Izmir where we hung out in Basmane Square, a place famous among the Syrians for meeting smugglers. When we got to Izmir, things were very quiet, as it was just after the EU-Turkey deal, but while drinking tea in a cafe we started talking to a Syrian refugee, Hassan, who shared his story with us. We also interviewed politicians from two of the biggest parties in Turkey and a professor of economics working for the Chamber of Commerce. The fact that we were a foreign team made getting access easier. I have reproduced excerpts from some of our interviews below.

> We know that Syrian children are working as an illegal workforce, and because they are underage, they are working for an even lower price. Turkish workers see them as, let's say enemies, like the Turkish migrants in Germany. . . . There is huge sexual and work exploitation of this population. In the guise of adoption, small female children are getting married and they are forced to become sex slaves.
>
> (Gülsüm Ağaoğlu HDP's Migration and Refugee Commissioner)

> Syrians are not considered refugees in Turkey, they are considered guests. The Turkish government supports the people in the camps, but if you are outside you are on your own. I think 2.5 million are outside the camps and 600,000 in camps. People don't want to stay in camps anymore, you can stay 2–3 months, but after that you need to go to work, to educate your kids if you have kids. Life here in Turkey is really, really difficult and the situation is really horrible. . . . Nowadays, everyone wants to take advantage of refugees. Everyone.
>
> (Syrian refugee Hassan)

> The first 20 days here (in Turkey) my kids were really comfortable, no more sounds of bullets and fire and chaos. We had water, everything was ok, a normal life. After that, they started asking about school. I feel bad and I don't know what to do, I might be forced to lie to get the identification number in order to be able to enrol them in school. My daughter is 8 years old, my youngest son is 7 years old, oldest 11. For this generation it's really hard for them to forget what's going on. They have fear, they suffer from anxiety. I try to tell them how it used to be before. 'Do you remember when we used to on holiday to Turkey?'
>
> (Samir Abboud, Syrian refugee waiter in Istanbul, former businessman)

My background is in documentary filmmaking, so I decided to make the project multimedia. Multimedia can give audiences a more immersive experience with the characters featured in the story, especially when reporting stories from a foreign country. Also, by the time we went to Turkey, the migration crisis had been covered extensively in the media, and I felt that combining audio, visual, and text offered a better chance to grab the attention of readers who might have grown weary of stories about migration.

We received a lot of help from other journalists, and from Syrians who acted as translators for us. The project would have been impossible without them. We were up front from the beginning that we were students and freelancers and could not afford to pay them, and that we could not afford to hire a fixer. Our trip to Turkey was supported by a 'Reporters in the Field' Fellowship from the Robert Bosch Foundation which covered our expenses (travel, accommodation, food). Without such small grants, freelancers could never afford to conduct such extensive reporting on issues like refugees and the migration crisis.

Covering the migration crisis did not just pose practical challenges. There were psychological consequences, too. My colleague and I talked at the end of each day about who we interviewed, how we interacted with the refugees, what they thought of us, and how we could do better next time. Nevertheless, a feeling of powerlessness in the face of their suffering persisted. Whilst writing and re-writing my MA project, I frequently felt emotional distress from what I had seen and heard. One moment stays with me to this day.

Figure 9.6 Girl's English class in Syrian school in Istanbul, Turkey.
Source: Brindusa Ioana Nastasa, April 2016.

I was sitting in an Arabic restaurant in Istanbul listening to the story of a Syrian waiter, who had previously been a lawyer, and his economic hardships living in Turkey. Our conversation was interrupted by a young child selling chocolate. This was one of the many Syrian kids who tried to scrape a living on the streets of Istanbul at night. I have seen children begging before, but in this case, I know nothing had changed for this child. I eventually wrote the second half of my MA dissertation on Trauma and Journalism, focusing on the reporting of refugees.

'A Second Syria' told these stories through a 2,000-word piece augmented by still photographs and video and audio recordings, all of which were carried on *The Ferret*. The story was created using Pageflow, which is one of the many online tools that allows users to create interactive multimedia stories (www.pageflow.io). Pageflow is particularly attractive for pitching multimedia stories to editors. Once the project is published, it can be reshaped to fit the specific website. In the case of *The Ferret*, their editors took all the elements (text, videos, photos, sound bites) and published the story in a format suitable for their site. 'A Second Syria' was the first multimedia project I created in Pageflow, and since then my technique has improved – I now use the minimum amount of text, and when I shoot the visual material (video or photo), I have the composition of an online site in mind and the possibility that text can be added on top of it.

After trying unsuccessfully to place 'A Second Syria' with more established outlets, I was put in touch with *The Ferret* by a colleague from *The Times* – where I had been interning. *The Ferret*'s editorial team were very interested in the piece, and my approach to the subject, and not long after making contact, the story was published. *The Ferret*'s innovative approach to journalism and its interest in online storytelling was important for getting my story about Syrian refugees in Turkey out to a wide audience. Since its publication the project received the Erasmus Award from City University for best dissertation and was selected as runner-up in the Multimedia Category at the 2017 Scottish Refugee Media Awards. After receiving a lot of positive feedback for 'A Second Syria', Annabella Stieren and I started a company (Springroll Media) specialising in feature-length multimedia storytelling.

Conclusion

Initially conceived of as a response to the diminishing commitment to investigative journalism at a national level in the Scottish media, *The Ferret* has also developed a focus on foreign reporting. This reflects both audience demands and gaps in the coverage offered by traditional media outlets. The international stories commissioned by the website mirror *The Ferret*'s broader concerns with public interest journalism based on human rights, inequality, and conflict. Foreign reporting has given *The Ferret* the opportunity to cover major international news stories – such as the Battle of Mosul – as well as the chance to showcase innovative multimedia story-telling approaches, such as the first-hand accounts of Syrian refugees in Turkey in 'A Second Syria'. Such international work has also helped *The Ferret* to develop its own unique news brand among members and potential subscribers. Being in a position to send journalists to places like Iraqi Kurdistan has validated *The Ferret*'s approach for subscribers but also for the journalists involved in the project and the wider journalistic community in Scotland. Stakeholder media have been identified by some as a possible solution to the crisis of funding journalism amid the decline of traditional revenue streams (Hunter et al., 2013). *The Ferret*'s experience suggests co-operative approaches to journalism can help to build trust and legitimacy with audiences (Rottwilm, 2014). In giving readers a say in both the running of the organisation and the stories covered, *The Ferret* could be said to contribute to active citizenship and more engaged relationships between journalists and their readers.

There are, however, limits to *The Ferret*'s capacity to support foreign coverage, and original journalism in general. Having built sustainable revenue streams over a relatively short timescale, *The Ferret*'s experience chimes with research that indicates a growing willingness among the public to pay for news online (Picard, 2013). *The Ferret* has also had some success in diversifying income streams, with revenue raised from a variety of sources including subscriptions, crowdfunding, grants, training and events. But *The Ferret* does not yet support any full-time staff beyond a fact-checker funded through a year-long Google grant. The organisation manages to keep its overheads below £150 per month – the vast majority of *The Ferret*'s revenue is spent on journalism – but budgets are tightly constrained. Most of the journalistic labour is carried out on a *pro-bono* basis, which has made it difficult to attract new active members. While subscribers are keen to provide funding for *The Ferret*'s journalism, they are often more reluctant to become involved in the quotidian workings of the project. Whether *The Ferret* can reach genuine sustainability – the true test of any new media approach – remains to be seen (Price, 2017).

References

Birnbauer, Bill (2011) 'Student muckrakers: Applying lessons from non-profit investigative reporting in the US', in *Pacific Journalism Review*, Vol. 17, Issue: 1, pp. 26–44.

Carlson, Matt and Usher, Nikki (2016) 'News startups as agents of innovation: For-profit digital news startup manifestos as metajournalistic discourse', in *Digital Journalism*, Vol. 4, Issue: 5, pp. 563–581.

Franklin, Bob (2014) 'The future of journalism in an age of digital media and economic uncertainty', in *Journalism Studies*, Vol. 15, Issue: 5, pp 481–499.

Geoghegan, Peter (2014) *The People's Referendum: Why Scotland Will Never Be the Same Again*, Edinburgh: Luath Press.

——— (2016) 'The end of the Scottish press?' in *London Review of Books*, Vol. 38, Issue: 8, pp. 201–221.

——— (2017) 'Data journalism in a cold place: The case of the Ferret', in Mair, John, Keeble, Richard Lance and Lucero, Megan [editors], *Data Journalism*, Bury St Edmonds: Abramis.

Hassan, Gerry (2017) 'Minority interest nation: The changing contours of reporting Scotland on BBC and STV', in *The Political Quarterly*, Vol. 89, Issue: 1, August.

Hunter, Mark Lee and Van Wassenhove, Luk (2010) *Disruptive News Technologies: Stakeholder Media and the Future of Watchdog Journalism Business Models*, Fontainebleau, France: Insead The Business School.

Hunter, Mark Lee, Van Wassenhove, Luk, Besiou, Maria and Van Halderen, Mignon (2013) 'The agenda-setting power of stakeholder media', *California Management Review*, Vol. 56, Issue: 1, pp. 24–49.

Jarvis, Jeff (2011) *Public Parts: How Sharing in the Digital Age Improves the Way We Work and Live*, New York: Simon and Schuster.

Kaye, Jeff and Quinn, Stephen (2010) *Funding Journalism in the Digital Age: Business Models, Strategies, Issues and Trends*, Bern, Switzerland: Peter Lang.

McChesney, Robert (2016) 'Journalism is dead! Long live journalism? Why democratic societies will need to subsidise future news production', in *Journal of Media Business Studies*, Vol. 13, Issue: 3, pp. 128–135.

Moe, Hallvard (2010) 'Everyone a pamphleteer? Reconsidering comparisons of mediated public participation in the print age and the digital era', in *Media, Culture & Society*, Vol. 32, Issue: 4, pp. 691–700.

Picard, Robert, G. (2011) *Mapping Digital Media: Digitization and Media Business Models*, Cambridge: Open Society Foundation.

——— (2013) *The Bottom Line: Do and Will Consumers Pay for Digital News*, Oxford: University of Oxford, Reuters Institute for the Study of Journalism.

Price, John (2017) 'Can the ferret be a Watchdog? Understanding the launch, growth and prospects of a digital, investigative journalism start-up', in *Digital Journalism*, pp. 1–15.

Rottwilm, Philipp (2014) *The Future of Journalistic Work: Its Changing Nature and Implications*, Oxford: University of Oxford, Reuters Institute for the Study of Journalism.

Smith, Maurice (1994) *Paper Lions: The Scottish Press and National Identity*, Edinburgh: Polygon.

10 After the Arab revolts

Social media and the journalist in Egypt

Zahera Harb

Introduction

This chapter examines the role social media played in the Tunisian and Egyptian revolts in 2011, but concentrates more on the interface between *journalistic* activity and the political structures of the Egyptian state post-January 2011. According to Howard and Hussain, the Arab revolts came about because authoritarian regimes were undermined by 'investigating their corrupt practices' (2011: 6). In their opinion, however, 'investigative journalism' was not an established feature of mainstream media practice, but was 'almost solely the work of average citizens using the Internet in creative ways' (2). These authors argue that, considering the circumstances faced by journalists and activists, 'the best and perhaps the only place that critics could use to achieve reform, was the internet' (6). The situation in each country was, however, determined by a number of factors: Bebawi, discussing developments a few years later in Syria and Yemen, noted that 'political conflict and unrest' in some parts of the region (2015: 2) acted as a brake on the development of investigative journalism. In discussing the relationship between political protest and journalism, a great deal has been written on the crucial importance of social media use (see Khamis and Vaughn, 2011; Comunello and Anzera, 2012; Rinnawi, 2012; Khamis and Vaughn, 2013; Wolfsfeld et al., 2013; El-Nawawy and Khamis, 2013; Brym et al., 2014; Herrera, 2014; Wolver, 2016). For my part, I argued in an article published in 2011 that social media had been taken up as a mobilising tool to bring people to the streets of Tunis and Cairo (Harb, 2011).

In that same article I argued that 'what happened in Tunisia and Egypt was effectively the seizure of power by the people as part of a collective will to overthrow dictators and autocratic regimes and to effect democratic change from within' (np). Social media networks did not of themselves generate revolutions, but they were able to facilitate them, helping to generate a sense of connectedness. They created a space where people shared grievances against those in positions of authority: groups of young people, in particular, used that newly shared virtual space to demand that a corrupt political elite be held responsible for their misuse and abuse of power.

Della Porta and Diani noted that 'collective identity is strongly associated with recognition and the creation of connectedness' (1999: 21). Sharing Facebook posts and Twitter hashtags provided exactly that essential bond between protestors. Della Porta and Diani also argued that 'identity is not an immutable characteristic, pre-existing action . . . it is through action that certain feelings of belonging come to be either reinforced or weakened . . . collective action produces and encourages continuous redefinitions of identity' (1999: 93). In this particular case, protest was the form of action that brought people together to form a collective identity, while social media was the platform that enabled the youth of the region to form an underlying bond.

The problem is that in many Arab countries, with the exception of Tunisia (where the democratic process is still developing despite many obstacles [Ghannoushi, 2014]) the strength of popular power has been reduced. Egypt, for example, has been hit by the return of military rule, despite the fact that on 30 June 2013, Egyptians again took to the streets in their millions, demanding the removal of the Muslim Brotherhood president Mohamad Morsi (since jailed, prosecuted and at one point facing the death sentence [Kingsley, 2015]). No sooner had he been removed, than his successor, President Abed El Fatah El Sisi (former head of the Egyptian army) used what he described as 'the people's mandate' to oversee a crackdown on most forms of opposition (2015). Political freedom and freedom of speech in Egypt have undergone a major setback. This chapter will concentrate, therefore, on the state of journalism in Egypt post-January 2011, and the space social media occupies in the lives of a group of journalists struggling to stand up to power and hold it to account. It will also draw on the problems facing investigative journalism in Egypt, amid the clampdown on freedom of expression.

Parallel states: media and politics in Egypt

After January 2011, Egypt witnessed an influx of newly established TV stations – among these were channels supported and financed by the Muslim Brotherhood. At one point, there had been a shift away from the homogenised messages issued (in both print and broadcast media), in support of the government and the country's leaders (Diab, 2012). This healthy development, however, did not last long. Following the 30 June revolt, the media were used as a mobilising tool in the hands of the military, led by Abed Al Fatah al Sisi. Journalistic notions of fairness and balance in covering events vanished. The country's media was then divided into two extreme media clusters – one in support of the Brotherhood, including Al-Jazeera *Mubasher Misr* (Egypt Live), and the other in support of the military. Hate speech against 'the other' on both sides came to dominate public discourse, until the military-led authorities closed down the channels linked to the Brotherhood and other Salafi affiliated religious channels.

The prevailing message and its associated terminology became seamless. Slogans such as 'the people want to execute the supporters of the Muslim Brotherhood', were turned into a celebratory message. There had been several attempts to provide some discursive balance in Egypt, including the creation of a satirical programme produced and presented by Bassem Yousef (who became known as the Jon Stewart of the Arab world), the appearance of a current affairs programme produced and presented by Reem Majed, and another produced and presented by Yousri Fouda. Within two years, the increase of private satellite TV stations in Egypt, which had seemed at first to represent an explosion of media diversity, foundered on a new reality; print and broadcast media ended up singing from the same hymn sheet, that produced by the ruling military elite. The three programmes just mentioned were taken off air for presenting what was assumed to be an attack on the country's political and military leadership.

This situation, where the media realm runs parallel to political organisation (rather than acting as an instrument of critique), can generate poor levels of professionalism in journalists (Hallin and Mancini, 2004). These authors maintain that, conversely, a high degree of professionalism in journalistic enquiry occurs when journalism is clearly differentiated as an institution from other bodies and forms of practice – including, of course, politics (38). This lack of autonomy has created a dominant mindset among a majority of Egyptian journalists; they have become tied to the political actor(s) to whom they lend their support. To borrow Hallin and Mancini's term, the media in Egypt became 'instrumentalized' (37). Journalists in Egypt (mainly broadcasters) identify themselves with particular points of view, which meant that they were not serving the public (even though they claimed to be doing so), contradicting their own standards of practice as specified in the Code of the Profession, ratified in 1986.

The Egyptian airwaves are these days dominated with hours and hours of one-man or one-woman shows, talking heads claiming that they represent wisdom and the truth, as though audiences should be grateful to them for sharing their insights. Some of these talk shows have generated hours and hours of hate speech against the 'other', which in the Egyptian case is seen as those critical of military rule – such people are described as traitors. As prominent broadcast journalist Reem Majed put it, in a paper presented at a conference in Berlin, 'the media is playing the lapdog role rather than the watchdog role, keeping an un-informed populace – that can be easily confused – deceived and directed' (Majed, 2015). The newcomer to the TV market in Egypt is a channel called DMC. Journalists I spoke to in Cairo refer to it as the 'Defence Ministry Channel', in reference to the direct funding it receives from the Ministry of Defence. Egyptian journalists, therefore, are divided into two groups. There are those who fully ally themselves with the regime and act as its mouthpiece, defending its political and economic activities, and those who are trying hard to defend their journalistic integrity and values. Many of the latter have lost their jobs and have been told to stay at home, while others decided to resign when accurate reporting became harder and harder to achieve.

Young people in Egypt were among the first of the Arab youth to use the internet as a political platform, and as a tool to mobilise people for change. Egypt has the largest and most active blogosphere in the Arab world. The Egyptian bloggers were the first to reveal corruption and initiated calls for change as early as 2007 (Saleh, 2007 see also El-Nawawy and Khamis, 2014). A few victories were achieved, such as the firing and sentencing of two police officers condemned for torturing Imad Al Kabeer in 2007 (BBC Arabic, 2007). However, these early Egyptian bloggers faced significant jail sentences and prosecution (BBC News, 2007). In their book *Egyptian Revolution 2.0*, El-Nawawy and Khamis (2013) highlighted the role played by Egyptian political blogs in encouraging civic engagement and public participation through the use of these methods:

> *1)* acting as effective tools for supporting the capabilities of the democratic activists by allowing forums for free speech and political networking opportunities and *2)* providing a virtual space for assembly, which allows for the exchange of civic discourse, deliberation, and articulation that goes beyond simply supporting the capability of the protestors to plan, organize, and execute peaceful protests on the ground.
>
> (3)

El-Nawawy and Khamis studied the blogs of Egyptian activists (describing them as citizen journalists). Although the use of blogs, and other forms of online agitation and commentary, are usually associated with the growth of citizen journalism, I know several professional journalists who took to the blogosphere during the Mubarak era, in order to publish information and raise questions about political and economic misconduct in the country. They adopted this approach because they were denied space in their own media institutions. Some of those journalists used pseudonyms to escape prosecution or the loss of their jobs. The blogosphere in Egypt has come to be dominated by social media outlets, and mainly by Facebook, where note publishing has given both journalists and activists the space they need to publish their stories.

Some ten years after these events, the prosecution of journalists and social media activists is still a regular occurrence. In January 2016, the Egyptian authorities arrested three Facebook admins and 'accused them of using the "networking website to incite against state institutions"' (Shearlaw, 2016). There are up to 35 journalists in detention right now for 'publishing offences', as one Egyptian journalist told me (S, interview with author, 2016) in a discussion that was part of a wider study of Journalism and Culture in Egypt.[1] In November 2016, an Egyptian court sentenced the head of the country's journalists' union and two board members to two years in prison. Another Egyptian journalist summarises the situation as 'journalists live in a state of fear. . . . Big Brother is watching' (M, interview with author, 2016). The Egyptian government is now planning to introduce a new law that criminalises what it calls 'illegal trading of ideas', which comes as an addition to the law on 'Electronic Crime' and can lead to the prosecution of journalists and activists who might do no more than exchange ideas that the regime might deem harmful to 'national interests' (B, interview with author, 2016).

Despite the depth of political gloom in Egypt, some journalists have taken their arguments to the virtual space, establishing journalistic online news ventures that are acting as an alternative forum to that provided by mainstream media. Among those ventures are *Mada Masr, Aswat Masriyah, Minasah*, and a newcomer to the market called *Madina*. *Mada Masr*, for example, became known for investigative reporting that shed light on corruption and misconduct among politicians and the military. According to journalist B (interview with author, 2016), the online news website gained credibility among whistleblowers in the Egyptian civil service. However, that didn't come without a price, because Hosam Bahgat, one of their leading investigative journalists, was arrested and detained for publishing a story in *Mada Masr* on 13 October 2015 with the headline 'A coup busted?'. The article spoke of 'the conviction in August of a group of military officers for plotting a coup with the banned Muslim Brotherhood' (*BBC News*, 2015).

After his release, Hosam posted a statement on Facebook detailing what had happened, informing his readers that he faced 'charges of deliberately broadcasting false news that harms national interests and involuntarily disseminating information that harms the public interest, as per Articles 102 and 188 of the [Egyptian] Penal Code' (*Mada Masr*, 2015). In Egypt, 31% of the population use Facebook, meaning there are some 28 million users of the service. The most notable year-on-year increase, however, was between July 2013 and July 2014, with the user figures jumping by 6.4 million to reach 22.4 million users (*Daily News Egypt*, 2016). Bahgat knew, as did other journalists and activists in Egypt, that the penetration of social media (mainly Facebook) has become far bigger than the readership of online or print news outlets in Egypt.[2]

According to Enrico De Angelis (2015), many journalists were forced to abandon mainstream platforms such as *Al-Shouroq* and *Al-Masri Al-Youm* newspapers, and began writing for alternative media outlets such as *Mada Masr*. However, 'the public recognition of the relevance of the internet is rapidly bringing to the online world the same constraints from which print media suffer' (119). De Angelis situated Egypt's media system within Chadwick's (2013) hybrid model, 'in which old and new media logics coexist' (Chadwick, 2013: 112). Yet this hybrid model seems to be fading from view, with the reproduction in the online news world of 'the existing networks of hierarchies, loyalties, and patronage' (De Angelis, 2015: 109). Naila Hamdy argues in her study on networked journalism in Egypt that 'traditional journalism workers continue their intentional attempt to maintain hegemony over information in a networked journalism environment through their use of gatekeeping practices' (Hamdy, 2015: 16). New media outlets in Egypt do enjoy a level of independence that is almost non-existent in traditional outlets, but as Journalist W put it, 'in the Egyptian experience, professional journalism has little to do with the platform' (interview with author, 2016).

As the case of Hosam Bahgat indicates, investigative journalism in Egypt has taken the form of advocacy journalism. Very few journalists are engaged with or willing to work on investigative stories, mostly because of fear for their safety, but also for lack of media platforms that are willing to publish those stories. Most investigative journalism activities in Egypt are now based on individual initiatives. Some of those journalists are trained by the Arab Investigative Journalists Network (ARIJ) based in Amman, Jordan, while others have not undertaken any professional training. The ARIJ covers stories in Bahrain, Egypt, Iraq, Jordan, Lebanon, Tunisia, Palestine, Syria, and Yemen, and its website allows prospective reporters to download resources and to gain advice. The ARIJ website highlights the essential elements of a typical investigative process: 'the existence of a problem (an action), the presence of victims (object) and the responsibility of a certain party or parties (subject)' (nd). In the opinion of one Egyptian journalist I spoke to, who has worked with the ARIJ and prefers to remain anonymous, the organisation should not be deemed as independent and impartial as it claims to be (personal communication, 2017). According to this journalist, the ARIJ refuses to publish or commission any investigation that involves the Jordanian army or the security apparatus in Jordan. ARIJ, on the other hand, had commissioned Egyptian journalists to investigate corruption in the Egyptian army, and the revelation that it led to arms being smuggled to ISIS operatives in Sinai. One prominent Egyptian investigative journalist and TV presenter, Yosri Fouda, had left the country and moved to Germany to produce and present a show on Deutsche Welle, the German TV broadcasting in Arabic. Fouda has been advised not to return to Egypt, and fears for his safety (journalist M, personal communication, 2016).

Pan Arab TV news and the Egyptian journalism scene

We cannot explore Egypt's media and journalism scene without dedicating some space to the two most prominent Pan Arab news channels – Al-Jazeera Arabic, and Al Arabiya. These channels have both become directly involved in the political struggle that is taking place in Egypt, as they are elsewhere in the Arab world (see Harb, 2011). Despite the fact that they follow the same editorial line on Syria, Yemen, and Bahrain, they actually differ in their treatment of Egypt. Al-Jazeera Arabic in Egypt has become the voice of the Muslim Brotherhood, promoting the organisation through a separate dedicated channel called *Mubasher Misr* (Arabic for Egypt Live). In Egypt, unfortunately, Al-Jazeera Arabic failed its own professional standards. The station broadcast old videos claiming them that they were new, and exaggerated the number of protests held and protesters against the military. They dedicated considerable air-time to voices from the Muslim Brotherhood, ignoring those that did not share its perspective. Despite the fact that they followed the same broadcast style as they did during the 2011 revolt (dedicating screen space for user generated content), coverage was one-sided and their credibility in Egypt has been harmed as a result. The Egyptian regime, meanwhile, shut down all Al-Jazeera offices and operations, including Al-Jazeera English, which was accompanied by the arrest and prosecution in 2014, of three of its journalists for 'operating in Egypt without a licence' (Al-Jazeera, 2015).

However, in 2015, when the relationship and political rivalry between Qatar (which owns Al-Jazeera network) and Egypt softened, Al-Jazeera decided to shut down *Mubasher Misr* and to take it off air (Shams El-Din, 2015). Nevertheless, that failed to stop the reproduction of anti-Qatar sentiments in Egypt, and Al-Jazeera remains a major target of those sentiments. In November 2016, a number of Egyptian TV hosts and journalists launched a campaign against Qatar, over a critical documentary on Egypt's compulsory military service, that was produced by Al-Jazeera (Abdallah, 2016). The documentary featured several testimonies given by army conscripts, claiming ill-treatment and abuse by army officers.

The anti-Qatar and anti-Al-Jazeera campaign was fuelled by large numbers of social media users, who lashed out at Qatar and started 'a storm of mockery on Twitter of the Emir of Qatar Tamim bin Hamad Al Thani' while 'another hashtag was also used to praise the Egyptian army; both of which were among the top trending hashtags in Egypt' (Abdallah, 2016). Many of the Egyptian journalists working for Al-Jazeera have left the network after Al-Jazeera adopted a fully pro-Muslim Brotherhood stand, or were otherwise forced into exile in Doha or Turkey. Al Arabiya and its sister channel Al-Hadath, on the other hand, adopted anti-Muslim Brotherhood sentiments, and hence received support from the Egyptian regime, its military, and a large number of Egyptian journalists, who as mentioned previously have accepted the role of apologists for the regime.

Social media and the journalist

In-depth interviews were conducted with seven Egyptian journalists as part of a study I am conducting on Journalism Culture in the Arab world. All seven journalists work or used to work for newsrooms supported by professional organisational structures. They range between mid-career to senior journalists (those that have been in the profession between 10 and 20 years), to the top echelon who work in the role of editors and deputy editors. Respondents were based in both state-run and privately owned news organisations. None of my interviewees works for Al-Jazeera or Al-Arabiya. Questions posed to these journalists included how social media has affected their way of conducting journalism, how they use it, and what content they tend to generate.

As stated earlier, the journalists interviewed have been anonymised and random letters have been used to refer to each individual. Interviews were conducted via email, Skype and face to face. It is worth mentioning that all of these journalists, except one, had taken part in the protests in Tahrir Square in 2011. At that time, they thought it extremely important to fulfil their role as citizens first, and then as journalists. Like all other activists at the time, they took to social media to express their views. One of them was later identified as a rising star of Egypt's 'online opinion journalism' (a term coined by De Angelis, 2015). Despite this accolade, the journalist himself told me that the phenomena reached its zenith between 2012 and 2015, and has now ended. Some of this decline, according to journalist E, has been due to 'the *negative* impact of social media' (my emphasis). For him, social media played the role of censor, where journalists are judged by users according to their own perception of what how journalists should be practicing their profession. 'Some users tend to classify and attack you according to their political beliefs and perceptions of political reality' (interview with author, 2016). Still, social media was seen by all as a significant source of news and information in a country where accessing information is restricted and sometimes impossible (M, interview with author, 2016), which coincide with Naila Hamdy's study (2015) on networked journalism in Egypt. Journalist W argued that social media had alerted her to stories as they were happening, even before they became news. She, however, points out that because of 'the government propaganda' in mainstream outlets, she has now turned to social media.

> Like many reporters, I've been able to contact sources through their social media accounts or identify a story simply by following actors on the ground tweeting about what they're seeing or what is happening around them. And because I can no longer read the papers regularly (the government propaganda could be a put off) I keep track of read-worthy content when it's shared on social media.
>
> (W, interview with author, 2016)

Journalist M (interview with author, 2016) gave credit to social media users, because it was these people who were altering her production team to stories and issues that needed to be brought to the public domain, and that would not otherwise have gained attention.

> We also used it to find guests for our show away from the official voice and the elite. It enabled us to disclose many human rights violations. We investigated those and verified the accusations and in most cases they were reliable stories. We cannot consider social media users as representative of public opinion, but they do represent one fraction of the society.
>
> (ibid.)

Journalists S and B, being senior editors, speak of the role of social media in bypassing censorship. Facebook is used to post full articles by journalists who have had to remove information from their articles that was deemed not in the 'national interest' before they are published in mainstream newspapers. Readers and users are able to see the two versions of the same article and realise what has been censored in the printed edition.

> Social media helps in raising the bar of freedom of expression and in confronting censorship in Egypt. Social Media is also helping in opening up the space on mainstream media to discuss issues that are usually not permissible to be discussed in the public domain. We use social media trending stories to talk about political or economic issues and publish stories that are perceived by the censor as crossing the line. That is why we are now witnessing an orchestrated campaign against social media.
>
> (B, interview with author, 2016)

Journalist S confirms that some pages on Facebook, such as Al-Mouqef Al Masri, have followers that are approaching one million, 'which exceeds all national Egyptian newspapers' daily distribution' (interview with author, 2016).

Social media is being used, therefore, as a tool to help many Egyptian journalists resist the official discourse that is being recycled through mainstream media, especially TV. At the same time, social media is being used as a platform to distribute lies or what is now being called 'fake news', items that attempt to justify government failures or policies. Journalist A, despite depending on social media interaction for certain stories, said he is mostly sceptical of stories posted on social media.

> Social media is also used as marketing tool for some journalists, and as a measuring device to discover how interested and engaged the public are, in one topic or the other.
>
> (D, interview with author, 2016)

Social media users in Egypt are as divided as the journalistic scene, between those acting as a mouthpiece for the regime, and those whose voices are critical of the economic hardship, political corruption and social injustice in the country.

The role of social media in bringing about democratic change

Wolfsfeld et al. (2013) state that 'one cannot understand the role of social media in collective action without first taking into account the political environment in which they operate' (119). This proved true in the case of Egypt. During the January 2011 revolution, the political and economic situation was at its worst, and the public had become tired of a handful of people in the political elite, who hung on to power and benefitted from the country's wealth, while depriving the public of their basic needs. This nationwide anger and disdain were growing and social media (mainly Facebook) were used as the tool to pass on and share that anger, and to facilitate calls for action (Harb 2011; see also El-Nawawy and Kahmis, 2013). These days, much of the social media scene in Egypt is centred on nationalistic and patriotic sentiments, and the fear of the insecurity that just one year of Muslim Brotherhood rule brought to the country. The regime has succeeded in manipulating that fear and in using it every time voices of dissent (mainly through social media) rise to prominence.

Social media, as one of the journalists interviewed here noted, could be a destructive tool directed at journalists, used to undermine their professional integrity and keep the political status quo intact. A clear example of that is the story of the Lebanese British journalist Liliane Daoud. After the 2011 revolts, Daoud (whose daughter is Egyptian), decided to leave the BBC Arabic service in London and move to host a TV show on one of the rising channels in Egypt (OnTV, owned by Egyptian Businessman Najeeb Saweris). Her talk show, 'The Full Picture', aired critical views of Sisi's government and hosted protesters and youth leaders as well as government officials (the *Guardian*, 2016). In February 2015, Daoud issued a tweet, calling on those Egyptian youth who had been sentenced to five years in jail for protesting, 'not to despair as the slayer will keep trying to deprive you of your will to live and your will for a better life'. Following this tweet, a hashtag on Twitter appeared, which called for the deportation of Daoud. '#Lilian_must_leave' went viral, and became the highest trending hashtag on twitter in Egypt for two days (*Elmawke3 News*, 2015). The hostile tweets that attacked Dauod included death threats. Users believed she was mocking El Sisi (the Egyptian President) and referring to him as the 'slayer' (see earlier). Many Egyptian journalists jumped on this bandwagon, attacking Daoud, while articles published in publications like *El Youm El Saba'a* fabricated information about her.

Nevertheless, some Egyptian journalists took also to Twitter and social media to support Daoud against the hate campaign to which she was subjected. They tweeted and posted on Facebook defending her professionalism and journalistic integrity, reminding the Egyptians that during the rule of Morsi's Muslim Brotherhood she also hosted critics of the Islamist group and, just like the majority of the Egyptian people, she celebrated the ousting of Morsi. That however, didn't deter the authorities form deporting Liliane Daoud in June 2016, claiming that 'she was deported because her residency has expired' (the *Guardian*, 2016). Daoud was deported hours after her contract with OnTV was terminated. One of OnTV officials told *Al Monitor*:

> The decision to stop broadcasting Daoud's show and the termination of her contact, which was supposed to continue until the end of the

year, came as the result of 'editorial policy' and conditions that the new ownership tried to impose on her. She was said to have rejected this, with the contract ending in an amicable manner.

(Saied, 2016)

The termination of the contract came a month after the channel was sold to another businessman who had close ties to the Sisi regime. In this instance, social media was used as a 'coordinating tool', to borrow Clay Shirky's term (2011), to spread hate and mobilise dissent against journalists who did not agree to the 'Hail Caesar' attitude to public life. Despite the negative impact social media might have in silencing voices that are critical of the regime, the journalists interviewed for this chapter still believed that social media provided them with a space to launch campaigns based on the dissemination of information that the authorities and their protégés do not want to reach the public domain. Egyptian journalist Hisham Allam, a member of the International Consortium of Investigative Journalists, and the only Egyptian journalist who took part in the Panama papers and Swiss leaks investigations, told me that it is too hard for investigative journalists in Egypt and the Arab world to get access to information through traditional routes, 'so we take to social media, looking for sources and people willing to provide us with information' (interview with author, 2017). Allam said that sometimes social media is used to publish material mainstream media in Egypt won't accept to publish. He reveals that:

> While working on the Panama Papers investigation, I had information that related to members of the royal families in Saudi Arabia, the United Arab Emirates and Kuwait, to the 'tax haven' investigation. Mainstream media in Egypt refused to give me space to publish these materials, because of the good economic and political relationship Egypt holds with these countries, while they would agree on me publishing anything that will condemn Qatar. I refused and to keep my journalistic integrity I used my Facebook and twitter accounts to publish the material I have investigated. There were no space restrictions.
>
> (Allam, interview with author, 2017)

Investigative reporting, the cornerstone of critical journalism and an essential element in holding those in power to account, cannot operate adequately in an atmosphere of fear for safety and security. Journalism needs to operate as an independent body from political institutions, if democracy is to function (see Hallin and Mancini, 2004; McQuail, 2013). Despite the fact that these are Western ideals of journalism, they resonate within the Egyptian context. Egyptian media are directly connected to the political institutions in the country. As Journalist W (interview with author, 2016) put it, 'in Egypt we don't have independent media, we have independent journalists'. Independent journalists are paving the way using online ventures and social media in order to keep holding those in power to account. Social media users and January 2011 revolution activists are not singing from the same hymn sheet anymore, but the situation is not going to go back to the way it was before January 2011. Independent journalists in Egypt (despite their limited numbers) will continue to fight to safeguard democratic change. If denied space on mainstream media, social media is there for them as an alternative space and an accessible tool of public communication.

Notes

1 Journalists interviewed are anonymised and are referred to by random letters to protect their identities.
2 Television is by far the most common source of news for Egyptians, with 84.2 % using it daily or several times a week to get news (Broadcast Board of Governors, 2014)

References

Abdallah, Salma (2016) 'Al-Jazeera documentary on Egyptian conscripts reignites media war with Qatar', *Aswat Masriya*, 27 November, https://egyptianstreets.com/2016/11/27/al-jazeera-documentary-on-egyptian-conscripts-reignites-media-war-with-qatar/ [accessed 10 March 2017].

Al-Jazeera (2015) 'Egypt releases jailed Al Jazeera reporter Peter Greste', *Al Jazeera Online*, 2 February, www.aljazeera.com/news/middleeast/2015/02/egypt-deports-jailed-al-jazeera-journalist-peter-greste-150201140209881.html [accessed 10 March 2017].

ARIJ: Arab Reporters for Investigative Journalism (nd) 'How to carry out an investigative report with ARIJ', http://en.arij.net/how-to-carry-out-an-investigation/ [accessed 30 March 2018].

BBC Arabic (2007) 'Three years jail sentence for two police officers in Egypt in a torture case', 5 November, http://news.bbc.co.uk/hi/arabic/middle_east_news/newsid_7079000/7079123.stm [accessed 26 March 2011].

BBC News (2007) 'Egypt blogger jailed for "Insult"', 22 February, http://news.bbc.co.uk/go/pr/fr/-/1/hi/world/middle_east/6385849.stm [accessed 1 March 2011].

——— (2015) 'Independent Egypt journalist Hossam Bahgat "arrested"', 8 November, www.bbc.co.uk/news/world-middle-east-34761624 [accessed 24 February 2017].

Bebawi, Saba (2015) *Investigative Journalism in the Arab World: Issues and Challenges*, London: Palgrave Macmillan.

Broadcasting Board of Governors (2014) 'Contemporary media use in Egypt', no date, www.bbg.gov/wp-content/media/2014/03/Egypt-research-brief.pdf [accessed 24 February 2017].

Brym, Robert, Godbout, Melissa, Hoffbauer, Andreas, Menard, Gabe and Zhang, Tony Huiquan (2014) 'Social media in the 2011 Egyptian uprising', in *The British Journal of Sociology*, Vol. 65, Issue: 2, pp. 266–292.

Chadwick, Andrew (2013) *The Hybrid Media System: Politics and Power*, Oxford: Oxford University Press.

Comunello, Francesca and Anzera, Giuseppe (2012) 'Will the revolution be tweeted? A conceptual framework for understanding the social media and the Arab spring', in *Islam and Christian – Muslim Relations*, Vol. 23, Issue: 4, pp. 453–470.

Daily News Egypt (2016) 'Report details internet and social media use among Egyptians', 4 January 2016, www.dailynewsegypt.com/2016/01/04/report-details-internet-and-social-media-use-among-egyptians/ [accessed 24 February 2017].
De Angelis, Enrico (2015) 'The new opinion journalism in Egypt', in *Afriche e Orienti*, Vol. 1, Issue: 2, pp. 103–120.
Della Porta, Donatella and Diani, Mario (1999) *Social Movements: An Introduction*, Oxford: Blackwell.
Diab, Khaled (2012) 'Egypt's heavily censored media continues to take on the regime', *The Guardian*, online, 9 February, www.theguardian.com/commentisfree/2012/feb/09/arabic-press-freedom-censorship [accessed 10 March 2017].
Elmawke3 news (2015) 'For the second day . . . twitter wants Liliane to leave', (translated from Arabic) 25 February, from www.elmawke3.com, [accessed 10 March 2017].
El-Nawawy, Mohammed and Khamis, Sahar (2013) *Egyptian Revolution 2.0 Political Blogging, Civic Engagement, and Citizen Journalism*, London: Palgrave Macmillan.
―――― (2014) 'Governmental corruption through the Egyptian bloggers' lens: A qualitative study of four Egyptian political blogs', in *Journal of Arab & Muslim Media Research*, Vol. 7, Issue: 1, pp. 39–58.
Ghannoushi, Soumaya (2014) 'Tunisia is showing the Arab world how to nurture democracy', 25 October, www.theguardian.com/commentisfree/2014/oct/25/tunisia-arab-world-democracy-elections [accessed 25 February 2017].
The Guardian (2016) 'Journalist critical of Egyptian government deported from Cairo', 28 June, www.theguardian.com/world/2016/jun/28/liliane-daoud-journalist-egypt-deported-cairo-lebanon [accessed 10 March 2017].
Hallin, Daniel (1989) *The Uncensored War: The Media and Vietnam*, Berkeley: University of California Press.
Hallin, Daniel and Mancini, Paolo (2004) *Comparing Media Systems, Three Models of Media and Politics*, Cambridge and New York: Cambridge University Press.
Hamdy, Naila (2015) 'Egypt shifts towards a networked journalism paradigm', in *Journal of Arab & Muslim Media Research*, Vol. 8, Issue: 1, pp. 3–20.
Harb, Zahera (2011) 'Arab revolutions and the social media effect', in *M/C Journal*, Vol. 4, Issue: 2, np, http://journal.media-culture.org.au/index.php/mcjournal/article/view/364%3E/0 [accessed 10 February 2017].
Herrea, Linda (2014) *Revolution in the Age of Social Media: The Egyptian Popular Insurrection and the Internet*, London: Verso.
Howard, Philip and Hussain, Muzammil (2011) 'Digital media and the Arab spring', in *Journal of Democracy*, Vol. 22, Issue: 3, pp. 35–48.
Khamis, Sahar and Vaughn, Katherine (2011) '"We Are All Khaled Said": The potentials and limitations of cyberactivism in triggering public mobilization and promoting political change', in *Journal of Arab & Muslim Media Research*, Vol. 4, Issue: 2–3, pp. 145–163.
―――― (2013) 'Cyber activism in the Tunisian and Egyptian revolutions: Potentials, limitations, overlaps and divergences', in *Journal of African Media Studies*, Vol. 5, Issue: 1, pp. 69–86.
Kingsley, Patrick (2015) 'How Mohamed Morsi, Egypt's first elected president, ended up on death row', *The Guardian*, online, 1 June, www.theguardian.com/world/2015/jun/01/mohamed-morsi-execution-death-sentence-egypt [accessed 24 February 2017].

Mada Masr (2015), 'A statement by Hossam Bahgat on his military detention, interrogation', 10 November, www.madamasr.com/en/2015/11/10/feature/politics/a-statement-by-hossam-bahgat-on-his-military-detention-interrogation/ [accessed 15 February 2017].

Majed, Reem (2015) Paper presented at Freie Universität conference, Berlin, November.

McQuail, Denis (2013) *Journalism and Society*, London: Sage Publications.

Rinnawi, Khalil (2012) 'Cyber uprising: Al-Jazeera TV channel and the Egyptian uprising', *Language and Intercultural Communication*, Vol. 12, Issue: 2, pp. 118–132.

Saied, Mohamed (2016) 'Why did Egypt deport this British-Lebanese TV host?' *Al Monitor*, 3 July, www.al-monitor.com/pulse/originals/2016/07/egypt-deport-british-lebanese-tv-host-liliane-daoud-sisi.html [accessed 10 March 2017].

Saleh, Heba (2007) 'Egypt bloggers fear state curbs', *BBC News*, 22 February, http://news.bbc.co.uk/go/pr/fr/-/1/hi/world/middle_east/6386613.stm [accessed 28 January 2011].

Shams El-Din, Mai (2015) 'As Egypt-Qatar relations thaw, Al Jazeera pulls Mubasher Misr off air', *Mada Masr*, 22 December, www.madamasr.com/en/2014/12/22/feature/politics/as-egypt-qatar-relations-thaw-al-jazeera-pulls-mubasher-misr-off-air/ [accessed 22 December 2017].

Shearlaw, Maeve (2016) 'Egypt five years on: Was it ever a "social media revolution"?' *The Guardian*, online, 25 January, www.theguardian.com/world/2016/jan/25/egypt-5-years-on-was-it-ever-a-social-media-revolution [accessed 24 February 2017].

Shirky, Clay (2011) 'The political power of Social Media', in *Foreign Affairs*, Vol. 90, Issue: 1, pp. 28–41.

Wolfsfeld Gadi, Segev, Elad and Sheafer, Tamir (2013) 'Social media and the Arab spring: Politics comes first', *The International Journal of Press/Politics*, Vol. 18, Issue: 2, pp. 115–137.

Wolver, David J. (2016) 'An issue of attribution: The Tunisian revolution, media interaction, and agency', *New Media & Society*, Vol. 18, Issue: 2, pp. 185–200.

11 Protecting the colony
Bermuda's national image and media censorship

Dana Selassie

Introduction

Seventeen-year-old Rebecca Middleton took her last few breaths of life on a quiet, dark road on the island of Bermuda. The brutal rape and murder of the Canadian tourist on 3 July 1996 not only horrified the local community, but exposed the small British colony to what would become one of the most controversial and internationally probed murder cases in Bermuda (since the killing of the Island's British Governor and his aide in 1973, when two local men were hanged for the crime). What made the Rebecca Middleton story such an international spectacle was the fact that the two key suspects, a teenager from Bermuda and a 21-year-old Jamaican man, had not actually been charged with her murder, due to the mismanagement of evidence and inaccuracies within the investigation, which led in turn to a double jeopardy ruling (where an individual cannot be tried twice for the same crime) and an unsolved case.

During the early stages of the investigation, and only days after being arrested in connection with Middleton's murder, 21-year-old Kirk Mundy admitted to being at the scene, and claimed to have had consensual sex with the victim. He argued that it was actually his friend, a local teenager called Justice Smith, who was responsible for the more than 30 stab wounds found on Rebecca's body. As Mundy agreed to testify against Smith, and before actual DNA evidence had been confirmed, local prosecutors charged Mundy with the lesser crime of accessory to murder, while Smith was charged with the premeditated murder of the victim. As new evidence emerged, however, it was revealed that DNA on the victim was actually linked to Mundy.

Considering the extreme violence used against the victim, prosecutors and the local police force were heavily censured for not having investigated the crime thoroughly before charging the two male suspects (both of whom were black). After fresh attempts were made to prosecute Mundy for Rebecca's murder, the charges were subsequently thrown out on the grounds of double jeopardy, which, as noted previously, states that no one can be tried for the same crime twice. As Mundy served his five-year sentence as an accessory to murder, local courts also found that there was insufficient evidence proving that Smith was solely responsible for the premeditated murder of Middleton, meaning that he was acquitted in 1998 of all charges: this meant, in turn, that the murder of the Canadian schoolgirl was in effect unpunished, and unresolved.

This was not the first time a young woman had been murdered on Bermuda's shores. Nor was it the first unsolved murder case recorded in Britain's oldest colony. It was, however, the first time that Bermuda had been drawn so extensively into the international spotlight for the mishandling of a case of this nature. As a result of this attention, the island's judicial system and its archaic laws were harshly criticised, and the competence of the colonial government called into question. With Bermuda's tourism industry generating 'hundreds of millions of dollars in government revenue' (Bermuda Economic Statistics, nd), the international coverage of the Rebecca Middleton trial not only tarnished Bermuda's national image, but challenged the island's supposedly impeccable reputation as a safe and tranquil paradise for overseas visitors. Furthermore, in the years following Rebecca's murder, Canadian news media continued to reprimand Bermuda for not doing more to address the errors within the case.

When, in 2007, Rebecca's family hired Cherie Booth (wife of former British Prime Minister Tony Blair) as their legal counsellor, more publicity was generated. The violation of Rebecca's human rights had been raised as justifiable grounds for revisiting the now high-profile story. While Booth's presence significantly raised awareness of the Rebecca Middleton tragedy, she was unsuccessful in her appeals to have the more than ten-year old case reopened. Booth argued that this was a huge injustice to Rebecca, as the two culprits had 'expressed no remorse for the fact that Rebecca was abused, dehumanized and killed' (CBC News, 2007), and had not been adequately punished for the crime, even with the submission of new evidence. Yet, it was perhaps the events surrounding the production of an investigative television documentary nearly 20 years after Rebecca's brutal murder, which most clearly demonstrated the values espoused by the island's government. By refusing work permits – justified under the Bermuda Immigration and Protection Act of 1956 – to a Canadian film crew investigating the case of Rebecca Middleton, the government's priority (preserving the island's image) was once again thrown into sharp relief.

Throughout the 1950s and 1960s, Bermuda's institutionalised forms of censorship created serious impediments to any form of journalism that challenged colonial authority or disturbed the status quo. In practice, therefore, contemporary problems were based on a long-standing tradition of government censorship of the media: as this chapter attempts to illustrate, this has been evident at every stage of Bermuda's developing media industry. Most often imposed during key periods of identity contestation, seen for example with government imposed safeguards introduced with the arrival of American military television, and in instances where radio programmes promoting progressive black politics were cut off air, the censoring of both local and foreign newspapers, radio, and television throughout the island's media history, indicates the level of threat perceived by Bermuda's colonial government.

This chapter examines the ways in which producers of the 'Murder in Paradise' series circumvented the local government's restrictions on filming on the island, and were able to create an investigative documentary that brought to life the tragic story of Rebecca Middleton. While this chapter does not address re-enactments and the sensationalising of murder cases on television, it does, however, point out a few of the key techniques used in television documentary production (intended to help an audience gain a better understanding of the events surrounding her murder) and looks at how the producers tried to demonstrate their objectivity within the film, so that they could meet any accusations of bias head on.

This form of enquiry will be supported by the use of a historical framework, which highlights events surrounding the introduction of television on the island (first set up by the American military). I will then discuss the safeguards imposed by the Bermuda government on this TV station as it prepared to open. Through an analysis of the Rebecca Middleton story and a focus on the events surrounding the arrival of television in the colony, this chapter offers both historical and contemporary evidence demonstrating how Britain's oldest colony enforced the censorship of the media, as well as how various media organisations had to navigate through the restrictive practices of a system that, in effect, censored an entire nation.

Censorship and the use of the Bermuda Immigration and Protection Act, 1956

In Spring 2014, Bermuda's Immigration and Home Affairs Minister, Michael Fahy, was openly criticised in the island's local newspapers, for refusing a Canadian film crew work permits (Bernews, 2014a). As noted earlier, the Canadians wanted to shoot a television documentary on the unsolved case of Rebecca Middleton. Cineflix Productions, producers of the 'Murder in Paradise' series, investigates murders taking place in various vacation spots around the world. One local media source reported that Fahy's decision was due to 'potential reputational risks to Bermuda' (Bernews, 2014b). The film crew, which had hoped to capture vital interviews and footage in Bermuda, in preparation for a television episode which featured the story of the murdered teenager, had been denied the right to hire crew, and to film within the British territory. The Minister argued that his decision was for the 'protection of local interest' (Bermuda Immigration and Protection Act, 1956 61.4.e-f, 1956) and, as another media source reported, was 'in accordance with what is legislatively available under the law' (Bell, 2014). The decision by Bermuda's Immigration and Home Affairs Minister, however, ushered in accusations that media freedom was being suppressed, while generating yet more negative publicity for Bermuda in the aftermath of an already contentious murder case.

Local news media highlighted the numerous criticisms of the ban on the Canadian production team, with *The Royal Gazette* reporting a number of comments and concerns vocalised by both the public and the opposition party. Bermuda's Shadow Attorney General, for example, addressed the fact that Minister Fahy, in his capacity as a government representative, 'had the legal power to consider "generally the requirements of the community as a whole" before granting a work permit', but was 'appalled by the rationale given' in regards to this case (Bell, 2014). Yet, in spite of the various criticisms, Bermuda's Immigration Minister stated that his decision was not a case of censoring the media, but rather a means of safeguarding the island. According to *The Royal Gazette*, Fahy argued that the production of the Rebecca Middleton story (which he called 'a brutal, horrific event') by a *foreign* company, would mean that there was no way to ensure that the representation of Bermuda would be unbiased: there was, he said, 'no guarantee that Bermuda's side would be portrayed in a balanced way' (Bell, 2014). Further, while this restriction would stop the Canadian film crew from possibly misrepresenting Bermuda, Fahy told local media, 'there was nothing preventing a local film crew from producing a documentary on this incident' (Bell, 2014).

As far as the colonial government was concerned, any documentary produced by the Canadian team had the potential to worsen international attitudes towards Bermuda, when the priority in its view was the protection of the island's reputation as a tourist destination. But critics argued that allowing the film crew access could be an opportunity for the colony to acknowledge its role in the case, and could offer a way for the nation to move forward. However, the fact that the colonial government tried to distance itself further from the Rebecca Middleton case, proved that this point of view carried no weight. The use of the Bermuda Immigration and Protection Act, 1956 to block the filming of the documentary, was, in essence, the simple use of state censorship.

Yet, while the restriction of work permits by the Bermuda government presented a number of barriers for the documentary's production team, the denial of access failed to stop the project. As narrator and executive producer Jacqueline Bynon revealed in an interview with *The Royal Gazette*, at no time had there been any plans to 'shelve the hour-long show, which will include interviews with Rebecca's parents' (Strangeways, 2014). Acknowledging the Bermuda government's resistance in granting work permits (on the grounds of potential bias and harm to local interest), Bynon told *The Royal Gazette* that her team had 'a really good journalistic track record' (Strangeways, 2014). This experience helped to demonstrate their commitment to good research practices and objectivity, as they investigated the time that Rebecca spent in Bermuda.

The challenge of investigation

Good intentions and experience, however, are not always enough to guarantee success. As Ayo Johnson (a Bermudian filmmaker and independent journalist) acknowledged, the challenges that reporters often face in investigating contentious stories, is such that, even when they have conducted extensive research, they must recognise that sometimes their theories will simply not pan out. Hostile to the idea that there is a difference between *investigative journalism* as a subgenre of *journalism,* Johnson argued that the term investigative journalism is 'redundant and somewhat elitist', because the role of any journalist is to question power, and 'hold [those in power] to account' (Johnson, interview with author, 2016). This view of journalism is essentially quite idealistic: while it may well be desirable that all journalism is conducted in a principled manner, if this does not actually occur, then it is not surprising that media professionals and the public will put their faith in a mode of enquiry that seems to promise a more rigorous approach (see the Introduction to this book).

Sheila Bernard, in her work on documentary storytelling, takes a practical view of the whole question, arguing that 'good research is a sequence of questions, answers, and more questions' (2007: 114). In order to address injustices, the journalist or filmmaker must confront the story head on, and remain devoted to the task despite setbacks. As Johnson notes, you have to 'challenge [those in power] on the facts that they don't want you to know' since it is exactly this information that 'may be in the . . . public interest' (Johnson, 2016, interview with author). The facts, acquired through extensive research, arm the journalist and the documentary filmmaker with an essential foundation, from which they can meet accusations of bias.

Additionally, as Navarro and Spence argue, viewers need to be assured that 'events did take place in such and such a way, and that the images and sounds on the screen are accurate and reliable' (2011: 13). If the documentary does not accurately represent the events, they suggest that the viewer will 'dismiss it as false, biased, or unreliable' (21). But, as Bernard indicates, 'balance and accuracy do not mean that you can't, as the filmmaker, take a particular position, or that your subjects can't take one' (2007: 113). However, if your work is going to be credible, with viewers 'tak[ing] you seriously', then, she argues, 'you must allow them to weigh the evidence for themselves, which means that you need to research and present the evidence' (113).

The first stage of the investigation had, inevitably, to establish the facts about Rebecca's background, helping to establish who she was, as a daughter, sister, and friend. In Bermuda itself, interviews would need to be conducted with the family that had acted as her hosts. The producer/director would have had to ask difficult, critical questions about the circumstances that meant that an under-age Rebecca had been out drinking with friends, and how that in turn had led, in the early hours of the morning, to her riding away on a motorcycle with two strangers. Researchers would then have had to find any publicly accessible forensic reports, and would have had to obtain interviews with forensic pathologists to explain how she was killed. Additionally, there would have to be a detailed assessment of the numerous witness accounts, taken from the police department, the court proceedings, and the testimony of the two suspects. All of these elements would be essential for establishing a chronology of events and constructing Rebecca's documentary narrative, and crucial in demonstrating credibility in the telling of her story.

After securing key interviews with Rebecca's parents, her friend Jasmine, and Bermuda's Ex-Commissioner of Police, along with a number of specialists and witnesses, the story of Rebecca Middleton was released in the 'Murder in Paradise' series, with the episode entitled *Stranger Danger* broadcast throughout the United States and Canada on channel Discovery ID (Bernews, 2014b). In spite of accusations of potential bias, and with the Cineflix production team restricted from obtaining work permits, it was clear that by Autumn 2014, the more than 50-year-old Bermuda Immigration and Protection Act of 1956,[1] no longer formed an obstacle to the investigation. Denied access to the crime scene, and to key interviews in Bermuda, the production company relied heavily on documentary techniques such as visualisation, using re-enactments, photographs from various sources, graphic simulations, and alternative locations to replace unobtainable material. These techniques, used when 'shooting is not possible – prohibited or [with the] subject inaccessible' (Millerson and Owens, 2009: 319), as in key parts of the Rebecca Middleton story, were essential to the production of the documentary.

Following a dramatic opening sequence and title, showing a graphic re-enactment of the murder, the television programme, which according to executive producer Bynon features 'people who go to beautiful places and then sometimes things can happen' (in Strangeways, 2014), moves into a lighter phase, filled with the typical generic picturesque scenes of tourists on the beach and vibrant shots of Bermuda's multi-coloured houses. The very bright, scenic, and visually stimulating shots of Bermuda, promoted heavily within its tourist industry, are in line with Bynon's claim that the programme highlights 'beautiful places' but where unexpected tragedy may occur. As calypso music plays in the background, the narrator establishes Bermuda's geographical location and proximity to the United States, while also emphasising the island's colonial ties with Britain.[2] As demonstrated in the opening moments of the programme, the establishment of location is essential to the production, as it helps give the viewer a sense of place, an insight into the environment, and also provides key features which Millerson and Owens describe as 'visual clues' (2009).

However, as the documentary narrative continues to build, the idyllic and vibrant footage of Bermuda's beaches and houses,[3] together with the cheerful visuals of Rebecca's arrival, are intentionally juxtaposed with narrative techniques that might be regarded as 'sensationalist', uncomfortable elements that seem to compete with the seriousness of its overall purpose. The music then shifts from lively calypso sounds to a dramatic score that indicates the gravity of what is to come. Over the next 40 minutes, the final moments of Rebecca's murder come to life through a series of reconstructions and emotional testimonies. Re-enactments of Rebecca at different stages of her vacation, edited alongside photographs of her as a child, give the viewer a sense of Rebecca as a person as the events surrounding her murder unfold.

The various formal interviews throughout the piece are structured in traditional documentary style, with the subjects mostly framed off-centre looking out of shot at the interviewer (the questions posed to the subjects are omitted, so that the viewer can concentrate on the statements of informants and witnesses). The visual elements are tied together effectively through the narrator, Bynon, as she guides the viewer through Rebecca's last days and fills in gaps in the story. The narration also helps to provide clarity where complex information is presented, such as the explanation offered for the series of knife marks found on Rebecca's head.[4]

While the narration is invaluable in linking all the elements of the story together, the interviews and first-hand accounts obtained from Rebecca's parents and friends, experts very close to the case, and witnesses, all provide an additional dimension to the story and add to the credibility of the documentary. The author Carol Shuman, for example, who had covered the Rebecca Middleton story extensively, notes that the trainee police officers at the crime scene were inexperienced in cases of this nature, and suggests that this may have contributed to the contamination of evidence that, in turn, affected the outcome of the trial. However, the ex-Commissioner of Police, Colin Coxall, argues in his interview that it was his belief that 'the officers did the job to the very best of their capability', while indicating that 'things could have been done differently'. By providing various perspectives on the events surrounding Rebecca's murder, the director is able to maintain a sense of objectivity. The decision to add Shuman's comments, which drew attention to the incompetence of local police officers, followed by Coxall's claim that he believed that they did the best that they could, provides viewers with various angles from which to assess the evidence, enabling them to draw their own conclusions. As Navarro and Spence argue, 'any representation is a selective view of the world' (Navarro and Spence, 2011: 129).

Yet, as the programme comes to a close, ex-Commissioner Coxall highlights the fact that the tragedy of Rebecca Middleton 'was a failure of the entire Bermuda criminal justice process'. And, addressing the fact that the Bermuda government was resistant to the documentary being filmed in Bermuda, he argues, 'they don't want this case revived . . . because its interference with its tourism. I am not slightest bit surprised that Bermuda would deny access'. The director chose to make an explicit acknowledgement that the production team had been refused permission to film in Bermuda by the colony's government. The refusal letter sent from the Bermuda Immigration office appears on screen, dated 2 April 2014:

> Subject: Middleton Film Crew: Temporary Work Permit Applications
>
> I write to formally advise you that the Minister responsible for Immigration has duly considered the temporary work permit applications for the above-captioned and has taken the decision to refuse the applications pursuant to Section 61 (4) (e) and (f) of the Bermuda Immigration and Protection Act 1956.
>
> (Valentin, 2014)

The narrator then indicates that although the production team had been denied their application, they still created an opportunity for the Bermuda government to comment on the events surrounding the Rebecca Middleton case. But, as the narrator argues, 'Government authorities also turned down our request for interviews'. In providing this evidence for the viewer, the producers were able to demonstrate that they had offered officials a platform to address the issue. This was an essential part of their attempt to prove their aim of being objective, while at the same time dispelling the accusations of bias circulated by the Bermuda government's Minister of Immigration. While the first part of this chapter offered an analysis of Bermuda's colonial authority, and how it tried to curtail perceived external threats to national identity, the next section will discuss censorship in its historic context – the introduction of television to Bermuda.

Censoring the nation: the Television Aerials Control Act 1955[5]

Control over the media through censorship and government policy has historically impacted and shaped the way that controversial events have been both covered and disseminated within the British island of Bermuda. This was particularly evident at a time when Britain was struggling to manage external threats to national identity during WWII, and many of her overseas territories were having to negotiate their colonial relationship with the mother country. To complicate these relations further, significant developments in the United States lessened the cultural stronghold that Britain had maintained over her territories, as many of them openly embraced America's influence.

Bermuda, like many of Britain's colonies in the 1940s, 1950s and 1960s, drew upon the technological and economic support offered by America, which ultimately helped to shape the island's cultural, political, and media landscape. The numerous relationships that Bermuda had with the United States not only supported the colony's affluence and technological development but, consequently, strengthened articulations of a culturally hybrid Bermudian-British-American national identity. The Defenders for Base Agreement in 1940, for example, was a pact between the UK and the United States that would essentially rent out part of Bermuda to the American military for 99 years, in exchange for a number of naval destroyers. While the deal was struck to help rectify some of Britain's financial challenges, created as a result of the war, the extensive impact of American culture in the small British colony, helped challenge colonial dominance, a development that could be exemplified in the expansion of its broadcasting industry.

Within three years of the Defenders for Base Agreement taking place, with the arrival of Kindley U.S. base in Bermuda, the island saw the introduction of its first national radio broadcasting company, the Bermuda Broadcasting Company (Radio), in 1943. Although a private initiative, the Bermuda Broadcasting Company relied heavily on support from Bermuda's local government, and received most of its technological expertise from military personnel stationed at Kindley, who also provided the majority of on-air radio programming for the budding station. As a result of the significant contribution by Kindley, in the early days of the Bermuda Broadcasting Company, Bermuda's airwaves were dominated by an American presence. By 1952, Bermuda's radio audience had reached approximately 40,000 people, with more than 90% of the island's homes having access to a radio set. According to Steve Mann of Adam Young International, there were '10,200 homes with 10,150 having radios in the home' and a reported 15,000 radios throughout the island (1952: 19). With the Bermuda Broadcasting Company's *ZBM* channel broadcasting predominantly American content, the island's British-Bermudian radio presence became secondary. This was further accentuated by the fact that the Bermuda Broadcasting Company continued to increase in popularity, and opened its second station, *ZBM-2*, in February 1952. Although there was a series of local radio shows being produced, and a number of radio programmes were supplied by the British Broadcasting Corporation for Bermuda's national radio service, Bermuda's first major radio station was more Americanised than it was Bermudian or British. It was no surprise, therefore, that when officers from Kindley military suggested opening Bermuda's first television service, the colonial government created a series of strict guidelines that would curtail the amount of American influence being disseminated throughout the colony.

According to Michele Hilmes, 'from its inception, radio and then television broadcasting developed in deeply nationalist contexts, guided by the twentieth-century imperatives of national definition, unification and defence' (2003: 13) She adds, however, that radio was 'carefully kept from crossing national lines, crafted to address only its own citizens and no others, shaped and regulated by national governments' (13). Yet the American military's proposed *ZBK-TV* did in fact cross national lines and did impact the surrounding non-military Bermudian community. In 1955, with the

American military's introduction of Bermuda's first television station, the colonial government devised new methods of censorship, deemed necessary to protect the nation from excessive U.S. influence. As the Americans at the Kindley base made their application to the Bermuda government, 'to set up a television broadcasting station', they argued that television on the base would be 'designed for the purpose of providing entertainment for Armed Forces personnel and as an assistance to morale' (*The Royal Gazette*, 1955a). Although the proposed broadcast from the Kindley base would cater mainly to its base personnel, government officials recognised that the television signal, which would be island-wide, would also allow Bermudians full access to American television programming. As a result, officials came up with three specific conditions that were considered to represent 'certain Bermuda Government safeguards' (*The Royal Gazette*, 1955a), needed in order for the United States to receive permission to start up a television station in the British colony.

The first safeguard presented by the Bermuda government was the *right of censorship*, which allowed the local government to prevent Kindley from broadcasting specific content that in some way or another threatened the colony. The second safeguard, the *removal of advertising material*, would be the Bermuda government's way of limiting the impact of America's commercialised broadcasting culture. Although Bermuda's national radio service was privately owned, it operated in a public service capacity much like the British Broadcasting Corporation, showing hostility towards America's commercialised broadcasting system. This expression of Britain's 'moral' superiority also permeated the colony, and was used as the justification for the restriction of advertisements on the American owned television station.

The first two safeguards indicate the length to which the Bermuda government would go in order to protect the colony from perceived risks to British-Bermudian colonial identity. However, the final safeguard was a clear attempt by the Bermuda government to ensure that its presence was regularly reflected and disseminated throughout the colony on the new television station. It demanded *the right to use a period of time each day to broadcast material of community interest.* This right would guarantee that articulations of Bermudian colonial identity and British nationalism (in effect, a form of propaganda) would be reinforced through the medium of television. As Hilmes noted, it was 'first radio, then television, [that] was defined by such states [United States and Great Britain] as a uniquely national medium, confined to the borders of the nation . . . and meant to construct and address a national public' (2003: 1). For Bermuda, this meant that while the Kindley base would incur most of the costs and maintain control over the operations of its television station, the safeguards imposed by Bermuda's government would secure the ability to censor military programming, and to exercise control over the use of the new medium. However, while the safeguards were felt to be 'more theoretical than practical', both parties agreed on the terms, and Kindley was granted its television licence (*The Royal Gazette*, 1955a).

Yet, as plans were underway for the construction of Kindley's *ZBK-TV*, the first television station in the British colony, a technicality in the agreement made between the U.S. military and television producers in the United States, unexpectedly revoked the right to broadcast to the local community. Arrangements between the United States Department of Defense and various television networks, denied the distribution of their television shows to anyone outside their own military bases. Furthermore, it had been determined that, even if the signal was available to the local community, it would be 'a practical impossibility to remove advertising material from the programmes' (*The Royal Gazette*, 1955a). With Kindley being unable to meet the demands of the Bermuda government's safeguards, and with the military television signal being inaccessible to Bermudians, *ZBK-TV* became a base-only television station, excluding Bermuda's population.

Kindley's broadcast signal, which was now supposed to be restricted to the base itself, was adjusted with 'a specially designed antenna and a transmitter of suitable low power' (*The Royal Gazette*, 1955a). It would be worth noting here that Bermuda is approximately 24 miles long and roughly 7 miles wide at the widest point. To restrict a television broadcast signal to only a small portion of the island would be futile, especially when the island's radio channels had in the past picked up signals from as far away as the United States. However, with permission granted by the colonial government, Kindley's *ZBK-TV* launched on 4 July 1955. Although this was the opening of the island's first television station, the Bermudian public was not a part of the festivities, and on the first live broadcast to the military base personnel, only the American and Bermudian flags were seen at the opening ceremonies, not the British.

Within the first few days of its maiden broadcast, however, there had been reports of broadcast leakage from *ZBK-TV* throughout various parts of the island. Navy personnel and other military personnel living off-base were reportedly able to access the television signal, although this was supposed to be restricted to Kindley itself. Officers who had purchased television sets from the base, found that they were able to pick up the signal from Kindley, although in some parts of the island the broadcast was not particularly clear, with *The Royal Gazette*'s 17 July 1955 headlines confirming the problem:

Reports of TV 'Leakage' Spreading In Colony
Reception Off Kindley Base
Kindley Air Force Base's 'dream boat'- ZBK-TV appears to be leaking . . .

Not only were off-base personnel watching *ZBK-TV* with their American television sets, but it was reported that in various parts of the island, 'TV programmes [had] been received direct from America and from Cuba', although the occurrences had been classified as 'freak reception' (*The

Royal Gazette, 1955a). Government officials met with Kindley officers and instructed them to lower the strength of the television signal to stop it from spreading throughout the colony. Then, to make matters worse, a number of Bermudians had begun to import American television sets into the country to try to access the television signal for themselves. This in turn caused the government to impose a ban on the importation of all American television sets onto the island by Bermudians, which was to be monitored by the Bermuda Customs department. *The Royal Gazette* reported that one set had already been brought into the island by a Bermudian, but it had been confiscated and 'sent back' (*The Royal Gazette*, 1955a). As a result of the ban, it was reported that several Bermudians were attempting to import unrestricted television sets from Britain, then were modifying the set to be able to receive Kindley's signal. By September 1955, *The Royal Gazette's* report, 'Kindley to Prevent TV "Leakage"' stated:

> The first two television sets have been imported into Bermuda by a local businessman and it is believed that Hamilton merchants have ordered a number of television sets from England, specially adjusted for reception of telecasts from Kindley.
> (*The Royal Gazette*, 1955b)

Many locals were using 'rabbit ears', a type of antenna placed on top of the television set that helped to get a clear picture. However, the increase in local access to the American television station from friendships made with off-base personnel, together with the rise in modified television sets being imported from the UK, 'spurred the Bermuda Government into action' (*The Royal Gazette*, 1955b).

With the increase in television sets arriving from Britain, new attempts were made at restricting the colony from accessing the signal. Reflectors, aimed at stopping the signal from '"leaking" off the base', and the lowering of the 'power of the Transmissions in response to Bermuda Government requests' (*The Royal Gazette*, 1955c), demonstrated the determination of the authorities to guard its colony from the uncensored television signal. But a number of Bermudians installed antennas on their roofs, in order to 'steal' the broadcast signal from the American base. This final act of defiance by Bermuda's local community, however, pushed the Bermuda government into introducing the Television Aerials (Control) Act 1955, which made it a punishable crime to access American military TV.

The act stated that 'No person shall erect or cause to be erected any outside television aerial' without a permit, with anyone found guilty of this offence being prosecuted and having to pay 'a fine not exceeding ten pounds' (The Television Aerials [Control] Act, 1955. No.114). If found guilty of repeated offences, individuals would 'be liable in respect of the day during which the offence continues, to a fine not exceeding five pounds', with the Television Aerials Act remaining enforced until 31 December 1956

(The Television Aerials [Control] Act, 1955. No.114). The introduction of the Act was the first major step that the colonial government took in regaining control over projections of American culture and identity, as Bermuda entered the age of television. While the Act may have provided a short-term solution for the colonial government, one year later, however, the Kindley Air Force Base television service, *ZBK-TV* was operating in Bermuda throughout the Island. Kindley remained the only television service in Bermuda until the island saw the arrival of Britain's first colonial television service, the Bermuda Broadcasting Company's *ZBM-TV* in 1958.

While the local government attempted to protect the island from extensive foreign cultural influences, such as America's military television programming, the local community's demand for television access proved greater than the diktats that colonial authorities were able to enforce. With the import of modified televisions and with the fixing of illegal aerials on local homes, it had been demonstrated that many islanders wanted access to American television, and did not agree with the island's colonial powers, that this desire was somehow detrimental to Bermudian national identity.

Rebecca Middleton's story, likewise, provides an illustration as to how a more contemporary external media entity navigated censorship imposed under Bermuda's colonial government, as it attempted to protect the colony from not only foreign influence, but also from outside criticism. The Bermuda Immigration and Protection Act, 1956, much like the Television Aerials Control Act in 1955, had been used by the colonial government as justification for restricting the Canadian production company from fully investigating their production of the television programme highlighting the murder of Rebecca Middleton. Fearing that the North American television programme would unfairly portray Bermuda in the aftermath of Rebecca's brutal murder, the documentary production team was refused permission to film. Yet, as has been discussed within this chapter, government restrictions such as these do not necessarily ensure 'protection' from outside critique and investigation. As the Cineflix production team demonstrated, it is through quality documentary filmmaking techniques and skills that the story can still be exposed, regardless of the obstacles that are created. With extensive research, re-enactments, personal interviews and graphic simulations, a powerful story can still be told, in spite of restrictions that operate, as in this case, as forms of censorship.

Thus, from the example of the Rebecca Middleton story and from the examination of the arrival of television in the colony, it can be seen that Bermuda's colonial government has historically used justified methods of censorship through various governmental policies to support its mission of safeguarding the colony and protecting national image. However, as many Bermudians demonstrated in 1955, and Cineflix Productions proved in 2014, colonial censorship of media, just like colonial hegemony, will always be contested.

Notes

1 The Bermuda Immigration and Protection Act, 1956 was implemented two years before Bermuda established its own national television broadcasting company in 1958.
2 The choice of calypso music, common amongst the Caribbean islands but not particularly relevant to Bermuda, suggests that the creators were attempting to use the familiar sounds associated with island life.
3 General footage of Bermuda is obtainable without requiring a work permit. Some of the content was provided by local sources.
4 Along with the forensic specialist's testimony, a graphic simulation of a body was used, showing how a knife was used to carve a series of 'x's on Rebecca's forehead, while the narrator indicated that the extremely painful process is known as 'Jamaican torture', used to subdue and control a victim.
5 The material used within the section 'Censoring the Nation: The Television Aerials Control Act 1955', comes from the PhD thesis 'Broadcasting in the Triangle: Negotiating Colonial Identity and Race in Bermuda's Emerging Media Industries', by Dana Selassie (submitted September 2016).

References

Bell, Jonathan (2014) 'Decision to ban film crew is condemned', 7 April, www.royalgazette.com/article/20140407/NEWS/140409815 [accessed January 2017].
Bermuda Economic Statistics (nd) www.gov.bm [accessed January 2017].
Bermuda Immigration and Protection Act 1956. No. 61.4.e-f. (1956). *Act E and F*, Bermuda.
—— (1955) The Television Aerials (Control) Act 1955. No.114, 31 December, Bermuda.
Bernard, Sheila (2007) *Documentary Storytelling* [2nd edition], Oxford: Focal Press.
Bernews (2014a) 'Middleton film crew denied work permits', 5 April, http://bernews.com/2014/04/middleto-film-crew-denied-work-permit [accessed January 2017].
—— (2014b) 'Rebecca Middleton documentary airs on TV', 8 September, http://bernews.com/2014/09/rebecca-middleton-documentary-airs-on-tv [accessed December 2016].
CBC News (2007) 'Blair's wife asks Bermudian court to reopen case of slain Canadian', 16 April, www.cbc.ca/news/world/blair-s-wife-asks-bermudian-court-to-reopen-case-of-slain-canadian-1.668711 [accessed December 2016].
Johnson, Ayo (2016) Independent journalist/filmmaker: Interview with author.
Mann, Steve (1952) 'International reports to sponsors: Bermuda station starts year with over 60 accounts', Adam Young International, Sponsor.
Millerson, Gerald and Owens, Jim (2009) *Television Production* [14th edition], Oxford: Focal Press.
Navarro, Vinicius and Spence, Louise (2011) *Crafting Truth, Documentary Form and Meaning*, London: Rutgers University Press.
The Royal Gazette (1955a) 'Reports of TV "Leakage" spreading in colony', 17 July.
—— (1955b) 'Kindley To Prevent TV "Leakage"', 16 September.
—— (1955c) 'No word yet of action on TV "Leakage"', 19 September.
Strangeways, Sam (2014) 'Middleton documentary makers run into immigration trouble', *The Royal Gazette*, 25 March, www.royalgazette.com/article/20140325/NEWS/140329861 [accessed January 2017].
Valentin, Marcus [Director] (2014) *Murder in Paradise, Stranger Danger* [television episode], Canada: Cineflix Productions.

Part IV
An industry in turmoil
Fake news, leaks, and economic challenges

This final section is devoted to an overview of recent developments in journalism, starting with Chapter 12, which examines the challenge posed to the profession by the appearance of 'alternative facts', and by the accusation that mainstream media forms produce 'fake news'. Chapter 13 presents a thorough account of the rise and fall of WikiLeaks as a moral force, while the final contribution, Chapter 14, examines the overall state of the industry. All three pieces demonstrate an acute awareness of those forces that appear to threaten or disrupt honest reporting, yet which have also provoked a fierce defence of journalism and calls for a return to some of its basic principles.

This section begins with Birks' detailed analysis (see Chapter 12) of the 'fake news' phenomenon, and the response of those media outlets that are determined to maintain the basic standards of journalistic enquiry. Birks argues that, while the verification of substantial claims through procedures like double sourcing, are 'central to investigative journalism', there are limits to the mechanisms associated with 'fact-checking' but also definite dangers in a reliance on 'press releases or news wires'. Birks also examines the notion that journalists operate in a highly subjective environment – their primary source is often other people, but they themselves work on assumptions that are not always subjected to critique. Individual reporters, therefore, may give a particular weight to the testimony of one type of social actor, while assuming that another source, who is almost unconsciously assigned to a separate category, is regarded as less reliable. The appearance of these factors does not, according to Birks, necessarily mean that the 'moral and emotional foundation behind investigative journalism' is wrong, but it does suggest that this model of commitment is quite alien to 'the professional ideology of the liberal model of journalism, especially the North American tradition, which is most highly wedded to the notion of objectivity'.

Chapter 13 is the work of Lisa Lynch, a Canadian academic, who examines a burning issue that dominates contemporary discussions of the role of WikiLeaks as a social and political force. If not quite at its inception, then certainly during the spectacular release of material that revealed the iniquity of the U.S. state, the organisation was regarded very highly in many quarters. Since the period when WikiLeaks seems to have moved closer to authoritarian regimes, enthusiasm for its brand of bold (or reckless) intervention, has waned. Lynch's purpose in this chapter is to examine WikiLeaks trajectory 'in the light of its ongoing contributions to, and clashes with, the process and institutions of investigative journalism'. In other words, while WikiLeaks has made a substantial contribution to public understanding of the 'deep state', and thus to the knowledge base from which investigative teams can draw their arguments, it does not necessarily comply with the more measured and responsible approach associated with the work of serious journalism. That may not be WikiLeaks' role, but Lynch recognises the moral dilemma created by its release of un-redacted material. She also recognises the ability of the group's operatives to undertake complex projects using relatively simple forms of technology to increase its profile, noting that 'WikiLeaks began to use Twitter not only to announce leaks, but to build a community of like-minded information activists that could serve as a research resource and source of operating funds'. Here, then, is an interesting parallel with the more decidedly democratic system adopted by organisations like *The Ferret* (see Chapter 9).

The journalist David Hayward provides the final contribution to this book (Chapter 14), turning his attention to the current state of journalism as a viable economic proposition. Identifying some of the major disruptions in the industry, he offers a perspective that recognises the dangers inherent in the breakdown of traditional modes of communication, while remaining optimistic about the future of a practice that has always been able to re-invent itself. Hayward is, however, completely open about a subject that some authors do not wish to discuss in depth – the apparent *disadvantages* of a more open communication system. In Hayward's opinion, the 'turn to more "democratic" new media forms allows propaganda, fake news and misinformation to reach a massive audience'. If, however, this development is 'combined this with a raft of new independent investigative journalism organisations, the collaboration of global media houses, and new techniques of verification', then Hayward believes that trust in the Fourth Estate can return and 'journalism can regain its role and reputation'. Using examples from his own extensive experience as a journalist and filmmaker, and practical guidance from initiatives he has witnessed, Hayward provides a note of optimism, one that shows a continued faith in the ability of individuals and institutions to renew the true virtues of the profession.

12 Fact-checking, false balance, and 'fake news'

The discourse and practice of verification in political communication

Jen Birks

Since journalism is often understood as a 'discipline of verification', fact-checking would seem to be fairly central to news-making, but in practice it is limited to testing the basic accuracy of names and dates (Shapiro et al., 2013). Therefore, while mainstream news media have been fascinated by the 'fake news' scandal that has undermined trust in social media, they should not be complacent about public doubt in their own ability to 'separate fact from fiction'.[1] Indeed, journalists' ability to do so has traditionally been hampered by their reluctance to make a judgement on the extent to which their sources' assertions stand up. In particular, the reliance on direct quotation of news sources – used as a 'strategic ritual' against accusations of subjectivity (Tuchman, 1972) – defers responsibility for accuracy and truthfulness to the source, and takes refuge in what is often (especially in the United States) disparagingly referred to as 'he said, she said journalism'.

Sharpiro et al. (2013) argue that verification is as much a strategic ritual as objectivity (Tuchman, 1972), that is to say, it is not about seeking the truth, but avoiding criticism. The principle of conveying 'just the facts' is central to the 'newspaper of record' tradition, but if 'facts' are interpreted as accurate quotes conveying the words and deeds of authorities then it risks becoming a form of uncritical stenography. Investigative journalism often recognises that 'the facts' are not self-evident but must be established, whereas day-to-day reporting often treats conflicting truth-claims as opinions that need only be balanced. In practice, then, dubious claims are challenged only by other sources, typically political opponents, with no adjudication between the two 'sides'.

Verification of substantial claims through double sourcing, checking the credibility of sources, and seeking corroboration are central to investigative journalism, when journalists are setting the agenda and defining a problem, but not when they are simply reporting 'on diary', when they seek not corroboration but *controversy*. There is little that citizens can do in this situation other than make an intuitive judgement about which source they trust more or find more credible. Research indicates, however, that a heuristic approach (reliance on factors such as party affiliation, ideology, and endorsements as shortcuts) is of limited use for voters in understanding which political candidates reflect their policy preferences, and is actively unhelpful for those who are least politically knowledgeable (Lau and Redlawsk, 2001). At the same time, audiences will not necessarily accept journalists' assertion of particular facts, even when solid evidence is offered, if this conflicts with their prior beliefs (Dunwoody and Konieczna, 2013) or contradicts established assertions (Nyhan and Reifler, 2010). Yet, without reliable verification, even those open to making an informed decision can be placed at a severe disadvantage.

A countervailing trend is the recent emergence of a separate genre of 'fact-checking' journalism – a more modest endeavour than investigative journalism, but also more practical and affordable. There has been some scholarly attention devoted to American fact-checking organisations (Graves, 2016) and the influence of this process on politicians and voters, especially Brendan Nyhan's influential work in the field of political psychology (Nyhan and Reifler, 2014; Nyhan et al., 2017), but so far this has been limited to U.S. politics. This chapter examines fact-checking in the UK in comparative context with the United States, and also locates the development of fact-checking as a separate genre of news in wider debates around verification, including source credibility, expert knowledge and 'false balance'.

Verification in journalism: theory and practice

Studies of American and European newsrooms have found the practice of verification to be limited. Drawing on interviews with Canadian journalists, Shapiro et al. (2013) argued that whilst journalists strongly identified with the notion of journalism as 'a discipline of verification', in practice the requirement was more limited than this suggests.

> It would seem fair, based on our research so far, to say that zeal for accuracy is a professional norm, but also that it is a norm of compromise – the compromise being simply understood rather than articulated. A small, easily checkable, fact needs to be checked, a larger but greyer assertion, not so much, unless it is defamation.
> (Shapiro et al., 2013: 668)

This means accuracy in dates, places, and the spelling of sources' names rather than interrogating the substance of the assertions. In the UK, Lewis et al. (2008) identified a high proportion of stories that appeared in 'quality' broadcast and press news, that had been drawn wholly or principally from press releases or news wires, and that '*in only half these cases did the press make any discernible attempt to contextualise or verify this information, and in less than one in five cases was this done meaningfully*' (Lewis et al. 2008: 15, emphasis in original). Diekerhof and Bakker (2012: 244) reported a surprisingly credulous attitude among Dutch journalists toward 'highly placed' sources, with journalists believing that elite social actors had no reason to lie, and could not afford to do so, indicating that the deferential assumptions identified by Gans (1979: 130) still persist.

Although the investigative tradition retains a more serious attitude to verification, corroboration tended to be limited to the 'pivotal facts' drawn from a witness' testimony (Ettema and Glasser, 1998: 142–143). What constitutes corroboration is anyway quite ambiguous, and journalists must decide how much of a discrepancy between sources' accounts can be tolerated. The common factor across news genres, though, is that journalists are for the most part dealing with human sources rather than documents, statistics, or direct evidence,[2] and this involves the possibility of relying upon subjective, flawed, or misleading accounts.

The principle established in investigative journalism, and recognised as an ideal more generally, is that every claim must be double sourced. However, Godler and Reich (2017) question this definition of verification and suggest that other scholars have set the bar too high. They point to 'second-order evidence', or 'evidence of evidence' as – at least in some circumstances – an equally sound evidentiary base. In this category, Godler and Reich include 'procedural evidence' of the source's reasoning and evidence, as well as 'social evidence' about their position or qualifications, and 'psychological evidence' of their (in)sincerity, such as being 'evasive, contradictory or otherwise incoherent' (Godler and Reich, 2017: 564–565).

These authors also acknowledge that in some circumstances, 'due to complexity', journalists may not have the specialist knowledge required to evaluate the source's evidence, but suggest that, in this event, 'the source's record on similar matters can be drawn upon' (2017: 564). Elsewhere, however, Reich (2011) finds limited support for the assumption that journalists base their perception of credibility on past contact with a source. Indeed, studies of scientists as news sources indicate journalists are at least as likely to select the most prominent, outspoken or controversial individual, as they would the most reliable (Peters, 2014), and that they rarely choose the most appropriate specialist (Dunwoody and Ryan, 1987).

Studies on source credibility tend to focus on those providing expert testimony of some sort, but another important source of information is testimony from eyewitness accounts or reports of personal experience. As with experts, we are rarely able – depending on our own knowledge and experience – to judge the validity of witnesses' claims directly, but need to parse their credibility based on other factors, to decide whether to accord them 'cognitive authority' (Wilson, 1983; Turner, 2001); that is to say, to regard their influence on our beliefs and understanding as legitimate.

Journalists attribute slightly more credibility to passers-by eyewitnesses with no 'axe to grind' (Ettema and Glasser, 1998: 146; see also Langer, 1992), as they do to disinterested sources more generally (Diekerhof and Bakker, 2012: 246–247), though reporters are not always good at identifying experts' conflicts of interest (Holland et al., 2014). In terms of investigative journalism, those who are deemed culpable of wrongdoing – the targets of investigation in particular – are accorded least credibility by this measure, but nonetheless may be given the opportunity to present their own version of events (Ettema and Glasser, 1998: 147). This might involve allowing them to deny the allegations, but that is not to say that these denials will be presented as credible.

Effective investigative journalism is not just about detecting, verifying, and revealing new information, but about telling a story to show why that information is important. Kovach (2001: 51) picks out the Pentagon Papers exposé as an example of 'interpretative investigative reporting' without the analysis of which the papers 'would have meant little to most of the public'. But he also defines investigative journalism as exemplifying 'the role of the press as activist, reformer and exposer' (2001: 50), highlighting the moral and political aspect of this interpretation. Ettema and Glasser agree that it is important to establish not only events but also the 'moral facts' (1998: 148) of intentionality (guilt) and the impact on victims – what they call the 'motive-action-consequence schema' (1998: 144).

Journalists are reluctant to acknowledge this substantive foundation, or regard it as part of the social consensus (Ettema and Glasser, 1998: 8–10), but they are also conscious of the risk that readers could *reject* the moral framing. To manage that risk, there is a careful narrative construction of the innocence of those 'victims' – establishing them as what Langer (1992) calls 'good victims' – and equally prudent selection of the most compelling stories that may generate audience empathy (Ettema and Glasser, 1998: 115). As with the weight of evidence, the moral narrative must also cohere around a specific conclusion, rather than leaving it for the reader to decide, as expected in 'objective' reporting (Ryan, 2001: 5).[3] Investigative journalists might present a range of subjective perspectives,[4] but they also 'convey their sense of the evidentiary and moral weight to be allocated to various interpretations' (Ettema and Glasser 1998: 147).

This moral and emotional foundation behind investigative journalism does not sit well with the professional ideology of the liberal model of journalism, especially the North American tradition, which is most highly wedded to the notion of objectivity, yet it is broadly accepted and even valourised by industry prizes (Wahl-Jorgensen, 2013). The more modest, but more news-focused and *novel* genre of fact-checking could be more vulnerable to accusations of subjectivity and editorialising, especially if these efforts are integrated into 'straight' news. Nonetheless, some U.S. journalists are becoming increasingly conscious of the need to take greater responsibility for the truth of what they publish, faced with a President whose relationship with the truth is tenuous at best.

Since Donald Trump entered politics, he has upended dominant assumptions, for instance that even deceitful sources 'will tend not to lie about readily refutable points' (Godler and Reich, 2017: 565), or that senior and prominent political figures can't afford to be caught in a lie (Diekerhof and

Bakker, 2012). Whilst many politicians may be 'economical with the truth' or dissemble, Trump seems to have a complete disregard for the truth. Journalists in the United States have had to reflect on whether their routines and rituals are equal to this challenge. For instance, an editorial on digital news site *Talking Points Memo*[5] argued that 'Trump's campaign has been so different, so indifferent to clear factual claims, so unbridled that he has frequently put this whole edifice under strain to breaking point', and a Nicholas Kristof op-ed in *The New York Times* (2016b) called him a crackpot and a mythomaniac – essentially an unhinged compulsive liar – and agonised over how to 'signal' this to readers.

Much of this reflective meta-journalism has drawn on a wider debate that has appeared in the opinion and editorial pages of several major U.S. newspapers over the issue of 'false balance'. A Nexis sample assembled from the last 20 full years (1997–2016) in major U.S. newspapers, showed that there were 136 mentions of 'false balance' or 'false equivalence',[6] 43 of which occurred in 2016, and most of which were related to the presidential campaigns.[7] In the national UK press over the same period, there were 67 uses of 'false balance', all since 2010, and with a particular spike in 2014. Whilst not necessarily representative of journalists' practice in general, these articles illustrate the conflicts in norms and expectations of journalistic verification, the limits of 'just the facts' reporting, and of conventional measures of source credibility. The following section therefore offers an analysis of this sample of newspaper articles.

Balancing versus weighting and verifying truth claims: false balance and false equivalence

In both the United States and UK, the term *false balance* is used to refer to the inappropriate application of balance to a matter of established fact (such as that the earth is round), or settled scientific consensus (such as climate change), rather than to opinion, values, and subjective beliefs. Daniel Hallin (1989) observed that the norms set by the social responsibility model of journalism, including balance, do not apply universally to every assertion, but only to those located in the 'sphere of legitimate controversy', whilst those in the 'sphere of consensus' can simply be stated or assumed. His point was that some socially and politically contentious issues, such as the U.S. role in the Vietnam War, were inappropriately located in the sphere of consensus, simply because they were not contentious among elites. With false balance, the problem is reversed: simply because some people (often but perhaps not always elites) contest climate change, evolution, vaccine safety, or even that President Obama was really born in the United States, some journalists frame those things as controversies. This suggests that attribution and balance are stronger strategic rituals than verification, certainly of those 'larger, greyer' facts. Hallin was, of course, talking more about value consensus than acceptance of fact grounded in evidence, but as Ettema and Glasser (1998) observe, the two are more closely related than journalists like to acknowledge.

In the United States, false balance is used interchangeably with the overlapping concept of *false equivalence* (e.g., by Paul Krugman in *The New York Times* 2006, 2016a). The latter term is used to refer to the inappropriate weighting of unequally significant or legitimate sources, but on political as well as scientific questions, and also (variously and confusingly) to false analogies and inappropriate comparisons or moral equivalences. It is therefore a term applied at least as much to value-based judgements (especially of political legitimacy) as judgements of expert interpretation of evidence (which hinge more on credibility).

False *balance* has been used in the United States, as it has in the UK, to refer to the undue attention given to ill-informed or self-interested commentators who question established climate change science, but only four of the 136 articles in the U.S. sample, or 3%, actually did so, in contrast to the 50% of mentions in UK nationals. Other examples of scientific truth claims that critics argued were inappropriately 'balanced' with sceptical voices included evolution (letter, *The Philadelphia Inquirer*, 2005), and more contentiously the safety of genetically modified crops (*St. Louis Post-Dispatch* [Missouri], 2003). However, whilst critics agree that 'false balance' is unhelpful, there is no apparent consensus about how to assert facts or dispute lies and misrepresentations. An obvious solution would be to simply state assertions such as climate change as fact and exclude inexpert critics as lacking credibility, but this can be interpreted as censorship (e.g. *Daily Express*, 2011).

Nonetheless, even the most vociferous critics of false balance within journalism, such as *The New York Times'* Public Editor, Margaret Sullivan, tend to call for just such opaque adjudications. For example, one issue that Sullivan returned to several times was the allegation of voter fraud repeatedly made by Republicans, dating back long before Trump's candidacy (*The New York Times*, 2012b, 2014b, 2014c), which was a matter of both factual and political dispute. The factual argument was over whether voter fraud was really a problem, with Democrats pointing out that there was no evidence of this offence actually occurring. Whilst it is difficult to prove a negative – and it is not unreasonable to suggest it was incumbent on Republican critics to provide evidence – it would have helped the reader if news reports had detailed what attempts had been made to detect voter fraud, to give a sense of how likely it was to have been detected if it had occurred. The *political* argument was that Republicans wanted to introduce more stringent voter registration measures, which Democrats argued was intended to suppress minority votes. This requires another form of evidence, though predictions and forecasts do not enjoy the certainty of 'facts'. Sullivan's intervention was limited, however, to encouraging and then praising the inclusion of the statement that there was no evidence of voter fraud, which does assert a verified fact, but excludes the more ambiguous arguments and evidence that fact-checking would draw upon.[8]

Other truth claims were not directly verifiable, so could only be judged in terms of the credibility of the source. On this basis, Sullivan was repeatedly critical of anonymous sources, where readers had to trust journalists' credibility judgements. However, she reconsidered her most forceful criticisms – of the use of anonymous police sources in the investigation into the Ferguson police shooting that were supposed to 'balance' the evidence of two named eyewitnesses[9] (*The New York Times*, 2014a) once the Justice Department report supported the police account with 'the testimony of more than 40 witnesses' (*The New York Times*, 2015). There is a certain pragmatism, then, when a story is reported before the evidence has been fully considered but, as Kovach (2001: 53) reflects, there is also a risk for journalists when reporting on an official investigation, of being the servant of the authorities rather than holding them to account.

Where sources contradict one another on claims that are difficult or impossible to verify, comparative credibility judgements are of particular importance. For example, a freelance journalist writing in *USA Today* (2002) complained that in a story about the war in Afghanistan, 'Pentagon denials coming out of Washington are given equal credibility with eyewitness reports from anti-Taliban villagers on the ground; the story dissolves into a false balance of he-said, she-said', which the freelancer interpreted as evidence of post-9/11 'hyperpatriotism'. Journalists had, she suggests, undervalued authenticity and the moral status of victimhood in their credibility judgements.

However, even when claims are based on expert knowledge and research, they can be politicised. The most obvious example is climate change, which is the subject of half of the references to 'false balance' which occur in the British press (and a further 10% on science more broadly, including the MMR scare, during which public disquiet was caused by the publication of a research paper that suggested that the MMR vaccine was responsible for causing major illnesses). Interestingly, however, the two spikes in coverage of the issue in the press focus on a BBC Trust report (July 2011) and a Parliamentary report (Science and Technology Select Committee, April 2014), as well as a complaint upheld by the BBC Trust (July 2014), that criticised the corporation for giving too much air-time to sceptics such as Lord Lawson (Chancellor of the Exchequer under Prime Minister Margaret Thatcher, essentially a representative of business interests). These complaints were framed by the conservative press as the liberal BBC muzzling critics (*Express*, 2011) and 'tak[ing] its orders from the green lobby' (*The Times*, 2014). The only sustained reflection on journalism as a whole appears in *The Independent*'s (2015) 'The Only Way Is Ethics' column, by ex-regulator Will Gore.

More recently, the EU referendum campaign illustrated the ways in which expert evidence could be misused, manipulated, undermined, and dismissed, or marshalled to support an account of the EU as either essential to the British economy or a burden on the state (based on supranational agreements like the free movement of people). But whilst there was much media analysis of Conservative MP and Vote Leave campaigner Michael Gove's assertion that 'the British people have had enough of experts' (Mance, 2016), again there was little reflection by journalists on their own role in the impoverishment of public debate. In contrast, there has been a significant amount of soul-searching in the United States about the 2016 presidential election coverage. In this instance, however, the focus was principally on false equivalence between the candidates' moral legitimacy or wrongdoing, rather than between their conflicting truth claims.

One significant difficulty for journalists is the general operating assumption that 'facts do speak for themselves. If one side is more compelling, that is apparent from the objective journalist's report' (Ryan, 2001: 7), and that objective journalists do not need to 'shout, "this side is superior", as some critics seem to suggest they should, but the superiority is apparent' (9). Given the audacity of Trump's lies and 'bullshitting', that is, having no regard for the truth (Davis, 2017), journalists assumed that this would be clear to the audience. Hence, as Josh Marshall editor's blog at online news site *Talking Points Memo*[10] points out, most of the 'damaging press' that Trump has received 'has been simply publishing or airing things he's said publicly' without explicit criticism. In contrast, they believed that Clinton's sophisticated spin machine required more digging, giving the impression, on her part, of disproportionate wrongdoing.

Moreover, *The New York Times*'s Sullivan had long argued that it is *readers* (voters, citizens) who are demanding the new approach to verification, and driving it through social and other digital media. Citing Stevenson, *The Times*'s political editor, she recounted his interest in:

> fact-checking . . . [which is] one of the most positive trends in journalism that I can remember. It's . . . brought about, in part, by a more demanding public, fuelled by media critics, bloggers and denizens of the social media world – to present the truth, not just conflicting arguments leading to confusion.
>
> (*The New York Times*, 2012b)

However, this 'movement' has remained on the sidelines of journalism, in online enclaves, signalled as a separate journalistic practice from straight news.

Fact-checking the small statistical facts

Fact-checking websites and blogs originated in the United States in 2003 with 'FactCheck.org' – a project of the Annenberg Public Policy Center of the University of Pennsylvania – which inspired the British *Channel 4 News* 'FactCheck' blog in 2005. The *Washington Post*'s 'Fact Checker' and *Tampa Bay Times*' 'Politifacts' both followed in 2007, independent British organisation 'Full Fact' in 2009, and the *BBC*'s 'Reality Check' in 2010. The British sites have grown significantly over the last three general elections: C4

FactCheck doubled the number of fact-check articles between 2015 and the snap Election of 2017, and Reality Check issued more quick response items on specific debate claims. The most remarkable, however, was independent fact-checker Full Fact – in 2015 they aimed to raise £25,000 through crowd-funding to kit out an election office for their volunteers; two years later they raised over £100,000 and were able to add to their permanent staff of 11 to create a 30-strong election team. In between 2015 and 2017, there was a highly contested referendum on EU membership that is likely to have increased public frustration at politicians twisting facts with impunity, an example I will return to below.

It is interesting that elections are the context in which news organisations recognise that they could do more to inform their audience (suggesting a limited view of citizens' political participation, perhaps), but equally that 'fact-checking' emerged from outside the industry and remains a separate news genre. Journalists and editors are consciously reluctant to incorporate fact-checking into their general practice, not for practical, resource-related reasons, but because accusing a politician of lying looks too much like bias. A Public Editor column in *The New York Times* (2012a) cites Executive Editor Jill Abramson's concern that if fact-checking became a 'reflexive element of too many news stories, our readers would find the *Times* was being tendentious' and may even see it 'as a combatant, not an arbiter of what the facts were'. In the UK, Full Fact battled for five years to gain charitable status from the charity commission because of concerns that their aim of promoting 'civic responsibility and engagement' could involve political controversy.[11] In a review of U.S. fact-checking, Lucas Graves (2016: 10) describes this tension, noting 'theirs is a story of shifting institutional norms and practices: fact-checkers enact a deliberate critique of conventional reporting and its practice of objectivity'. This function is all the more important, he argues, in a digital world where journalists can no longer 'decide what's *news*' (Gans, 1979), because of competition from social media, so they can only 'decide what's *true*'.

This suggests a rather grander process than the practical reality, which is limited to deciding whether a given politician's claim is accurate, with a focus on statistics and other 'hard' factual claims. In his study of 'hybrid media' combining traditional news and digital innovations, Chadwick (2017: 201) cites Alice Tartleton, a member of the C4 FactCheck team, who explained that the purpose of his approach is 'about 'having the small scoop' by puncturing the bubble of politicians' often selective use of statistics'. This can, however, risk neglecting the bigger, greyer, assertions that have more political punch. Having said that, Cushion and Lewis (2016) found that only 4% of statistics used in the general broadcast news coverage of the British EU referendum campaign were challenged or verified (at least explicitly), and that more statistical claims came from politicians than any other group, especially experts from think tanks and universities, so it is significant that fact-checkers attempted to do this.

The EU referendum provides an interesting case for analysis, because of the highly contested claims made on both sides. Rather than making manifesto pledges, arguments both in favour of remaining in the EU (from the government-backed Remain campaign and others) and leaving (from a range of competing and conflicting Leave campaigns) made predictions about *the impact of either outcome* on growth, jobs, wages, public services and so on. On both sides, those claims were highly politicised, and used to back up their chosen narratives – for Remain, that leaving would cause a recession, and for Leave that continued 'uncontrolled' immigration was the biggest threat to future prosperity and that only an exit from the EU would allow the country to 'take back control'.

Campaigners' dubious and outright false claims frequently went unchallenged in the mainstream news reporting because their political opponents made a strategic choice to turn their focus elsewhere. For instance, Remain campaigners rarely challenged the notorious claim that the UK sends £350 million a week to Brussels because the real figure also sounded quite high (around £161 million, according to Reality Check, though assessments differed). Although BBC and Channel 4 fact-checkers disputed the figure online, in their news bulletins politicians were allowed to continue to make the claim, as well as suggesting it would otherwise be used to fund the NHS, though they were not in a position to make that pledge. Embalzoned on the side of a double-decker bus, the claim was used as a backdrop for television interviews.

One particularly interesting fact-check concerned the claim that rising immigrant labour drives down wages. This exemplified politicians' attempts to rationalise the hostility to immigration that seemed to be at the heart of the 'Leave' campaign. Whilst references to this assertion in the press in the final three weeks of the campaign provided scant evidence – only a third mentioned a source, and just 18% offered data – all three UK fact-checkers addressed the claim. They focused on a report from the Bank of England[12] that found that in unskilled and semi-skilled service sectors, a 10-percentage-point increase in the proportion of immigrants in a given workforce corresponded to a 1.88% decrease in wages. This was leapt upon by leave campaigners who misinterpreted (or purposely misrepresented) it as the consequence of a 10% increase in immigration. This small difference in wording changed the meaning from a very large change in immigrant population to a much more plausible one.

Reality Check (2016b) pointed out that 'a 10 percentage point increase in immigrants working in a sector is a lot' and put the overall increase in the proportion of non-UK nationals in work in the UK at just 6.4 percentage points over 18 years. Full Fact (2016) gave a more specific context, in terms of the low-skilled and semi-skilled service occupations in question (though across all of the UK, where the report specified certain regions), which was rather higher at 8% over eight years, but calculated this effect as 'a drop of between 1 and 2 pence per hour, each year'. FactCheck (2016b), meanwhile, estimated a 10% rise in the EU-born population at 300,000 and a 10-percentage-point rise at nine million. All of these attempt to explain the statistics in a meaningful way, but even though FactCheck and Full Fact frame their checks as responding to Boris Johnson's misrepresentation of the figure in a televised debate, they do not point this out explicitly. FactCheck even buried the point in a parenthetical aside, whilst suggesting that Johnson had merely omitted a caveat, and 'if he had talked about 'a reduction in wages for the low-skilled' rather than just "a reduction in wages" he would have been right', which is a very lax interpretation that does not challenge political misuse of statistics.

However, in the press, the only reported challenge to Johnson's assertion was from 'Remain' campaigner Alex Salmond during a TV debate. Salmond was declared as the victor in this case on the basis that he had read the report, whilst Johnson was forced to admit that he had not. Furthermore, the relevant statistics were only cited twice in the press sample, and though they did so accurately, they were mediated and politicised by campaigning sources, which omitted statistical explanation and caveats, and framed the impact as significant. A report in *The Sunday Times* noted that:

> the pitfalls of mass immigration disproportionately affect the poorest sector of the population, [as] MacKinnon [a member of campaign group Economists for Brexit] points out, citing a Bank of England study last year that showed a 10% increase in the proportion of immigrants was associated with a 2% drop in pay among unskilled service workers. 'The negative effects come through at the lower end of the scale. That's why you get this social resentment', he says.
>
> (2016)

The report was also bandied about as support for even more sweeping generalisations, such as the statement made by Vote Leave chair, Gisela Stuart (quoted in the *Guardian*, 2016a), who said, 'as the Bank of England has confirmed, uncontrolled immigration has played a key role in bringing down wages'.

Of course, partisan commentators do not need to use statistics at all – several columnists in *The Telegraph* and *The Daily Mail* simply stated as fact the claim that immigration drives wages down, a position supported in two *Sun* editorials. The notion was also circulated by reluctant 'Remainers' on the Left like Len McCluskey, General Secretary of Unite the Union (see the *Guardian*, 2016a) and Jeremy Corbyn, the Labour leader (the *Independent*, 2016c). Even some pro-immigration Remainers accepted the immigration/wage depression argument as common sense, or at least as one element of a persistent public belief (*The Times*, 2016b; the *Guardian*, 2016b; the *Independent*, 2016a).

The newspaper articles that did *not* start from a specific political angle were able to consider, not only the evidence of an impact of immigration on wages, but also the claim that the economic impact of leaving the EU would have a greater effect: this included TUC (Trade Union Council) research which indicated that leaving the EU would cost £38 per week in average wages. These reports were based on the many economic forecasts that predicted a fall in GDP growth as a consequence of Brexit, which were then politicised by campaigners.

Politicians in the Remain camp – especially then Prime Minister David Cameron and Chancellor George Osbourne – tended to frame economic forecasts as *fact* rather than informed (but fallible) *opinion or judgement*. Channel 4's FactCheck (2016a) described Cameron's phrasing in one such speech as 'overcooking it slightly' and pointed out that 'obviously we're talking about predicting the future here and there's no way the Treasury or anyone else can "confirm" that something will or won't happen'. Another problem with the political interpretation of the statistics was the dubious framing of GDP growth forecasts in terms of a cost per household, as pointed out by Reality Check (2016b).

However, the principal objection to these economic forecasts was based on doubts about the cognitive authority of economists, which varied from scepticism to cynicism. By comparison, whilst there was some acknowledgement of uncertainty and ambiguity in the treatment of claims on immigration and wages, they were not framed in such a way that undermined the research altogether. For instance, political commentators remarked that 'evidence on wage impacts is a bit less conclusive' (*The Times*, 2016a) and that 'the truth of the competing claims is hard to establish' (*The Independent*, 2016b). In contrast, references to economic forecasts cast aspersions on the whole discipline: 'our elite, brilliant economists have a solid record of getting it wrong' (*The Telegraph*, 2016) and dismissed the figures as political scaremongering: 'the Leave campaign has used civil servants, paid for by us, to trawl up all sorts of economic forecasts' (*Sunday Express*, 2016).

Interestingly, economic forecasts were also treated with significant scepticism by the BBC fact-checker, Reality Check. Several fact-checks on economic questions referred back to an 'explainer' on economic modelling that cast doubt on the validity of the entire enterprise. This source presented its argument in somewhat patronising tones, as follows: 'Q: Economic models – are they like fashion models? A: No, they're a bit more realistic than that. But not much' (Reality Check, 2016a). It also advised the concerned voter to examine various measures of credibility such as 'how well-respected the people conducting the research are', the existence of any evidence of an association with a particular side in the debate, and any hint of bias motivated by past support from the EU, such as funding. Ultimately, however, the 'explainer' concluded with a recommendation, not on how to make an informed judgement in the face of uncertain evidence and the doubtful credibility of experts, but on how to make an instinctive judgement on whether to trust particular arguments, regardless of the credentials of those making them.

And remember there's also the option to decide that you don't care what even the finest economists predict, or even that you don't think the economic impact is the most important thing about EU membership.

(Reality Check, 2016a)

At the same time, however, voters do have alternative sources of information besides that offered by experts, such as their own experience of past 'economic growth' that might not correspond with rising wages and secure jobs, despite the assurances provided by economists.[13]

Effectiveness of fact-checking

In the United States, President Trump has capitalised on the trust that people place in their own observations and extrapolations, and has traded on the corresponding fall in trust shown in experts and authorities, including the media. For this reason, Chadwick argues, no amount of fact-checking would undermine his supporters' approval.

> When Trump made racist, sexist, or xenophobic remarks, exaggerated claims or massaged statistical evidence, elite media had treated him as either an amateur to be ridiculed, or had responded with manufactured outrage that further fuelled Trump's publicity-hungry campaign and its theme that elite media were biased.
>
> (Chadwick, 2017: 253)

That is not necessarily to say, however, that Trump's supporters are impervious to factual correction, but that the small, checkable facts are of less importance to them than the larger, more ambiguous assertions about America's place in the world and what would make it 'great again'. Davis (2017) argues that they 'simply decide that it's better to support someone who is on their side rather than someone who has a grasp of the facts'. In a widely quoted remark, Salena Zito (2016) argued that when Trump makes a claim such as that 58% of black youths cannot get a job, a figure that 'drive[s] fact-checkers to distraction' as it includes those in full-time education, 'the press takes him literally, but not seriously; his supporters take him seriously, but not literally'.

Nyhan et al. (2017) responded to this by testing three hypotheses on responses to fact-checking indicated by previous conflicting research findings. The first of these is 'motivated resistance' – that people are 'highly resistant to unwelcome information' that contradicts their ideological convictions, and indeed double down on the misbelief in a 'backfire' effect. The second is 'differential acceptance' – that people can adjust their factual beliefs even against their ideological convictions, but to a lesser degree than those for whom the correction confirms their beliefs. Finally, the third is 'differential interpretation' – that people can adjust their factual beliefs but interpret those facts differentially according to their ideological convictions.

The researchers compared survey responses from those exposed only to Trump's assertions on rising crime, with those of another group that were also provided corrections from FBI crime data stating crime had fallen, and another provided with both plus a denial and criticism of FBI credibility, as well as a control group. They found that Trump supporters' assessment of the amount of crime on a five-point scale was the same whether they had read Trump's statement or not (though interestingly, Clinton supporters *reduced* their estimate in response to Trump's assertion that it had risen), suggesting that he was reflecting their instinctive views rather than influencing them (2017: 6–8). Trump supporters *did* adjust their assessment of crime levels down in response to the correction, however, although to a lesser degree than Clinton supporters. At the same time, they also thought the article slightly less accurate with the correction and were more doubtful of FBI statistics when used as a correction to their candidate (2017: 9–10). However, Trump supporters did not adjust their belief in the need for tougher law and order measures, or their favourability toward Trump. The authors conclude that like the media's response to Trump, his supporters in return 'took the corrections literally, but apparently not seriously'. In other words, their policy convictions do not appear to have a factual basis.

The discourse of 'fake news': discrediting rather than disproving

Prior political beliefs are therefore often more influential on our credibility judgements than evidence and expertise of the source. Politicians can succeed by claiming to share those beliefs, but that relates to another dimension of credibility – *sincerity* (or *authenticity*). Trump's supporters probably see him as more honest and trustworthy than his opponent, not because they thought his statements accurate, but because they felt that his politics were sincere, unfiltered, and unspun. This is not necessarily an attitude that is confined to the Right. One of the founders of the Left-wing website *The Canary*, Kerry-Anne Mendoza, argues that the British Left-liberal press lost the trust of many of its readers over its negative framing of Labour leader Jeremy Corbyn, especially on the basis of judging him unelectable, despite apparently sharing his political position. Because of this, she argues, 'people stopped trusting their motives'.[14] However, headline statistics showing low trust in mainstream news mask huge differences in the trust placed in individual channels, publications, and platforms. In addition, one purported reason for the decline in trust in mainstream media is that people experience greater exposure to the established media outlets that they don't ordinarily read, *via social media*,[15] therefore increasing their awareness of aspects of the mainstream media they find politically distasteful. This suggests that a pluralistic media environment *increases* people's distrust of the media, rather than exposing them to a wider range of viewpoints to better inform their beliefs.

This distrust is what allowed Trump to turn the 'fake news' label back against the mainstream media. Politifact remarked that 'In the short time we've been devoted to fact-checking "fake news", the phrase has been overused and misappropriated to the point that it's become pretty much meaningless'.[16] Trump's modus operandi has not been to refute hostile claims, however, but to muddy the waters, a long-established tactic used by propagandists and PR professionals, for instance in casting doubt on climate change science, or on the evidence that tobacco is carcinogenic.

Nonetheless, Trump shows some signs of being sensitive to fact-checking – one *Washington Post* Fact-checker article (Kessler et al., 2017) quotes him hedging, 'I better say "think", otherwise they'll give you a Pinocchio. . . . And I don't like those – I don't like Pinocchios', though this suggests a very narrow definition of fact-checkable truth claims. In other words, he suggests that you can turn a factual assertion into an *opinion* – which need not be verified or challenged, but merely 'balanced' with other opinions – simply by prefacing it with the word 'think'. More predictably, Donald Trump's alt-Right media supporters (principally Breitbart,[17] whose Executive Chairman, Steve Bannon, once served as Trump's Chief Strategist) have accused U.S. fact-checkers of liberal bias, as has Sean Spicer, then White House Press Secretary, who coined the term 'alternative facts' in a dispute over media debunking of his claim that Trump's was the most watched inauguration ever,[18] though his later arguments were less obviously counterfactual.

Disproving and debunking false claims, myths, and bad assumptions is important for rational political debate, but also contributes to the general sense that all public claims can be discredited, which turns healthy scepticism into cynicism. *The Times* columnist Hugo Rifkind argued that fact-checking itself plays into the hands of those trying to spread misinformation via doubt.

> Nor, depressingly, are fact-checkers [the answer]. It is a naive fallacy to assume fake news is all just the work of the odd enterprising crank or charlatan. . . . NATO's Handbook of Russian Information Warfare discusses fake news as a distinctive part of the Kremlin's cyberwarfare strategy. Crucially, the point is not merely to deceive; rather, it is to sow seeds of doubt and create a background hum of mistrust.
>
> (*The Times*, 2017)

There certainly is evidence of what Nyhan and Reifler (2010) call the 'backfire effect' in response to fact-checking of news circulated on social media, because it is interpreted as an act of censorship, carried out by the liberal mainstream media, against 'conservative' free speech. A *Guardian* article featuring interviews with writers of 'fake news' stories related examples where conservative groups on Facebook had increased traffic to disputed stories – according to one writer, 'with Facebook trying to throttle it and say, "don't share it", it actually had the opposite effect'.

> He [Jestin Coler, fake news publisher] also noted that many consumers of fake news won't be swayed by a 'disputed' tag given their distrust of the media and fact-checkers: 'A far-right individual who sees it's been disputed by Snopes, that adds fuel to the fire and entrenches them more in their belief'.
>
> (*Guardian*, 2017)

The bloggers interviewed were, like Trump, unconcerned with the truth, and see an emotional engagement with the claim as just as important: 'A lot of people think Obama is Muslim. That's what it plays on. Is it real? I don't know. . . .] The fact is a lot of people thought it was real or it reflects their sentiment' (*Guardian*, 2017).

The problems with journalistic verification in contemporary politics are not, therefore, wholly or even mainly about accuracy of small, particular facts, but about the credibility of the bigger, greyer claims and their moral ordering. Ettema and Glasser (1998: 151) argue that in investigative journalism this depends, ultimately, on the implicit values of the journalist. In an increasingly polarised society, any moral interpretation is increasingly contested and resisted, to the extent that facts no longer constrain the moral or narrative interpretation of an event. Where once alternative *interpretations* were widespread, now the existence of 'alternative facts' threatens to become a commonplace assertion.

Primary references (press sources)

U.S. newspaper articles

The New York Times (2006) 'A False Balance', Editorial Desk, P23, by Paul Krugman, 30 January 2006.

The New York Times (2012a) 'Keeping Them Honest', The Public Editor, P14, by Arthur S. Brisbane, 22 January 2012.

The New York Times (2012b) 'He Said, She Said, and the Truth', The Public Editor, P12, by Margaret Sullivan, 16 September 2012.

The New York Times (2014a) 'A Ferguson Story on "Conflicting Accounts" Seems to Say "Trust Us"', The Public Editor's Blog, by Margaret Sullivan, 21 August 2014.

The New York Times (2014b) 'He Said, She Said, and Getting It Right About Voter ID', The Public Editor, by Margaret Sullivan, 2 September 2014.

The New York Times (2014c) 'So We Beat On: Another Year in the Hot Seat', Public Editor, P12, by Margaret Sullivan, 19 October 2014.

The New York Times (2015) 'Reconsidering My August Post on Ferguson and "Conflicting Accounts"', The Public Editor's Blog, by Margaret Sullivan, 23 March 2015.

The New York Times (2016a) 'All the Nominee's Enablers', Op-Ed Columnist, P27, by Paul Krugman, 8 July 2016.

The New York Times (2016b) 'When a Crackpot Seeks Office', Op-Ed Columnist, P27, by Nicholas Kristof, 15 September 2016.
The Philadelphia Inquirer (2005) 'Letters', Editorial, P18, 20 October 2005.
St. Louis Post-Dispatch (Missouri) (2003) 'Letters to the Editor: Biotech Foes Falsely Viewed as Luddites', Editorial, P31, 31 May 2003.
USA Today (2002) 'Armchair anti-American warrior aims, shoots duds', by Walter Shapiro, 8 May 2002.

UK newspaper articles

Express (2011) 'Uproar as BBC muzzles climate change sceptics', News, P5, by Nathan Rao, 21 July 2011.
Guardian (2016a) 'TUC chief ridicules "phoney" Brexit campaigners', Politics, P7, by Heather Stewart and Angela Monaghan, 1 June 2016.
Guardian (2016b) 'David Cameron's fatal mistakes on immigration threaten our country's future', Opinion, by Owen Jones, 21 June 2016.
Guardian (2017) 'Facebook promised to tackle fake news: But the evidence shows it's not working', Technology, by Sam Levin, 16 May 2017.
Independent (2015) 'With facts on the Sinai crash hard to come by, journalists have a right to set out theories'. The Only Way is Ethics, Opinion, by Will Gore, 9 November 2015.
Independent (2016a) 'Target funding to ease immigration fears, says Labour', News, P6, by Rob Hastings, 13 June 2016.
Independent (2016b) 'Is freedom of movement a principle to be upheld or reformed?' News, P21, by John Lichfield, 21 June 2016.
Independent (2016c) 'Corbyn: Remain will help bring reforms', June 23, 2016, News, P4, by Arj Singh, 23 June 2016.
Sunday Express (2016) 'Analysis', P9, by Marco Giannangeli, 5 June 2016.
The Sunday Times (2016) 'Immigration is working: The influx of foreign workers has boosted the economy but curbed wages of low-paid workers', Business P7, by Tommy Stubbington, 12 June 2016.
Telegraph (2016) 'August bodies such as the IMF say Brexit would be a disaster. James Bartholomew explains why they are all wrong', Diary of a private investor, Your Money P10, 4 June 2016.
The Times (2014) 'BBC has lost its balance over climate change; The corporation now seems to take its orders from the green lobby and is generating alarm over the environment', opinion, P17, by Matt Ridley, 7 July 2014.
The Times (2016a) 'Limiting immigration won't lift Britain to top of the Premier League', Business, P43, by Paul Johnson, 14 June 2016.
The Times (2016b) 'Killer flaw at the heart of Brexit campaign', Opinion, P27, by Daniel Finkelstein, 22 June 2016.
The Times (2017) 'Populism and fake news are a two-headed beast', Opinion, P19, by Hugo Rifkind, 9 May 2017.

Fact-check blogs

FactCheck (2016a) 'FactCheck Q&A: Are we really heading for a DIY recession?' 23rd May 2015 www.channel4.com/news/factcheck/factcheck-qa-heading-diy-recession.

FactCheck (2016b) 'Does immigration drive down wages?' 15 June 2016 www.channel4.com/news/factcheck/factcheck-boris-johnson-alex-salmond-does-eu-immigration-drive-down-wages.
Full Fact (2016) 'Does a 10% rise in immigration lead to a 2% reduction in wages?' 21 June 2016 https://fullfact.org/immigration/does-immigration-reduce-wages/.
Reality Check (2016a) 'Reality check: Should you care about economic models?' 21 March 2016 www.bbc.co.uk/news/business-35862618.
Reality Check (2016b) 'Reality check: Would Brexit cost your family £4,300?' 18 April 2016 www.bbc.co.uk/news/uk-politics-eu-referendum-36073201.

Notes

1. www.digitalnewsreport.org/
2. Journalists trust their own direct experience and witnesses more than any second-hand information (Ettema and Glasser, 1998: 146; Reich 2011: 61), but this is a very limited source in practice: one study put it at just 4% of articles (Reich 2011: 61).
3. Ryan argues that factual verification is not contrary to his definition of objective journalism, but his is an idealised defence of objectivity from a critical realist perspective (against relativist critics and the proponents of advocacy journalism), whilst acknowledging that there may be a problem with implementation.
4. One investigative reporter explained 'I present [all the points of view] in such a way that readers will have the advantage of the information that I had in order to make up my mind' (quoted in Ettema and Glasser, 1998: 147).
5. http://talkingpointsmemo.com/edblog/the-crisis-at-the-times-and-that-public-editor-piece
6. From a search on Nexis using its category of 'major US newspapers' grouped by moderate similarity, and manually excluding those relating to sport or entertainment and references to 'false balance sheets'.
7. In the first five years (1997–2001) there was on average just under one reference per year, 2.6 over the next five years (2002–2006), rising to 3.6 (2007–2011), and leaping to 19 mentions in 2012, and an average 20.2 in the five years to and including 2016.
8. For example, see this more recent fact-check on voter fraud claims: www.politifact.com/truth-o-meter/statements/2016/oct/17/donald-trump/donald-trumps-pants-fire-claim-large-scale-voter-f/
9. The eyewitnesses said that the victim had his hands up when he was shot by police, whilst the authorities reported support for the officer's account that the man was advancing on him.
10. http://talkingpointsmemo.com/edblog/the-crisis-at-the-times-and-that-public-editor-piece
11. www.civilsociety.co.uk/news/full-fact-gets-charity-status-after-being-rejected-twice.html
12. www.bankofengland.co.uk/research/Documents/workingpapers/2015/swp574.pdf
13. Stephen Turner (2001: 132) contrasts economics with the physical sciences, arguing that letters to newspapers signed by hundreds of economists shows how little they can claim to speak representatively on behalf of the discipline.
14. www.theguardian.com/media/2017/aug/06/can-you-trust-mainstream-media
15. www.theguardian.com/media/2017/aug/06/can-you-trust-mainstream-media
16. www.politifact.com/punditfact/article/2017/jan/27/fact-checking-fake-news-reveals-how-hard-it-kill-p/

17 www.breitbart.com/tech/2016/12/15/facebook-introduce-warning-labels-stories-deemed-fake-news/
18 www.politifact.com/truth-o-meter/statements/2017/jan/21/sean-spicer/trump-had-biggest-inaugural-crowd-ever-metrics-don/–atfhead

References

Chadwick, Andrew (2017) *Hybrid Media: Politics and Power*, Oxford: Oxford University Press.

Cushion, Stephen and Lewis, Justin (2016) 'Lies, damned lies and statistics: Why reporters must handle data with care', *The Conversation*, 28 November, http://theconversation.com/lies-damned-lies-and-statistics-why-reporters-must-handle-data-with-care-69314.

Davis, Evan (2017) *Post-Truth: Why We Have Reached Peak Bullshit and What We Can Do About It*, London: Little Brown.

Diekerhof, Els and Bakker, Piet (2012) 'To check or check not to check: An exploratory study on source checking by Dutch journalists', *Journal of Applied Journalism and Media Studies*, Vol. 1, Issue: 2, pp. 241–253.

Dunwoody, Sharon and Konieczna, Magda (2013) 'The role of global media in telling the climate change story', in Ward, Stephen J. A. [editor], *Global Media Ethics: Problems and Perspectives*, Hoboken, NJ: Blackwell, pp. 171–190.

Dunwoody, Sharon and Ryan, Michael (1987) 'The credible scientific source', *Journalism Quarterly*, Vol. 64, pp. 21–27.

Ettema, James S. and Glasser, Theodore L. (1998) *Custodians of Conscience*, New York: Columbia University Press.

Gans, Herbert J. (1979) *Deciding What's News*, Evanston, IL: Northwestern University Press.

Godler, Yigal and Reich, Zvi (2017) 'Journalistic evidence: Cross-verification as a constituent of mediated knowledge', *Journalism*, Vol. 18, Issue: 5, pp. 558–574.

Graves, Lucas (2016) *Deciding What's True: The Rise of Political Fact-Checking in American Journalism*, New York: Columbia University Press.

Hallin, Daniel (1989) *The uncensored war: the media and Vietnam*. Oakland: University of California Press.

Holland, Kate, Sweet, Melissa, Blood, R. Warwick and Fogarty, Andrea (2014) 'A legacy of the swine flu global pandemic: Journalists, expert sources, and conflicts of interest', *Journalism*, Vol. 15, Issue: 1, pp. 53–71.

Kessler, Glenn, Ye Hee Lee, Michelle and Kelly, Meg (2017) 'President Trump's first six months: The fact-check tally', *Washington Post Fact-checker*, 20 July, www.washingtonpost.com/news/fact-checker/wp/2017/07/20/president-trumps-first-six-months-the-fact-check-tally/?utm_term=.74ce46a170ab.

Kovach, Bill (2001) 'Toward a new journalism with verification', *Nieman Reports*, Winter 2006, http://niemanreports.org/articles/toward-a-new-journalism-with-verification/.

Langer, John (1992) 'Truly awful news on television', in Dahlgren, P. and Sparks, C. [editors], *Journalism and Popular Culture*. London: Sage Publications, pp. 113–129.

Lau, Richard R. and Redlawsk, David P. (2001) 'Advantages and disadvantages of cognitive heuristics in political decision making', *American Journal of Political Science*, Vol. 45, Issue: 4, pp. 951–971.

Lewis, Justin, Williams, Andrew and Franklin, Bob (2008) 'A compromised fourth estate? UK news journalism, public relations and news sources', *Journalism Studies*, Vol. 9, Issue: 1, pp. 1–20.

Mance, Henry (2016) 'Britain has had enough of experts, says Gove', in *Financial Times*, 6 June 2016, https://www.ft.com/content/3be49734-29cb-11e6-83e4-abc22d5d108c [accessed 16 November 2018].

Nyhan, Brendan and Reifler, Jason (2010) 'When corrections fail: The persistence of political misperceptions', *Political Behaviour*, Vol. 32, pp. 303–330.

——— (2014) 'The effect of fact-checking on elites: A field experiment on US state legislators', *American Journal of Political Science*, Vol. 59, Issue: 3, pp. 628–640.

Nyhan, Brendan, Reifler, Jason, Porter, Ethan and Wood, Thomas J. (2017) 'Taking corrections literally but not seriously? The effects of information on factual beliefs and candidate favorability', SSRN, https://ssrn.com/abstract=2995128.

Peters, Hans Peter (2014) 'Scientists as public experts: Expectations and responsibilities', in *Routledge Handbook of Public Communication of Science and Technology*, London: Routledge, pp. 70–82.

Reich, Zvi (2011) 'Source credibility and journalism: Between visceral and discretional judgement', *Journalism Practice*, Vol. 5, Issue: 1, pp. 51–67.

Ryan, Michael (2001) 'Journalistic ethics, objectivity, existential journalism, standpoint epistemology, and public journalism', *Journal of Mass Media Ethics*, Vol. 16, Issue: 1, pp. 3–32.

Shapiro, Ivor, Brin, Colette, Bédard-Brûlé, Isabelle and Mychajlowycz, Kasia (2013) 'Verification as strategic ritual: How journalists retrospectively describe processes for ensuring accuracy', *Journalism Practice*, Vol. 7, Issue: 6, pp. 657–673.

Tuchman, Gaye (1972) 'Objectivity as strategic ritual: An examination of newsmen's notions of objectivity', *The American Journal of Sociology*, Vol. 77, Issue: 4, pp. 660–679.

Turner, Stephen (2001) 'What is the problem with experts?' *Social Studies of Science*, Vol. 31, Issue: 1, pp. 123–149.

Wahl-Jorgensen, Karin (2013) 'The strategic ritual of emotionality: A case study of Pulitzer prize-winning articles', *Journalism*, Vol. 14, Issue: 1, pp. 129–145.

Wilson, Patrick (1983) *Second-Hand Knowledge: An Inquiry into Cognitive Authority*, Westport, CT: Greenwood Press.

Zito, Salena (2016) 'Taking Trump seriously, not literally', *The Atlantic*, 23 September, www.theatlantic.com/politics/archive/2016/09/trump-makes-his-case-in-pittsburgh/501335/.

13 WikiLeaks and investigative journalism

The organisation's effects and unfinished legacy[1]

Lisa Lynch

Introduction: what happened to WikiLeaks?

In July 2016, WikiLeaks released the first of what would become a series of leaks related to the campaigning activities of the U.S. Democratic National Committee; 44,053 emails and 17,761 attachments were obtained from a DNC central server. WikiLeaks' 'DNC Leaks' (WikiLeaks, 2016b) would eventually include emails from DNC Chair John Podesta (WikiLeaks, 2016c), former U.S. Secretary of Defense Colin Powell, and texts of speeches that Hilary Clinton – then the Democratic Party candidate for the U.S. presidency – had delivered to audiences at Goldman Sachs and other corporate venues. The leaks were greeted with delight by Republican campaign operatives, who used them to argue that the Clinton campaign was dishonest, if not criminally corrupt. In order to maximise their impact, WikiLeaks timed the last release of emails (those belonging to John Podesta) to coincide with the final weeks before the election, generating a flood of negative media attention for Clinton and her campaign. As U.S. media outlets digested the leaks, some journalists had trouble accepting the notion that WikiLeaks, long regarded by liberals as a champion of transparency in the service of good governance, might be attempting to throw the election to Republican candidate Donald Trump, generally regarded by progressive thinkers as a demagogue. Claims by U.S. intelligence agencies that the Australian hacker Julian Assange received the material via a state-authorised Russian hack – and not, as Assange had declared, via a DNC intermediary – deepened the sense that the group had somehow been co-opted. 'What happened to WikiLeaks?' asked a series of articles (Zoom, 2017; Bhuiyan, 2016; Samuelson, 2016; Turton, 2016), most of which concluded that WikiLeaks' release of the DNC emails provided evidence that the whistleblowing organisation had lost sight of its social mission.

As troubling as the DNC leaks were in the context of the 2016 U.S. elections, the argument that they represented a fundamental shift in WikiLeaks' mission or strategy was a misreading of WikiLeaks' decade-long history. Indeed, the leaked emails reflected WikiLeaks' long-standing intention to disrupt government institutions through a strategy of radical transparency that prioritises the broadest possible distribution of leaked disclosures and disregards journalistic conventions regarding the sourcing and redaction of such disclosures. This chapter will look at WikiLeaks in the light of its ongoing contributions to, and clashes with, the process and institutions of investigative journalism. There is no doubt that WikiLeaks has helped to facilitate the rise of the sort of globally based, internationally focused investigative journalism that is the subject of this volume, both by serving as a central source for disclosures of global consequence and by indirectly prompting the creation of investigative networks in various countries, as reporters across the world worked to unpack the significance of these disclosures. At the same time, however, WikiLeaks' emergence on the international stage has focused attention on some of the more intractable problems now faced by investigative reporters, highlighting the tensions between legacy media institutions and newer methods of obtaining and circulating information. The Clinton leaks and their aftermath have made the chaos that erupts in the information ecosystem especially evident, as legacy institutions are increasingly defunded and delegitimised and as 'news' is increasingly routed through alternative media outlets and social media.

The beginnings of WikiLeaks

When WikiLeaks launched in late 2006, it initially claimed to be a collective of 'dissidents, journalists, mathematicians, and start-up company technologists' organised by the Australian hacker Julian Assange (Altman, 2008). By the time of their public launch, WikiLeaks had already stockpiled a trove of leaked information, with plans to solicit further leaks through a web-based portal relying on modified Pretty Good Privacy (PGP) and Tor encryption technologies to allow leakers to upload documents anonymously. This portal was attached to a public-facing site built on a Wikimedia platform that allowed interested parties to comment on, or even authenticate, published leaks. WikiLeaks' decision to operate as a 'wiki' (a move that would be reversed in 2010) contributed to the site's initial characterisation as a place for an engaged global community to publish and comment on material that would shed light on corporate and government corruption; indeed, Assange has referred to the site as 'an intelligence agency of the people' (Assange, 2011).

However, WikiLeaks' expansive ambitions for the site were initially thwarted by a tepid public response. Their first release – a leaked letter from a member of the Somali Islamic Court laying out a civil war strategy, allegedly obtained from a Chinese dissident – failed to attract anyone who might authenticate the document, and its contents received minimal media attention. Indeed, in the months following the launch of the site, less attention was paid to WikiLeaks' initial leaks than to the novelty of its format. Though some of the attention was flattering – an early article, for example, described the site 'as important a journalistic tool as the [U.S.] Freedom of

Information Act' (Schmidt, 2007), while another called it an example of 'the brave new world of investigative journalism' (Gonsalves, 2008) – press coverage of WikiLeaks generally identified the site as cyber-activism, not as a journalistic enterprise (Kleeman, 2007; Schmidt, 2007).

Reading through correspondence between WikiLeaks volunteers during this period reveals that their frustration over this misdirected media attention made them wary of press contact. One volunteer suggested that WikiLeaks refer reporters to the site's 'About' section in order to pre-empt certain questions, arguing that 'reporters – and keep in mind that they are competitors with WikiLeaks as much as any keepers of secrets and peddlers of inside information – will most likely dig for unfriendly aspects of WikiLeaks' (WikiLeaks, 2007). At the same time, when a WikiLeaks-authored article describing the Somali leak was distributed, to no effect, to publications including CounterPunch, Zmag, and the Christian Science Monitor, another volunteer complained that until the site was certified by someone with 'a gold plated reputation', it might be hard for them to gain media credibility (ibid.).

Uncertain about how to win media attention, and unsure whether the media ought to be trusted, WikiLeaks cautiously courted a few journalists via email during the early months of their operation, drawing their attention to new disclosures on the platform. For the most part, however, the first wave of reporters who wrote about WikiLeaks disclosures did so because they were tipped off about the existence of documents on the site, not because checking the WikiLeaks website was a part of their reporting routine (Lynch, 2010). But as interesting material continued to arrive on the site – such as a series of U.S. Congressional reports, or the operating manual from Guantanamo – U.S. and British journalists began to pay closer attention.

One incident during this early period is notable for catalysing a shift towards an acknowledgement that WikiLeaks and similar sites might play an important, if nascent, role in the journalism ecosystem. In 2008, after legal action by a Swiss bank resulted in the WikiLeaks.org domain being temporarily suspended by a California judge, a group of media advocacy organisations and media outlets – including the American Society of News Editors, the Associated Press, the Hearst Corporation, the Los Angeles Times, the Newspaper Association of America, and the Society of Professional Journalists – filed an amicus brief on behalf of WikiLeaks, declaring the shutdown to be a violation of the First Amendment. The suspension was described in *The New York Times* as a 'major test of First Amendment Rights in the Internet Age' (Liptak and Stone, 2008). Elsewhere, journalists described it as an attack on press freedom (Arnoldy, 2008; Egelko, 2008; Hendler, 2008), acknowledging WikiLeaks' journalistic role. After the injunction was reversed, WikiLeaks thanked their media supporters in a press release posted to their site. The press release also quoted U.S. Supreme Court Justice Louis Brandeis's assertion that 'sunlight was the best medicine', and declared WikiLeaks would 'continue to be a forum for the citizens of the world to disclose issues of social, moral and ethical concern' (Kiss, 2008). The message of the press release was clear: WikiLeaks had been recognised as a new force in the media, one that was dedicated to ethical oversight through transparency and direct engagement with the public.

Routing around conventional media

Though bolstered by the attention they received after the Baer case, WikiLeaks' struggle for acceptance and recognition continued throughout 2008 and 2009. Searching for new ways to push information out to audiences, at the end of 2008 they turned to Twitter, and soon the social media platform became an essential part of the organisation's strategy. Though the impact of WikiLeaks' Twitter use was slow in coming (the site built followers gradually, at first attracting more technologists than journalists), in time WikiLeaks began to use Twitter not only to announce leaks, but to build a community of like-minded information activists that could serve as a research resource and source of operating funds (Lynch, 2014). And as their follower base grew, the organisation also experimented with a potentially transformative use of Twitter – using the platform to transmit information suppressed through media censorship.

WikiLeaks' first attempt to use Twitter to bypass censorship came in July 2009, when WikiLeaks posted a 266-page report about corruption in Turks and Caicos (a British overseas territory consisting of a number of coral islands near the Bahamas). When a suppression order issued by a local judge prevented local and British media from discussing the report's findings, WikiLeaks campaigned to increase media coverage of the report by using Twitter. Over the course of several days, the group tweeted 15 times about the report and (when they learned of it) the media injunction. In the end, the judge responsible for the injunction changed his position, declaring the media blackout ineffective due to the coverage of the report on social platforms. In effect, the media coverage of the report was most likely increased by the failed injunction, providing a cautionary tale for those who might try to seek similar forms of press suppression in the British courts.

Several months later, WikiLeaks again turned to Twitter to help overturn a British court injunction, participating in a larger Twitter campaign related to the oil-trading company Trafigura. In October 2009, Trafigura obtained a 'super-injunction' to prevent the *Guardian* and other British press from publishing or discussing a leaked report showing that the company had engaged in toxic waste dumping in West Africa (Cohen, 2009). When the report was taken down from the *Guardian*'s website, WikiLeaks reposted their own link to the report and launched a volley of tweets related to Trafigura. They urged British media outlets to defy the injunction, tweeting that it was 'time for UK journalists to grow some balls and start violating censorship injunctions' (WikiLeaks Twitter Feed, 2009). Their efforts caused the *Guardian* technology journalist Charles Arthur (@charlesarthur) to tweet in response, 'Oh, @WikiLeaks, how I would love to retweet you, but I would get in so much trouble if I did' (Cohen, 2009). This exchange made the clash between old media constraints and the liberties claimed by WikiLeaks painfully clear; while the *Guardian* was forced merely to allude to documents procured by their own reporters, WikiLeaks – a site the *Guardian* was enjoined from even mentioning – became the primary destination for members of the public who wished to see the documents.

WikiLeaks' adroit use of its own site and the Twitter platform to circumvent censorship did not go unnoticed. Ian Douglas, technology blogger for Telegraph.com.uk and a close follower of the site, speculated at the time that journalists and the public might increasingly consider WikiLeaks as the repository of choice for sensitive documents, something that might have sweeping implications for traditional pathways of leaked material. Douglas noticed that his colleagues were beginning to remark that those who had sensitive documents should 'upload [them] to WikiLeaks', while in the past, they would have suggested that such material should be 'hand[ed] ... to the BBC' (Douglas, 2009).

WikiLeaks 'goes mainstream'

Throughout 2009 and early 2010, as the legacy press was beginning to accept that WikiLeaks might be useful, WikiLeaks increasingly began to emphasise their usefulness to journalists, positioning themselves more clearly as a media outlet in their own right and as a supportive resource for the media. They changed their mission definition on their site's 'About' page to describe themselves as a 'not-for-profit media organization' (WikiLeaks, 2010), a sentiment echoed by WikiLeaks spokesman Daniel Schmitt (a pseudonym: the spokesperson was later revealed to be Daniel Domschiet-Berg) at both journalism and tech conferences (Gulli Staff, 2009). In late 2009, they applied for a half-million-dollar Knight News Challenge grant intended to fund innovative uses of technology in the media. The grant, WikiLeaks claimed, would be used to create an integrated leaking portal that would allow the mainstream press to gather and distribute leaked material more securely. On the voting platform that allowed members of the public to weigh in on the News Challenge applications, supporters rated the project highly, suggesting that the group might be a finalist for the grant. Despite WikiLeaks' repositioning as a media outlet, however, the group remained too secretive about its own operations, its staff, and its budget to appeal to U.S. foundations. When the Knight Foundation turned WikiLeaks down, WikiLeaks used Twitter to express their surprise and disappointment, writing that 'WikiLeaks was highest rated project in the Knight challenge, strongly recommended to the board but gets no funding. Go figure' (WikiLeaks Twitter Feed, 2010).

The megaleaks period

WikiLeaks might have expressed surprise at losing the Knight Challenge, but by the time awards were distributed in June of 2010, the group was already at odds with the U.S. government and both its funding and its legal status were brought into question. That WikiLeaks was and would remain a journalistic outlier would become abundantly clear over the following months, during WikiLeaks' mass leak of documents related to U.S. diplomatic and military operations. By November 2009, the group had made contact with Chelsea (formerly Bradley) Manning, a U.S. soldier who had access to U.S. intelligence databases. Over the next few months, Manning provided WikiLeaks with a videotape of a U.S. military helicopter seemingly opening fire on civilians, 92,000 field reports from Afghanistan, 400,000 field reports from Iraq, 251,287 U.S. diplomatic cables and 700 case reports on prisoners at Guantanamo. In April 2010, WikiLeaks released the video (which they dubbed the 'Collateral Murder' tape), accompanied by an investigative package that featured the work of an international team of professional journalists. On the day of the release, reporters filled the room at a press conference in Washington D.C.'s National Press Club, where Assange appeared personally to introduce the video. Stories about the video and WikiLeaks' role in the release appeared in most major U.S. print and broadcast outlets and many international outlets as well; WikiLeaks, it seemed, had finally achieved its goal of disrupting legacy media and providing a sensational 'scoop' that routed around conventional channels of access and distribution.

As Danish media scholar Mette Mortensen noted, this disruption, to some extent, overshadowed the leak itself. Media reporting on the leaked video was overwhelmingly preoccupied with WikiLeaks itself as a phenomenon, as reporting on the leak focused largely on how the video was obtained, published, and circulated (Mortensen, 2012). While much earlier reporting about WikiLeaks' methods and aims had been sceptical, a fair amount of the coverage of WikiLeaks in the spring of 2010 was celebratory, heralding the site as a potentially new force in investigative and political journalism. In *Newsweek*, Jonathan Stray argued that 'at its best, the rise of WikiLeaks represents the type of accountability journalism made famous in the 1970s by Carl Bernstein and Bob Woodward' (Stray, 2010). And in a *Guardian* online report, Stephen Moss opined that Assange might be seen as then impresario of a new form of news, quoting Assange's declaration that:

> for the financial and specialist press, it'll still look mostly the same – your daily briefing about what you need to know to run your business. But for political and social analysis, that's going to be movements and networks. You can already see this happening.
>
> (Moss, 2010)

The *Guardian's* enthusiasm for WikiLeaks – which would prove transient – was motivated by more than just WikiLeaks' Twitter campaigns and the 'Collateral Murder' video. By the time Moss's *The Guardian* interview with Assange came out, Assange had already begun collaborating with other the *Guardian* journalists on what would become the organisation's most significant series of leaks to date – the 'War Logs' material released later in July, and the 'Cablegate' leaks that emerged at the beginning of November 2010. Unlike the Collateral video release, these large leaks were circulated through what Assange described as 'partnerships' with major international media outlets, including the *Guardian* as well as *The New York Times*, Al Jazeera, and *Der Spiegel*. The releases were governed by a complicated series of embargo agreements, including assurances by WikiLeaks that they would not release material in advance of media coverage.

Largely, these relationships proved highly beneficial for media outlets, which dedicated both investigative reporters and data analysts to the leaks. WikiLeaks' mass disclosures came at a time when data journalism was just emerging as a force in newsrooms, and the complex, visually striking visualisations of the leaked data proved to be – in the words of the *Guardian* data editor Simon Rogers – a 'game changer' for the emerging field (Rogers, 2011). Elaborate data visualisations based on WikiLeaks' SIGACT (Special Interest Group on Algorithms and Computation Theory) data from Iraq and Afghanistan, and on the U.S. diplomatic cables, appeared in *The New York Times* and the *Guardian*, and the *Guardian*'s public release of the dataset allowed data scientists to submit their own visualisations to The *Guardian*'s Datablog. The French data journalism organisation OWNI created WikiLeaks' own database for the SIGACTs material, as well as an app for searching the data, and the UK-based Bureau of Investigative Journalism undertook data journalism for Al Jazeera, *Le Monde*, and Channel 4.

If the first wave of cable releases was helpful in spurring the adoption of data journalism in newsrooms, a second round of releases helped to catalyse another significant development in investigative reporting – the rise of internationally based collaborations. In late 2010, after WikiLeaks' initial news partners slowed in their coverage of WikiLeaks cables, the organisation began approaching journalists and media outlets based in regions not represented in the initial releases. These outlets were given flash drives containing a select number of geographically relevant cables. In many cases, these releases resulted in stories of local significance, but a few noteworthy partnerships resulted in strong regional or international reporting. In the United States, the newsmagazine *The Nation* partnered with the journal *Haiti Liberte* to distribute their reports on cables concerning Haiti, drawing on the local expertise of those reporters while bringing the cables to a wider audience. In Central America, Costa Rican journalists requested and received permission to collaborate with Nicaraguan journalists to analyse cables (Buzenberg, 2015). Though some of these partnerships lasted for the duration of the investigation, the ability of journalists to share Cablegate resources through both formal and informal international partnerships became one of the defining features of the second phase of cable distribution, as journalists drew on and expanded existing networks of investigative practitioners to share new disclosures, suggest search practices for cable databases, and discuss the implications of Cablegate in their home regions.

Despite the promise of these partnerships, however, a survey of the sourcing and coverage of the reporting conducted on Cablegate by these outlets suggests the difficulty of producing 'global journalism' in a media environment dominated by segmented market interests. Though Assange argued that distribution of cables to a second set of media partners had 'subverted the filter of the mainstream press' (Goodman, 2011), what actually happened was that these newer partners wrote stories that circulated in the regional press or in the blogosphere, but which rarely attracted the attention of international media outlets. In part because they had already chosen the cables they found newsworthy, WikiLeaks' initial media partners rarely picked up stories from this second round of reporting. In addition, regions that did not have a fairly robust media system in place – such as much of Africa – were left out of the second round of cable releases. This lack of access was keenly felt by some who felt that the diplomatic cables might hold key information otherwise inaccessible in areas with weak media systems. For example, the diasporic community of the Democratic Republic of Congo (DRC) complained that WikiLeaks was withholding information that might be important in the project of political reform.

The DRC and other countries finally got access to the U.S. cables in August of 2011, when WikiLeaks, breaking its agreement with its original media partners, released all of the cables in a downloadable file. In response, the media outlets which had overseen the redaction and gradual release of the first cables authored a letter of protest condemning the mass leak, saying they 'deplore[d]' WikiLeaks' decision (Ball, 2011). The acerbic letter was one of the more public manifestations of a long-simmering conflict between WikiLeaks and the media outlets that had published the megaleaks. Given the volatile nature of the media industry and the mercurial personality of Assange, it was hardly a surprise that personal tensions had emerged over the course of the U.S. releases, but the tensions were far more than personal: they were also institutional and political.

The megaleaks backlash

In part, the breakdown in communication between WikiLeaks and those publishing the first wave of cables was tied to a resurgence of the debate over whether or not WikiLeaks should be seen as a media outlet. This time, the stakes of the debate were higher; as a Justice Department Task force debated whether Assange might be tried under the U.S. Espionage Act, legal observers noted WikiLeaks' claim that their actions constituted journalistic activity protected by the U.S. First Amendment, might be their only viable defence

(Samuels, 2010). Yet despite the threat posed by such a prosecution, the journalistic community was less straightforward in their support of WikiLeaks than they had been when their hosting had been suspended during the 2009 Baer case. As Karin Wahl-Jorgensen notes, journalists performed 'boundary work' on WikiLeaks as the disclosures' impact grew, describing the site as outside the boundaries of journalistic practice (Wahl-Jorgensen, 2014). Media |outlets – the *Guardian* especially – pointed to WikiLeaks' ethical lapses as a sign that the professional media should remain in charge of analysing and distributing leaks. Journalists writing about WikiLeaks had raised ethical flags from the time of the site's initial launch, expressing concern about the ability of WikiLeaks to guarantee the sort of source protection it professed to offer (Austin Thomas, 2007; Leigh et al., 2011; Garfield, 2009). But during the megaleaks period, further questions were raised about WikiLeaks' care in presenting sensitive documents. The Afghan War Logs, in particular, contained thousands of names of individuals that were edited out of media reports but printed unreacted by WikiLeaks, raising concerns among several human rights organisation. WikiLeaks defended itself by claiming to have asked the U.S. government for help with redaction, arguing the 'Pentagon wants to bankrupt us by refusing to assist review' (Weaver, 2010).

In most instances in which WikiLeaks faced criticism from the press, Assange responded defensively and often acrimoniously, accusing his media partners of deliberately seeking to distance themselves from WikiLeaks. Attempting to secure his journalistic credentials, he argued that WikiLeaks was the proponent of a new and superior sort of journalism termed 'scientific journalism', based on the principle that original source documents must be available to readers at all times so they could draw their own conclusions about claims made by reporters. In an article for the *New Statesman*, he also made a historical argument for WikiLeaks' legitimacy, tracing the lineage of WikiLeaks directly back to the radical British press dating from the 1640s and claiming the site was 'firmly in the tradition of those radical publishers who tried to lay 'all the Mysteries and secrets of Government' before the public' (Assange, 2011).

During this period, aside from Assange himself, the strongest defenders of the idea that WikiLeaks itself was a journalistic endeavour were those scholars and media observers who supported the digital disruption of the news industry. Soon after the 'Collateral Murder' video was released, Jay Rosen, known for his work on online citizen journalism, coined the oft-repeated phrase 'stateless news agency' to describe how WikiLeaks was able to evade state censorship (Rosen, 2010). As WikiLeaks proceeded to collaborate with its media partners, first on the War Logs and then on Cablegate, other observers similarly enfolded WikiLeaks within the journalistic camp, often describing WikiLeaks as an incidence of 'networked' journalism (Beckett and Ball, 2012; Benkler, 2013) or as part of a 'media ecosystem' (Ingram, 2010; Jarvis, 2010). Writing a column on the benefits of Cablegate for the Nieman Lab, Nikki Usher argued that Cablegate demonstrated how new media forms could allow 'one person to change the conversation', but also helped bolster the status of legacy media by showing the value of 'parsing through complicated details' and showing the ability of legacy media to set the news agenda (Usher, 2010).

As Cablegate wore on, the responses to WikiLeaks among U.S. media – ranging from tepid to distinctly icy – became itself the focus of media discussion. Some journalists sympathetic to WikiLeaks attributed the attack on the organisation to the economic decline and corporatisation that had weakened the U.S. press (Yelvington, 2010; Outing, 2011). Still others found the negative response to be more political than professional/ethical. Glenn Greenwald, a Salon columnist and the most vigorous press defender of WikiLeaks, was perhaps the most scathing in his discussion of the media response, arguing that the government had trained 'a nation's journalist class to despise above all else those who shine a light on what the most powerful factions do in the dark and who expose their corruption and deceit' (Greenwald, 2010).

Greenwald's criticism may have been overblown, but he had a point: the same media groups that had flocked to defend WikiLeaks during the Dynadot takedown in 2008 – when the Swiss bank Julius Bayer filed a (rapidly abandoned) lawsuit against WikiLeaks and Dynadot, a web services provider – now hesitated to defend the site in the face of far more serious threats. By the end of the megaleaks period, WikiLeaks itself was financially and operationally crippled by both legal and extra-judicial responses. The first serious trouble for WikiLeaks had, on the face of it, less to do with its leaking activities than with the behaviour of its founder; beginning in the summer of 2010, Assange was investigated on a series of sexual assault charges in Sweden that by mid-November resulted in a European Arrest Warrant. Assange, who was living in Britain at the time, was placed under house arrest. He then pressed unsuccessfully to reverse an extradition order that would send him to Sweden, claiming that Sweden would then extradite him to the United States to face trail for WikiLeaks' U.S. military and diplomatic leaks. For the next year, Assange remained under house arrest at Ellingham Hall, Norfolk, an estate owned by British journalist and Frontline Club owner Vaughn Smith. Though the estate proved to be a useful base of operations for the following year, the sexual assault charges were used further to discredit Assange and WikiLeaks.

While Assange adjusted to his new living conditions, the end of 2010 also saw a series of attack on WikiLeaks related directly to its U.S. disclosures. In November 2010, WikiLeaks itself was taken offline by a DOS (Denial of Service) attack; a U.S.-based hacker known as 'The Jester' claimed responsibility saying that, in circulating the U.S. and Afghan SIGACT leaks WikiLeaks was 'attempting to endanger the lives of our [U.S.] troops, "other assets" & foreign relations' (Greene and Hughes, 2010). Then, after stories on U.S. diplomatic cables began appearing in media outlets, U.S. Senator Joseph Lieberman issued a call for U.S.-based companies to stop doing business with WikiLeaks. As a result, Amazon Web Servers stopped hosting a portion of the WikiLeaks site, and Visa, MasterCard, and PayPal cut off WikiLeaks' access to funds. Since the organisation was relying primarily on volunteer donations at the time, this financial freeze proved crippling – especially given that WikiLeaks had lost the hosting service they had partly relied upon, in the wake of the DDOS attack. In order to preserve the site, WikiLeaks asked volunteers to create 'mirror sites' that would host WikiLeaks' disclosures in the event of continued takedown; in the end, over 1,200 such sites were created around the globe. And as a response to the financial blockade, a group of hackers from the collective Anonymous launched Operation Avenge Assange, a series of DDOS attacks against the financial institutions in question.[2] In the end, PayPal restored some funds to WikiLeaks, but the sites' ability to continue to collect donations remained severely restricted.

A series of internal conflicts within the organisation added to these external challenges. Most notably, WikiLeaks spokesman Daniel Domscheitt-Berg left the organisation, taking with him the architecture for the site's leaking platform and a large collection of unpublished material (allegedly), including documents related to Bank of America and the U.S. Department of Homeland Security (DHS) No-Fly List. After leaving, Domscheitt-Berg published a book that cast Assange as a capricious, irresponsible leader of the organisation. Other defections followed. At the end of the megaleaks period, WikiLeaks was perhaps as well-known as any media outlet in the world, but it had lost most of its funds, several key figures, and the technology which it claimed made it the most attractive alternative for potential whistleblowers. After losing a court appeal, Assange himself took refuge in the Ecuadorian embassy in London to avoid extradition to Sweden, where he remained as WikiLeaks entered its 'post-megaleaks' period.

WikiLeaks after megaleaks

It would hardly have been surprising if WikiLeaks had folded at the end of 2011, given the challenges the organisation faced. Instead, it has persisted and continued to disclose leaks of global interest, despite the fact that its secure leaking portal remained offline between 2011 and 2015. In the months following the mass release of the U.S. diplomatic cables, WikiLeaks released the first of three collections of documents relating to the surveillance industry: though these documents were not technically 'leaked' material, they drew attention to the sales of surveillance equipment to repressive regimes around the world. Beginning in 2012, they released over two million emails from Syrian political figures and ministries, working with the Associated Press, Spain's Publico.es, and Egypt's *al-Masry al-Youm* to publish stories. In 2013, WikiLeaks created a searchable database of U.S. diplomatic documents the contents of which included the 2011 cable releases as well as a large set of (publicly available) cables related to former U.S. Secretary of State Henry Kissinger,[3] labelling the collection the PLOD, or 'Public Library of U.S. Diplomacy' (WikiLeaks, 2013).

In 2015, they leaked a draft copy of the proposed Trans-Pacific Partnership Trade Agreement, drawing further attention to the controversial agreement in the lead-up to the U.S. presidential elections. A new version of the online portal was also launched in May of that year; in typical fashion, WikiLeaks declared their leak portal to be more secure than ever, asserting cryptically that 'the full-spectrum attack surface of WikiLeaks' submission system is significantly lower than other systems and is optimised for our secure deployment and development environment' (WikiLeaks, 2015a)

For the most part, WikiLeaks' activities between late 2011 and early 2016, though less spectacular than the Cablegate leaks, remained recognisably aligned with the organisation's stated function of whistleblowing and transparency; the TPP leak, in particular, was seen as a valuable intervention into a secretive trade deal negotiation that had made citizens of the United States, Canada, Australia, and elsewhere anxious about its terms. In mid-2006, however, WikiLeaks began to release material that would shift how both journalists and followers perceived its motives and methods. The first, and arguably most significant, of these leaks was the DNC emails that began to emerge in mid-July.

WikiLeaks' involvement in Clinton's bid for the presidency began in March of 2016, when the organisation published a searchable archive of 30,000 emails sent to and from Clinton's private email server during her tenure as Secretary of State. Like the Kissinger Cables, these emails were not leaked material, nor were they exclusive to WikiLeaks: rather, they were part of an ongoing investigation regarding the appropriateness of Clinton's communications protocols and had been released through a FOIA (the U.S. Freedom of Information Act) request. And, like the Kissinger Cables, Assange archived them in order to chronicle what he identified as corrupt behaviour and poor policy choices. In an interview, he claimed that emails provided evidence of Clinton's complicity in 'the disastrous, absolutely disastrous intervention in Libya, the destruction of the Gaddafi government, which led to the occupation of ISIS of large segments of that country [and] weapons flows going over to Syria' (Democracy Now Staff, 2016). Elsewhere, conservative media outlets such as Breitbart relied on the database to discuss Clinton's role in deaths of State Department workers in Benghazi, Libya in 2012, and speculated that the database might lead to the candidate's downfall.

These efforts aside, the searchable email database scarcely made it into the news during the first part of 2016. In July, however, WikiLeaks struck again, releasing the first of a series of leaks culled directly from the DNC central server. This time, the media attention was significant and constant. Perhaps unsurprisingly, the U.S. news outlets most sharply critical of the content of the leaked emails occupied the Right of the political spectrum, including Fox News (Fox News, 2016a), *The Washington Times* (Riddell,

2016), and a newspaper published by Trump's son-in-law Jared Kushner, the *New York Observer* (Sainato, 2016).

Though they also covered the leaks avidly, Left or centrist media outlets in the United States and elsewhere were more temperate in their criticism of Clinton, treating the leaks more as a news phenomenon than as politically fatal revelations. Reporters, did however, find evidence in the emails of the uncomfortable interplay between the Clinton Foundation and Clinton's work as Secretary of State (BBC Staff, 2016), but also noted that the material revealed that the Clinton campaign was efficiently run, a contrast to the chaotic Trump campaign that might possibly reflect each candidate's management potential (Smith, 2016). Indeed, the leaks seemed to create a conundrum for the centrist press – reporters felt a responsibility to report on the material, but also expressed anxiety about the motivation for the leak and the net effect of the revelations.

The effect of these disclosures on Clinton's campaign is still a matter for debate, but clearly the emails served to bolster claims that Clinton was corrupt, made by Republican political operatives, supporters of the Republican candidate Donald Trump, and frequently by Trump himself. Some on the political Right who had condemned WikiLeaks during the Cablegate disclosures began to champion the organisation for its ability to reveal harsh truths that were being suppressed by a pro-Clinton media. Dinesh D'Souza, a conservative commentator whose documentary *Hillary's America* had also contributed to anti-Clinton sentiment, claimed on Fox News that 'WikiLeaks has become the investigative journalism of America . . . the mainstream media is not doing it' (Fox News, 2016b). Emboldened by the idea that the emails contained evidence of multiple conspiracies, 'investigations' conducted by conspiracy theorists – many of them originating on WikiLeaks' 'Research Community' sub-site, which itself was initiated in the wake of the DNC leaks – reached bizarre conclusions, including allegations that the Clinton campaign ran a child trafficking campaign from a local Washington pizzeria (Kang, 2016). This claim escalated from the bizarre to the ominous after a gunman arrived at the pizzeria to investigate the situation[4], firing shots from his military-grade rifle before surrendering to police (Goldman, 2016).

Given these often hysterical interpretations, some journalists and scholars who had previously expressed measured or even enthusiastic support for WikiLeaks voiced their ambivalence about the DNC leak. After writing a column for *The Intercept* insisting that journalists simply needed to disregard motives once the Clinton information was in the public domain, Glenn Greenwald followed up with an online conversation with Naomi Klein, in which Klein expressed concerns about Assange's motivations and Greenwald admitted that he was having his own doubts about the ethics of writing about the leak (Greenwald, 2016a, 2016b). The Sunlight Foundation, an organisation that had been tentatively supportive of WikiLeaks during the megaleaks period, wrote an editorial decrying what it identified as 'weaponized transparency' (Howard and Wonderlich, 2016) or the increased publishing of leaked material on non-traditional platforms that were not bound by journalistic ethics or political norms. And Zeynep Tufecki, a media scholar and critic who had once expressed hopes for WikiLeaks' power to reinvigorate journalism, pointed out that the disclosures held helped to fuel 'viral misinformation' and were interfering with, not facilitating, the journalistic process (Tufecki, 2016).

Underlying all the praise for and ambivalence over the *contents* of the DNC leaks were a series of questions about the *motives* for the leaks that seemed more urgent in this instance than in any previous instance of WikiLeaks disclosures. By the time that WikiLeaks began releasing DNC materials, intelligence reports suggested that Russian hackers had penetrated the DNC servers; this meant that the material in question might not be the work of a 'whistleblower', but instead part of a Russian attempt to interfere with the U.S. election process. Assange sharply resisted such speculation. The emails, he insisted, were delivered to him by Craig Murray, the former British Ambassador to Uzbekistan; Murray, in turn, insisted that he was handed the documents by a disaffected DNC member during a clandestine meeting in the woods outside the American University in Washington. In the aftermath of the elections, Assange's account was disputed by U.S. intelligence officials, who claimed to have identified Russian intermediaries that delivered the material to WikiLeaks instead (Entous et al., 2016). Assange has maintained that the email leak was the work of a whistleblower (Owen, 2017), though sceptical media observers pointed to his long-standing relationship to Russia and his continual skittishness about any suggestion of a connection between Russia and the Trump campaign (Beauchamp, 2017; Cameron and O'Neill, 2016; Daileda, 2017).

A series of disclosures in the wake of the U.S. elections raised further concerns about possible collaboration with Russian. The first leak was, once again, a cache of emails, this time in the region of 6,000 messages belonging to senior Turkish government minister Berat Albayrak, son-in-law of the country's president, Recep Tayyip Erdogan. This material received limited Western press coverage, though the *Independent* identified evidence in the emails that Albayrak had strong links to the oil trade (McKernan, 2016). A second leak, more widely covered in the international press, was a cache of documents from a German parliamentary inquiry into the collaboration between Germany's BND foreign intelligence service and the U.S. National Security Agency (WikiLeaks, 2016a). These documents cast a negative light on Angela Merkel, the German Prime Minister who was up for re-election in 2017; according to intelligence reports, they were possibly obtained via a Russian government hack with the intention of influencing the German federal election (Delcker, 2016). And in early March 2017, WikiLeaks began releasing materials connected to the CIA hacking programme, part of a tranche of leaked material that they claimed was their largest release to date. In the explanatory material accompanying the release, they argued that the documents provided evidence that the CIA had an internal group which carried out 'false flag' hacking attacks; computer security experts, however, contested this interpretation of the documents and suggested that WikiLeaks was laying the groundwork for the claim that the DNC hack might have been a CIA effort – a claim that was circulating widely in the U.S. far-Right media-sphere within hours of the release (Zetter, 2017).

For those invested in WikiLeaks as a force for transparency and accountability, the idea that the group might be actively concealing connections with Russian officials represented a fundamental breach of trust, and relationships between WikiLeaks and its original (formal and informal) support community eroded considerably as a result. A widely publicised AP article criticising WikiLeaks' increasing issues with publicising sensitive material – and WikiLeaks' subsequent intemperate response (Wemple, 2016) – did not help with the organisation's reputation. By the end of 2016, long-time WikiLeaks spokesperson Kristinn Hranfsson quietly stepped down, leaving Assange alone as the spokesperson for and representative of WikiLeaks.

Conclusion: what happened to WikiLeaks?

In January 2017, outgoing U.S. President Barack Obama formally commuted the sentence of Chelsea Manning, the U.S. soldier who had turned to WikiLeaks in 2010 as a publisher of, and advocate for, the leaked documents she felt had the power to shed light on U.S. abuses of military and diplomatic power. Obama's commutation, celebrated by some and condemned by others, brought to an end a pivotal chapter in the history of U.S. journalism – a moment during which the promised potential of digitally facilitated leaking galvanised journalists around the globe and permanently transformed how media outlets obtain and report on sensitive materials.

No matter what happens to WikiLeaks in the future, much of the legacy of that moment should be seen as positive for journalists. As mentioned earlier, the megaleaks moment itself helped to spur the rise of data journalism and international investigative collaboration. The power of both of these investigative strategies was amply demonstrated in April of 2014, when journalists from 107 media organisations worked together to analyse a leak of documents from the Panamanian legal firm Moseck Fonseca, revealing a global network of offshore shell corporations (Greenberg, 2016).

It should also be noted that Manning's choice to entrust WikiLeaks instead of a mainstream media organisation with what proved to be one of the larger media stories in history – and the fraught relationships that emerged between WikiLeaks and legacy media as a consequence – helped to popularise the idea that media outlets should develop their own secure, anonymous leaking technologies in order to remain attractive to potential whistleblowers. In time, this spurred a series of independent efforts towards secure leaking technology that are have proved remarkably resilient and successful (Greenberg, 2012). The most successful of these, SecureDrop, was initially developed by the U.S. programmer and activist Aaron Schwarz and *Wired* editor Kevin Poulsen. In the wake of Schwarz's suicide in 2013, it was taken over by the Freedom of the Press Foundation. By the end of 2015, *Aftenposten*, the Associated Press, and *The New York Times* had added SecureDrop portals and GlobaLeaks had developed a roster of 60 users in 20 languages. During the U.S. presidential election, *Washington Post* reporter David Farenthold frequently promoted the *Post*'s SecureDrop portal on Twitter as a place to submit election-related leaks, and in the wake of the elections several outlets have relied on it as a source of leaked material. Though the *Post* has not mentioned specific stories emerging from the portal, *The Intercept* and Associated Press have been more forthcoming, identifying several stories that emerged from SecureDrop leaks.

Despite these positives, however, WikiLeaks could be said to have played a somewhat darker role in the transformation of the media landscape: as much as they have given investigative journalists new material, new tools, and new methods for reporting, they have also cheered on the delegitimisation of the legacy press. This is not to say they have caused it: the political, economic, social and technological forces behind the media's delegitimisation are far beyond WikiLeaks' control. But Assange's hope that WikiLeaks would help usher in a world in which 'scientific journalism' presented audiences with raw documents to interpret as they wished seems to be coming true, with a dystopic abruptness. Without investigative journalists to provide context, unpack motive, and imbue their analysis with an ethical drive to make the world a better place – without voices that can be trusted to be telling the truth in a sea of misinformation – what emerges from such interpretation is not journalism; it is Pizzagate. WikiLeaks, born of the sincere intention of bringing sunshine to bear on darkness, bears not a little responsibility for leaving a trail of fog in its wake.

Notes

1 Portions of this chapter have been adapted from previous articles and book chapters I have published on WikiLeaks: see Lynch 2010 and 2011.
2 This Anonymous operation was one of a series of operations known collectively as Operation Payback.
3 The Kissinger documents were released as part of the U.S. National Records and Archives Act.
4 Shortly after the gunman incident, a note was added to the page explaining that WikiLeaks did not endorse the Pizzagate conspiracy, but the page remains in use. The WikiLeaks Research Community is located at https://our.wikileaks.org/Main_Page.

References

Altman, Alex (2008) 'A coming chill over internet freedom?' *Time*, 20 February, http://content.time.com/time/health/article/0,8599,1714980,00.html [accessed 9 April 2017].

Arnoldy, Ben (2008) 'Close of WikiLeaks website raises free speech concerns', *Christian Science Monitor*, 22 February, www.csmonitor.com/2008/0222/p02s02-usgn.html [accessed 10 March 2017].

Assange, Julian (2011) 'What's new about WikiLeaks?' *New Statesman*, 14 April, www.newstatesman.com/digital/2011/04/civil-war-wikileaks-newspapers [accessed 10 March 2017].

Austin Thomas, Mark (2007) 'Whistleblowing made easier . . . not necessarily safer', *NPR Marketplace*, 7 March, http://marketplace.publicradio.org/shows/2007/03/07/AM200703072.html [accessed 10 March 2017].

Ball, James (2011) 'WikiLeaks publishes full cache of unredacted cables', *The Guardian*, 2 September, www.theguardian.com/media/2011/sep/02/wikileaks-publishes-cache-unredacted-cables [accessed 10 March 2017].

BBC Staff (2016) '18 revelations from WikiLeaks' hacked Clinton emails', *BBC News*, 27 October, www.bbc.com/news/world-us-canada-37639370 [accessed 10 March 2017].

Beauchamp, Zack (2017) 'The WikiLeaks-Russia connection started way before the 2016 election', *Vox*, 6 January, www.vox.com/world/2017/1/6/14179240/wikileaks-russia-ties [accessed 10 March 2017].

Beckett, C. and Ball, J. (2012) WikiLeaks: News in the networked era. *Polity*.

Benkler, Yochai (2013) 'WikiLeaks and the networked fourth estate', in Brevini, Benedetta, Hintz, Arne and McCurdy, Patrick [editors], *Beyond WikiLeaks: Implications for the Future of Communications, Journalism and Society*, Basingstoke: Palgrave Macmillan.

Bhuiyan, Johana (2016) 'What happened to WikiLeaks? BuzzFeed UK Editor Janine Gibson has a theory', *Recode*, 30 November, www.recode.net/2016/11/30/13799334/julian-assange-janine-gibson-wikileaks-buzzfeed-guardia [accessed 10 March 2017].

Buzenberg, William, E. (2015) 'Anatomy of a global investigation: Collaborative, data-driven, without borders', Shorenstein Center, 5 July, https://shorensteincenter.org/anatomy-of-a-global-investigation-william-buzenberg/ [accessed 10 March 2017].

Cameron, Dell and O'Neill, Patrick Howell (2016) 'WikiLeaks release excludes evidence of €2 billion transfer from Syria to Russia', 12 September, www.dailydot.com/layer8/wikileaks-syria-files-syria-russia-bank-2-billion/ [accessed 10 March 2017].

Cohen, Noam (2009) 'Twitter and a newspaper untie a gag order', *New York Times*, 19 October, www.nytimes.com/2009/10/19/technology/internet/19link.html [accessed 10 March 2017].

Daileda, Colin (2017) 'Attention internet: WikiLeaks is now anti-leaks', *Mashable*, 6 January, http://mashable.com/2017/01/06/wikileaks-nbc-hack-report/#zgY2XmmJLiqZ [accessed 10 March 2017].

Delcker, Janosch (2016) 'Russian hacking looms over Germany's election', *Politico*, 19 December, www.politico.eu/article/russian-influence-german-election-hacking-cyberattack-news-merkel-putin/ [accessed 10 March 2017].

Democracy Now Staff (2016) 'Assange: Why I created WikiLeaks' searchable database of 30,000 emails from Clinton's private server', *Democracy Now*, 25 July, www.democracynow.org/2016/7/25/assange_why_i_created_wikileaks_searchable [accessed 10 March 2017].

Douglas, Ian (2009) Personal email exchange with the author, 22 June.

Egelko, Bob (2008) 'Whistle-blower web site ordered shut down', *SFGate*, 20 February, http://m.sfgate.com/bayarea/article/Whistle-blower-Web-site-ordered-shut-down-3293995.php [accessed 10 March 2017].

Entous, Adam, Nakashima, Ellen and Miller, Greg (2016) 'Secret CIA assessment says Russia was trying to help Trump win White House', *The Washington Post*, 9 December, www.washingtonpost.com/world/national-security/obama-orders-review-of-russian-hacking-during-presidential-campaign/2016/12/09/31d6b300-be2a-11e6–94ac-3d324840106c_story.html?utm_term=.21f8fed3cf0f [accessed 10 March 2017].

Fox News Network (2016a) 'Filmmaker Dinesh D'Souza reacts to Clinton campaign leaks', *YouTube*, www.youtube.com/watch?v=tbVqtmQ4slQ [accessed 10 March 2017].

—— (2016b) 'Trump, GOP seize on new Clinton Cash revelations to revive "pay-to-play" Charge', *Fox*, 28 October, www.foxnews.com/politics/2016/10/28/trump-gop-seize-on-new-clinton-cash-revelations-to-revive-pay-to-play-charge.html [accessed 10 March 2017].

Garfield, Bob (2009) 'Transcript of "Leak Proof"', *NPR on the Media*, 13 March, www.onthemedia.org/transcripts/2009/03/13/04 [accessed 10 March 2017].

Goldman, Adam (2016) 'The comet ping pong gunman answers our reporter's questions', *New York Times*, 12 December, www.nytimes.com/2016/12/07/us/edgar-welch-comet-pizza-fake-news.html [accessed 10 March 2017].

Gonsalves, Sean (2008) 'Will WikiLeaks revolutionize journalism?' *Alternet*, 7 July, www.alternet.org/story/90641/will_wikileaks_revolutionize_journalism [accessed 10 March 2017].

Goodman, Amy (2011) 'Exclusive: Julian Assange of WikiLeaks & Philosopher Slavoj Žižek in conversation with Amy Goodman', *Democracy Now!*, 5 July, www.democracynow.org/2011/7/5/exclusive_julian_assange_of_wikileaks_philosopher [accessed 10 March 2017].

Greenberg, Andy (2012) *This Machine Kills Secrets: How WikiLeakers, Cypherpunks and Hacktivists Aim to Free the World's Information*, New York: Penguin.

—— (2016) 'How reporters pulled off the panama papers, the biggest leak in whistleblower history', *Wired*, 5 April, www.wired.com/2016/04/reporters-pulled-off-panama-papers-biggest-leak-whistleblower-history/ [accessed 10 March 2017].

Greene, Richard Allen and Hughes, Nicola (2010) '"Hacktivist for good" claims WikiLeaks takedown', *CNN*, 29 November, www.cnn.com/2010/US/11/29/wikileaks.hacker/ [accessed 10 March 2017].

Greenwald, Glenn (2010) 'The media's authoritarianism and WikiLeaks', *Salon*, 10 December, www.salon.com/2010/12/10/wikileaks_media/ [accessed 10 March 2017].

—— (2016a) 'On WikiLeaks, journalism, and privacy: Reporting on the Podesta archive is an easy call', *Intercept*, 13 October, https://theintercept.com/2016/10/13/on-wikileaks-journalism-and-privacy-reporting-on-the-podesta-archive-is-an-easy-call/ [accessed 10 March 2017].

—— (2016b) 'Is disclosure of Podesta's emails a step too far? A conversation with Naomi Klein', *Intercept*, 19 October, https://theintercept.com/2016/10/19/is-disclosure-of-podestas-emails-a-step-too-far-a-conversation-with-naomi-klein/ [accessed 10 March 2017].

Gulli Staff (2009) 'WikiLeaks: Daniel Schmitt interviewed', *News gulli.com*, Der IT – und Tech-Kanal, 5 July, www.gulli.com/news/974-wikileaks-daniel-schmitt-interviewed-english-2009-07-05 [accessed 10 March 2017].

Hendler, Clint (2008) 'Don't worry, WikiLeaks', *Columbia Journalism Review*, 20 February, http://archives.cjr.org/the_kicker/dont_worry_wikileaks.php [accessed 10 March 2017].

Howard, Alex, and Wonderlich, John (2016) 'On weaponized transparency', *Sunlight Foundation*, 28 July, https://sunlightfoundation.com/2016/07/28/on-weaponized-transparency/ [accessed 10 March 2017].

Ingram, Mathew (2010) 'Is what WikiLeaks does journalism? Good question', *GigaOm*, 24 December, https://gigaom.com/2010/12/24/wikileaks-journalism/ [accessed 10 March 2017].

Jarvis, J. (2010) 'Value-added journalism', *BuzzMachine*, 27 July, http://buzzmachine.com/2010/07/27/value-added-journalism/ [accessed 10 March 2017].

Kang, Cecilia (2016) 'Fake news onslaught targets Pizzeria as nest of child-trafficking', *New York Times*, 21 November, www.nytimes.com/2016/11/21/technology/fact-check-this-pizzeria-is-not-a-child-trafficking-site.html [accessed 10 March 2017].

Kiss, Jemima (2008) 'US judge reverses WikiLeaks injunction', *The Guardian*, 3 March, www.theguardian.com/technology/2008/mar/03/wikipedia.web20 [accessed 10 March 2017].

Kleeman, Jenny (2007) 'WikiLeaks – whistleblowing made easy', *The Guardian*, 17 September, www.guardian.co.uk/media/2007/sep/17/digitalmedia.humanrights [accessed 10 March 2017].

Leigh, David, Harding, Luke, Pilkington, Booth, Robert and Arthur, Charles [editors] (2011) *WikiLeaks: Inside Julian Assange's War on Secrecy*, London: Guardian.

Liptak, Adam and Stone, Brad (2008) 'Judge shuts down web site specializing in leaks, raising constitutional issues', *New York Times*, 20 February, www.nytimes.com/2008/02/20/us/20wiki.html [accessed 10 March 2017].

Lynch, Lisa (2010) 'We're going to crack the world open', *Journalism Practice*, Vol. 4, pp. 309–318. doi:10.1080/17512781003640752.

——— (2011) '"That's Not Leaking, It's Pure Editorial": WikiLeaks, scientific journalism, and journalistic expertise', *Canadian Journal of Media Studies*, Fall, pp. 40–68, http://cjms.fims.uwo.ca/issues/special/Lynch.pdf [accessed 10 March 2017].

——— (2014) '"Oh, WikiLeaks, I would so love to RT you": WikiLeaks, Twitter, and information activism', *International Journal of Communication*, Vol. 8, Issue: 10, pp. 2679–2692.

McKernan, Bethan (2016) 'Email cache proves Turkish oil minister's links to Isis oil trade, WikiLeaks claims', *Independent*, www.independent.co.uk/news/world/middle-east/wikileaks-turkey-isis-oil-minister-email-cache-leaks-claims-a7460736.html [accessed 10 March 2017].

Mortensen, Mette (2012) 'Metacoverage taking the place of coverage: WikiLeaks as a source for the production of news in the digital age', *Northern Lights: Film and Media Studies Yearbook 10*, pp. 91–106. doi:10.1386/nl.10.1.91_1 [accessed 10 March 2017].

Moss, Stephen (2010) 'Julian Assange: The whistleblower', *The Guardian*, 14 July, www.theguardian.com/media/2010/jul/14/julian-assange-whistleblower-wikileaks [accessed 10 March 2017].

Outing, Steve (2011) 'How could journalists disagree with Assange?' *Media Disruptus*, 1 January, http://steveouting.com/2011/01/01/how-could-journalists-disagree-with-assange/ [accessed 10 March 2017].

Owen, Tess (2017) 'Julian Assange says the FBI and CIA are wrong about Russians hacking the DNC', *VICE News*, 3 January, https://news.vice.com/story/julian-assange-says-the-fbi-and-cia-are-wrong-about-russians-hacking-the-dnc?utm_source=vicenewstwitter [accessed 10 March 2017].

Riddell, Kelly (2016) 'Top 10 Clinton scandals exposed by WikiLeaks', *Washington Times*, 12 October, www.washingtontimes.com/news/2016/oct/12/top-10-hillary-clinton-scandals-exposed-wikileaks/ [accessed 10 March 2017].

Rogers, Simon (2011) 'WikiLeaks data journalism: How we handled the data', *The Guardian*, Datablog, 31 January, www.theguardian.com/news/datablog/2011/jan/31/wikileaks-data-journalism [accessed 10 March 2017].

Rosen, Jay (2010) 'From Judith Miller to Julian Assange', *Pressthink*, 9 December, http://pressthink.org/2010/12/from-judith-miller-to-julian-assange/ [accessed 9 April 2013].

Sainato, Michael (2016) 'Corruption recap: The first half of WikiLeaks' Podesta emails', *Observer*, 10 July, http://observer.com/2016/10/corruption-recap-the-first-half-of-wikileaks-podesta-emails/ [accessed 10 March 2017].

Samuels, David (2010) 'The shameful attacks on Julian Assange', *The Atlantic*, 5 December, www.theatlantic.com/international/archive/2010/12/the-shameful-attacks-on-julian-assange/67440/ [accessed 10 March 2017].

Samuelson, Kate (2016) 'Julian Assange dead? 4 theories following WikiLeaks claims', *Time*, 16 October, http://time.com/4532984/wikileaks-julian-assange-theories/ [accessed 10 March 2017].

Schmidt, Tracey Samantha (2007) 'A wiki for whistle-blowers', *Time*, 22 July, www.time.com/time/nation/article/0,8599,1581189,00.html [accessed 10 March 2017].

Smith, David (2016) 'WikiLeaks emails: What they revealed about the Clinton campaign's mechanics', *The Guardian*, 6 November, www.theguardian.com/us-news/2016/nov/06/wikileaks-emails-hillary-clinton-campaign-john-podesta [accessed 10 March 2017].

Stray, Jonathan (2010) 'Is this the future of journalism?' *Foreign Policy*, 7 April, http://foreignpolicy.com/2010/04/07/is-this-the-future-of-journalism/ [accessed 10 March 2017].

Tufekci, Zeynep (2016) 'WikiLeaks isn't whistleblowing', *New York Times*, 10 November, www.nytimes.com/2016/11/05/opinion/what-were-missing-while-we-obsess-over-john-podestas-email.html [accessed 10 March 2017].

Turton, William (2016) 'What happened to WikiLeaks?' *Gizmodo*, 29 July, http://gizmodo.com/what-happened-to-wikileaks-1784455507 [accessed 10 March 2017].

Wahl-Jorgensen, Karin (2014) 'Is WikiLeaks challenging the paradigm of journalism? boundary work and beyond', in *International Journal of Communication*, Vol. 8, 12. http://ijoc.org/index.php/ijoc/article/view/2771 [accessed 9 March 2017].

Weaver, Matthew (2010) 'Afghanistan war logs: WikiLeaks urged to remove thousands of names', *The Guardian*, 10 August, www.theguardian.com/world/2010/aug/10/afghanistan-war-logs-wikileaks-human-rights-groups [accessed 9 March 2017].

WikiLeaks Files (2007) 'Internal development mailing list', http://cryptome.org/wikileaks/wikileaks-leak.htm [accessed 10 March 2017].

―――― (2010) 'Collateral murder', 5 April, https://collateralmurder.wikileaks.org [accessed 3 January 2017].

—— (2013) 'Public library of US diplomacy', April, https://wikileaks.org/plusd/about/ [accessed 3 January 2017].

—— (2015a) 'Trans-pacific partnership final texts', 16 November, https://wikileaks.org/tpp-final/ [accessed 3 January 2017].

—— (2016a) 'German BND-NSA inquiry exhibits', 1 December, https://wikileaks.org/bnd-inquiry/ [accessed 3 January 2017].

—— (2016b) 'DNC email database', 22 July, https://wikileaks.org/dnc-emails/ [accessed 3 January 2017].

—— (2016c) 'The Podesta emails', [nd], https://wikileaks.org/podesta-emails/ [accessed 3 January 2017].

WikiLeaks Twitter Feed (2009) Tweet on 14 October, 1:05 p.m., https://twitter.com/wikileaks/status/4867836901.

—— (2010) Tweet on 17 July, 6:03 a.m., https://twitter.com/wikileaks/status/16379729990.

Usher, Nikki (2010) 'Why WikiLeaks' latest document dump makes everyone in journalism – and the public – a winner', *Nieman Journalism Lab*, [n.d.], www.niemanlab.org/2010/12/why-wikileaks-latest-document-dump-makes-everyone-in-journalism-and-the-public-a-winner/ [accessed 9 April 2013].

Wemple, E. (2016) 'The AP and WikiLeaks are brawling over a privacy story', *The Washington Post*, www.washingtonpost.com/blogs/erik-wemple/wp/2016/08/25/the-ap-and-wikileaks-are-brawling-over-a-privacy-story/?utm_term=.34849350da8a [accessed 12 March 2017].

Yelvington, Steve (2010) 'Five sad reasons American press isn't outraged', *Yelvington.com*, www.yelvington.com/content/12-12-2010/five-sad-reasons-american-press-isnt-outraged [accessed 10 March 2017].

Zetter, K. (2017) 'WikiLeaks files show the CIA repurposing hacking code to save time, not to frame Russia', *The Intercept*, https://theintercept.com/2017/03/08/wikileaks-files-show-the-cia-repurposing-foreign-hacking-code-to-save-time-not-to-frame-russia/ [accessed 11 March 2017].

Zoom, Doktor (2017) 'What the hell has happened to WikiLeaks?' *Wonkette*, http://wonkette.com/607209/what-the-hell-has-happened-to-wikileaks [accessed 9 March 2017].

14 Online news video, collaboration, and social networks

The disruption of the media industry

David Hayward

Introduction: technology and investigative journalism

Online and digital news video is revolutionising the journalism and media industry. More than 330 billion videos are watched every month on social media platforms (Wochit Team, 2018). On Facebook alone, more than 10 billion videos are viewed every day (Savage, 2016). With such huge audiences, online social video has become the key battleground for an industry that is struggling with failing business models and out-of-date cultures. For the first time, start-ups and digital 'native' news organisations are challenging the traditional press, media, publishing houses, and broadcasters. As a result, a new era of collaboration has emerged in investigative journalism, one that is radically changing the way reporters operate. But with this democratisation of the news and media industry comes considerable danger. Does the post-truth world and malicious, fake news pose the greatest threat that journalism has ever faced?

This chapter will explore the role video and social media networks are playing in disrupting the business of journalism and news, looking at what the future holds at a local, national and international level, and how the digital landscape can be verified and held to account itself. It will investigate how 'digital natives' and organisations outside the 'mainstream media' are driving investigative journalism.

The role of the 'Fourth Estate'

Has the Fourth Estate seen a time when it has been more under attack, when it has been less trusted and where its role has been questioned to the extent that it is today? This is a time when the President of the United States can use a press conference to attack journalists for producing 'fake news' and 'the media' are blamed every time their narratives counter those produced by the authorities. There is an imbalance in the power structure, one that poses very serious questions (Jamieson, 2017). The Fourth Estate, journalists, and the media industry are there to hold power to account, to keep politicians and the authorities honest, and to expose wrongdoing at the highest level. They exist to tell the truth, to inform people, and report in a fair, balanced, and accurate way. The democratisation of the means of production and content distribution has been seen in general terms as a good thing – but there are also some significant dangers.

This turn to more 'democratic', new media forms allows propaganda, fake news, and misinformation to reach a massive audience. It makes it more difficult to separate the truth from the lies and the myths from facts. There is, however, the promise of renewal. A new generation of 'digital natives' has joined respected news organisations in producing quality material and innovative content. The mainstream media are learning from these examples and following suit: together, the new media forms are gaining extraordinary new audiences – no longer measured in millions, but in billions.

If this development is combined with a raft of new independent investigative journalism organisations, the collaboration of global media houses, and new techniques of verification, trust in the Fourth Estate can return and journalism can regain its role and reputation. This chapter contends that there is hope: that the power of digital media can add to the great tradition of investigative journalism, and that First Draft News (2018), the Bureau for Investigative Journalism, ProPublica, Nowthisnews, AJ+, the Organized Crime and Corruption Reporting Project, Buzzfeed, and even UNILAD have a big role to play in this development.

Witnessing the dangers of state control

There is no doubt the explosion of digital media and access to information has had a revolutionary influence on our understanding of the world. It is no longer easy for the authorities to mislead an entire population on the basis that they control the means of communication.

I want to underline this observation by recounting a story from my time living in Sarajevo during the late 1990s. I was working for the BBC World Service Trust in Bosnia. One weekend I arranged to meet a friend at a cafe in the town of Pale. Geographically it was a just a short distance away, a little over 10 miles from my flat in the centre of Sarajevo. But the metaphorical gulf was huge – it was across the border in Republika Srpska. It seems difficult to believe now how different the world was there and then. This was before widespread access to the internet and mobile phones, even international satellite TV and broadcasters.

This was not a place that CNN and BBC World were universally available and more importantly it was not a place where the mainstream Western media were trusted. I met my colleague and got talking to a woman who was serving us the thick, black, viscous coffee, the slivovitz – a potent, local plum brandy – and the bootleg cigarettes that we were consuming with vigour. She asked me where I was living – I said Sarajevo. She said it had been many years since she had visited Sarajevo, and asked how was it now.

I replied, 'well fairly damaged and broken since the siege and the deaths of so many thousands of people'. This is where she took me aback. She said she didn't believe me. That I was pedalling Western propaganda spread by those evil leaders, Blair and Clinton. I asked her how she had come to this opinion – she said – and this is the chilling phrase I will never forget: 'The man on the radio told me'. These seven words explain so much about the power of the media, the power of misinformation and the effect that control of the means of communication can have. This was not the last time I experienced the mistrust of the West and the narrative of the Western media in Bosnia. I would have lengthy arguments with people about the 1995 Markale Market bomb in Sarajevo (that led to the NATO airstrikes), and about the role Ratko Mladic and Radovan Karadzic played in the Srebrenica massacre.

Journalism is under attack

I relate this story, because in many ways 'the man on the radio' has been replaced by Facebook and social media. 'I read it on Facebook' has become a popular refrain. Social media has become the way in which the modern world gets its information. But if this information is wrong, misleading, and fake, we are in very serious trouble. The director of the Centre for Journalism at Cardiff University, and former director of BBC News, Richard Sambrook wrote recently:

> Information is the currency of our world. Business, politics, social discourse, international relations and more rest on the assumption of shared, accurate information. But we learned in 2016 how that currency is being debased in an alarming number of ways . . . the problems are driven by structural issues which the developed world has yet to address. These include digital accountability of algorithms and the dominant market power of the big technology companies that devise them; the failed business model for serious news and information; [and] deep public confusion about the differences between facts and opinion . . . All of which has created a vacuum of trust which is undermining many of the institutions upon which open, democratic societies rest. If we are to have confidence in what we learn about the world and how it works, these structural issues need serious attention.
>
> (2017)

There is little doubt, these are dangerous times. Journalism and the media as a whole are in a precarious situation. The industry is under attack and faces a fight for its reputation. Fake news and misinformation has become big business. It is growing, and all sides of the political divide are trying to exploit it. Every day there emerges a new line of fake news and new ways in which it is being manipulated. It is astonishing how clever it can get. The recent case of Cambridge Analytica is the most obvious case, but over the past couple of years, there have been some astonishing examples. As the journalists from Buzzfeed discovered in 2016, there one small town in the former Yugoslavia became the centre of a fake news explosion:

> Over the past year, the Macedonian town of Veles (population 45,000) has experienced a digital gold rush as locals launched at least 140 US. politics websites. These sites have American-sounding domain names such as WorldPoliticus.com, TrumpVision365.com, USConservativeToday.com, DonaldTrumpNews.co, and USADailyPolitics.com. They almost all publish aggressively pro-Trump content aimed at conservatives and Trump supporters in the US. The young Macedonians who run these sites say they don't care about Donald Trump. They are responding to straightforward economic incentives.
>
> (Silverman, 2016)

The article just cited describes a sophisticated network, reaching huge audiences because they know how to influence the digital landscape. But this is far from the sole source of fake news. The very same techniques are being used by governments, pressure groups, marketing agencies, businesses, lone individuals, and activists to exploit the means of communication (Reid, 2016). This is why every mistake made by the mainstream media is so important, and why errors like the one made by Channel 4 News in March 2017, which wrongly named the Westminster terror suspect as Abu Izzadeen, are so serious (Glenday, 2017).

Journalism fighting back

However, journalism is not dead, and it could have a bright future. The threat of fake news and attempts to discredit and undermine the industry are very real at the moment, but will ultimately fail. They will fail for the same reasons they are succeeding at the moment – the existence of digital and social media. Arianna Huffington – the founder of the Huffington Post – has been making this point about new media for the past ten years.

During my previous role at the BBC, I was lucky enough meet her a number of times. She spoke at an internal event I ran in 2009. The key point she was making was about the shift in power from the mainstream to the new media. It was a wake-up call for the BBC. She saw the BBC and the legacy media as oil tankers. Very powerful when going in one direction, but when they need to change route, it takes a long time to turn. The new media by contrast is a nimble speedboat – not so powerful quite yet – but able to follow the direction of change very quickly.

Huffington's most important point – and one that still resonates with me – was in response to a question about the new media and investigative journalism. Her answer was that the old media had missed the biggest two stories of the first decade of the twenty-first century: the financial crash and the misinformation spread by the U.S. and UK governments, which led to the start of the Second Gulf War. Without the trust of the people, politicians can exploit this idea of the post-truth world, that the media peddle fake news and are irrelevant. The media need to act to regain control and to regain trust.

Verification and fact-checking

In 2013, I was part of a BBC and *The New York Times* initiative to analyse the relationship between the mainstream and social media. The discussion took place at a conference called the New York Social Media Summit #smsnyc (Hayward, 2013a). The event had all the essential ingredients, and many of the key players were involved – senior editorial figures from the mainstream media (MSM) and senior editorial figures from the social media platforms. A few days before the conference, there was an event that highlighted so many of the problems, showing the way in which the mainstream media and social media forms combined to cover a large breaking news story.

On Monday 15 April 2013, two homemade bombs were detonated close to the finishing line of the Boston Marathon. Three people were killed and hundreds injured. There was a massive challenge in reporting this. In the thirst for information and breaking news, the mainstream media allowed a level of trust in certain elements of social media that was simply wrong (Editor, Trusted Reviews, 2013). This was the beginning of a collaboration between the mainstream media and social platforms – the discussion to create a new era of trust and verification.

Some of the suggestions that emerged from the conference were (Hayward, 2013b):

- A colour-coded system for rating verification. People and organisations are rated on their ability to verify content and information: green, high; red, low
- Verified and trusted organisations get more space on Twitter
- News organisations have a duty to provide a guide/code of conduct to help people to understand ethical reporting
- An 'eBay-style' trust/verification rating system for individual users
- Credit-style rating systems for news organisations, similar to Moody's/Fitch financial credit ratings for organisations
- Set up a verification task force
- Have a verification button – saying what and how people have verified the material
- Barometer for verification – can Twitter provide a heat map/dashboard?
- Downgrade unverified content so it doesn't show up on a social search
- Warnings of graphic images

So many of these have come into use. The Twitter and Facebook verification ticks and the verification taskforces are just two examples. Whether directly or indirectly, great things were to follow this conference: the formation of organisations like First Draft News (Reid, 2016) and the appearance of the excellent Verification Handbook (Silverman, 2015).

It is one thing, however, to establish a code of conduct and encourage the self-regulation of the responsible, independent media. But it is a very different challenge to secure the involvement of the big beasts – in other words, to obtain the full engagement of the platforms and search engines. There is still a misconception about the role of the platforms. Facebook and Google have always maintained that they are no more than platforms, with the content provided by third parties.

But at the end of 2016, in the face of the explosion of fake news, Facebook and Google were forced to act. They needed to protect their image and reputation. They also needed to accept responsibility as arbiters of information. Facebook was the first to act:

> Facebook is going to start fact-checking, labelling, and burying fake news and hoaxes in its News Feed, the company said Thursday.
>
> (Heath, 2016)

The announcement that it would work with a number of independent, fact-checking organisations, to analyse disputed material was very significant. Those organisations are part of the group that signs up to the Poynter Institute guidelines (nd). They include Snopes, Factcheck.org, Associated Press, ABC News and Politifact. On 22 March 2017, Facebook rolled out its new alert to combat 'fake news'. It was reported across the global media, including this article in *the Guardian*:

> Titled 'The Irish slave trade – the slaves that time forgot', the story published by the Rhode Island entertainment blog Newport Buzz was widely shared on the platform in the lead-up to St Patrick's Day on 17 March. For some users, attempting to share the story prompts a red alert stating the article has been disputed by both Snopes.com and the Associated Press.
>
> (Hunt, 2017)

And now Google is joining forces. In April 2017, it announced its own fact-checking process. Like Facebook the company is using the expertise of third-party fact-checking services.

> The world's largest search engine is rolling out a new feature that places 'Fact Check' tags on snippets of articles in its News results. The Alphabet Inc. unit had already run limited tests. On Friday (7th April 2017), it extended the capability to every listing in its News pages and massive search catalog. . . . The company plans to reserve the label for search results about addressable public claims of fact, rather than opinion. Publishers can write the labels that appear next to results. Examples include 'True', 'Mostly False', or 'Pants on Fire!'
>
> (Bergen, 2017)

The importance of the moves by Google and Facebook cannot be underestimated. It marks a change of responsibility of two of the most powerful media companies in the world, and their understanding and acceptance that they have a role to play in truth and trust in the dissemination of information in the digital age. This is a recognition of the importance of fact and against the idea of post-truth world and the freedom this gives the distributors of fake news, propaganda, and misinformation.

Clearly there is still some way to go for Facebook and Google. The early positive signs have been discredited by numerous scandals, most notably that of Cambridge Analytica. The allegations are that personal data was minded on social media platforms and used by firms to manipulate the outcomes of elections and referendums. The U.S. elections, the EU referendum and the 2017 UK general elections are all thought to have been targeted, while Facebook stood by and did little to combat this. The *Guardian* has done some sterling work investigating the crisis, talking to whistleblowers including the former Facebook executive Sandy Parakilas:

> Hundreds of millions of Facebook users are likely to have had their private information harvested by companies that exploited the same terms as the firm that collected data and passed it on to Cambridge Analytica.
> (Lewis, 2018)

These damaging stories, however, can be countered in a more collaborative and open media that works together to expose wrongdoing and highlight misinformation. Verification is central to this.

Verification case studies

At this point, two examples of verification will be used to show how simple journalistic techniques, combined with the latest online tools, can help to check whether a story is true or false. In the 18 months leading up to the 2016 presidential election, one of the most shared pictures of Donald Trump was him in 1998, accompanied by a quote from an interview in *People Magazine*, in which he is meant to have said:

> If I were to run, I'd run as a Republican. They're the dumbest group of voters in the country, they love anything on Fox News, I could lie and they'd still eat it up. I bet my numbers would be terrific.

It was (and continues to be) shared hundreds of thousands of times on social media. But of course the story is not true. It was a great example of propaganda, and close enough to the truth, for people to believe what is being said, without actually being genuine. The fact-checking organisation Snopes (La Capria, 2017) conducted the analysis on this item. Going back to the source material, via *People Magazine*'s extensive online archive, it found no evidence of the interview and certainly no evidence of the offending quote. Snopes also combined this with reverse image searches, via Google Image search and TinEye (nd). These are very simple steps to ensure verification.

A more complicated example of verification came from the social media news agency Storyful (nd). It was investigating the validity of a video that emerged from the Syrian conflict, claiming to show troops loyal to President Assad burying a rebel soldier alive (YouTube, 2012). It was shown on dozens of mainstream media organisations. It fitted the dominant narrative, appearing to prove that war crimes were being committed by Syrian government forces. The team of journalists began checking the origin of the video, trying to establish when it first appeared online, and the publishing accounts from which it came.

They also conducted a close examination of the participants shown in the video. Were the accents and language used in the video consistent with the story? There was also an element of collaboration. Storyful communicated with experts in other news organisations, including the BBC, to see what they had discovered and whether they also had concerns. This conversation took place in the open, via social media on Twitter and Facebook groups, drawing on the expertise of a vast pool of journalists and fact-checkers.

They also looked at the video itself. Was there meta-data available that indicated where and when the video was shot? Did the weather conditions match those on the day the video was taken, and in the place it was shot? They concluded that, while they were unable to declare definitively that it was false, the overriding evidence suggested that it was – and that news organisations should use it with great care (Browne, 2012).

The world needs a free, fair, and independent media, but above all one that is trusted by the audience. The power of the media is shifting. The audience is in flux and consuming news and information in different formats and on different platforms. With this change in form, comes a change in style and a new form of journalism and media, which could represent the beginning of a new industry in communication and information that will revive the Fourth Estate.

Investment and new sources of investigative journalism

As we begin to look at the investment in online investigative journalism, the one organisation that continues to be spoken of very highly is Buzzfeed:

> following a succession of scoops over match-fixing in tennis, the children's charity scandal at KidsCo, and the failings of the National Crime Agency (NCA), BuzzFeed News UK finds itself regularly featured on prestige outlets from the Radio 4 Today programme to the Andrew Marr Show.
>
> (Burrell, 2016)

The often much derided 'listicle' website has become a serious player when it comes to investigative journalism. Buzzfeed made a very clear statement of intent when it appointed the significant figures in the world of journalism, like Heidi Blake and Janine Gibson. Gibson is a former senior executive at the *Guardian*. She started the *Guardian US* and was the brains behind the *Guardian*'s online success, and won numerous awards for her work covering the Snowden leaks. Blake is the former head of the *The Sunday Times* 'Insight' team, which broke the FIFA scandal on allegations that Qatar had given out bribes to stage the 2022 World Cup (Blake, nd). In the United States, the social media news video publisher NowThis News is beginning to invest heavily in investigative journalism and long-form video (NowThis News, nd). The publishers came to prominence producing short form, text-based social video – and were very successful in the use of this mode.

Speaking at the BBC Fusion 'Social Broadcasting – What Next?' conference in December 2016, Ashish Patel outlined the plans to expand into longer form content to build on the 2.5 billion video views that NowThis News get every month (Live Stream, 2016). A central part of this initiative is quality content and investigative journalism. A further announcement was made by their president, Athan Stephanopoulos, in March 2017:

> 'We're not moving away from what we know', Stephanopoulos said of NowThis, which has grown to 2.5 billion monthly video views largely by creating short, text-on-screen news video clips that dominate the Facebook news feed. 'This is an opportunity for us to extend and amplify the NowThis brand by going deeper into longer-form programming around key issues and topics that do well in the social feed'.
>
> (Patel, 2017)

Meanwhile AJ+, Al Jazeera's U.S.-based digital publisher, which targets the millennial audience, is showing a renewed and close interest in investigative journalism. Also speaking at the BBC Fusion 'Social Broadcasting – What Next?' conference, Shadi Rahimi explained why AJ+ was building on quality content and investigative journalism, holding power to account (Norris, 2017)

If you add Channel 4 into the mix, and the way it is supporting and producing the next generation of investigative journalists, things do begin to look much better. Channel 4, led by the Head of News and Current Affairs, Dorothy Byrne, is investing heavily in teaching and training, with its investigative journalism scheme and the MA for investigative journalism at De Montfort University (Investigative Journalism MA, nd). Meanwhile, independent, non-profit organisations are proving to be more and more powerful. They are taking on a new role in the media, supporting and supplementing the investigations being carried out by the legacy press and broadcasters:

> The survivors among the big newspapers will not be without support from the nonprofit sector. ProPublica . . . hopes to provide the

mainstream media with the investigative reporting that so many have chosen to forgo.

(Alterman, 2008)

This was an outline of ProPublica from an article in *The New Yorker* magazine in 2008. Today, ProPublica continues to be a mainstay in the world of investigative journalism, upholding the core traditions of the Fourth Estate and doing so in the best possible way (ProPublica, nd). In response to an article ProPublica published on the Huffington Post: 'Trump Can Pull Money From His Businesses Whenever He Wants – Without Ever Telling Us' (Kravitz and Shaw, 2017) Sean Spicer, White House Press Secretary, dismissed ProPublica as a 'Left-wing blog', to which it responded.

'What we do is hold people in power accountable, no matter who they are, or what names they call us', the news outlet wrote. 'We do it with facts'. They then tweeted 15 times – 15 different stories to illustrate just this.

(D'Angelo, 2017).

The received narrative is that journalism is failing, and that with the decline of the mainstream media and the press, there is an associated decline in investigative journalism and of the Fourth Estate in general. This is far from the case: over the past few years, new trends of investigative journalism have been emerging and are now beginning to bear fruit.

Collaboration is king

As Charles Lewis, the founder of the International Consortium of Investigative Journalism (nd), puts it so eloquently – collaboration is absolutely key to the future of the Fourth Estate. He argued that 'the concept of public accountability should not be confined by the borders and orthodoxies of traditional journalism' (Lewis, 2016). All the best and finest examples of investigative journalism in the past five years have depended upon collaboration: the original WikiLeaks disclosure, the Panama Papers, and the Snowden affair.

Each one of these stories involved news organisations around the world, working together to produce a ground-breaking agenda and the type of journalism that can hold power to account. The new breed of investigative journalists not only uses the traditional tools of their trade, but also the new techniques of data analysis, data manipulation and data illustration. These techniques allow quantities of data that would be impossible to analyse only a few years previously. By working together, news organisations throughout the world are able to challenge the global authorities. This *Guardian* article on the Russian Laundromat crisis, from March 2017, provides a useful example:

Britain's high street banks processed nearly $740m from a vast money-laundering operation run by Russian criminals with links to the Russian government and the KGB, the Guardian can reveal. HSBC, the Royal Bank of Scotland, Lloyds, Barclays and Coutts are among 17 banks based in the UK, or with branches here, that are facing questions over what they knew about the international scheme.

(Harding et al., 2017)

It was only by working with dozens of media partners – and the independent innovative journalism projects – that this revelation could be made:

The Global Laundromat banking records were obtained by the Organized Crime and Corruption Reporting Project (OCCRP) and Novaya Gazeta from sources who wish to remain anonymous. OCCRP shared the data with the Guardian and media partners in 32 countries.

(Harding et al., 2017)

The OCCRP is one of several independent and much valued organisations. The Bureau for Investigative Journalism and ProPublica are two others from a range of dedicated organisations, which include The Organized Crime and Corruption Reporting Project, The African Forum for Investigative Reporting, and The Global investigative Journalism Network.

Conclusion

There is no point in pretending that even the most prominent revelations have secured the future of investigative journalism, or that we are about to enter a revival of the period when stories that could have been produced by Woodward and Bernstein, are going to appear every week. There is still a lot to achieve and a lot for the mainstream media and digital-native publishers to agree upon. The analogy that I referred to earlier, about the oil tanker changing course, is only the beginning. There are a number of troubling issues and much disagreement about the way forward.

Back in 2009, Paul Bradshaw, the author of the online journalism blog and digital news guru, came to speak to the BBC about his new project helpmeinvestigate. The title of his talk was the 'future of investigative journalism'. The idea was a collaborative project to work in the open on investigations. This did not go down well with the traditional journalists, such as the reporters and editors from 'Panorama', 'Newsnight', and the 'Today' programme. Suspicion does still exist and a conflict of approaches, between the open publication of material and the closed mode of reporting, remains a live issue. The decision by Buzzfeed to publish an intelligence dossier on Donald Trump in full may illustrate this tension. Buzzfeed justified this by opening the fact to the public. The journalists, Ken Bensinger (BuzzFeed News Reporter), Miriam Elder (BuzzFeed News World Editor), and Mark Schoofs (BuzzFeed News Investigations Editor), explained that:

BuzzFeed News is publishing the full document so that Americans can make up their own minds about allegations about the President-elect . . . the document was prepared for political opponents of Trump by a person who is understood to be a former British intelligence agent. It is not just unconfirmed: it includes some clear errors.

(Bensinger et al., 2017)

There is concern and unease about the publication of unverified material and content. It goes against the instincts of traditional journalism. In the same vein, there is huge concern about the way in which un-redacted information is published by organisations such as WikiLeaks. However, the evolution of investigative journalism is underway. There is a revolution in online and digital media – and investigative journalism is an essential part of this.

References

Alterman, Eric (2008) 'The death of the American newspaper', 31 March, newyorker.com at www.newyorker.com/magazine/2008/03/31/out-of-print (accessed 22 July 2018).

Bensinger, Ken, Elder, Miriam and Schoofs, Mark (2017) 'These reports allege Trump has deep ties to Russia', *buzzfeed.com*, www.buzzfeed.com/kenbensinger/these-reports-allege-trump-has-deep-ties-to-russia?utm_term=.hkNkaPrYZ#.avEXYlDKN [accessed 11 January 2017].

Bergen, Mark (2017) 'Google brings fake news fact-checker to search results', *bloomberg.com*, www.bloomberg.com/news/articles/2017-04-07/google-brings-fake-news-fact-checking-to-search-results [accessed 7 April 2017].

Blake, Heidi (nd) 'Heidi Blake UK posts', www.buzzfeed.com/heidiblake [accessed 22 July 2018].

Browne, Malachy (2012) 'Doubt cast on video of Syrian "buried" activist', *storyful.com*, 26 April, http://web.archive.org/web/20120428112946/http://storyful.com/stories/26986 [accessed 22 July 2018].

Brouwer, Bree (2017) 'Top online video creators across social: September 2017', *Tubular Insights*, 27 October, http://tubularinsights.com/top-online-video-creators/ [accessed 22 June 2018].

Burrell, Ian (2016) 'Buzzfeed to Fleet Street – "We're figuring out the future of journalism"', *thedrum.com*, 9 June, www.thedrum.com/opinion/2016/06/09/buzzfeed-fleet-street-were-figuring-out-future-journalism [accessed 22 July 2018].

D'Angelo, Chris (2017) 'ProPublica expertly claps back at Sean Spicer for calling it a "Left Wing Blog"', *huffingtonpost.co.uk*, www.huffingtonpost.com/entry/propublica-sean-spicer-left-wing-blog_us_58e2cbe5e4b03a26a36557fc [accessed 4 April 2017].

Editor, Trusted Reviews (2013) 'Boston Bombings: How twitter fed the mainstream media lies', *trustedreviews.com*, 22 April, www.trustedreviews.com/opinions/hard-news-everyone-misreported-the-boston-bombings-the-internet-just-did-it-faster [accessed 20 June 2017].

First Draft News (2018) Shorenstein Centre, Harvard Kennedy School, https://firstdraftnews.org, [accessed 22 July 2018].

Glenday, John (2017) 'Channel 4 News falsely identified Westminster attacker', *thedrum.com*, 23 March, www.thedrum.com/news/2017/03/23/channel-4-news-falsely-identified-westminster-attacker [accessed 23 March 2017].

Greenfield, Patrick (2018) 'The Cambridge Analytica files: The story so far', *guardian.co.uk*, 26 March, www.theguardian.com/news/2018/mar/26/the-cambridge-analytica-files-the-story-so-far [accessed 22 July 2018].

Harding, Luke, Hopkins, Nick and Caelainn, Barr (2017) 'British banks handled vast sums of laundered Russian money', *guardian.co.uk*, www.theguardian.com/world/2017/mar/20/british-banks-handled-vast-sums-of-laundered-russian-money [accessed 30 March 2017].

Hayward, David (2013a) 'Future of news organisations in a social world: The big guns discuss', 23 April, #smsnyc at bbc.co.uk, www.bbc.co.uk/blogs/collegeofjournalism/entries/ee9e9a77-e673-3200-b303-6608a40bbafd [accessed 20 March 2018].

—— (2013b) 'After Boston, brainstorming better verification #smsnyc', bbc.co.uk, 22 April, www.bbc.co.uk/blogs/collegeofjournalism/entries/41555703-68f9-3697-a496-b734e8c4e5d1 [accessed 20 March 2018].

Heath, Alex (2016) 'Facebook is going to use Snopes and other fact-checkers to combat and bury "fake news"', *uk.businessinsider.com*, http://uk.businessinsider.com/facebook-will-fact-check-label-fake-news-in-news-feed-2016-12 [accessed 15 December 2016].

Hunt, Ellie (2017) 'Disputed by multiple face-checkers: Facebook rolls out new alerts to combat fake news', *guardian.co.uk*, 22 March, www.theguardian.com/technology/2017/mar/22/facebook-fact-checking-tool-fake-news [accessed 28 March 2017].

International Consortium of Investigative Journalists (nd) www.icij.org/ [accessed 22 July 2018].

Investigative Journalism MA (nd) De Montfort University Masters course, www.dmu.ac.uk/study/courses/postgraduate-courses/investigative-journalism/investigative-journalism-ma-degree.aspx [accessed 20 July 2018].

Jamieson, Amber (2017) '"You are fake news": Trump attacks CNN and Buzzfeed at press conference', *The Guardian*, online, at guardian.co.uk, www.theguardian.com/us-news/2017/jan/11/trump-attacks-cnn-buzzfeed-at-press-conference [accessed 11 January 2017].

Kravitz, Derek and Shaw, Al (2017) 'Trump can pull money from his businesses whenever he wants – without ever telling us', *huffintgonpost.com*, 3 April, www.huffingtonpost.com/entry/trump-trust-business_us_58e24b74e4b0b3918c84ebb8 [accessed 10 April 2017].

LaCapria, Kim (2017) 'Did Donald Trump say Republicans are the "Dumbest Group of Voters"?' *snopes.com*, 30 November, www.snopes.com/1998-trump-people-quote/ [accessed 22 July 2018].

Lewis, Charles (2016) 'The future of journalism in three words: Collaboration, collaboration, collaboration', *The Guardian*, online, 18 April, www.theguardian.com/commentisfree/2016/apr/18/future-of-journalism-collaboration-panama-papers [accessed 22 July 2018].

Lewis, Paul (2018) '"Utterly horrifying": Ex-Facebook insider says covert data harvesting was routine', 20 March, www.theguardian.com/news/2018/mar/20/facebook-data-cambridge-analytica-sandy-parakilas [accessed 22 July 2018].

Live Stream (2016) 'Live stream: Social broadcasting – where next? conference #BBCSocial16', www.bbc.co.uk/academy/technology/article/art20161121112513441 [accessed 20 June 2017].

Norris, Ashley (2017) 'A look at AJ+ – Al Jazeera's unique approach to engaging millennials', fipp.com, 26 January, www.fipp.com/news/features/a-look-at-al-jazeeras-unique-approach-millennials [accessed 20 July 2017].

NowThis News (nd) https://nowthisnews.com [accessed 20 July 2017].

Patel, Sahil (2017) 'NowThis to expand in investigative journalism and long form video', *digiday.co.uk*, 6 March, https://digiday.com/media/nowthis-is-investing-in-investigative-journalism-and-long-form-video/ [accessed 20 July 2018].

Poynter (nd) 'International fact-checking network: Fact-checkers' code of principles', www.poynter.org/international-fact-checking-network-fact-checkers-code-principles [accessed 22 July 2018].

ProPublica (nd) www.propublica.org [accessed 22 July 2018].

Reid, Alastair (2016) 'The five sources of fake news everyone needs to look out for online', *firstdraftnews.com*, 10 May, https://firstdraftnews.com/the-5-sources-of-fake-news-everyone-needs-to-look-out-for-online/ [accessed 10 May 2016].

Sambrook, Richard (2017) 'Trust and news', *medium.com*, https://medium.com/@sambrook/trust-and-news-310e978f82b [accessed 6 April 2017].

Savage, Jonathan (2016) 'Top 5 Facebook Video Statistics for 2016', https://www.socialmediatoday.com/marketing/top-5-facebook-video-statistics-2016-infographic [accessed 20 July 2018].

Silverman, Craig (2015) *Verification Handbook for Investigative Reporting*, on Creative Commons, http://verificationhandbook.com/book2/chapter1.php# [accessed 22 July 2018].

——— (2016) 'How teens in the Balkans are duping trump supporters with fake news', *buzzfeed.com*, www.buzzfeed.com/craigsilverman/how-macedonia-became-a-global-hub-for-pro-trump-misinfo?utm_term=.pcb1NJQWL#.vlaOvwMrD [accessed 3 November 2016].

Snopes (nd) News website, www.snopes.com [accessed 22 July 2018].

Storyful (nd) https://storyful.com [accessed 22 July 2018].

Thomson, Alex (2011) 'Ratko Mladic and the Srebrenica Massacre', *channel4.com*, www.channel4.com/news/ratko-mladic-and-the-srebrenica-massacre [accessed 26 May 2011].

TinEye (nd) Image search website, www.tineye.com [accessed 22 July 2018].

YouTube (2012) 'Syrian soldier buried alive', www.youtube.com/verify_controversy?next_url=%252Fwatch%253Ftime_continue%253D10%2526v%253D8vlv0jbm7vo [accessed 22 July 2018].

Wochit Team (2018) '2018 Social Video Statistics for the Video Savvy Brand', at *Video Insider*, https://www.wochit.com/blog/2018-social-video-statistics-video-savvy-brand/ [accessed 22 July 2018].

Index

Note: Page numbers in *italic* indicate a figure on the corresponding page.

ABC News 291
Abercrombie, Nicholas 21, 78
Abreu, Mauricio de Almeida 163
Abreu, Sabrina 160
activism 113–115, 155–157, 218–219, 267–268; and the deep state 59–61, 65–66, 68–69
Afghanistan 143, 187, 251, 270–271
Aftenposten 280
agency *see* political agency
Ahrne, Göran 82
Al Arabiya 220–221
Al-Jazeera 216, 220–221
Allan, Stuart 12, 167
Al-Marashi, Ibrahim 184
al-Masry al-Youm 275
al Qaeda 60, 62, 68, 120
Al-Qarawee, Harith Hasan 181
Alterman, Eric 294–295
Alvito, Marcos *see* Zaluar, Alba
Amnesty International 168, 171
Amos, Deborah 184–185
antagonism *see under* structural factors
Arab Investigative Journalists Network (ARIJ) 220
Arab revolts 176, 215
Assange, Julian 57, 70, 265–266, 279–280; and the megaleaks backlash 272–275; in the megaleaks period 270–272; and WikiLeaks after megaleaks 275–279
Associated Press 267, 275, 280, 291
Association of Chief Police Officers (ACPO) 61, 68–69
Athayde, Celso *see* Meirelles, Renato
austerity 12, 26, 79, 81, 89n9, 123
authoritarianism 11
authority 27n11, 77–79, 81–82, 86–88, 109n3, 109n4

Bahrain 220
Baiense, Carla *see* Vaz, Paulo
Bakker, Piet *see* Diekerhof, Els
balance 10–11, 96–103, 216–217, 232–233; *see also* false balance
Barber, Marsha *see* Bernier, Marc-François
Barisione, Mauro 7
Battle of Mosul 176, 200–208, *204*, *207*, 212
BBC 18, 37, 53n5, 75, 79; and the Arab revolts 224; and disruption of the media industry 287–290, 293–294, 296; and verification 251–252, 254, 256; and WikiLeaks 269
Beano 198
Bebawi, Saba 215
Beer, David 17
Beevor, Anthony 121
Bengio, Ofra 182
Bensinger, Ken 196
Bergen, Mark 291
Berglez, Peter 2–3
Bermuda 175–177, 229, 233, 235–241, 242n2; Bermuda Immigration and Protection Act 230–232, 234, 241, 242n1
Bernard, Sheila 233
Bernier, Marc-François 77
Bingham, Tom 13, 26n1
Blair, Tony 230, 288
Blake, Heidi 294
bloggers 23, 97, 218, 260, 269
Borel massacre 171–173
Bradley, Jane 156
Brazil 18–20, 113–115; dictatorship in 164–165; ethnicity and poverty in 162–163; and the internet 167–169; media attitudes and

171–173; mediating Brazilian favelas 160–161; news agendas and 165–166; perspectives of journalists and residents on 161–162; the problems of community journalism and 170; the *Viva Favela* portal 169–170
Brexit 73, 146, 198, 255–256
Briggs, Billy 176, 196, 200–208
British overseas territory 268; *see also* Bermuda
Broersma, Marcel *see* Peters, Chris
Burrell, Ian 293
Byrne, Dorothy 90n25, 294

Cambodia 114, 128; and Global Witness 137–138, 143, 147–149, *148*, 151–156, *152*
Cambridge Analytica 6, 20, 289, 292
Cameron, David 147, 256
Campbell, Duncan 56, 58, 70
Canada 59–60, 64, 234, 276
Canadian Security and Intelligence Service (CSIS) 64–65
capitalism 20–22, 27n2, 78, 81, 87, 89n5
Capriglione, Laura 172
Carlson, Matt 12
Carpentier, Nico 11
case studies 24, 95, 114, 176, 200, 292–293; Global Witness and 143–149, 153–156
Catalonia 132
censorship 69–70, 155–156, 222–223, 231–232, 268–269
Chadwick, Andrew 11, 253–257
Channel 4 6, 147, 156, 271, 289, 294; FactCheck 252–256, 291
Chayes, Sarah 157
China 9–10, 27n6, 36, 74, 80, 266; Global Witness and 139, 150
citizen investigations 117–120; *see also* Memory Movement
citizen journalism 24, 77, 88n1, 97, 173, 218, 273
citizens 6–7, 16, 18–20, 22–23, 162–163, 167–168, 252–253; *see also* citizen investigations; citizen journalism
Clarke, Charles 39–40, 43, 53n4
class 17, 20; class and working-class autonomy 20, 119; mobility 18–20; and the political class 6, 22; and subordinate 28
Clinton, Hillary 6, 252, 258, 265–266, 276–277
Cohen, Jared *see* Schmidt, Eric

collaboration 86–87, 130–131, 278–279, 286–287, 291–293, 295–296
communication 1–2, 4–7, 13–21, 27n15
Conboy, Martin 23
Connell, Christopher 138–139
control 16–18, 20–21, 25–26, 27n15, 137–139, 182–183; and the deep state 64–5; and journalists under duress 75–78, 81–82, 89n3, 89n8, 90n17, 90n20; and 'voluntary' obedience 84–85
corruption 113–114; and Brazilian favelas 164–165; Global Witness and 137–142, 144–147; and investigative journalism 156–157; and Iraq 188–189, 191–192; WikiLeaks and 265–266, 276–277
Counter-Intelligence Programmes (COINTELPROs) 65
Cram, Ian 43, 46
Credit Suisse 150
Cushion, Stephen 253
Custodio, Leonardo 167

Daily Mail, The 146, 255
Daily Record 198
data 63–64, 69–71, 99–102, 153–154, 184–185, 292–293; data-gathering 142–143; data-mining 143
Davis, Aeron 24
Davis, Evan 257
De Angelis, Enrico 219, 222
Dean, Jodi 19
Debord, Guy 14–15, 27n10
de Burgh, Hugo 2, 140–141, 147–148, 151, 156
deep state 56–58; key research methods for investigating 62–69
Deibert, Ron 18, 74–75
Della Porta, Donatella 216
democracy 1, 7–9, 11–12, 14–15, 24–26, 28n18; 'arrested democracy' 12; binary character of 18, 19, 26; democratic change 215, 223–226; 'democratic deficit' 5–7; 'emerging democracies' 184–186; and 'insurgent' perspectives 11; minimalist and maximalist 11; as public ritual 8; as rhetoric 5; systemic 8; trans-national notions of 8–10
Department of Homeland Security (DHS) 58–59, 62–63, 66, 275
Deutsche Bank 150–152
Deuze, Mark 9, 27n5

Diani, Mario *see* Della Porta, Donatella
dictatorship 117–118, 125, 164–165; *see also* Brazil; Spain
Diekerhof, Els 246–247
Die Tageszeitung 196–197
dissent 58–62, 66, 75, 77, 82, 224–225
Douglas, Ian 269
duty *see* proactive duty

economic factors 19–22, 25–26; Brazilian favelas and 163–165; economic crisis 90n14; Egypt and 217–218, 223–225; *The Ferret* and 197–198, 208–209; Global Witness and 148–149; journalists under duress and 79–83, 87–88, 89n10; Spain and 122–123; verification and 256–257
Economist, The 199
Egypt 175–176, 215–216, 275; media and politics in 216–220; and Pan Arab TV news 220–221; and social media 221–226
elasticity 20–22
elite, the 8–9, 11–12, 18–21, 24–26, 28n17; Global Witness and 146–147; verification and 256–257
El-Nawawy, Mohammed 218
Escudero, Rafael Baena 121, 125
ethnicity 17, 20, 162–163
Ettema, James S. 24, 140, 248, 250, 260
EU referendum 251, 253–254
European Convention on Human Rights (ECoHR) 98, 100–104, 107, 102–103
European Court of Human Rights (ECoHR) 43, 51, 98, 102
European Union (EU) 7, 110, 200, 209–210, 253–257, 292
Evans, Rob 57, 60, 65–66, 71
executive power 7–8, 14, 17, 73, 76, 78-82, 85, 88

Facebook 4, 20, 286, 288–293; Brazilian favelas and 167; Egypt and 216, 218–219, 223–225; *The Ferret* and 209; Global Witness and 137, 155; verification and 259–260
fact-checking 197, 213, 243, 245–246, 293; and the discourse of 'face news' 259–260; effectiveness of 257–258; and the small statistical fact 252–257; theory and practice of 246–249; verification and 290–292

fake news 16, 223, 243–244, 245, 286–292; the discourse of 258–260
false balance 246, 249–251, 262n6
false equivalence 249–252
favelas 113–114; alternative perspectives on 161–162; and community journalism 170; development of 162–165; internet use and 167–169; and media attitudes 171–173; mediating the Brazilian favelas 160–161; news agendas and 165–166; the *Viva Favela* portal 169–170
Ferret, The 175, 197, 212–213; and the Battle of Mosul 200–208, *204*, *207*; co-operative approach of 197–199; international reporting of 199–200; and 'A Second Syria' 208–212, *208*, *209*, *211*
financial backing 150–153
First Amendment 267, 272
foreign reporting 176, 230, 271; *see also Ferret, The*
Fotopoulos, Takis 20
Fourth Estate 244, 286–288, 293, 295
Fox News 276–277, 292
Franco, Francisco 113, 118, 120–122, 125–126, 130, 133–134, 135n4
Freedom of Information Act (UK) 66, 69
Freedom of Information Act (U.S.) 276
Freedom of Information (FOI) requests 35, 60, 67–70, 88, 198, 276
Freedom of the Press Foundation 280
freelance journalists 88n1, 107, 109n5, 197, 200, 211, 251
Full Fact 252–255
fusion centres 35, 58–60, 62–63, 66

Gans, Herbert J. 247
Geoghegan, Peter 175
Gerbaudo, Paolo 119
Gerbner, George 82
Germany 171, 210, 220, 278
Glasser, Theodore L. *see* Ettema, James S.
GlobaLeaks 280
Global Witness 113–114, 137–141, 156–157; and data- and text-mining 143; 'Hostile Takeover' 153–156; 'No Safe Haven' 143–147; and open data-gathering 142–143; and

research 150–153; 'Rubber Barons' 147–149, *148*
Godler, Yigal 247
Goldman Sachs 150, 265
Google 18–19, 63, 150, 153, 198, 213, 291–293
Gore, Will 251
government 3–5, 7–10, 20–22, 289–290; Bermuda and 230–232, 235–241; and the deep state 68–71; Egypt and 222–224; Global Witness and 139–140, 143–144; Iraq and 180–182, 184–186, 188–189; and journalists under duress 74–76, 80–81, 83–84; and the proactive duty to report 42–43; WikiLeaks and 265–266, 273–274; and social justice 113–114; Spain and 132–133
Grassegger, Hannes 101
Graves, Lucas 253
Greenwald, Glenn 18, 73, 76, 106–107, 274, 277; and the deep state 56, 70–71
Guardian, the 6, 259–260, 268–273, 291–295; and Global Witness 156; and journalists under duress 57, 60, 66
Guardian News and Media 95–96
Guardian Weekend 114

Hadhum, Haider S. 183
Hagan, John 181
Haiven, Max 21
Hallin, Daniel 217, 249
Hama-Saeed, Mariwan *see* Kim, Hun Shik
Hamdy, Naila 219–220, 222
Hansen, Ejvind 2
Harb, Zahera 176
Harbisher, Ben 35
Harding, Luke 295–296
Hassan, Hashim 182, 192
Hayward, David 244
Hearst Corporation 267
Heath, Alex 291
Hepp, Andreas 15
Herald, The 198, 200
Hermida, Alfeed 16
Hibou, Béatrice 81
Hickman, Tom 104
hierarchy 15, 21–22, 25, 81–82, 85, 88, 90n15, 90n20; and hierarchical organisation of consensual rule 85
Hoang Anh Gia Lai (HAGL) 147–153, *148*

Holston, James 19–20
'Hostile Takeover' 153–156
Howard, Philip 176, 215
human rights 3, 75, 135n2, 154–155, 200–201; *see also* European Convention on Human Rights(ECoHR)
Hunt, Ellie 291
Hunter, Mark Lee 199
Hussain, Muzammil *see* Howard, Philip
Hussein, Saddam 181–183

ideology 9, 78, 182; professional ideology 82, 243, 248; *see* liberal ideology
immigration 254–255; *see also under* Bermuda
impunity 154–155, 185, 253
Independent, The 278
information economy 36, 85–87
institutional pressures 77
Integrated Security Units and Joint Intelligence Groups (ISU-JIG) 60, 64
Integrated Threat Assessment Centre (ITAC) 60, 64–65
Intercept, The 106, 277, 280
international coverage *see* foreign reporting
International Federation of Journalists, The (IFJ) 185–186
International Finance Corporation (IFC) 150–151
internet 13–14, 16–19, 23–24, 286–287, 292–294, 296–297; and Brazilian favelas 167–169; and the deep state 57–58; and Egypt 218–219; and *The Ferret* 196–199, 212–213; and Global Witness 142–143, 153–155; and protecting sources 105–106; and WikiLeaks 276–277
interview 292–293; Bermuda and 231–236; Egypt and 221–225; *The Ferret* and 202–203, 205–207, 209–210; Iraq and 186–188; and the proactive duty to report 37–38; verification and 259–260
intrusive practices 75–77
investigative journalism 15, 37; and Chinese tradition 9; and democratic deficit 5; as a global discipline 23–24; as a mode of enquiry 2; and murders of journalists 4; and serious crime 101; and the state 56, 58, 60–66; and terrorism 37–41, 43, 46–47

304 *Index*

Investigative reporters and editors 13
Iraq 12, 46, 175, 179, 191–192, 270–271; the emergence of sectarianism in 181–182; investigative journalism in 184–190; and media post-Saddam 183–184; and media under Saddam Hussein 182–183; Radio Free Iraq 179–180; *see also* Iraqi Kurdistan
Iraqi Kurdistan (Northern Iraq) 1, 176, 200–207, *204*, 213
Isin, Engin 18

Jawad, Rana 75, 79
Johnson, Ayo 233
Johnson, Boris 255
Jordan 191, 220
journalism and austerity 79; and authority (ten fields of influence) 77–79; and structural antagonism 75–76
Journalistic Freedom Observatory 185
justice 19, 86, 95–98, 122–125; *see also* social justice

Kaplan, David E. 189
Keeble, Richard 190
Khamis, Sahar *see* El-Nawawy, Mohammed
Khashoggi, Jamal 4
Kim, Hun Shik 192
Kissinger, Henry 276
Kitschelt, Herbert 27n3
Kovach, Bill 12–13, 248, 251
Krogerus, Mikael *see* Grassegger, Hannes
Kushner, Jared 277

Langer, John 248
Laos 147, 151, 158
law 38–41, 109n3, 109n4, 150–151; application of 44–46; and balancing interests 96–100; practical legal responses 102; source protection laws 51, 96, 104–105; *see also* European Convention on Human Rights (ECoHR); law enforcement; proactive duty; Terrorism Act
law enforcement 39, 59–60, 64
leaks 2, 70, 225, 243, 294; *see also* megaleaks; WikiLeaks
Lee, Micah 106
Leeds, Elizabeth 165

Left, the 119, 125–128, 255, 258
Leftist 89n11, 119
Lessa, Carlos 163–164
Leveson, Brian 99
Levin, Sam 156
Lewis, Charles 295
Lewis, Justin 246; *see also* Cushion, Stephen
Lewis, Paul 60, 65–66, 71
LexisNexis 35, 63, 145
liberal ideology 20–22
libertarian communists 121, 126
Lloyd, Anthony (Baron Lloyd of Berwick) 39–41, 45
Lloyd, John 73, 75
Lopes, Tim 170
Los Angeles Times 267
Lynch, Lisa 243–244

Mahdawi, Arwa 20
Majed, Reem 217
Malaysia 23, 36, 74
management 77, 82–83, 86–88, 90n23
managerialism 78, 81–83, 85, 88, 90n17
Mancini, Paul *see* Hallin, Daniel
Mann, Steve 237
Manning, Chelsea 270, 279
Manning, Paul 7
'Mansions' campaign *see* 'No Safe Haven' campaign
McGuiness, Anthony 81
McNair, Brian 78, 83
media forms 8–10, 15, 243–244, 287
megaleaks 270–275, 279
Meirelles, Renato 163
Memory Associations *see* Memory Movement
Memory Movement 113, 117, 120–123, 125–129, 131–134
Meyen, Michael 77, 79–80
Middleton, Rebecca 176, 229–232, 234–236, 241
Millar, Gavin 46
Mills, C. Wright 14, 21
Monaghan, Jeffrey 56, 60, 64–65, 69–70
Monahan, Torin 56, 58–64, 68
Mortensen, Mette 270
Moss, Stephen 270–271
Mubasher Misr 216, 220–221
multi-issue extremism (MIE) 35, 59–62, 64, 66–68
Muslim Brotherhood 176, 216–217, 219–221, 224
Myanmar (Burma) 147

narcocracy 164–165
Nastasa, Brindusa Ioana 175–176, 200, 208–212, *208, 209, 211*
National Public Order Intelligence Unit (NPOIU) 61, 69
national security 36, 43, 65, 67, 96–98
National Security Agency 57, 278
Navarro, Vinicius 233, 235–236
neoliberalism 12, 21–22
New Internationalist 196
Newkirk, Anthony 56
new media 16–19, 219–220, 244, 274, 287, 289
news: news agendas 165–166; production of 12–13, 74, 77, 172, 175; *see also* fake news
Newspaper Association of America 267
Newsweek 270
New York Observer 277
New York Times, The 186, 249–250, 252–253, 267, 271, 280, 290
networked journalism 219–220, 222
'No Safe Haven' campaign 143–147
Nyhan, Brendan 257, 259

Obama, Barack 142, 249, 260, 279
Obermaier, Frederik *see* Obermayer, Bastian
Obermayer, Bastian 10, 13
Observer 6
Office of the Police and Crime Commissioner (OPCC) 84
Oldroyd, Rachel 156
online journalism *see* internet
organising 128–133
ownership 18–19, 77, 183, 191, 197, 199

Paiva, Anabela *see* Ramos, Silvia
Pan Arab news 220; *see also* Al Arabiya; Al-Jazeera Arabic
Patel, Ashish 294
patriarchy 22, 25, 74, 81, 89; state patriarchy 78, 89n5
Paxman, Jeremy 53n5
People Magazine 292–293
Peters, Chris 12
Petraeus, David H. 188
Pickard, Victor 20
police: Bermuda and 234–235; Brazilian favelas and 160–168, 170–173; and the deep state 60–62, 64–70; proactive duties to report to 38–42, 46–47; and protecting sources 95–96, 99–101; social justice and 114–115; and spies 69
political agency 16–18
political culture 73, 88, 119
Politifact 259, 291
popular rule 7–8, 10–12
portals 266, 269, 275–276, 280; *Viva Favela* portal 169–172
post-truth 286, 290, 292
poverty 20, 89n5, 151, 160, 162–163, 166
power 7; authoritarian 9, 14; executive 8; exercise of 19; generative 14; and money 10; and representation 15; symbolic and material 24
Poynter Institute 291
pressures *see* institutional pressures
Price, Stuart 9, 16, 26, 36
proactive duty 38–42
professional standards 75, 82–83
ProPublica 196, 287, 294–296
protecting sources 36, 95–98, 100–108, 140, 190, 273; the proactive duty to report and 40–41, 44, 49, 51
Public Library of U.S. Diplomacy (PLOD) 276
Publico.es 275
public relations (PR) 14, 25–26, 86, 259

'Radio Free Iraq' 179–180
Ramalho, Cristiane 169–171
Ramos, Silvia 166
Read, Alastair 26
Reality Check 254–257
Reich, Zvi 247; *see also* Godler, Yigal
reparation 122–125
representation 5–6, 15, 165–166, 232, 235
research 2–4; Bermuda and 232–234; desk research 150, 153; *The Ferret* and 208–209; Global Witness and 139–141, 146–151; Iraq and 189–190; and the proactive duty to report 50–51; researching the deep state 56–62, 69–71; research methods 62–69; Spain and 117–118; and verification 245–246, 256–258
Research Information and Communications Unit (RICU) 68–69

resourcing 126, 128–133
revolution 176; 'digital' 195, 286-287, 297; in Egypt 218, 224, 226; in Libya 79; and social media 215
resistance 4, 60, 82, 119, 257
Ribeiro, Denise 172
Right, the 119, 127, 258, 276
Rio de Janeiro *see* favelas
Rogers, Simon 271
Rosen, Jay 273
Rosenstiel, Tom *see* Kovach, Bill
Royal Canadian Mounted Police (RCMP) 64
'Rubber Barons' investigation 114, 147–149, *148*, 153
Rugh, William A. 283
Russell, Adrienne 17, 119
Ryan, Michael 262n3
Ryfe, David M. 23

Saied, Mohamed 224–225
Sanz Sabido, Ruth 113–114, 116
Schmidt, Eric 18–19
Scotsman, The 198
sectarianism 175; *see also* Iraq
SecureDrop 105, 279–280
Seib, Philip 75
Shapiro, Ivor 246
Shirky, Clay 225
Silverman, Craig 291
smartphones 161, 167–168, 173
Smith, Maurice 198
Snopes 260, 291–293
Snowden, Edward 16, 18, 21, 76, 106–108, 294–295; the deep state and 57–58, 66, 70–71
social justice 3, 8, 13, 25
social media 16–19, 23–24, 288–290, 292–294; and Brazilian favelas 167–168; and democratic change 223–226; and the journalist 221–223; and social justice 113–114; in the Tunisian and Egyptian revolts 215–216, 218–219, 221; and verification 252–253; *see also* Facebook; Google; Twitter
social networks 168–169, 172–173
Society of Professional Journalists 108, 267
sources *see* protecting sources
Spain 117–120, *118*; *see also* Memory Movement
Spence, Louise *see* Navarro, Vinicius
standards *see* professional standards

Starkman, Dean 12–13
state, the 9–10, 27n11, 87, 99; authoritarian 1, 5, 10; Global Witness and 146–147; and the proactive duty to report 38–40; Spain and 127–128, 134; state control 287–288; *see also* deep state
Stephanopoulos, Athan 294
Stray, Jonathan 270
structural factors: structural antagonism 75–77; structural contradiction 36, 85–87; structural complicity 16; *see also* institutional pressures
structure 6; command structure 78; democratic 197; dependent communicative structures 15; economic 165; of governance, 88; hierarchical 81, 85, 286; legal 100; political 176, 215
Sullivan, Drew 4, 189–190
Sullivan, Margaret 250–252
Sunday Post 198
Sunday Times, The 255, 294
surveillance 17–18, 35, 57–59, 62–66, 100–105, 153
Syria 275–276, 293; *The Ferret* and 200–201, 208–213, *208, 209, 211*; and the hazards of investigation 175–176; and the proactive duty to report 46, 48, 50

Tampa Bay Times 252
technology 23–24; Bermuda and 236–237; and protecting journalistic sources 95–96, 98–102, 104–108; WikiLeaks and 268–269, 279–280; *see also* internet; social media
Telegraph, The 156, 255
Television Aerials Control Act 236–241
terrorism 58–61, 65–70; *see also* Terrorism Act
Terrorism Act 38–41, 43–52, 99–100
text-mining 143
Thailand 114, 138–139
threat assessment 59–60, 64
Times, The 95, 186, 212, 252–253, 259
Tong, Jingrong 9–10, 139
torture 126, 135n2, 170, 186, 188, 190
Trump campaign 6, 277–278
Trump, Donald 22, 289, 292, 295–297; Global Witness and 156–157; verification and 248–250, 252, 257–260; WikiLeaks and 265; *see also* Trump campaign

truth claims 249–252, 259
Tufte, Thomas 20
Tunisia 215–216, 220
Turkey 23, 176, 208–213, *209*, 221
Turner, Stephen 262n13
Twitter 17, 115, 244, 290, 293; Brazilian favelas and 161–162, 172; Egypt and 216, 221, 224–225; WikiLeaks and 268–269, 271, 280

United Kingdom (UK) 22, 35–36, 89, 176; Bermuda and 237, 240; and the deep state 57, 60–62, 65–70; *The Ferret* and 196, 198–199, 201, 207; and Global Witness 142–144, 146–147, 151, 156; Iraq and 183–184; and the proactive duty to report 37–38, 46–51; and protecting sources 95–98, 101–102, 104–105, 107; and verification 246, 249–250, 253–254
United Nations (UN) 78, 128, 155, 171, 187
United Nations Educational, Scientific and Cultural Organization (UNESCO) 24, 186
United States (U.S.) 3, 76, 243, 290, 292; Bermuda and 237–239; Global Witness 142, 156–157; Iraq and 179, 181, 183–184, 187; and the proactive duty to report 39, 51; verification and 246, 248–250, 259; WikiLeaks and 265, 257, 259–276, 278–280
Universal Declaration of Human Rights 76
USA Today 251
Usher, Nikki 273–274

Valentin, Marcus 236
Van Wassenhove, Luk *see* Hunter, Mark Lee
Vaz, Paulo 166
verification 62–63, 243–252, 260, 262n3, 287, 290; case studies related to 292–293; and fact-checking 290–292

violence 4, 19; in Bermuda 229; in Brazil 160–173; in Cambodia 137; and sectarian violence in Iraq 181, 185, 191; and Spanish history, 124, 130; and terrorism 39
Vietnam 114, 151; *see also* 'Rubber Barons' investigation
Vietnam Rubber Group (VRG) 147, 157–162
'voluntary' obedience 84–85

Wahl-Jorgensen, Karin 273
Waisbord, Silvio 24, 155
Walby, Kevin *see* Monaghan, Jeffrey
Walker, Clive 53n5
Washington Post 199, 252, 259, 280, 282
Washington Times, The 276–277
Weaver, David H. 85
weighting 249–252
'Western' paradigm 10–12
West Highland Free Press 196
whistleblowers 2, 36, 75, 219; the deep state and 57, 66, 70–71; and protecting sources 95, 106; WikiLeaks and 275, 278–279
WikiLeaks 143, 243–244, 265–266, 279–280, 295, 297; the beginnings of 266–268; and conventional media 268–269; and going mainstream 269; after megaleaks 275–279; *see also* Assange, Julian; megaleaks
Willnat, Lars *see* Weaver, David H.
Wired 280
witnesses 167–169, 234–235, 247, 251, 262n2
Wolfsfeld, Gadi 223
World Bank 150–151

Yemen 200, 215, 220

Zaluar, Alba 162–163
Zelizer, Barbie 12
Zito, Salena 257

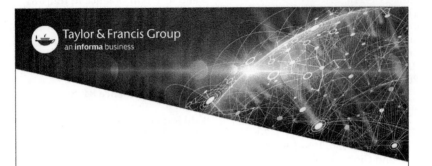